Web Technology

Theory and Practice

Brief Contents

Contents

Foreword *xv*
Preface *xvii*

1 Web Foundations 1

1.1 The Evolution of the Web 01
1.2 A Peek into the History of the Web 02
1.3 Internet Applications 03
1.4 Networks 04
1.4.1 From Moore to Metcalf 04
1.5 TCP/IP 04
1.5.1 Internet Address Structure 05
1.5.2 IPv6 06
1.6 Higher Level Protocols 07
1.6.1 FTP 07
1.6.2 Telnet 08
1.6.3 E-mail Related Protocols 08
1.6.4 HTTP 10
1.7 Important Components of the Web 15
1.7.1 Firewalls 15
1.7.2 Routers 15
1.7.3 Browser 16
1.7.4 Browser Caches 17
1.8 Web Search Engines 17
1.9 Web Servers 17
1.10 Application Server 18
1.11 Internet Organizations' Who's Who 18
1.11.1 ISOC – Internet Society 18
1.11.2 IETF – Internet Engineering Task Force 19
1.11.3 IESG – Internet Engineering Steering Group 20
1.11.4 IANA – Internet Assigned Numbers Authority 20
1.11.5 IAB – Internet Architecture Board 21

1.11.6 IRTF – Internet Research Task Force 21

1.11.7 W3C – World Wide Web Consortium 21

1.12 Summary 21

Exercises 21

Caselet Activity 23

2 Client-Side—HTML 24

2.1 SGML Framework 24

2.2 HTML 25

2.3 HTML Tags 26

2.3.1 Attributes 27

2.4 HTML File Structure 28

2.5 Common HTML Tags 30

2.5.1 HTML Tag 31

2.5.2 Meta 31

2.5.3 Title 32

2.5.4 Body 32

2.5.5 Headings 32

2.5.6 Anchor 33

2.5.7 Lists 35

2.5.8 Table 38

2.5.9 Frames 40

2.5.10 HTML Forms 40

2.6 XHTML 43

2.6.1 HTML Validator 44

2.7 Block and Inline Elements 45

2.8 HTML5 45

2.9 Summary 46

Exercises 46

Project Activities 47

Caselet Activity 47

3 Client-Side—CSS 48

3.1 CSS Declarations 48

3.2 Using CSS 49

3.3 Sample CSS File 51

3.4 Selectors 52

3.5 Box Model 57

3.5.1 Concept 57

3.5.2 Padding 58

3.6 Float 58

3.6.1 Using Float and Clear 60

3.7 *Z*-Index 61

3.7.1 Websites 63

3.8 Benefits of CSS 64

3.9 Summary 64

Exercises 64

Project Activities 65

Caselet Activity 66

4 Client-Side—Behavior 67

4.1 JavaScript 67

4.2 A Bit of History About JavaScript 68

4.3 Organization of the Language 68

4.3.1 Basics of Client-side JavaScript 69

4.4 An Example 69

4.5 Data Types 73

4.5.1 Special Numbers 74

4.5.2 Boolean 75

4.5.3 Constants 75

4.5.4 Typeof 76

4.6 Conversions 78

4.7 Basic String Operations 80

4.7.1 Other Common String Operations 82

4.7.2 String Encoding for URIs 82

4.7.3 Reference or Value 83

4.7.4 Regular Expressions 84

4.8 Date Object 84

4.8.1 A Note on Including JavaScript File 85

4.9 Arrays 86

4.9.1 Array Implementation Basics 86

4.9.2 Array and String Operations 87

4.10 Variables and Functions 89

4.10.1 Function Literals 89

4.10.2 Function Arguments 90

4.10.3 Anonymous Functions 91

4.10.4 Inner Functions 92

4.10.5 Closures 92

4.11 Closure Scenarios 98

4.11.1 Simplify Scope 98

4.11.2 Return Methods from Functions 98

4.12 Summary of Ways to Use a Function 98

4.12.1 Client-side Cookies 99

4.13 The Concept of Classes 101

4.13.1 Creating Objects 101

4.13.2 Objects Through Function Constructors 102

4.13.3 Dynamic Addition of Methods—Prototype 103

4.13.4 Inheritance 104

4.14 Execution Contexts 112

4.15 DOM 112

4.15.1 The Bigger Picture of DOM 112

4.15.2 Representing DOM 113

4.15.3 DOM Traversal 114

4.15.4 Accessing Nodes Directly 117

4.15.5 Adding Dynamism—DOM Manipulation 117

4.16 Event Handling 119

4.16.1 Event Onclick 121

4.16.2 Event Onchange 121

4.16.3 Event Onload 122

4.16.4 Mouse Events 122

4.16.5 Default Event Listeners 123

4.16.6 Browser Specific Challenges 126

4.16.7 Event Propagation 127

4.16.8 Other Events 129

4.17 A Shopping Cart Table Sort Example 130

4.17.1 Method InnerHTML 136

4.18 Overall Observations About DOM 137

4.19 Ajax with JavaScript 137

4.19.1 Ajax Introduction 137

4.19.2 Scenarios 138

4.19.3 Technology Components Required for Ajax 138

4.19.4 XMLHttpRequest Object 138

4.19.5 A Look at the Steps Involved 139

4.19.6 Sample Ajax Code 139

4.19.7 Ajax – Points of Caution 141

4.20 JavaScript Security 141

4.20.1 File Handling and Execution 142

4.20.2 Same Origin Policy 142

4.20.3 Pop-up Windows 142

4.20.4 History 142

4.20.5 Mail Through a Form 142

4.20.6 Server Restriction 142

4.21 Closing Observations on JavaScript 143

4.21.1 Client Side Compatibility 143

4.21.2 Unobtrusive JavaScript 143

4.22 Summary 145

Exercises 146

Project Activities 147

Caselet Activity 148

5 The Server Side 149

5.1 A Broad Outline 149

5.2 Behind the Scenes 149

5.3 Client Side Vs. Server Side 151

5.4 Transformation from Static to Dynamic Sites 151

5.4.1 Embedded Server-side Scripts in HTML 153

5.5 Java Servlets 155

5.5.1 Servlet Creation and Lifecycle 156

5.5.2 Lifecycle of a Servlet 157

5.5.3 A Simple Servlet Example 158

5.5.4 An Intermediate Web Application Architecture 159

5.6 Example—Read Environment Parameters 165

5.7 Accessing Parameter Data 171

5.7.1 Sharing Data Through Servlet Context 171

5.7.2 Trip Pooling Example 172

5.7.3 Thread Safety 182

5.8 State Management 183

5.8.1 Example—Session Basics 184

5.8.2 Cookies 195

5.9 Event Driven Tracking 207

5.9.1 Listeners and Events 208

5.9.2 Steps 210

5.9.3 Session Tracking Example (FavConnect) 210

5.9.4 Attribute Scopes 232

5.10 Summary 233

Exercises 233

Project Activities 234

Caselet Activity 235

6 JSP 236

6.1 A Better Way 236

6.2 Why JSP? 237

6.3 A Brief History and Background 237

6.4 Overview 237
6.5 JSP Lifecycle 238
6.5.1 JSP Service Methods 239
6.6 Elements in a JSP Page 239
6.6.1 Declarations 239
6.6.2 Directives 239
6.6.3 Scriptlets 240
6.6.4 Expressions 240
6.6.5 Transfer Control 240
6.7 Implicit JSP Objects 240
6.8 JSP Object Scopes 240
6.9 FavConnect Example Modified 241
6.10 JSP Tags 244
6.10.1 Declarations 245
6.10.2 Directives 245
6.11 JSP Exceptions 246
6.11.1 Expressions 248
6.11.2 Scriptlet 249
6.11.3 Actions 249
6.12 Expression Language (EL) 249
6.13 JSP Standard Tag Library 250
6.14 A JSP Example 251
6.15 Custom Tag Library 259
6.16 JSP and Equivalent Technologies 262
6.17 Summary 264
Exercises 264
Project Activity 265
Caselet Activity 265

7 The Business Layer—EJB Fundamentals 266

7.1 Layering 266
7.2 With Servlets 268
7.3 EJB Versions 269
7.4 Usage Scenarios 269
7.5 EJB Components 269
7.5.1 Session Beans 270
7.5.2 Message Driven Beans 270
7.5.3 Entity Beans 270
7.6 Lifecycle of an EJ Bean 271
7.7 A Shopping Cart—Simplified Example 273

7.8 Summary 280
Exercises 280
Project Activity 281
Caselet Activity 281

8 XML 282

8.1 Introduction 282
8.2 The Need 282
8.3 XML Building Blocks 284
8.4 How It Works 285
8.4.1 Basic Structure 286
8.5 Characteristics 286
8.6 Scenarios for Handling XML 286
8.7 Valid XML Document 287
8.7.1 DTD 287
8.7.2 XSD—Schema 289
8.8 XML Transformations—XSL 290
8.8.1 XSLT 291
8.9 XML Parsing 295
8.9.1 SAX 295
8.9.2 DOM 296
8.9.3 Choosing Between DOM and SAX 296
8.9.4 Java Support for Parsing XML 297
8.10 JSON 297
8.11 Summary 304
Exercises 304
Project Activities 304
Caselet Activity 305

9 Web Services 306

9.1 Tracing the Path of a Request—a Different View 306
9.2 Evolution of the Concept 308
9.3 Purpose 309
9.4 Standards 310
9.5 Use Cases 310
9.5.1 Sample Scenarios 310
9.5.2 Roles 311
9.6 Programming Models 312
9.7 SOAP Based Web Services 312

9.7.1 WSDL 314
9.7.2 SOAP 318
9.7.3 Structure of SOAP Messages 318
9.8 A Basic Example 319
9.8.1 Generating a Web Service 322
9.9 REST Based Web Services 322
9.9.1 REST Principles 322
9.9.2 Resource Orientation 323
9.10 Rest Based Web Services—An Example 323
9.10.1 Service Provider Side 324
9.10.2 The XML Document from the Service 329
9.10.3 Client Side 330
9.11 SOAP vs. REST 336
9.12 Case Study of an Online Store 337
9.12.1 Online Store Front 337
9.13 Web Services Endnote 339
9.14 Summary 339
Exercises 339
Project Activities 340
Caselet Activity 340

Appendix 341

Index 365

Foreword

In the current information age, the Web plays an important role in connecting people, sharing relevant content and enabling us to conduct our daily activities with remarkable ease. In view of the widespread use of the Web for almost everything that we need for our comfortable day-to-day living, more and more demands are being placed on the technology. In this context, this book written by Mr. Srinivasan is a worthy contribution that delineates the concepts of web technology in a precise manner in a single volume. The book is logically organized, is quite enjoyable to read, and reflects the author's rich experience spanning two decades, in this domain.

To enable the students of computer science to be conversant with the latest approaches, tools and techniques prevalent in the industry, the academic community requires constant inputs from the practitioners of Web technology. Most often, the books and lecture notes on web technology tend to be verbose and students require enormous effort to filter out and highlight the main concepts and useful features. This book offers a refreshing change by bringing out the concepts from a practical perspective, all in a single volume, with illustrative diagrams and relevant code listings.

Dr V. Chandrasekaran PhD (UnMelb, Australia)
Professor and Head
Department of Mathematics and Computer Science
Sri Sathya Sai Institute of Higher Learning (Deemed to be University)
Prasanthinilayam-515134
Andhra Pradesh
India

Preface

This book encapsulates rich practical hands-on experience in developing web applications, combined with teaching the subject for graduate/post-graduate students. The book is therefore a culmination of putting together what has been both practiced as well as preached, which is the one of the most compelling differentiators for this book. But what is more fascinating is the nature of the web itself.

The web is all-pervasive. God created the five elements – Air, Water, Earth, Fire, and Ether. After Ether, we can consider the Web as the sixth – and the only man-made element, because it is also present everywhere – at least wherever there is civilization! Perhaps this is the only other difference with the other five elements, in that it is present (only) wherever civilization exists, whereas the others do not depend on the existence of civilization.

The web did not grow overnight to its present state. The web is changing the world since it influences all spheres of our lives. As a matter of fact, it changes the world, and changes itself too! In fact, each such change is perceived as if it is just the beginning of the web. Over the course of many "generations" of the web, every added set of functions adds a layer of abstraction to it, because that is how any software development takes place. Each such abstraction makes it simpler to use, but the flip side is that the fundamentals tend to be forgotten by those who have joined the bandwagon late. This book attempts to bridge the fundamentals, how it has evolved and how it is in its present form today. The book can be used by students to get a grasp of the fundamentals and also by professionals who want to brush up with the basics of the technology. It is written as concise as possible so that the reader need not skip any section, at the same time, can finish reading the book within a short period of time.

The reader may wonder that technology, especially in the web world, is getting obsolete faster than ever before. And then there are so many books on web technology. So why go through the trouble of reading another book? Well, it is true that technologies are changing fast but if one observes closely there is a pattern on how it changes. For instance, an abstraction of such a pattern is that most of the new advancements are happening by combining a few things together. And all of those things already exist. As a corollary and a direct proof of it, these innovations are observed to happen in waves rather than by sharp turns. So it actually makes sense for someone to take a snapshot of the current state which will be useful for extrapolation. A case in point is HTML5, which is being made public. In fact, HTML5 can be considered to be a combination of CSS3, HTML4 and JavaScript.

The first wave of the web (retrospectively termed Web 1.0, though there is no such term officially) brought about interconnecting **computers** together. The subsequent waves (Web 2.0 and 3.0) focused on bringing about **people** together. The phenomenon of Web 2.0 happened in stages and was not discovered or invented in one day. This holds true for Web 3.0 as well. In fact, the concept behind Web 3.0 is facilitating **collaboration** among people (read stakeholders in an extended enterprise). The power of the collaboration among people is not to be underestimated. Its counterpart in the world of innovation is worth observing where it has been proven that enabling interaction among people brings in remarkable progress in innovation. Similarly, the web will continue to change and the pace of change will only get faster. To catch up with it becomes a continuous process throughout one's life but to understand its mechanics is something that is a more lasting skill or achievement, giving rather a brief reprieve to forecasting trends. During the time the book is written and published, the world is already talking of the sixth sense where the concept is in fact talking about the web being dead!

Well, this is almost true when one considers the ubiquitous web – being not only on the browser but also on mobile phones, electronic gadgets like GPS, credit cards, and a host of such day-to-day stuff. The way people interact and collaborate using these devices is no longer dependent on logging on to a computer and browsing through – it is being made possible to directly connect to the servers and get the results without going through a browser. So, in fact, the web is used to make itself redundant! That is the true power of Web Technologies! Catch on...

THE INTENDED AUDIENCE

Here is a set of people who would be strongly benefited by this book.

- Graduate/post-graduate students in IT or Computer Science as a textbook providing an all-round perspective of the various technologies involved
- An aspiring IT architect who would like to understand or get refreshed with the fundamentals
- A business person or manager of an IT firm who would like to glance over certain topics in this book as a starting point for getting hands-on experience.

Whoever you are, you are most welcome!

ORGANIZATION OF THE BOOK

The book covers the fundamentals of the main technologies that make up the web. The organization of the book is represented by Figure 1.

The book is structured along the lines of the representation shown in the figure. Starting from Web Essentials in the top middle, it follows clockwise through, to Web Services. As technologies are changing very fast, specific areas of technology go obsolete faster than ever before. They are replaced by new areas of technology but the base concepts will remain more or less the same, so an understanding of these will be useful. For example, when we refer communication among systems connected to the internet, the protocol by default is TCP/IP. This will not change often, but, how this is used to service an application will change fast enough. Also, another example is in Ajax which is a technology that has brought in rich interfaces into the web, thus opening up new business possibilities.

The question that might come to the reader at this point is how web technologies are relevant in the current times. As a matter of fact, web technology has revolutionized the usage surpassing all other innovation cycles. Economists have come out with a theory of innovation cycles and its relation to the economy. In the past, the world has witnessed many innovation cycles – Industrial revolution, steam engine, steel industry, oil/auto and currently Internet or web technologies, as per Carlota Perez model. Furthermore, it is said that a 10% increase in broadband correlates to a 1.5% increase in economy. We are seeing this in our day-to-day life, without even realizing it.

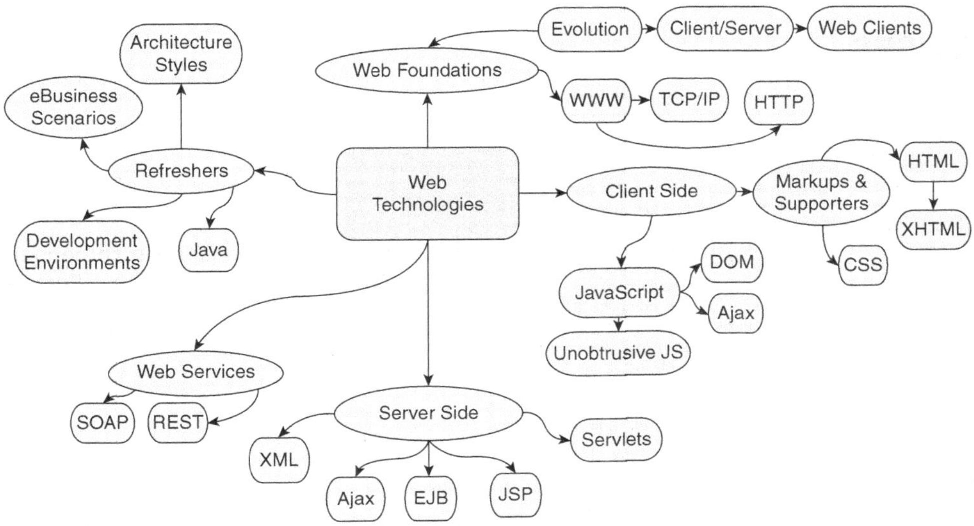

Fig. 1 *Broad outline of the book*

SPECIAL FEATURES

This book captures the essence of the various technologies that constitute the web. Rather than just focus on theory, the book brings out the concepts in the form of examples and illustrations. Just like how the web is linked to many resources, the exercises aid the reader for further reading pointing to the plethora of web resources available. The book is self-contained in the sense that the section on Refreshers provides a useful guide to the basics of the Java programming environment, which provides almost the complete ecosystem for developing web applications.

Side Notes

Aside note

Search engines can also be available for use within an enterprise. Google's GSA (Google Search Appliance) is an example of a Search so lution that involves a combination of hardware and software. It could be modeled as an Enter prise Search solution within the Intranet or for Internert facing sites. Link up to http://www. google.com/enterprise/search/gsa.html for addi tional information.

Numerous side notes in the form of "Aside Note" add to the bits of extra information, vital for additional reading or research.

The term "Aside" in "Aside Note" has been inspired by the HTML5 tag <aside>, signifying secondary content, related to the main theme of the page. It is interesting to note that today's secondary content could in all likelihood be tomorrow's primary topic, especially in web technologies.

EXERCISES

> **3.10 Exercises**
>
> 1. Tool-tips are small pieces of help text that act as a guide to fill up a field or such, when the cursor is hovered around the element. How are these achieved in HTML?
> 2. Construct a HTML table along with some data. Play around with some of the attributes of the table related tags and observe the outputs.
> 3. Imagine a scenario where you are going on a cycling tour around the country side. You have jotted down events and memorabilia in your diary and are now ready to publish in a web log of all the events. Design a set of HTML pages that can be used to create the log. Remember to include not just text but also images, videos and audio clips to make it interesting.

Exercises help the students to ponder over further, on each the topics. For teachers it helps in periodic evaluation of their students.

Exercises target both individual activity as well as team activity. The latter are the form of Project Activity questions.

Caselet Activities

Caselet Activity appears as part of Exercises, in (almost) every chapter.

An interesting facet with respect to Exercises is about Caselet Activities, which are ideally to be taken up by a team of students. These Activities, theme around a central idea of a project. The reason they are interesting is this: taken piecemeal, they are smaller, independent chunks of activity; taken together sequentially from each chapter, will result in a whole project. At the same time, there can be variations in each teams' implementation, thus fostering creativity. Furthermore, it helps emphasize the point any web project comprises of not just individual contributions but also team-based activities.

> **Caselet Activity**
>
> 11. Design a Website conforming to a theme. Read the notes below to get an idea of the theme. You may follow the given theme or better still, imagine your own theme, becase the design of creating a web site is more creative than the process it takes to do! Here are the basics.
>
> ■ A website is a collection of Web pages that are of course related to each other and also related to the purpose of the website. The landing page when . . .

Teachers' Resources

For teachers, this book comes with a website containing slides that can be used to jump start on the course right away. Indicative answer clues to exercise questions (excluding caselets and team work assignments) are also made available. Teachers will find this book handy since all information required for teaching is available in the book, including a section on Refreshers.

Refreshers

To make the book self contained, basics on core Java are included as part of the book. A lot of material is available on the web on Java, but it was felt that at least the basics of the language be covered in as much a concise way as possible.

ACKNOWLEDGEMENTS

This work was conceptualized and completed wholly under the Divine inspiration of our beloved Guru, Bhagawan Sri Sathya Sai Baba and is beyond any verbal quantification. Prof. V. Chandrasekaran (Department of Mathematics and Computer Science, Sri Sathya Sai Institute of Higher Learning) was instrumental in putting across to me the idea of writing this book. I am deeply indebted to him and to the University for providing me the opportunity to serve in His Divine institution as a visiting faculty member. The role played by my mentors, managers & subordinates at work and my students at the University, in shaping up my thought process is invaluable.

I owe my gratitude to my family members for their support and encouragement throughout the process of writing this book, especially Savitha for helping with the selection of the design of the book. I am also thankful to my parents, wife, brothers, and other members of the family for providing moral support on this initiative. I also express my thanks to my students and friends, who helped with the painstaking task of proof-reading.

I sincerely thank the editorial team at Pearson for their patience and support in working with me in this initiative. I am also extremely thankful to my colleagues at my workplace (Coextrix Technologies), to the University staff and all those who played roles in reviews and constructive criticisms. Comments and suggestions from faculties and students to enhance the contents of this book are welcome. I may be reached at msrini@computer.org.

M. Srinivasan

1

WEB FOUNDATIONS

Chapter Objectives:

- ***Understand the history of the web***
- ***The technologies that make the web***
- ***The standard bodies that govern the web***

The foundation of the web was laid around the 1960s in USA, when the ARPA (Advanced Research Projects Agency – renamed as DARPA – Defense Advanced Research Projects Agency) researched into a localized networking concept on how they can share text documents from one computer to another. The technology they researched was aimed at how these computers can communicate even if a portion of the phone network crashed during say a war or flood or any calamity. When the then phone network was based on circuit switching technology, this research actually gave rise to the birth of packet switching in networks. The new model aligned well with the fact with that information was sent in bursts or packets at some time intervals.

1.1 THE EVOLUTION OF THE WEB

It is reiterated that the web in its present state did not grow overnight, nor was it designed formally as in a roadmap. In fact one of the most critical success factors of the web can be attributed to the thought of independent innovations. According to this, smaller systems get architected and developed independent of each other in possibly different environments. Suddenly, they come together and when merged, throw open to form interesting applications in entirely different ways. According to Tim Berners-Lee, the following is an observation:

> Suppose someone had (and it was quite likely) invented a World Wide Web system somewhere else with the same principles. Suppose they called it the Multi Media Mesh(tm) and based it on Media Resource Identifiers(tm), the MultiMedia Transport Protocol(tm), and a Multi Media Markup Language(tm). After a few years, the Web and the Mesh meet. What is the damage?

- A huge battle, involving the abandonment of projects, conversion or loss of data?
- Division of the world by a border commission into two separate communities?
- Smooth integration with only incremental effort?

The last option is what is the most optimal and this is what the Web makes it possible to achieve. To quote again, Lee observes as follows:

> As the Web becomes the basis for many applications to be built on top of it, the phenomenon of independent invention will recur again and again. We have to build technology so as to make it easy for systems to pass the test, and so survive real life in an evolving world.

Owing to the fact that the older versions will be required to co-exist with the newer innovations, it appears as a continuous progress of evolution. In fact, it implies that the primary characteristic of the web is its ability to evolve. Well, product companies have solutions that also evolve. The market is used to seeing SAP release its ERP products from one version to another including its Netweaver™ based products. Same is the case with Oracle, Microsoft, i2/JDA or even other smaller sized products. Though the components of the web do have versions, the concept of evolution in the sense of the web is markedly different. It paves the way for further enhancing the web and at the same time, preserves or co-exists with the applications written in the previous versions. There is thus a greater degree of compatibility across different versions, and also there is loose coupling between systems, making them modular. In a sense the web can be compared to a mighty river that actually started off small, but accepting a lot of tributaries and sub-tributaries to join itself on the march towards the ocean! Likewise, many different sets of technologies form the web.

1.2 A PEEK INTO THE HISTORY OF THE WEB

The history goes back to the packet switching technology first used when two computers talked to each other (Figure 1.1). Multiple nodes operate independently thus reducing impact in case of point failures. Thus TCP/IP was developed. A few big companies like Cisco are specialized in networking technology and is a big science by itself. The first generation of the web was in the form of private networks. The networks were shared within the defence. Another set of networks (SURANET, etc.) was within the university campus. Here are some trivia bit of information:

- DARPA creates ARPANET – 1968
- First set of nodes connecting universities among UCLA, Stanford, and University of Utah – 1970
- First E-Mail sent – 1972
- Development on TCP/IP – 1973
- USENET – decentralized news group
- NSF creates CSFNET which is a 56 kbps network within institute
- TCP/IP made used in ARPANET
- IPv4 formal introduction – 1980
- IBM PC – 1981
- DNS – 1983
- Internet, WWW – 1992
- 1000s of new hosts added to internet – 1994
- the Federal Networking Council (FNC) defines the term 'Internet' – 1995

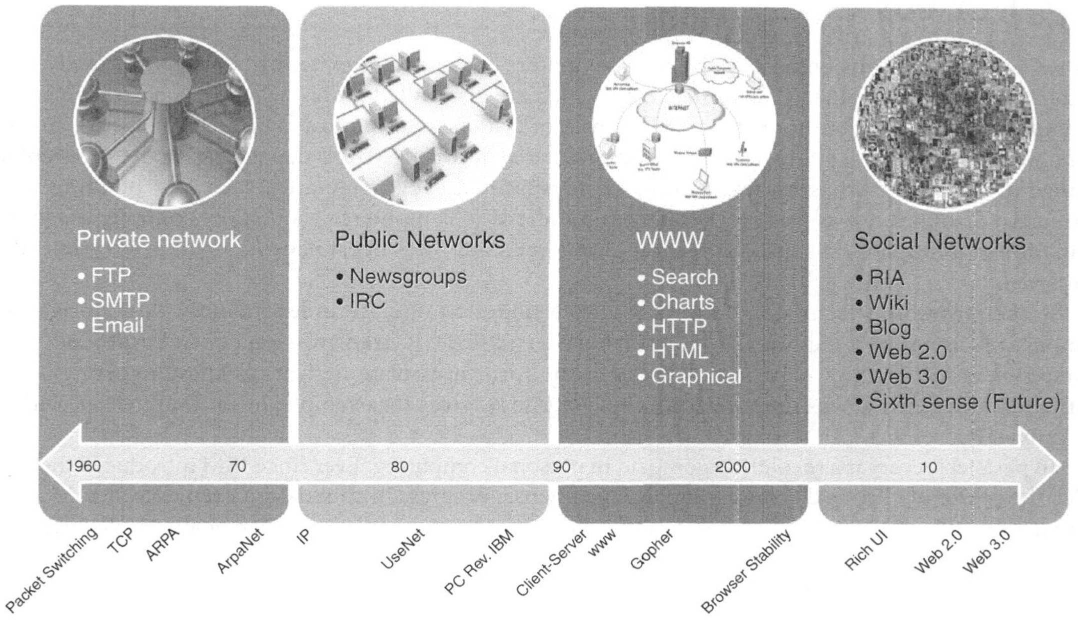

Fig. 1.1 *Web evolution*

The growth from private to public networks gave rise to the Internet. According to FNC the Internet is defined as follows:

Internet refers to the global information system that –

(i) is logically linked together by a globally unique address space based on the Internet Protocol (IP) or its subsequent extensions/follow-ons;

(ii) is able to support communications using the Transmission Control Protocol/Internet Protocol (TCP/IP) suite or its subsequent extensions/follow-ons, and/or other IP-compatible protocols; and

(iii) provides, uses or makes accessible, either publicly or privately, high level services layered on the communications and related infrastructure described herein.

Thus the Internet is a network of networks, joining many computers together from different organizations, providing an infrastructure for various applications.

1.3 INTERNET APPLICATIONS

Internet is the platform for connecting computers together, but what can be achieved? Well, in short it is the world as the World Wide Web (WWW) is the most popular and widely used Internet based application. But there can be other uses as well like E-Mail, FTP, Bulletin boards, hyper text documents, etc.

The focus of the book will be the WWW, although other applications will be covered to the extent that is required to understand the context.

1.4 NETWORKS

A network can be considered as a series of computers connected together physically or virtually. The internet connects together a set of networks which are also called nodes, when they abstract a set of computers (or even other nodes) together. A network can be referred to as a local area network (LAN) or a wide area network (WAN), or a metropolitan area network (MAN) depending on the geographic range it spans. A LAN is normally confined to a limited geographic area, such as a building, and comprises from as few as three to as many as hundreds of computers. A WAN, by contrast, is a combination of multiple LANs that are geographically separate. The largest network of all is, of course, the Internet.

Packet switching technology allows multiple nodes to operate independently thus mitigating impact in case of point failures. This in turn gave rise to TCP (transmission control protocol). The first generation of the web using this was in the form of private networks. These networks were private in the sense it was shared within the Defense services for example, or for that matter, within a University.

In parallel there was a revolution going on in personal computing. Ever since IBM introduced the first PC, the power of client side computing became intense. Progress in chip design even exceeded Moore's predictions about the power of processing. The PC became popular and personalized with laptops becoming commercially affordable to corporate as well as homes.

1.4.1 From Moore to Metcalf

As a result of the tremendous increase in processing power, the growth from private networks to public networks was achieved. With that, the growth in Internet became imminent. Literally, we witnessed Moore's law of computing in action and now, we are realizing Metcalf's law of communication networks getting true. According to Metcalf's theory, two communication devices (it is not yet a network!) can join to form one connection, whereas four of them can make 8 and sixteen of them can make 120 connections. Obviously, these are more theoretical connections rather than real useful ones but then Social networking will come into play to maximize the effectiveness of the connections.

By now, we have a few very big companies solely specialized in networking, like Cisco, Juniper Networks, etc.

1.5 TCP/IP

Coming back to TCP/IP, this deserves special mention since it is at the foundation of any computer network. It evolved from ARPANET which is a WAN protocol. Compared to the OSI model of seven layers, TCP/IP has four layers, though not as rigid a layering. Nevertheless, the layering is shown in Figure 1.2.

The success of TCP/IP as the major protocol for the Internet is largely because of IP which enables hosts to connect together geographically dispersed networks of computers irrespective of their size or types of links. The way in which this is done is through the concept of a host and a subnet. The IP protocol uses this concept. The Internet (IP) address is a means to uniquely identify a resource which could be a host computer, desktop, printer, etc., on the internet.

<table>
<tr><th>TCP/IP</th><th>OSI</th></tr>
<tr><td rowspan="3">Application</td><td>Application</td></tr>
<tr><td>Presentation</td></tr>
<tr><td>Session</td></tr>
<tr><td>Transport</td><td>Transport</td></tr>
<tr><td>Internet</td><td>Network</td></tr>
<tr><td rowspan="2">Link</td><td>Data Link</td></tr>
<tr><td>Physical</td></tr>
</table>

Fig. 1.2 *TCP/IP against the OSI layers*

1.5.1 Internet Address Structure

The IP forms the basis of communicating data using packets. IP version 4 (IPv4) is the version that is commonly used today, though IPv6 has been there for quite sometime, standardized in 1998. IPv4 uses 32-bit notation which allows up to 232 unique addresses. The IPv6 uses 128 bit notation and offers markedly more than what IPv4 offers but more importantly it addresses the requirements of subnet routing prefixes within the address (Figure 1.3).

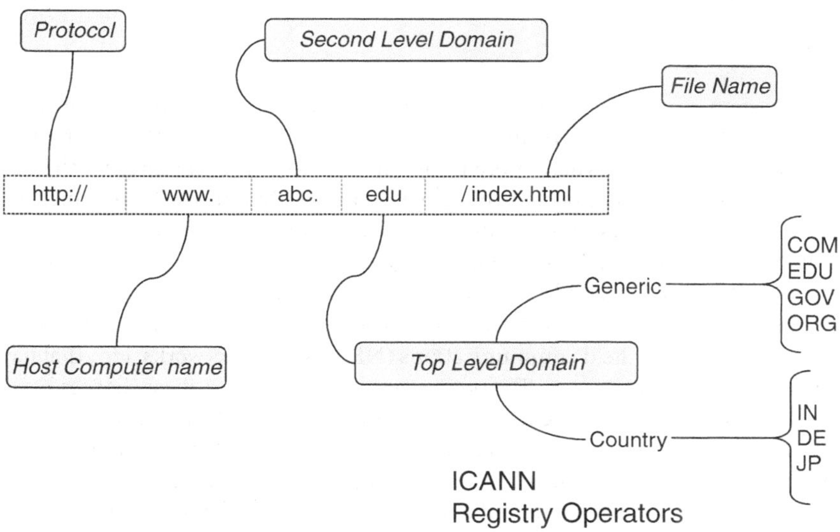

Fig. 1.3 *Address structure*

A 32-bit based address typically is represented as shown in the Address Structure figure. It consists of four sections with each section represented by an octet.

The domain name service (DNS) makes it easier for users to use the IP address. The unique logical IP address representing the host computer is rather cumbersome to type in and remember, so it is substituted by human friendly names like www.abc.com. Accordingly, it does Forward Lookup (from Hostname to IP address) and also Reverse Lookup (from IP address to Hostname). DNS also enables E-Mails to function properly. In summary, DNS is used for the following:

- IP name resolution
- Hostname resolution, enabling use of consistent names
- Internet domain support – to access servers through remote networks
- E-Mail through outbound SMTP server

The DNS is viewed as a huge, dynamic, scalable and reliable database, but distributed globally. There is no one server that has all the information and rightly kept! Logically, it comprises three items – a Namespace (which is the Domain), Servers which take that name space and Clients which seek clarifications within the name space.

Most top level domains (TLDs) with at least three characters are referred to as generic TLDs (gTLD). The earliest ones created, which are still in use, are .com, .gov, .net, .org and .edu. There were others created in the same period like .mil but have limited use. Later, it spawned a set of sponsored domains like .aero, .museum and .coop as also a set of unsponsored ones like .biz, .info, .name and .pro. The sponsored domains are represented by a specialized community.

In fact, the addresses, starting from any of these TLD, are similar to the physical address structure that we commonly find for residences. As we go down from the TLD (which could be the equivalent of a country in the residential address), it converges each level to a more narrow scope. It goes on until it finds the smallest entity. In the Internet this entity is referred by a resource (as the 'A' element).

1.5.2 IPv6

Though the IPv4 system can support up to 4.3 billion unique addresses theoretically, on its address space, it is not sufficient to meet the growing numbers of devices and users that are required. Now, we have almost reached the threshold where more things are connected to the Internet than people. Cisco predicts the number of Internet-connected things will reach 50 billion by 2020, which will equate to more than six devices for every person on Earth. Already, the numbers of possible devices that have been connected are quite many – laptops, PCs, mobiles, smartphones, tablet PCs, gaming devices, TV, etc. By February 2011, officially, all of IPv4 address space has been used up.

The trend is that many more types of devices are expected to come in the future that will be web-connected and they include near field communications (NFC), sensor networks, etc., that have the ability collect, transmit and analyze information. The point regarding IPv4 is that these devices have contributed to the depletion of IP addresses very quickly. Moreover, companies have blocked a larger number of address spaces than what they actually require or use. Furthermore security needs also require to be enhanced. All of these reasons justify the need towards IPv6. For the records, there was a move towards IPv5, but since the additional features were far fewer to warrant a new release, those were merged as part of IPv6 itself.

The advantages and features of IPv6 are summarized as below:

- Additional address space: IPv6 is based on 128 bits thus allowing for up to 2128 unique devices. This is the single most important advantage of IPv6. It also obviates the need for techniques like NAT which is used with IPv4.

- Dynamic auto configuration: In IPv4, when a new device is added, there is an additional work of reconfiguration whereas in IPv6 the network address can be obtained from the IPv6 router.
- Simpler header format in IPv6
- Enhanced security: IPSec is mandatory in IPv6
- Interoperability with IPv4

Aside note

Currently (as of early 2011) IPv6 is being deployed in stages and will continue to coexist with IPv4 during this transition. The website www.ipv6.com provides a single place for adequate information on ipv6, with links for comprehensive information.

1.6 HIGHER LEVEL PROTOCOLS

Protocols operate at multiple levels during communication between systems on the web as is seen in the OSI model. Key to using the web is various high level protocols like FTP, SMTP, Telnet and HTTP. Out of this list, perhaps the most ubiquitous and most used protocol is the HTTP, which will be discussed later in this chapter.

1.6.1 FTP

Files can easily be copied over another computer residing on the same network, through a shared folder. Transfer of files can even be sent over E-Mails but then the size is limited. However, if they are big and/or separated across the web, then transferring files can happen through the Internet in an effective way, but then for security reasons, it is not allowed to share folders over the web. Furthermore, it is not required for the source machine to have the same operating system as the target machine.

The most widely used is the FTP or the file transfer protocol to transfer files over TCP. It works on a client–server model. The client authenticates with a FTP Server which usually stores the files. Both text and binary files are possible to be handled. It can work both directions – meaning it can be used for upload as well as download, provided access is allowed. The client could be a software that needs to be installed (downloadable free), but sometimes even browsers can be used instead (Figure 1.4).

The client sends command over the command port which is usually port number 21. The address that is specified can be a named address or numeric (like 197.20.0.2). A username and password is generally required, some allow it to be connected anonymously.

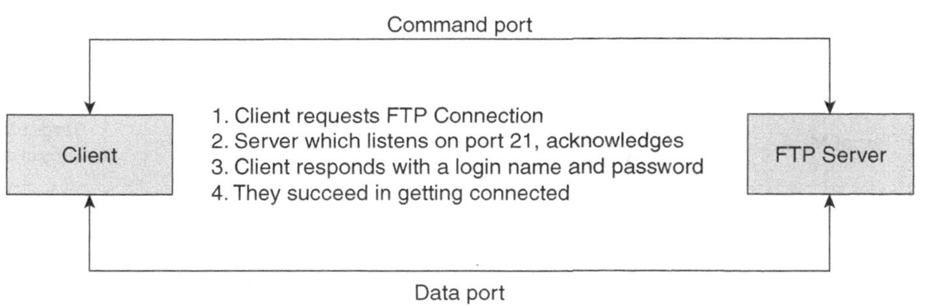

Fig. 1.4 *FTP connection*

Command line interfaces are common though there are some clients that run through a UI. Through a browser the address starts with ftp://.

1.6.2 Telnet

Telnet (which stands for terminal network) allows a user to login to a server and work off a window in the client's machine. As in FTP, there are two parts to it – a client and a server.

1.6.3 E-Mail Related Protocols

People need to communicate with one another through some formal means, including as much as to conduct business. Earlier, during the mainframe days, communication was done through connected systems one-to-one. As systems became interconnected, it was required to communicate irrespective of the underlying operating system. So, standard protocols began to emerge for E-Mail. There are two main protocol standards used for E-Mail over the Internet and it is important to make a mention of them – POP and SMTP.

1.6.3.1 SMTP SMTP which stands for simple mail transfer protocol; it is a text-based protocol. It works across TCP/IP from ports 25 or 587. It operates as the application layer, defining the transport as opposed to the mail content. Handling mails can again be thought of as a client–server system. The mail server uses SMTP to send and receive messages. The client uses SMTP to send mails. The mail client could be Microsoft Outlook, Notes, or any such software (including a browser) that are commonly familiar. For receiving, typically the client uses the POP or IMAP protocol over the web. The mail client could also belong to one of the proprietary tools like Lotus or Microsoft Outlook. POP stands for post office protocol in this context (not to be confused with point of presence, which denotes an access point to an Internet ISP) (Figure 1.5).

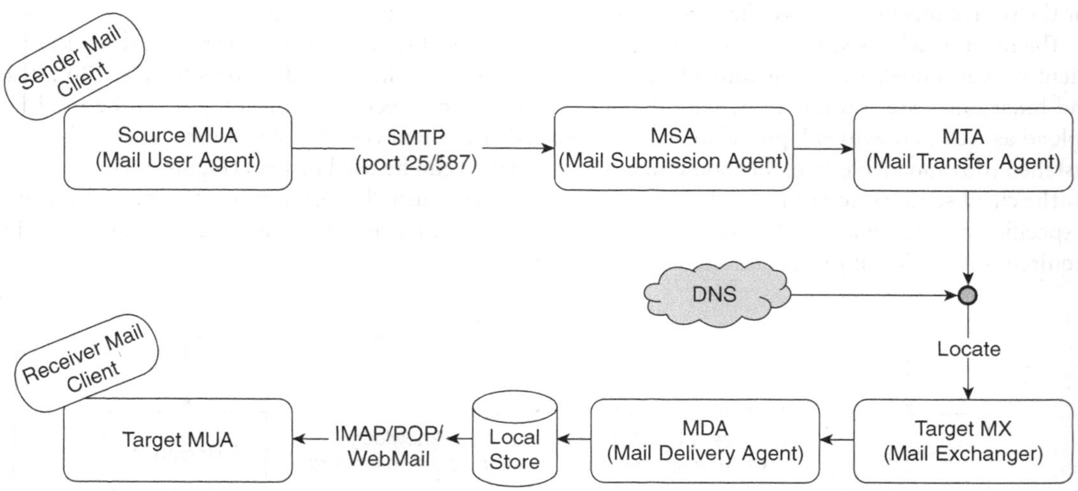

Fig. 1.5 *Mail handling flow*

The overall flow of mail from the sender (Source) to the receiver (target) is shown. The idea is not only to make the reader understand easily but also get used to a few terms that are used in the process. It is not necessary to know the details of each step for a web programmer, as each step is detailed in itself, best studied under networking. Notice that the client part on the receiving end can access mails through either IMAP or POP (or POP3 representing the version of POP) or WebMail.

The server is (required to be) online all the time for receiving messages and storing in a local store. However, this need not be the case for the client. As per POP, the recipient pulls his/her mails into a personal hard-disk, so that the user need not be online all the time for checking messages. It is similar to the process of chewing-the-cud in animals, wherein messages are downloaded at suitable intervals when online, and then each of these can be read and acted upon by the recipient offline.

1.6.3.2 IMAP Developed by Stanford University, IMAP stands for internet message access protocol. It is meant for accessing E-Mails through the internet. It was designed to work even on low bandwidth speeds, by downloading only the header – the user has the option to download in full only those messages that are required. The advantage is that unimportant messages like spam or anonymous messages need not be downloaded.

Advanced versions of IMAP (like IMAP4) has facilities to search through the body of mail messages for keywords which will further help in filtering messages.

1.6.3.3 MIME Traditionally, E-Mail handling was designed based on text types of files and hence were ASCII-based. However, it needed enhancements when binary messages needed to be transmitted, since they came about when mails were used in the context of business. It was then that standards like MIME were introduced. The purpose was to handle additional file types (in E-Mail) without having to change the then existing (E-Mail) infrastructure. It started as a means for encoding binary files for transfer through SMTP. However, usage of MIME has now grown into a generic content type to be used in communication protocols like HTTP. It is, in fact, designed to be extensible.

MIME stands for multipurpose internet mail extensions, its expansion still reflects just the older meaning, though.

IANA defines the standard MIME file types. This is manifested in the content-type, as part of the HTTP header. The standard types are mentioned below.

- application
- audio
- example
- image
- message
- model
- multipart
- text
- video

There are subtypes under each of the above types (except example). For example, text/html identifies an HTML file. Other examples include image/jpeg, application/xml, text/xml, etc.

1.6.4 HTTP

Hyper Text Transfer protocol (HTTP) is a protocol that utilizes TCP to transfer information between computers connected on the web – this includes web servers and clients as well. This is the communication mechanism that browsers use to exchange data from clients and servers. The client makes an HTTP request to a web server using a web browser, and the web server sends the requested information (website) to the client. The standard port used for connection between the client and server is 80.

Talking about connections, these are the most important features to note, which is unique to this protocol. They are mentioned below.

- HTTP is a predominantly text-based protocol, so it is easier handled by humans. However, it also handles binary data exchange.
- The connection is dynamic. What this means is that it is virtually connectionless. After a request is made the client disconnects from the server and waits until a response is received. The connection is re-established. As a matter of fact, the client is normally never directly connected to the server. The HTTP request is created by the browser and sent to the web server, which reaches the server through a network of computers.
- As the connection is dynamic, it follows that HTTP is a stateless protocol. This means the history is maintained neither by the server nor by the client. The requirement is necessary for being lean with respect to performance, however that does not mean the information between connections cannot be maintained. (This is done using a variety of ways like cookies, sessions, etc, which will be discussed in subsequent sections.)
- The connection is agnostic of the medium which is used to make the connection, that is, it is platform-neutral. This means the request could come from a browser or a mobile phone or any of the devices which can make a web connection. The MIME specification handles the content.

1.6.4.1 HTTP architectures Some of the common architectures are represented in Figure 1.6.

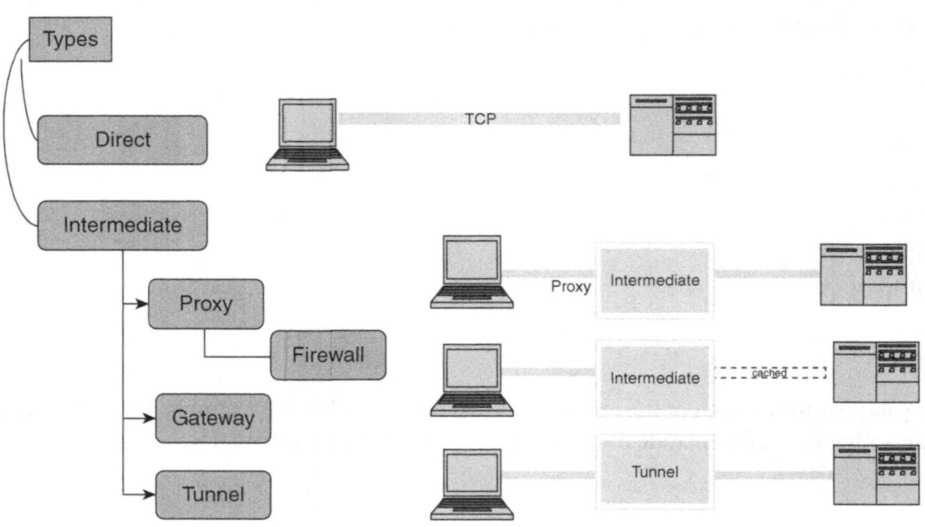

Fig. 1.6 *Common HTTP architectures*

Aside note

We take things for granted and tend to oversimplify the technologies behind them. Visualize, what happens internally when you switch on a light – think about all the infrastructure needed – the power plants, transmission systems, cables, internal wiring, etc.

On similar lines, think about what might happen internally when you enter an URL in a web browser or when you send an E-Mail. Imagine the kind of infrastructure that powers you from behind – the web servers, hardware switches, and software that works – all in a matter of seconds.

1.6.4.2 A simple scenario using HTTP The flow of a request through the browser is discussed in this sub-section.

The HTTP protocol aligns with the client–server model as shown in the diagram (Figure 1.7). A simplified set of steps are summarized as follows:

1. An HTTP client opens the connection through the browser. The browser recognizes the URI typed in by the user. It looks up the address as per the domain name, using the DNS (which is provided by the ISP).
2. The request triggers the connection. The browser retrieves information from as per the URL.
3. The processing is done by the resource as abstracted by the URI.
4. The response, as a result of the processing, is sent to the browser. It also performs additional processing as required for getting related and supplementary resources like images, etc.
5. The browser renders the information for display.

There are multiple types for a request, depending on the (HTTP) request method. The methods possible are one of GET, POST, PUT, HEAD, DELETE or TRACE. Out of these, the most common ones that are encountered by a typical user are GET and POST. The following table summarizes their meanings.

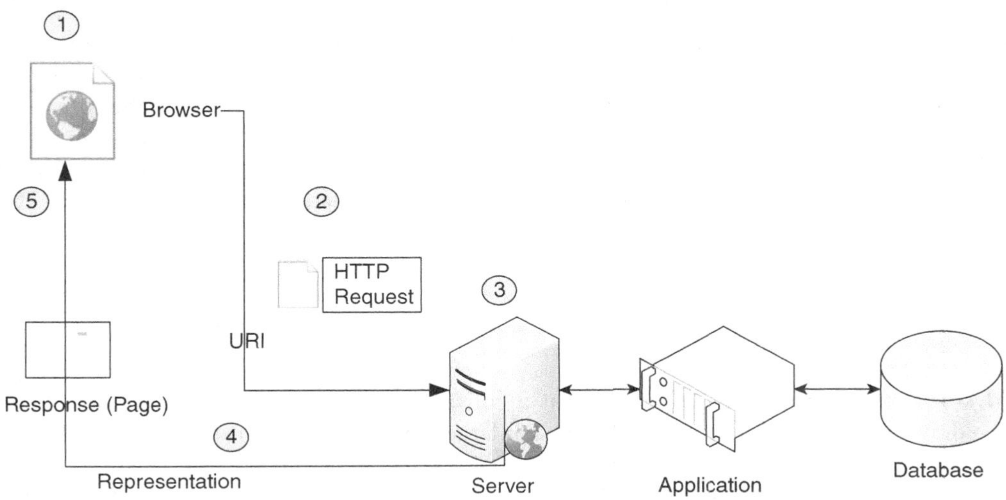

Fig. 1.7 *A simplified web communication scenario*

Method	Usage
GET	• retrieve a URL from the server • simple page request • run a CGI program • run a CGI with arguments attached to the URL
POST	• preferred method for forms processing • run a CGI program • parameterized data • more secure and private
PUT	• To transfer a file from the client to the server
HEAD	• requests URL's status header only • used for conditional URL handling for performance enhancement schemes • retrieve URL only if not in local cache or date more recent than cached copy
DELETE	• Request for deleting a resource
TRACE	• Request server to return whatever is received • Used for diagnostics

The most common methods are GET, POST, and HEAD.

1.6.4.3 Get method The GET method is used to retrieve web pages from the server, sent through the browser, by means of the URL. The URL is itself a string containing the address of the web page requested. Further information is passed as parameters after a question mark (?) sign. Parameters appear as Name-Value pairs, separated by an ampersand (&) sign. For example, if a flight number and date is to be passed as parameters, the URL will appear something like this. www.abc.com/reserve.html?flt=AA123&dt=12312010&seg=BOMDEL. Notice the parameters after the question mark (?) sign followed by the first parameter and then by the second parameter, separated by ampersand (&) sign. A pure query is an idempotent request and is an ideal candidate for GET as opposed to POST.

```
GET /reserve.html?flt=AA123&dt=12312010&seg=BOMDEL HTTP/1.1
Host: www.abc.com
User-Agent=Mozilla/5.0
```

1.6.4.4 Post method The GET method is a convenient way to pass parameters but obviously suffers a drawback in terms of security and size. For larger and more number of parameters, POST is a better option. This is achieved by means of a Form that is presented to the user who then fills it up and submits to the browser. There is no limitation to the size of data that is sent to the Server. Figure 1.8 illustrates the front end of the request (a blow up of the HTTP request portion referred in Figure 1.7).

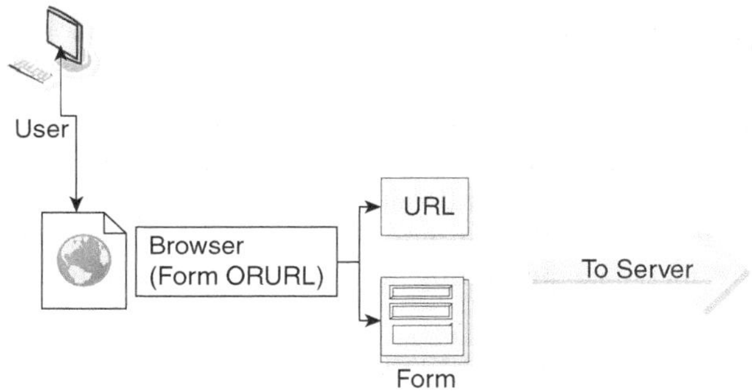

Fig. 1.8 *GET and POST from an HTTP request*

The same example when sent through a form (which is POST) will look like this below.

```
POST /reserve.html HTTP/1.1
Host: www.abc.com
User-Agent: Mozilla/5.0
Accept: text/xml
Content-Length: 22
Content-Type: application/x-www-form-urlencoded
...
flt=AA123&dt=12312010&seg=BOMDEL
```

1.6.4.5 Get vs. Post The HTML specifications (we will cover HTML in the next chapter) define the difference between GET and POST. GET involves parameter data encoded within the URL while POST implies parameter data appearing within the message body. As per HTML 2.0 and HTML 4.0 "If the processing of a form is idempotent (i.e. it has no lasting observable effect on the state of the world), then the form method should be GET. Many database searches have no visible side-effects and make ideal applications of query forms. If the service associated with the processing of a form has side effects (for example, modification of a database or subscription to a service), the method should be POST."

The point is that the right discretion should be used when deciding whether to use a GET or a POST method. However, most modern day browsers include a confirmation message to caution the user about a possible duplicate entry. For instance, the user tends to reload a page or to click on a submit button more than once in response to a delay that could perhaps be due to network congestion. This could in most instances cause an undesirable effect (like for instance money transfer over the net, or credit card payments, or ordering books from Amazon and so on). Most GET requests apply in areas like search or such read-only operations which are idempotent, that is, even if the user clicks the submit button more than once, there is not much undesirable effects – it is just that the search or whatever such operation is carried out that many times without causing change in any state of the system. It is for this reason that GET is often cacheable but a POST is not.

However, there could be instances where POST can be used for idempotent requests like, for instance, the parameters list is too long or if it contains non-ASCII characters. If in case you think that the parameters could be hidden from the user in case of a POST, you are probably wrong since 'view source' can reveal all of them. So choose your pick accordingly!

1.6.4.6 HTTP response Each time the browser seeks a page from the server, it (server) not only sends the HTML markup (document) of the page but also a set of header information (Figure 1.9). These (response) headers are not visible by default. However, they can be made visible through a few tools or a few browser plug-ins, if required. The format that is sent internally to the browser follows a structure. The metadata pertaining to the structure is aligned as per the following semantics.

- Status line along with status code
- Header fields consisting of meta information – one or more lines
- Message body which is optional

The response status codes are given off by the server to the browser. The following are the interpretations.

- 1xx – reserved for future use
- 2xx – successful, understood, and accepted
- 3xx – further action needed to complete
- 4xx – bad syntax in client request
- 5xx – server can't fulfil good request

Content-type is one of the most important headers. In the above example, it signifies that the information sent is text. The content-type is also called MIME type. Browsers get a clue on how to render a page by means of the MIME-type.

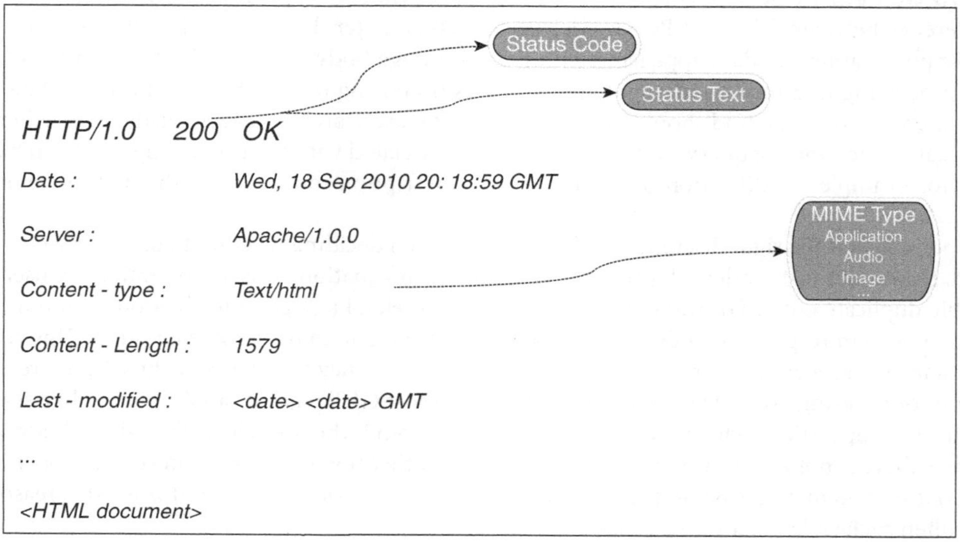

Fig. 1.9 *Response sample corresponding to an HTTP request*

1.7 IMPORTANT COMPONENTS OF THE WEB

1.7.1 Firewalls

Firewalls are software or hardware components that decide what messages can pass through and what cannot. It is like the gatekeeper with a set of rules and policies. They perform the following functions.

- Filter the incoming traffic
- Log events
- Detect intrusion attacks and alert
- Authenticate users
- Perform basic content screening
- Enforce corporate network security policy

In this context, some of the threats that can be reduced are Denial of Service (DOS) attacks, IP spoofing, data thefts, virus attacks, etc.

1.7.1.1 The growing importance of firewalls Firewalls have always been a part of the web due to the reasons mentioned above. However, the pattern of usage has been growing in such a way that a lot of information is exchanged between numerous components on the web. This is made possible by web Services and SOA that automate end-to-end business processes spanning organizational and geo-political boundaries. Simple firewalls, which does packet-filtering only operates on the periphery, but sophisticated firewalls using XML can be used to provide filtering at the web services layer. They can even perform security services like authentication, authorization, and auditing. In effect, the function of a firewall has grown into security gateways.

In practice, we can have simple firewalls, scaling up to a combination of software and hardware firewalls. In summary, these are the variations in usage:

- A simple packet filter (router) which is configured to allow exchange of packets between networks. This works on the network layer of the OSI model. At the transport layer, access to certain TCP/UDP ports can be blocked depending on the IP address of sender/receiver.
- Proxy, which is a set of programs to allow or reject access to application across networks. This operates on the application layer of the OSI. A DMZ* can act as a proxy as well.
- A complex system of proxy servers, hubs, routers, and packet filters to control traffic across networks.
- Security gateways to filter and transform outgoing traffic, and restrict incoming traffic.

*DMZ or de-militarized zone in networking is a small network or proxy that acts as a neutral zone between the internal and the external networks.

1.7.2 Routers

It is said that the internet is a huge network of hosts. Routers are the ones that hold them together, which creates the illusion of a unified set of computing resources. This is achieved by transferring packets of data from a set of input links to a set of output links. A router operates on a WAN as opposed to a switch, which operates typically on a LAN. Routing functions include route calculation, routing table management, and execution of routing protocols. They are found at many levels in the Internet:

- at homes, they allow users to get connected to the internet through the ISP;
- in the enterprise, they link intranets – computers within the enterprise
- backbone routers link the ISPs and enterprise networks

The detailed architecture and working of routers is beyond the scope of this book.

1.7.3 Browser

The browser is the most common interface available to the user to access resources from the web. It is the thinnest form of the client possible. A thin client does not need any extra installation on the client machine as a browser is normally available as part of the O/S (IE is available on Windows, but other browsers like Chrome or Firefox have to be installed in the system). On the other hand a thick client needs installation on each client. A pure internet architecture for a web-based application is supposed to work on thin clients like the browser. However, it is not just a line that separates thick vs. thin clients. There are a lot of degrees of states in between. Accordingly we see a lot of extensions in the form of Adobe Flash, Silver light, etc. that enhance the basic functionality. As long as they are standardized, there is little of an issue otherwise, there will be installation headaches. A bit of history on the evolution of today's browsers helps.

The early generations (Web 1.0?) of web browsers were predominantly text based, so even on low bandwidth the performance was good. An example of such browsers included Mosaic.

Although a J2EE application can consist of three or four tiers, J2EE multitier applications are generally considered to be three-tiered applications because they are distributed over three different locations – client machines, server machine(s), and the database machines. Three-tiered applications that run in this way extend the standard two-tiered client and server model by placing a multithreaded application server between the client application and database. Some web applications employ thicker client technologies that use custom binary code to extend the browser's built-in capabilities. Examples of such extensions include ActiveX controls, Java Applets, Shockwave, Flash, and Silverlight. These components may be deployed as byte code that is executed by a suitable browser plug-in, or may involve installing native executables onto the client computer itself. Over time, some of these (add-on) technologies is hoped to become part of the standard web browser itself so as to provide a RIA (rich Internet Architecture) based application to enjoy the benefits of a richer UI leading to greater productivity.

The commonly used browsers are Internet Explorer from Microsoft (IE), Mozilla Firefox from the Mozilla Foundation and Safari from Apple. All of them are meant to perform the basic task of browsing. They all do it well, but they are far from being standardized.

One very important point to note from the view of developers and architects is that the wide variety of choices possible on the browser adds a lot of complexity to the underlying software development scenario. This is because the software has to be made available over a wide variety of browsers and versions. Just imagine the permutations and combinations of the number of browsers and the versions in each that may have to be supported. The fact of the matter is that users belonging to either ends of the spectrum – the geek user who is working on the cutting edge of the versions of the browser available to the semi-literate user who is working on the pre-java script flavors of the browser – both of them have to be equally supported, which makes it challenging enough!

A traditional browser application is generally not rich in UI as compared to the older client-server application or a desktop application. Besides not being robust, the (traditional) interface was/is limited to hyperlinks on web pages, submitting forms, and waiting for the page to load after it retrieves information from the server. It did not have the controls like trees, tabs, intelligent grids, or any of the other interactive interfaces. Prior to Web 2.0 era, the question was why the browser-based applications were built this way. Well, the above sections sort of give a clue to the answer – in short browsers were not made for applications, but rather for linking up pieces of information or documents together. We saw that this was achieved through HTML. But then when people began to use them, it was realized that it was required to be dynamic rather than work off static pages/documents.

1.7.4 Browser Caches

Caches are meant to increase web speed by reusing information already retrieved. The Browser Cache has files stored in the temporary internet files folder. The files range from entire web pages to pieces of information like CSS (CSS will be described in the subsequent chapter) files, media files, etc.

1.8 WEB SEARCH ENGINES

The World Wide Web is a huge repository of distributed information, but can be searched as if the information is present in a single repository. A web search engine is used to search for information based on keywords entered by the user. Google, Yahoo! and Bing are the most popular search engines today and need no introduction about the way they is used and the way results are presented.

What is interesting about search engines is the algorithms that were developed, which contributed to shaping up the state of the web. Google's page ranking algorithm was the first of the lot which became widely used. It was effective as it ranked the results according to the number of links it had, because popular pages had more links than the rest. More advances have resulted in Google's MapReduce framework for parallel processing, which then gave rise to open source Hadoop algorithms.

A search engine consists of four functional elements – a spider which traverses the web in the background, and builds an index, which is used to retrieve relevant objects, arranged as per their ranking.

It is recognized that web search engine technology is a large subject by itself to warrant a separate book. This section is just to highlight the reader about the importance of this basic web component and provide suitable pointers into its study.

Aside note

Search engines can also be available for use within an enterprise. Google's GSA (Google Search Appliance) is an example of a search solution that involves a combination of hardware and software. It could be modeled as an Enterprise Search solution within the Intranet or for Internet facing sites. Link up to http://www.google.com/enterprise/search/gsa.html for additional information.

1.9 WEB SERVERS

Essentially, how are the web pages of a website hosted and made available to all clients 24×7? The simplest answer is a web server.

In the web context, the term server applies in different ways and relates to a piece of software rather than hardware. In a generic sense, a server refers to different contexts, performing different roles – a database server primarily hosts an RDBMS; a front-end server takes care of routing requests. Likewise a web server takes care of handling web requests. It does not matter whether these roles are served in the same physical hardware or distributed across multiple machines or even if a single role requires multiple machines to perform.

In its simplest sense, a web server is a software program that accepts HTTP requests from clients, passing it on to another server and serving the response back to the client. The response page is usually of a specific format called HTML.

Aside note

> Web servers have evolved over the years and there are quite a lot of different things they perform apart from essentially the functions mentioned above. The first web server evolved out of a project from CERN in 1989, thanks to Tim Berners-Lee. Some of the popular web servers include Apache, Tomcat, Lighttpd, Mongrel, etc.

1.10 APPLICATION SERVER

It is not just enough for a server to serve basic client requests alone, for dynamism to be built in, there has to be some processing on the server side through a servlet container or such means. An application server deploys and manages the web applications on the server. In other words, the application server (or App Server for short) is a superset of the web server. JBoss is one of the popular application servers in the open source category. Others include GlassFish (from Oracle), WebLogic (from Oracle, previously BEA Systems), WebSphere (from IBM), etc. Specialized application servers like SAP Netweaver acts as the application server for running SAP. It takes care of all core functions, divided into layers like Presentation, Business logic, Integration, Database, and Connectivity.

In a typical multi-tier architecture, the application server takes care of the Business Logic layer. Refer to the Appendix on N-Tier Architecture.

1.11 INTERNET ORGANIZATIONS' WHO'S WHO

An examination of the definitions and concepts related to the Internet will pose a question to the reader as to who makes it work and how. The question is genuine because there is no one single owner of the Internet, yet how does it provide a standardized platform. Howsoever it is done, such a massive concept will have high degrees of coordination that is required at multiple levels aligned by the following activities.

- Standardization – agreement on Internet Standards
- Allocation of Internet resources
- Defining policies

To manage these activities, there are central authorities, mostly not-for-profit, like W3C, IETF, RIR, etc. It is obligatory for anyone in the web business to understand the backbone organizations behind the Internet. As this is not meant to be an exhaustive list, readers are encouraged to do research on their own to understand further. The significant forums are given below.

1.11.1 ISOC – Internet Society

ISOC is an international, nonprofit membership-based organization founded in 1992 to provide leadership in Internet-related standards, education and policy. It provides financial and/or legal support to

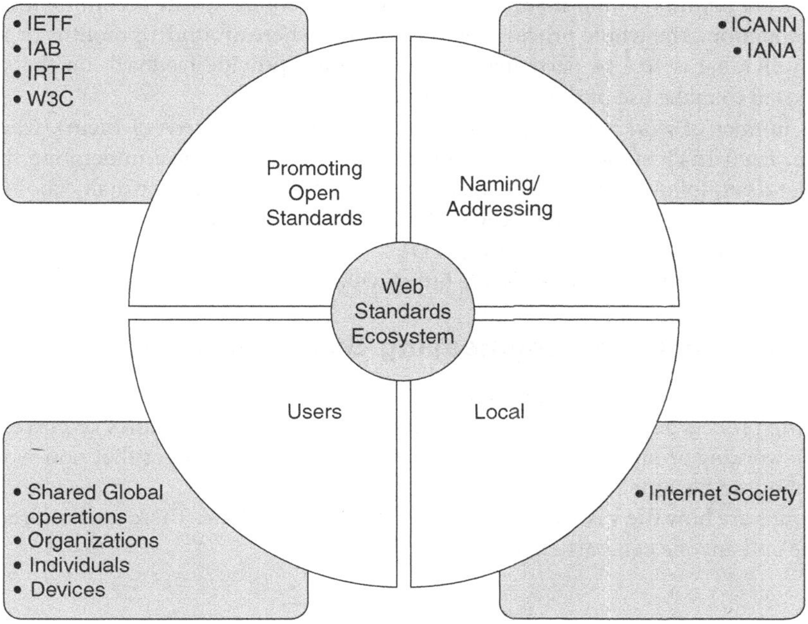

Fig. 1.10 *Web standards ecosystem*

other groups and task forces related to the Internet. Most of the Internet standards with respect to technology are developed and set by the Internet Society (ISOC) and the units operating under its auspices.

A concise view of the Internet (web) standards ecosystem, shown in Figure 1.10, gives an idea of what the Internet ecosystem involves.

1.11.2 IETF – Internet Engineering Task Force

The Internet Engineering Task Force is an international, self-organized group of people who contribute to the engineering and evolution of Internet technologies. It is the principal body engaged in the development of new Internet standard specifications. IETF are aligned or structured as per area groups. Each area is managed by an Area Director, who is a member of IESG (Internet Engineering Steering Group – more on this in forthcoming paragraph). The following are examples of some of the broad areas.

- APP – applications – concerned with protocols for E-Mail, etc.
- INT – Internet – concerned with ways of moving IP packets and DNS information
- SEC – Security – concerned with authentication, privacy, etc.

The first step in the process of a W3C technology specification is the formation of a working group, comprising members from W3C and the industry. This group develops the standards required for the technology to work, passing through a number of intermediate stages consisting of the following.

- Working draft
- Final working draft
- Recommendation

Sometimes there are additional intermediate steps in the form of candidate recommendation and proposed recommendation. The whole process could take somewhere around 18 months or more. During this time any individual is free to participate, comment, and provide feedback on the specifications. Readers are advised to make use of this opportunity.

There are a number of working groups under an area (about hundreds of them), where the actual work gets done. Each IETF standard that has been published would have undergone the stages of a working Internet draft, followed by an RFC (request for comments). This is usually coordinated by the Area Director or the working group chair. RFCs include best current practices (BCP), proposed standard (PS), draft standard (DS) or Internet standard (STD).

The reader is encouraged to visit the website http://www.ietf.org for more details.

1.11.3 IESG – Internet Engineering Steering Group

The IESG is responsible for technical management of IETF activities and the Internet standards process. It administers the process according as per ISOC procedures. The IESG ratifies or corrects the output from the IETF's working groups, gets them started and finished, and ensures that non-working-groups drafts that are about to become RFCs are correct (Figure 1.11).

Working groups are how the vast majority of the IETF's work is done. There are hundreds of working groups at a time and anyone can participate in their discussions.

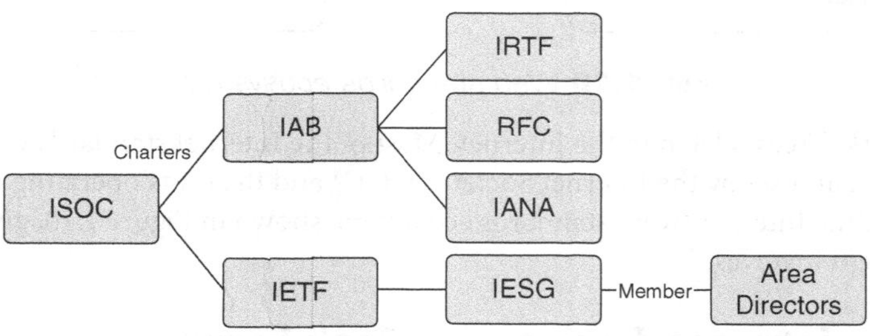

Fig. 1.11 *Internet offices*

1.11.4 IANA – Internet Assigned Numbers Authority

Some of the activities need to be monitored even after the protocol is finalized. Examples include registry activities for MIME, Port number, etc. IANA is the central coordinator for the assignment of unique parameter values for Internet protocols. The IANA is chartered by the Internet Society (ISOC) to act as the clearinghouse to assign and coordinate the use of numerous Internet protocol parameters.

It is responsible for domain names, IP addresses, and port numbers (default port numbers like 80). It delegates the administration to other bodies like the following:

- RIPE NCC (Réseaux IP Europeans Network Coordination Centre)
- ARIN (American Registry for Internet Numbers)
- APNIC (Asia Pacific Network Information Centre)
- LACNIC (Latin American and Caribbean IP address Regional Registry)
- AfriNIC (African Regional Registry for Internet Number Resources)

In 1998, another organization called ICANN (The Internet Corporation for Assigned Names and Numbers) was created as a private-sector, not-for-profit Internet stakeholder aimed at administering policy for Internet name and address system. ICANN operates under the US Department of the Commerce. As a result, it performs part of the previously assigned IANA functions – IP address allocation, top level domain name management (like .com, .net, .org), etc. It ensures that every IP address is unique and can be found on the Internet.

1.11.5 IAB – Internet Architecture Board

The IAB was earlier called the Internet Advisory Board, changed to the current one in 1989. The internet is vast and hence there is every possibility than a particular standard or policy loses sight of the global picture. The IAB is responsible to ensure that the big picture is intact and focus on long-term planning and coordination among the broad areas of the IETF. IAB thus reviews the activities (and formation of new) working groups for integrity and architectural consistency. Another offshoot of an important activity is the IRTF (Internet Research Task Force).

1.11.6 IRTF – Internet Research Task Force

IRTF's mission is to promote research of importance to the evolution of the future Internet. This is done by creating focused, long-term, and small research groups working on topics related to Internet protocols, applications, architecture, and technology. Some of the topics span security, anti-spam, network management, name space management, etc. One of the important architectural components include SNMP.

1.11.7 W3C – World Wide Web Consortium

The W3C was founded in 1994, by Tim Berners-Lee, in collaboration with CERN. Its mission is centered on the web and most of its work revolves around the standardization of web technologies to ensure interoperability. It achieves this by working on "recommendations" which are generated by members. When approved, it results into a proposal for either a new "Activity" or a "Working Group" charter. The terms within quotes mentioned here are some of the jargons that the reader will come across, when working in the industry.

1.12 SUMMARY

This chapter brought out the philosophy of the web, its history and its evolution to what we see today. The various technologies that interact with each other that form the web are also brought out. In the process, they are tied together by standards and the various organizations that are responsible for bringing up these standards are also highlighted.

EXERCISES

Q1. While learning the evolution of the web and how the internet has taken the world by storm, understand the history of how technology revolutions, in general, have shaped out in the past. Refer to the website http://www.carlotaperez.org/lecturesandvideos.html and take a look at the videos and slides available.

Q2. How is the evolution of the web different from that of the applications?

Q3. What is the new version of IP? What are its advantages over its previous version?

Q4. Which HTTP methods are NOT considered idempotent?

A. GET

B. DEL

C. PUT

D. HEAD

E. POST

Q5. Why are firewalls important in the context of a web application?

Q6. Differentiate between a web server and an application server.

Q7. What is MIME type? Where is it found in the HTTP header?

Q8. There is an architectural style called REST, meant for distributed systems. While it is not required at this stage to understand what REST is, all that can be said about it is that it is just a style, not a standard. Comment on whether the following statements are true or false. Justify your statement.

A. You will not see the W3C coming up with a REST specification.

B. You will see IBM or Microsoft or Oracle selling something like a developer's toolkit for REST.

Q9. Pick any two application servers that are available in open source stack. Compare and contrast them.

Q10. Pick any two application servers that are available commercially. Compare and contrast their features. How does that compare with the Open Source based application servers?

Q11. Install an application server in your environment and try to configure them. Write a simple HTML script for testing purposes.

Q12. What is a resource in the context of web? Give examples. What is the difference between URI and URL?

Q13. URIs that are identical, by character, refer to the same resource. Do different URIs necessarily point to different resources? Explain your answer.

Q14. What are the ways in which the web is identified as an open system?

Q15. Apart from Google, Yahoo!, and Bing, make a list of web search engines that are available.

Q16. Using your favourite search engine, come up with a study on how search engines work.

Q17. As mentioned in this chapter, RFC (request for comments) is one of the official ways to propose new standards for the Internet. Visualize this process as part of the entire life cycle of a standard. Represent this in a diagram and explain the steps involved.

Q18. An IP address is said to be unique, however, a client cannot be reliably located based on its IP address. Explain why it is so?

Q19. A "ping" command is used to test out connectivity between two systems. Technically speaking, a ping is an ICMP (internet control message protocol) request to another machine which echoes back an acknowledgement. Try out this command from your terminal. For example ping www.microsoft.com from a Linux or Windows shell and see the response. It also echoes back with the resolved IP address.

Q20. Research the web to find out about how software (or utilities) are available in open source. What are the types of licensing agreements that are commonly available?

Q21. Come up with your own report on why the web is often referred to as being ubiquitous. While making the report, analyze over multiple dimensions on how the web has played a role permeating our daily lives.

Q22. Gather information from the web about how a web spider can be implemented. A web spider (also referred to as a crawler) is a program that browses a site (or a group of sites) and navigates itself, used by search engines to index web pages.

Caselet Activity

Q23. Imagine an Internet-facing website to be designed as part of a web application. As part of preparatory work required for this initiative, there could be a need for domain name registration and a hosting provider. Prepare a report on what strategy you will adopt for this. What considerations you will include as part of this work? For testing and development purposes, a local host can be considered.

2

CLIENT-SIDE—HTML

Chapter Objectives:

- ***Understand the origin of markup languages***
- ***Get to know the basics of the basics of the web—HTML***
- ***Experiment with a few HTML tags***

We have so far seen the standard means of communication among computers over the web (using HTTP). We have also seen its characteristics like being stateless and being platform-neutral, for instance. Correspondingly, in the telecommunications industry, what has been discussed so far is quite like having all the telecom cables laid out along with switches and exchange system working together. But then, how do humans communicate amongst themselves. We still require a medium or a standard that both parties can understand, which is a language like English.

However, communication between computers (i.e. servers) and the end users is different than communication among computers themselves. In the context of the web, the process of communication among computers has been standardized, and accordingly the tool used for such purposes is standardized in the form of a browser, which communicates through a language called HTML (Hyper Text Markup Language). Consequently, HTML is the most popular and common language that the web understands. However, HTML is in reality not a single language but a combination of different conventions that have evolved over the years into the language that is understood by the system on the web.

HTML has been derived from SGML or Standard Generalized Markup Language, considered as the mother of all web-based mark-up languages. Though SGML can be used directly, it is complex to use. In practice, there are a number of markup languages and specialized markup languages that are derived from SGML.

2.1 SGML FRAMEWORK

Some of the most common relationships are represented in Figure 2.1.

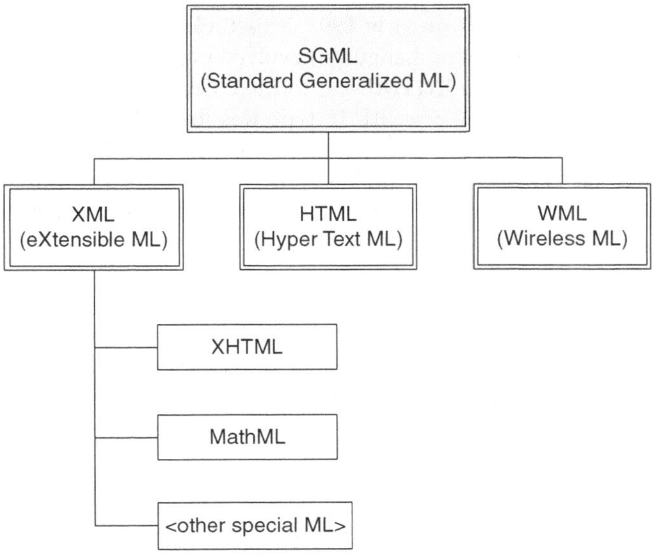

Fig. 2.1 *SGML and its derivatives–an example*

Figure 2.1 shows an example of what the inheritance structure looks like. There are various other derivatives that have evolved and are still evolving, aligning with the World Wide Web Consortium (W3C) principle of being evolving and open. For example some of the specialized XMLs are MathML, CML (Chemicals XML), X3D (3D Graphics ML), etc.

HTML is the most common means of browser-based communication. The web as it exists today—being vibrant and open—is predominantly due to HTTP and HTML. We will focus on HTML and XHTML throughout this chapter.

2.2 HTML

HTML is the predominant mark-up language for the web on the client side. It defines how a resource is linked together and organized. Though the term HTML refers specifically to text, in practice it has broadened to also refer to other resources like audio, images, files, or any other object. A web server or an application server communicates with the client through HTML, which is the language that a browser understands. Like the other technologies, HTML too has evolved over the years. It originated in the mid-1980s from SGML, first appearing as about a dozen tags in 1991. The Internet Engineering Task Force (IETF) initialized the first organized effort to standardize HTML with HTML 2.0 around 1995. Then the W3C took over standardization activities.

Around 1996, the W3C released HTML 2.2, which took care to standardize Microsoft's and Netscape's proprietary elements. The first substantial phase of HTML development took place roughly between 1994 and 1998. This period was characterized by the browser wars and involved a strange conflicting mix of standardization efforts and competition among the browser-based companies. The major differentiating factors in those days were that it was supposed to be both open as well as evolvable—two major characteristics of the W3C. These twin objectives, though simple to view, are indeed complex to satisfy.

HTML 4.0 evolved during late 1997 or early 1998. This took place under the W3C recommendations. Thereafter XML (eXtensible Markup Language) evolved in parallel and it was found to be a good idea to combine HTML and XML. Thus XHTML was formed. Consequently, the 4.01 version of HTML became the first version of XHTML. A new MIME type was formed for XHTML called application/xhtml+xml. To take care of the transition, there was *XHTML Transitional* which was different from the standard XHTML called the "Strict" version. In 2009, the W3C stopped working on XHTML 2.0 and worked towards the current version which is HTML5. As of 2011, development in HTML5 is picking up steam.

Aside note

Refer URL http://dev.w3.org/html5/spec/ for details of HTML5 specification. Refer http://www.w3.org/TR/html-design-principles/ to get an understanding of its design principles.

The technical specifications for all official versions of HTML are freely available from the W3C at its website (http://www.w3.org). These specifications may be difficult to read, being highly technical in nature and written primarily for computer scientists and system software vendors who program web user-agents.

2.3 HTML TAGS

HTML is text written in the form of XML tags. Tags appear in pairs with a start-tag and an end-tag. A start-tag or an end-tag begins with the less-than character (<) and ends with the greater-than character (>). Looking at tags does not give a sense of a true programming language—they are rather directives that instruct the browser. Tags are understood by the browser and the directives point at how a piece of text is to be displayed. The HTML file is itself a text file that can be written using any text editor like vi, notepad or gedit. There are also special editors available, to simplify the task of writing. However, if they are to be written by hand all the time, only static content can be delivered. So, instead, it is being generated by a system (or a server). In any case, it is important to get to know the overall syntax and get a feel for HTML. We will take a look at a sample HTML file in Figure 2.2.

```
<!DOCTYPE HTML PUBLIC "-//W3C//DTD HTML 4.01 Transitional//EN">

<html>
<head>
  <title> MyFirstHTML </title>
  <meta http-equiv="Content-Type" content="text/html; charset=UTF-8">
</head>
<body>
    <h1>Hello HTML<h1>
</body>
</html>
```

Fig. 2.2 *A simple HTML file–an example*

Fig. 2.3 *Output from IE*

The response that is produced in MS Internet Explorer is shown in Figure 2.3.

The response will be similar in other browsers as well.

HTML uses tags to create structured documents via semantics for text—such as headings, paragraphs, and lists—as well as for links and other elements. Each tag has a certain semantics associated with it and renders accordingly. HTML also lets authors embed images and objects in pages and can create interactive forms.

2.3.1 Attributes

Almost all of the tags can optionally have attributes associated with them. Attributes are *name-value* pairs. The attributes are specific to a tag, but different tags could have the same attributes that are permissible. The values attributes can have an impact on how the tag is displayed. The generic format is defined below.

```
<tag attribute1=value1 attribute2=value2> ... </tag>
```

For example, the Anchor tag <a> has an attribute called href, which specifies the link.

```
<a href="http://www.microsoft.com">
Click here to take to Microsoft
</a>
```

The above example creates a hyperlink with the given text which leads to the Microsoft site (www.microsoft.com).

Attributes *id* and *class* are applicable for all tags. *id* represents the identifier which is supposed to be unique within the web page. *class* represents the semantic class or category of the element. Since it is application-specific (or web page specific, in other words) the value can be anything that the application developer decides. This way elements with the same class name can be grouped together, which can be used to render a common style or do some sort of processing. Generally, a style is associated with the class (and not processing). Details of this can be seen in the section on CSS.

<fieldset> is a tag to support Form elements by logically grouping together a set of fields. A border is drawn along with a legend tag that defines the caption for the border (Figure 2.4).

```
<!DOCTYPE html PUBLIC “-//W3C//DTD XHTML 1.0 Transitional//EN”
“http://www.w3.org/TR/xhtml1/DTD/xhtml1-transitional.dtd”>
<html xmlns=”http://www.w3.org/1999/xhtml”>
<head><title> Documentation Collections </title></head>
<body>
    <form>
           <fieldset><legend>Basic Info</legend>
               Name: <input type=”text” size=”20” </input>
               Division: <input type=”text” size=”20” </input>
           </fieldset>
           <fieldset><legend>Location Info</legend>
               Location: <input type=”text” size=”20” </input>
               Country: <input type=”text” size=”20” </input>
           </fieldset>
           <button>Submit</button>
    </form>
</body>
</html>
```

Fig. 2.4 *Fieldset*

Notice the borders enclosing the legends (Basic Info and Location Info) shown in Figure 2.5.

Fig. 2.5 *The output in netscape*

2.4 HTML FILE STRUCTURE

<!DOCTYPE> tag: This is the first element—a special tag specifying the DTD (Document Type Definition) used by the document (file). In this case it specifies the version of the HTML that is followed.

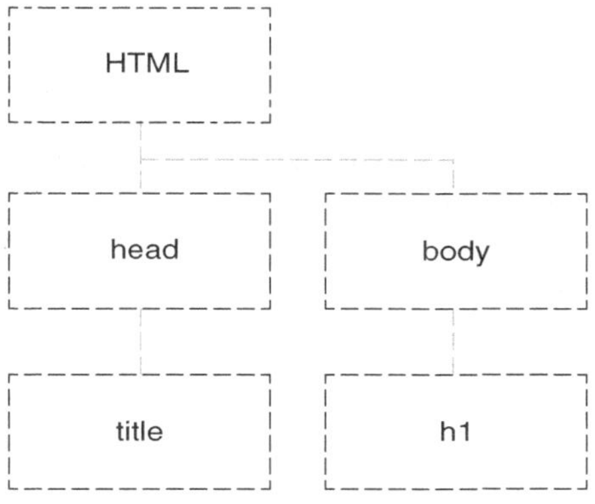

Fig. 2.6 *Sample HTML document structure*

There are 3 common versions followed—Strict, Transition and Frameset—all with HTML 4.01. In HTML5, this is simplified to just <!doctype html>.

<HTML>: Starting with this element, the document (file) follows a tree structure (Figure 2.6). The HTML element is considered the root of the document.

Referring to any of the example HTML files, the indentation in them (HTML file) is not mandatory but is essential for us to understand easily. The tags that are surrounded by <and> symbols are interpreted by the browser between the start and end tags. In this case the text between <h1>, signaling the start of h1 element and </h1>, signaling the end of the tag, is considered within HTML as first level heading and hence the response given off by the browser is accordingly bold and big. A tag can contain valid attributes which describe more about the data.

All text that is coming from the body element of the document will appear in the client area of the browser. The body can contain any number of elements like h1. In the strict flavor of HTML, all ending elements must be present corresponding to its start element. However, though there is provision for the non-stricter forms (transitional), it is strongly advised to follow the norms and not take advantage of its leniency.

Learning HTML is considered relatively easy, though complex HTML pages can look daunting at first. There are numerous tutorials available on the web to learn HTML, but it is really not necessary to remember each element and their syntax. A HTML document can be written using a simple text editor like Notepad or vi, but is rarely done that way since it is rather tedious to write and is without helpers to assist in using the right syntax. For development purposes, IDEs like Eclipse or Netbeans can be leveraged which offers auto-completion tips that are extremely helpful. Nevertheless, a basic understanding of their working and knowledge of the most commonly used tags will be greatly helpful for the aspiring web architect.

An HTML document is composed of a set of elements. Each element consists of a pair of tags—start tag and an end tag. Each tag is semantically defined (i.e.) it has its own meaning associated, that is understood by the browser. Each tag in turn can have specific attributes which describe their characteristics like color, class, id, etc. Attributes are optional and they are defined as name–value pairs. Content is displayed between the start and end tags.

Refer to the example HTML below.

```
<h1> This is the main heading </h1>
```

The start and end tags are represented as <h1> and </h1> respectively. The content is sandwiched between the tags. Semantically, it instructs the browser to display the content in the main heading (<h1>). There are six header tags ranging from h1 to h6 each signifying sub-levels.

Similarly, there are tags for paragraph element (<p>), table element (<table>), title element (<title>), etc. A tag called <div> is one of the most common tags that will be used in web programming. Content enclosed between <div> and </div> tags can be grouped together as representing a division over which a behaviour or style can be applied.

The reader is advised to go through basic HTML lessons to get an idea of the tags normally used in HTML. A total understanding of the syntax of HTML is beyond the scope of this book. It is sufficient to get an idea of the structure and importance of HTML. Most of the HTML tags, in practice, are encapsulated in a framework like Rails which are used as opposed to using raw tags.

2.5 COMMON HTML TAGS

We have seen that HTML is written in the form of tags and attributes that the browser interprets and renders the display. There are a number of tags that browsers recognize. In practice, the term *tag* is used

Functional Group	Name(s)	Qualifier (Tag/Attribute/Form)
Structural	Html	Tag
	Meta	Tag
	Title	Tag
	Comment	-
	Head	Tag
	Body	Tag
	Frameset	Tag
Link	Anchor	Tag
	Anchor with Image	Tag
	Image map	Tag
Content	Headings – H1 thru H6	Tag
	Paragraph	Tag
	Image	Tag
	Table	Tags
Formatting	Bold/Strong	Tag
	Font tag	Tag
	List tags	Tags
	Center	Tag
	Division	Tags
	Block quote	Tag
	Preformatted text	Tag
	Blink	Tag
	Super script (sup/sub)	Tags
	Fieldset	Tag
	Align	Attribute
	Vlink	Attribute
	Alink	Attribute
	Border	Attribute
Form	Input – text box	Form Tag
	Input – Radio buttons	Form Tag
	Input – Checkbox	Form Tag
	Select	
	Password	

Fig. 2.7 *Common tags*

interchangeably with the term *element* and the two terms are indeed used synonymously. However, there is a subtle difference that needs to be recognized. It is highlighted by the following statement—an *element* contains a *start tag* and an *end tag*. The most common ones are summarized by function in Figure 2.7.

The reader is encouraged to refer help on HTML from the web for an exhaustive listing. A description of some of these tags along with relevant attributes is described in the following paragraphs.

Aside note

Unlike in strict academic circles, in the context of programming it is customary to use a "Cheat-Sheet"! A Cheat Sheet is a concise set of notes for quick reference during programming. Numerous Cheat sheets are available for a number of topics and HTML is no exception. Refer to the web and keep an HTML Cheat sheet handy for reference.

2.5.1 HTML Tag

The HTML tag follows the <!DOCTYPE> element in an HTML document. It is the starting tag of the HTML page. So all other elements (except <!DOCTYPE>) of the page are contained within this tag. Applicable attributes include the following:

- dir—indicates direction of the text. Value ltr indicates left to right and rtl indicates right to left.
- Lang—represents language used for the tag
- Xmlns—defines the XML namespace for for the (XHTML) document. It points to a URI. For example, consider the following declaration.

```
<html xmlns=http://www.w3.org/1999/xhtml lang="en">
```

It indicates that the tags in the HTML documents follow the XHTML namespace as defined. However, note that for HTML5, this attribute is no longer required as all tags are in this namespace by default.

2.5.2 Meta

As the name suggests, it provides information about data. Typically, they are used by browsers to control the display of content, used by search engines or even web services or used to refine the information provided by the actual headers. An example is shown below.

```
<meta http-equiv="Content-Type" content="text/html; charset=utf-8">
```

It indicates that the content is an HTML document with a character encoding as mentioned. For better security, it is recommended to always specify a certain encoding (character set) mechanism. A shorter form in HTML5 is as follows.

```
<meta charset="utf-8" />
```

Aside note

The META tag in HTML5 is also used to display mobile content for a device like iPad or iPhone.

```
<meta name="viewport" width="device-width">
```

2.5.3 Title

The title appears on the Title bar of the browser. Accordingly, the title is to be chosen (short and precise). The title tag is defined within the Head element.

2.5.4 Body

The <body> tag contains the body of the HTML document. It includes the content that appears in the browser window. Some of the key attributes applicable are as follows.

- Background—specifies URL of a background image of the web page
- Alink—this is used with the Anchor tag and specifies the color of the linked text.
- Vlink—this is also used with the Anchor tag and specifies the color of the link when it has been visited
- Link—specifies the color of the link text (when not visited)

There are other attributes applicable to this tag.

2.5.5 Headings

H1 through H6 are tags meant for headings at various levels. H1 can be considered for main heading and H2 through H6 for sub-headings.

```
<h1>H1 Heading</h1>
<h2>H2 Heading</h2>
<h3>H3 Heading</h3>
<h4>H4 Heading</h4>
<h5>H5 Heading</h5>
<h6>H6 Heading</h6>
```

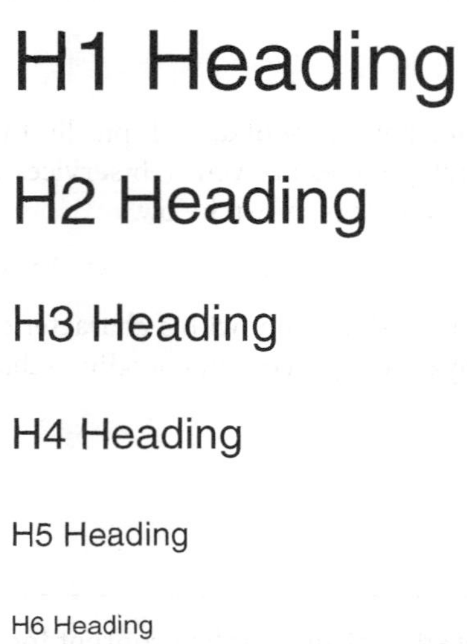

Fig. 2.8 *Headings H1 through H6*

They are typically displayed in a browser as shown in Figure 2.8. Note that the display can be changed by supplementing with a style element.

2.5.6 Anchor

The anchor tag is manifested as <a> tag, used to link to an url defined by a href attribute. An example is shown below.

```
<P>
Click <A HREF="http://pearsoned.com"> here </A> for a publisher of text
books
</P>
```

In a browser, it will manifest as follows.

Click here for a major publisher of text books

On clicking the anchor text, which is hyperlinked, it will lead to the address defined in HREF attribute. The address could be relative, internal or absolute (the example shown above is an absolute address). The choice of colors for the linked text can be customized. The control parameters include the following.

- Link—the default color of the linked text first time it is rendered
- Visited—the color it changes to, once the link is visited. Attribute name is vlink.
- Alink—this is used with the Anchor tag and specifies the color of the linked text.

They can be defined as attributes in the Body tag since it is applicable to the entire page. The details are covered in section on Body tag.

Another concept that is should be noted is the type of URL which can logically be Absolute, Relative or Internal.

Relative addresses operate based on the concept of a base URL. If the base URL is www.abc.com/d1/d2.html, then "../d3.html" will be equivalent to www.abc.com/d3.html.

Absolute address point to a complete URL.

Internal addresses refer to areas within a page so that the browser can scroll down (or up) the required point. It is referenced by a hash (#) prefix. For example www.abc.com/mydocument.html#chapter-2 is a valid address for the browser to attempt to navigate to chapter-2 of the document.

2.5.6.1 Target attribute If the URL pointed by the href attribute has to open the target in a specific window, use the attribute by name "target". Consider the following code.

```
<a href="www.abc.com/index.html" target="windowName">
```

The above line is interpreted by the browser to fetch the URL's index.html and position in the window named windowName. If this window does not exist, the browser will take the trouble (or pleasure!) of creating it. The value of windowName could be anything, but the following names have special semantics.

- _top
- _self
- _parent
- _blank

2.5.6.2 Image navigation

```
<?xml version="1.0" encoding="UTF-8"?>

<!DOCTYPE html PUBLIC "-//W3C//DTD XHTML 1.0 Strict//EN"
"http://www.w3.org/TR/xhtml1/DTD/xhtml1-strict.dtd">
<html xmlns="http://www.w3.org/1999/xhtml">
<head>
  <meta http-equiv="Content-Type" content="text/html; charset=UTF-8"/>
  <title>Anchor with Text or Image</title>
</head>
<body vlink="red" link="blue">
    <!-- Open a link in a specified window called mywin -->
    Click <a href="http://pearsoned.com" target="mywin"> here </a>
    for a major publisher of text books
    <br />
    <!-- This is a link in an area within the document -->
    Click <a href="#myref"> here </a> to jump to an internal page
    reference
    <br />
    <!-- Open the link by clicking a picture -->
    Click this image for link to Pearson
    <a href="http://pearsoned.com"> <img align="middle"
    src="flower.png" alt="flower" width="400" height="400" />
    </a>
    <br />
    <br />
    <!-- internal page reference address -->
    <div id=myref>This is the internal page reference that the
          browser visible area will jump to. The <i>id</i> of
          this element is the same as the <i>target</i> attribute
    </div>
</body>
</html>
```

Fig 2.9 *Links using anchor via text and image*

The output of the coding in figure 2.9 displays three links—one with the text and the other with the image, identified by flower.jpg (Figure 2.10). Both these locations point to the same site in this example.
The internal link (page reference) will display the portion identified by #href (not visible in the output figure).

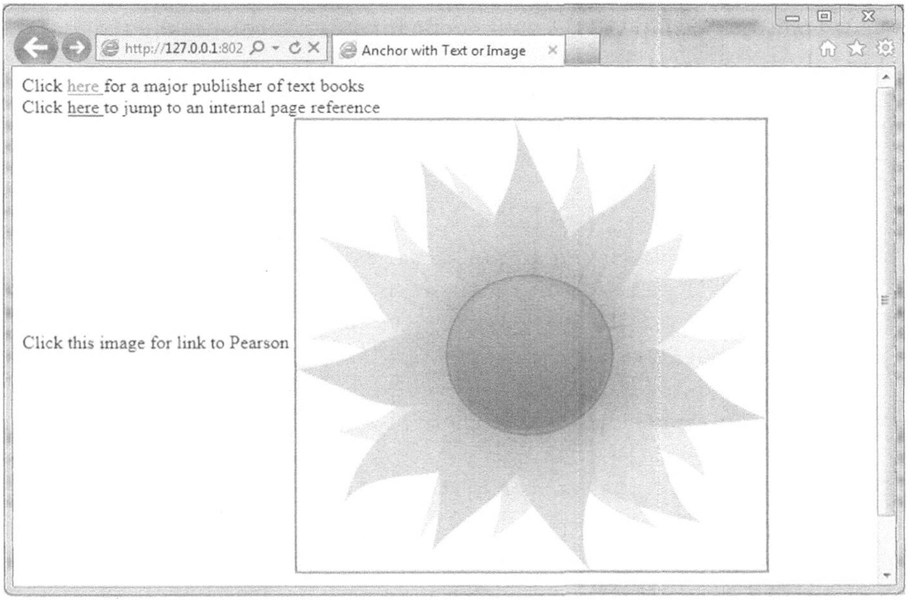

Fig. 2.10 *The output displaying the three links*

2.5.7 Lists

A list in a document refers to the arrangement of concise points in a textual format. The most popular example that is encountered in a word document is a bulleted list (of points). There are three types of Lists that are shown—Ordered list (ol), Unordered list (ul) and Definition list (dl).

An example of an ordered list is shown below.

```
<ol>
          <li> First in the list </li>
          <li> Second in the list </li>
          <li> Last but not the least </li>
</ol>
```

The ordered list starts off a numbered set of items, each item identified within <li> tags. There are options to arrange as per Roman numerals, Arabic numbers, etc, by specifying attributes. For example <ol type='I'> will arrange the list in Roman letters.

Unordered lists are specified by <ul> instead of the <ol> tag. In this case, they are listed out using bulleted lists. The Type attribute can still be used, with options for the shape of the bullet (Figure 2.11).

```
<!DOCTYPE html PUBLIC "-//W3C//DTD HTML 4.01//EN"
"http://www.w3.org/TR/html4/strict.dtd">
<html lang="en">
<head>
```

(Continued)

```
    <meta http-equiv="Content-Type" content="text/html; charset=utf-8">
    <title>L i s t s</title>
    <meta name="generator" content="Studio 3 http://aptana.com/">
    <meta name="author" content="srini">
    <!-- Date: 2011-07-02 -->
</head>
<body>
     <h1>Steps for developing a small Website </h1>
     <p> Following is the <b>structure</b> </p>
     <ol>
        <li> Lay out the main pages </li>
        <li> Sort out the templates </li>
        <li> Understand marketing theme, design Flash & other elements
        </li>
        <li> Decide on the <acronym title="content management system">
        CMS </acronym> </li>
        <li>Generate the HTML </li>
     </ol>
     <p> Spice yourself with some <acronym title="enthusiasm">enthu!
     </acronym> </p>
</body>
</html>
```

Fig. 2.11 *Ordered lists and other tags*

Fig. 2.12 *The output of lists in IE*

While observing the output (see Figure 2.12), notice how the acronym appears as a tool tip. Two acronyms are defined in the example, out of which the second acronym is shown.

There are numerous controls (tags) in HTML that need to be learnt that it becomes a tremendous task to tabulate all of them. Anyway, the fact is that usage of these tags is similar. With the kind of help and support available from the web as well as within most IDEs it makes the job of identifying HTML tags very easy. Nevertheless it is good to know the basic tags and understand their usage.

Definition lists are useful to define items as in a word (or a phrase), followed by its description. They are useful in coming up with a glossary. Definition tags are defined by dl, dt and dd tags. DL is the main heading for the definition list. DT specifies the title for which definition is defined. The definition itself is written down within the dd tags.

```
<?xml version="1.0" encoding="UTF-8"?>
<!DOCTYPE html PUBLIC "-//W3C//DTD XHTML 1.0 Strict//EN" "http://www.
w3.org/TR/xhtml1/DTD/xhtml1-strict.dtd">
<html xmlns="http://www.w3.org/1999/xhtml">
<head>
  <metahttp-equiv="Content-Type" content="text/html; charset=UTF-8"/>
  <title>Definitions</title>
</head>
<body>
    <dl>
      <dt>
        H<sub>2</sub>SO<sub>4</sub>
      </dt>
      <dd>
        Sulphuric Acid - this is a strong acid, will cause burns when
        gets in contact with a person's skin
      </dd>
      <dt>
        HCL
      </dt>
      <dd>
        Hydrochrolic acid - This is equally dangerous...
      </dd>
      <dt>
        [Ni(CN)<sub>4</sub>]<sup>-2</sup>
      </dt>
      <dd>
        Nickel chloride solutions are acidic, with a pH of around 4
        due to the hydrolysis of the Ni<sup>2+</sup> ion
      </dd>
    </dl>
</body>
</html>
```

Fig. 2.13 *Definition lists and other tags*

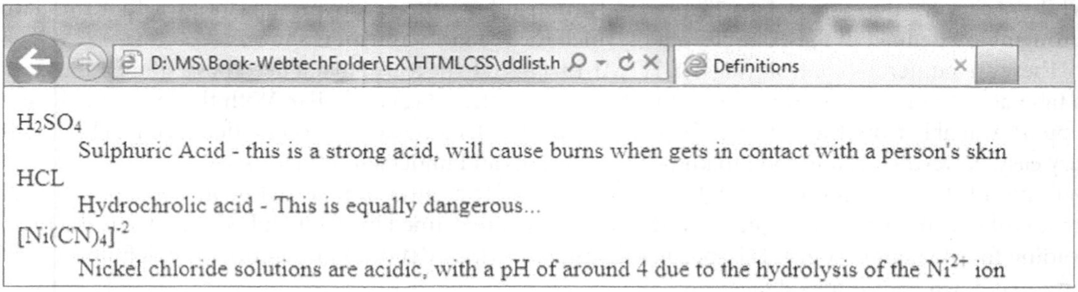

Fig. 2.14 *Definition lists output*

The HTML shown in Figure 2.13 includes a set of definitions within a DL tag. See the corresponding output in a browser (Figure 2.14).

Notice the indentation that is rendered by the browser automatically, because of the definition list.

As a side note, observe the way superscripts and subscripts are produced in the chemical formulae (as in H_2SO_4). They are achieved through the <sup> and <sub> tags respectively in the HTML code. For example the HTML snippet, **H₂SO₄** renders H_2SO_4 with the numerals appearing as subscripts.

2.5.8 Table

A **<table>** tag inserts a table (row–column tuple) in the HTML page. Within the table tag, there are a lot of tags applicable—for headers (heading row), rows (content row) and table data (corresponding to cell). Related to this are tags **<th>** for table header **,** **<tr>** for a table row, **<td>** for a table cell.

Tables are commonly used to format content within a page since there are a lot of alignment features that come native to a table. This obviates the need for (nbsp;) directives to insert spaces within the webpage. Formatting is achieved by using attributes that can be used along with table related tags (Figure 2.15).

Borders can be applied to the table (as an attribute in the Table definition tag [td]), but it is not compulsory to have one. Tables without borders are also elegant especially when designing a blog page or such, where the content is to be arranged in columns.

```
<?xml version="1.0" encoding="UTF-8"?>
<!DOCTYPE html PUBLIC "-//W3C//DTD XHTML 1.0 Strict//EN" "http://www.
w3.org/TR/xhtml1/DTD/xhtml1-strict.dtd">
<html xmlns="http://www.w3.org/1999/xhtml">
<head>
  <meta http-equiv="Content-Type" content="text/html; charset=UTF-8"/>
  <title>Table HTML</title>
</head>
<body>
  <h1>Table related tags and Attributes - example </h1>
  <table  border="solid" cellspacing="1px" title="Table" dir="LTR">
      <thead>
        <tr><strong>
          <td>Tag</td>
```

```
            <td>What it does</td>
            <td>Some attributes</td>
          </strong></tr>
        </thead>
          <tr>
            <td>table</td>
            <td>Basic tag for defining the table</td>
            <td>border, cellspacing, width, height, dir ...</td>
          </tr>
          <tr>
            <td>th</td>
            <td>Table Header Data Definition</td>
            <td>align </td>
          </tr>
          <tr>
            <td>td</td>
            <td>Table Data Definition</td>
            <td>colspan, rowspan, dir...</td>
          </tr>
          <tr>
            <td>tr</td>
            <td>Table Row Definition</td>
            <td></td>
          </tr>
    </table>
  </body>
</html>
```

Fig. 2.15 *Table tags*

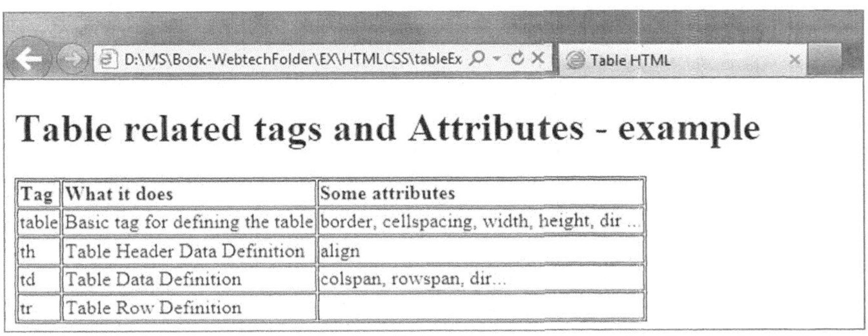

Table related tags and Attributes - example

Tag	What it does	Some attributes
table	Basic tag for defining the table	border, cellspacing, width, height, dir ...
th	Table Header Data Definition	align
td	Table Data Definition	colspan, rowspan, dir...
tr	Table Row Definition	

Fig. 2.16 *Table output*

Tables can be used not only to display the content but also to edit, along with HTML Form elements (Table 2.16).

2.5.9 Frames

Frames facilitate using multiple HTML documents to be displayed in a single page. The tag frameset is used. A word of caution—this tag is not recommended to be used as it has several drawbacks and the fact that there are better substitutes. It is more for cautioning the reader that this paragraph is included.

2.5.10 HTML Forms

All these aspects of HTML discussed so far dealt with the communication from the browser to the user (i.e.) how the browser treated these elements for it to render. Now an HTML (XHTML included!) form is a way for the user to interact and send his Responses. Of course, an HTML form isn't the only way to be interactive. There are other ways which will be subsequently mentioned.

A Form is a web page that is used by the user to enter information as in a registration process or such. The Form could contain many ways of soliciting information—typically called Controls like a text box, drop downs, etc. After the information is entered, the user submits the form (by clicking on a button, usually called Submit button), the browser packages and sends it to the appropriate Server, which could then be processed by a Web application.

```
<!DOCTYPE html PUBLIC "-//W3C//DTD XHTML 1.0 Strict//EN"
"http://www.w3.org/TR/xhtml1/DTD/xhtml1-strict.dtd">
<html>
<head>
<meta http-equiv="Content-Type"
content="text/html; charset=ISO-8859-1" />
<title>Simple Form example</title>
</head>
<body>
 <form action="serverURL" method="POST">
    Registration Form: <br /> <br />
    First name: <input type="text" name="firstname"></input> <br />
    Last name: <input type="text" name="lastname"> </input> <br />
    Gender: <input type="radio" name="gender">Male</input>
           <input type="radio" name="gender">Female</input>
    <br />
    EMail: <input type="text" name="email" value=""></input> <br />
    Country: <select name="country" size="1">
                 <option value="IN">India</option>
                 <option value="SIN">Singapore</option>
                 <option value="USA">USA</option>
          </select> <br />
    <br />
    <button type="submit">Submit</button>
 </form>
</body>
</html>
```

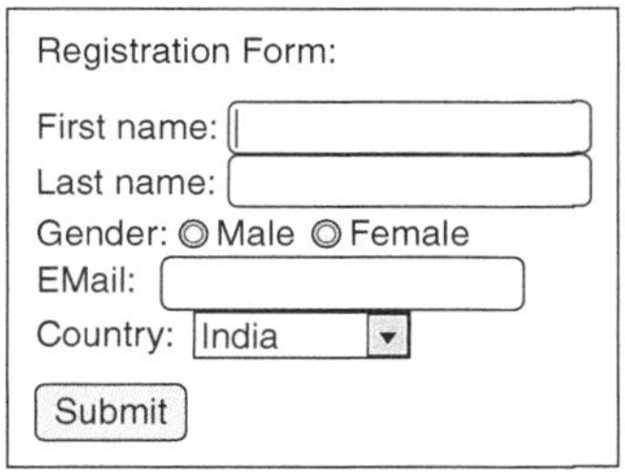

Fig. 2.17 *An example of an HTML form*

Notice the different tags (Figure 2.17) that are used to create the form and how they are rendered by the browser. The Form itself is created by the <form> tag which has *action* as one of the attributes. The action is a relative (or an absolute) URL which will be the target when the Submit button is clicked , that is when the Form is posted. The server side can be a PHP, or an ASP.NET or Java Servlet or a Rails program that accepts the Form values for further processing. Each of the Form elements are contained within—in this case includes text boxes, a check-box and a drop down list, besides the Submit button itself. In a simplistic scale, the browser can be thought to send the Form values as name–value pairs, with the names being defined in the HTML form (with name attribute). Hence it is required to have the name attribute unique within a web form. However, notice that the Radio buttons have the same name—this implies that only one of them can be in a clicked state at a time. Check boxes are similar but then multiple values can be checked at the same time.

An input text box which accepts a password, is not expected to echo the characters into the screen. An input box with type = password will enable this feature. (however, this is not shown in the example).

The code shown in Figure 2.18 shows the same Form that is formatted in a table structure.

```
<!DOCTYPE html PUBLIC "-//W3C//DTD XHTML 1.0 Strict//EN"
"http://www.w3.org/TR/xhtml1/DTD/xhtml1-strict.dtd">
<html>
<head>
  <meta http-equiv="Content-Type"
  content="text/html; charset=ISO-8859-1" />
  <title>Simple Form example with Table</title>
</head>
<body>
   <form action="serverURL" method="POST">
    <table id="regtab" bgcolor="#80DAEB" title="Registration Form">
      <tr>
          <th colspan="2">Registration Form</th>
      </tr>
      <tr>
          <td>First name</td>
```

(*Continued*)

```
            <td><input type="text" name="firstname"></input></td>
        </tr>
        <tr>
            <td>Last name</td>
            <td><input type="text" name="lastname"></input> </td>
        </tr>
        <tr>
            <td>Gender</td>
            <td>
                <input type="radio" name="gender">Male</input>
                <input type="radio" name="gender">Female</input>
            </td>
        </tr>
        <tr>
            <td>EMail</td>
            <td><input type="text" name="email" value=""></input> </td>
        </tr>
        <tr>
            <td>Country</td>
            <td> <select name="country" size="1">
                    <option value="IN">India</option>
                    <option value="SIN">Singapore</option>
                    <option value="USA">USA</option>
                </select>
            </td>
        </tr>
        <tr>
            <td colspan="2"><button type="submit">Submit</button>
            </td>
        </tr>
      </table>
    </form>
  </body>
  </html>
```

Fig. 2.18 *Example of the HTML form with table*

The button at the end of the Form definition is of type "Submit". When the user clicks the submit button, the browser sends the Form data to the URL specified in the *action* attribute of the Form. Similarly, there is another type of button, called "reset", which when clicked, will reset the values of the Form.

Notice the difference in output and the ease in adjusting the alignment. Needless to say, the formatted output in Figure 2.19 is more presentable.

Fig. 2.19 *Output*

2.6 XHTML

XHTML is HTML in a stricter form. In the initial period when HTML was introduced and used, a lot of badly formed HTML coding practices were common. Though the then browsers were tolerant of such badly formed code, it did not go well with advanced versions and rightly so. In parallel, during the same time, there were advances in a related technology called XML. XML is used to describe content while HTML is used to present content. The two technologies merged to form XHTML. The first version of XHTML was actually HTML 4.01 with XML. By default HTML has actually become to be referred to as XHTML, and as such the two terms are interchangeably used, including those in this book.

An example of a badly formed HTML is shown in Figure 2.20.

```
<!DOCTYPE html PUBLIC "-//W3C//DTD XHTML 1.0 Strict//EN"
"http://www.w3.org/TR/xhtml1/DTD/xhtml1-strict.dtd">
<html>
<head>
  <meta http-equiv="Content-Type"
  content="text/html; charset=ISO-8859-1" />
  <title>> not good HTML </title>
</head>
<body>
   <h1>This is a malformed heading
   <p> P Element without closing tag
</body>
</html>
```

Fig. 2.20 *An example of a malformed HTML code*

The reader would have noticed that the <h1>tag in the above example is not closed (with the</h1> tag). Similarly the <p> tag is not closed as well. However, if the program is run on a browser like Netscape, the above code will generate an output and will not indicate any error. This probably is considered a good behaviour since it is tolerant of errors, and is likely to be right (or harmless) in this context. But there are numerous other areas where it can behave in undesirable ways. For example, if there is a statement that follows the <h1>, then the browser will consider the text as a header, which is not likely to be correct. The end result is that errors are harder to detect, and cannot be automated by DOM manipulation. Therefore, the convention is to stick to stricter norms, enforced by XML's data/content definitions. The following are the conventions that are strictly followed in XHTML.

- An XHTML page should have one root element
- There are some mandatory elements in XHTML
  - DOCTYPE declaration is the first statement in the HTML, even before the <html> tag. This is a directive to the browser about the markup language
  - html,
  - body
  - title
- All tags must be properly closed
- Tags should be nested properly so that it can be represented as a hierarchy. The section on DOM or Document Object Model describes the structure and methods to navigate a HTML page.
- XHTML tags should all be in lower case, including attribute names.
- Some tags were deprecated in XHTML. Notable among them are <frameset>, <frame>, <center>, <iframe>, <ins>, <map>, <menu>, <strike>, etc.

XHTML documents (those defined with a MIME type of XML like application/xhtml+xml) are treated as XML documents by the corresponding Web browsers, and hence parsed by an XML processor. However, the XML processor differentiates in the processing when it is an XHTML document as compared to a pure XML document (more on XML in the section pertaining to Server Side in this book). The difference is in handling rendering errors.

2.6.1 HTML Validator

A software to validate how well-formed an (X)HTML document is, can be used to check the correctness. This is available in www.w3.org. It is free to use and reports out deficiencies in the HTML code. There are three ways of checking out the HTML code as follows.

- Validate by URI, in which the URL is given to the service to work on
- Validate by File upload in which the HTML file is uploaded for the service to check its code
- Validate by direct input in which the HTML code is pasted into a space provided by the service

The validation for the malformed HTML (Figure 2.20) is shown in Figure 2.21.

The output shows the area where the error occurred.

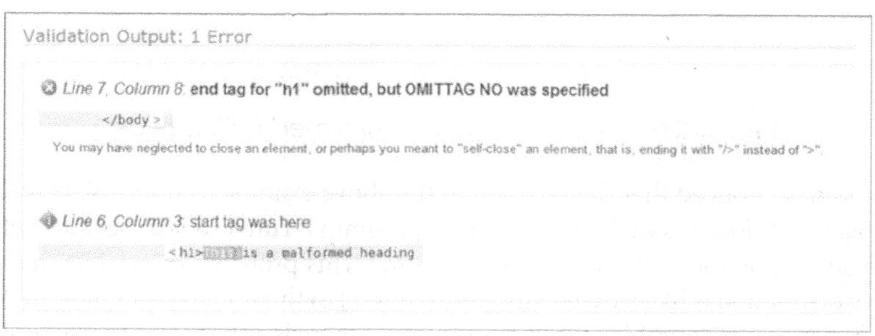

Fig. 2.21 *Output from HTML validator*

2.7 BLOCK AND INLINE ELEMENTS

A few of the tags cause new lines to be introduced during display (i.e. rendering by the browser). These are called Block elements or Block tags. Block tags create a block of element on an HTML page. A Paragraph tag is defined by <P> element. A DIV element groups a page into sections. It is normally used by developers to update specific DIV sections through Ajax. These are examples of Block elements.

A few others cause the display in-line. Examples include <span>, and <a> elements. The distinction between Block and Inline type of tags is made to facilitate understanding of how styling elements work and used in CSS.

2.8 HTML5

As HTML5 is being released, it is supported by some of the latest version of browsers in varying degrees of compliance. The new features of HTML5 has generated a lot of interest, it is just being introduced, as an overhaul for HTML4. Browsers will continue to support both versions for a lot more time as it will take a while before its usage becomes widespread. At this point of time there are variations in the degree of support for HTML5 in various browsers: IE, FireFox, Opera, Chrome and Safari. One of the goals of HTML5 is to enable moving away from proprietary technologies. So far, the trend has been to promote more and more capabilities towards rich interfaces, as is seen by plug-ins such as Flash, Silverlight, etc. But HTML5 promises to have all of these capabilities under a single standard, across computers and mobiles and without plug-in. The latter point, eliminating the need for a plug-in, is a significant advantage in the mobile world.

Aside note

W3C has issued a new logo for HTML5, shown below. It can be seen in sites that are HTML5-ready.

There are many new elements/features introduced as part of HTML5. The notable ones are included below.

- Canvas element which renders graphics. When Canvas is used, there is no need for plug-ins to be installed, as is being currently done.
- Video and Audio Elements which obviates the need for 3rd party plug-ins like Flash or QuickTime. In the current model of HTML, an Audio player has to be embedded, supported by some JavaScript code to load the player. In HTML5 an audio file can be directly loaded as in the following example.
    - <audio controls="controls">
    - <source src="mysong.wav" type="audio/mpeg" />

- </audio>
- Currently not all browsers support all audio formats, so it is a challenge to work around this.

- Geo Location to locate the user's location through GPS
- Support for Offline browsing
- New set of Form attributes and input types

Aside note

The level of conformance to HTML5 features can be checked in your browser from the following website:

www.html5test.com

See for yourself the set of standards, supported and unsupported.

2.9 SUMMARY

This chapter brought out the basic concepts of HTML (interchangeably referred to as XHTML), which itself is the basis of web technology. The most common tags classified into structural, link, content, formatting and Forms were presented. An introduction into the latest version, HTML5, is also made in this chapter.

EXERCISES

Q1. Tool-tips are small pieces of help text that act as a guide to fill up a field or such, when the cursor is hovered around the element. How are these achieved in HTML?

Q2. Construct a HTML table along with some data. Play around with some of the attributes of the table related tags and observe the outputs.

Q3. Imagine a scenario where you are going on a cycling tour around the country side. You have jotted down events and memorabilia in your diary and are now ready to publish in a web log of all the events. Design a set of HTML pages that can be used to create the log. Remember to include not just text but also images, videos and audio clips to make it interesting.

Q4. Design an XHTML Form for accepting inputs online for buying a pair of sports shoes. Include some of the most common brands (Reebok, Nike, etc), and an appropriate set of controls for capturing the order. Let this Form be simple enough, but doing its job essentially. Be as creative as possible while designing the Form.

Q5. Design a Login Form. The speciality of the login Form is the presence of a Password field. On typing the password, it shows itself as a set of stars, thus hiding the characters. Again, be as creative as possible while coming up with the login Form.

Q6. What is the technique to display chemical formulae using HTML?

Q7. Study the new features available in HTML5. Write down the merits and demerits of using HTML5. Analyze from multiple perspectives like usage, availability of skills, technical capability, and much more.

Q8. There are UI frameworks like JSF and ASP.NET. Form teams consisting of pairs of individuals to conduct a high level study on how HTML forms the basis for these technologies. Understand the importance of being familiar with HTML for web programming.

Project Activities

Q9. Investigate the additional Form input elements available in HTML5. Make a report.

Q10. Browsers come in different flavors. Each of them has its USP. As a web programmer or designer, you need to be aware of this variance and design accordingly. Keeping HTML5 in mind do an analysis of the various browsers. Team up to make a report on the analysis. Use sites like www.html5test.com while coming up with the report.

Caselet Activity

Q11. Design a Website conforming to a theme. Read the notes below to get an idea of the theme. You may follow the given theme or better still, imagine your own theme, because the design of creating a web site is more creative than the process it takes to do! Here are the basics.

- A website is a collection of Web pages that are of course related to each other and also related to the purpose of the website. The landing page when the user first enters the website is called the Home page. There will be a menu and a set of links to traverse to the other pages. The process of linking from one page to another set of pages is called site navigation. The question is how is a website designed? It starts with the purpose of the website. For example consider a theme involving people collaborating over coffee. The ultimate goal is to bring people together in your chain if café shops, book tables online and take orders.
- Leverage the preparatory work (Domain Name and the Hosting provider) that has been done as part of the Caselet Activity in the previous chapter.
- Organize the website into a series of pages. Starting with the Home page, visualize the primary pages for *About*, *Services*, *Stores*, *Customers* and *Online*. Create a Mock-up of these web pages.
- Preferably, first pencil out the important pages like Home page
- Then visualize the navigation links. The entire set of activities (layout as well as navigation) is called the Information Architecture for a site.
- While designing consider the future state of the website as well, like an e-commerce page, a site specific design, user personalization, etc.
- Refine the preparatory report if necessary.

3

CLIENT-SIDE—CSS

> *Chapter Objectives:*
> - ***Bring out the philosophy of CSS***
> - ***Learn CSS with a few examples***
> - ***The concept of the Box model***
> - ***Understand the rationale of CSS***

It has been seen in the preceding sections as to how the browser interprets an HTML file and renders output. While doing so, it uses its default settings on how each tag is to be rendered. CSS (Cascading Style Sheets) is a mechanism to override the default settings and render the output as per specific styles required by the user.

CSS is actually a language that defines style constructs. Examples of style constructs include font, color, positioning, background themes, etc. CSS Styles can be applied directly within an HTML page. Alternatively, they can be written in a separate text file with an extension of css.

The first version of CSS, called CSS1, came out in 1996. CSS2 evolved in 1998 and it continues to be most popular. CSS3 is the latest version. The reader is advised to check out the details from the website at http://www.w3.org/Style/CSS/.

3.1 CSS DECLARATIONS

The hierarchy of applying CSS styles work on an HTML page. An HTML page can have multiple styles. A style sheet document in turn can apply to multiple HTML pages as well. That is the advantage—styles can be uniformly applied as well as specifically controlled—a unique combination of centralized as well as a de-centralized approach to applying styles to documents.

Returning to the hierarchy of styles, an HTML document can have multiple styles or CSS documents, associated; each CSS document can have multiple style declarations; each declaration consists of a Rule. A Rule consists of a Selector and a set of name–value pairs.

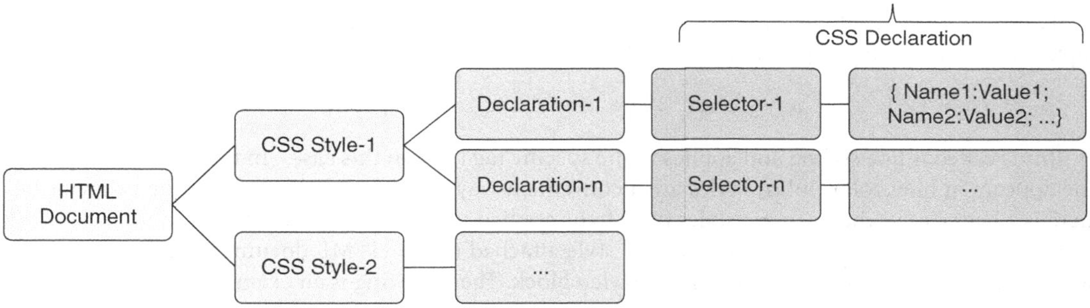

Fig. 3.1 *Hierarchy of CSS declarations*

Figure 3.1 shows how CSS Declarations are applied as styles to HTML. Each CSS Declaration takes the following format.

Selector {Name1 : value1; … }

Here Name is the name of a property (attribute) and Value signifies its value. Selector defines the criteria for applying the name–value pairs. The most common Selector is an HTML Tag. There are other selector types possible and will become clear as we progress through this chapter.

To reiterate, Style declarations are defined based on each (HTML) element and applied based on certain attributes like "id" and "class". Applying styles to elements can be thought of as applying colors and decorations to rooms in a house to make it appealing. However, it is not just for the appeal that CSS is for—there are a lot of innovations that have happened which make the web functionally more useful as well. For example, the concept of tabs and menus can wholly be implemented using CSS.

Consider a sample directive in CSS like the following.

```
p {
background-color :blue;
border: 2px dashed red;
}
```

It instructs all <p> tagged elements of the corresponding HTML file(s) to set the background color to blue. Then it applies a border of red color, 2 pixels thick. The style names are case-sensitive and are generally lower case. Examples of style names are font-family, text-decoration, margin, padding, width, etc.

When using attributes, it could filter further to an element or stand alone by itself. For example, p.myclass (instead of just "p" in the above instruction block) will apply to all "p" elements with a class attribute of "myclass". Similarly using p#myid will apply to "p" elements with the "id" of "myid".

3.2 USING CSS

Style sheets are thus templates, containing rules on how to apply styles to content. An understanding of the Document Object Model (DOM) model will make usage of CSS clearer. There is a separate section on DOM as part of JavaScript and the reader is encouraged to refer both these sections in parallel, if required. However, the reader may choose to mull over the topic of CSS and then revisit this chapter after DOM has been covered.

There are three ways to associate styles with content. They are inline, embedded and linked. The last option is the ideal method that is recommended in the interest of best practices for web development.

Styles can be used along with HTML (recall that HTML is used interchangeably with XHTML), applied directly on a tag as part of its attribute.

```
<p style="color:blue"> this line uses inline styling to color </p>
```

This is called inline styling and applies to the specific tag (<p> in this case). In the above example the line appears in blue color. Inline styles are a convenient way to apply for altering specific behavior but there is a better way when generic styles need to be applied to a group of elements.

To accomplish this, there is an embedded style attached to the HTML document. All style declarations are embedded within a <style> and </style> block. The following is an example.

```
<!DOCTYPE html PUBLIC "-//W3C//DTD XHTML 1.0 Transitional//EN"
"http://www.w3.org/TR/xhtml1/DTD/xhtml1-transitional.dtd">
<html xmlns="http://www.w3.org/1999/xhtml">
     <head><title> CSS Embedded Styling</title>

     <style type= "text/css">
     <!--
            p {color:blue;}/*set font color to blue */
     -->
     </style>

     </head>
     <body>
            <p> This line leverages emdedded styling to color me</p>
     </body>
```

The effect is similar with respect to coloring, but all <p> tags will get the color.

With the above arrangement, one generic style can work for all similar groupings—by tags (groups of tags), class (selective groups of tags) or id (individual tag). However, this model does not still vouch for the earlier mentioned goal of separating style from content. There should definitely be another model.

The most commonly used model of applying CSS styles to content is by having a separate CSS file and importing it in HTML file. This way, the same style can be used in several HTML files within or across websites. Some of reasons why Styles and Content need to be separate are summarized below:

- Promote common look and feel within a website
- It is easier to change styles as necessary to suit different needs
- Promote division of skills—a set of CSS styles can be designed by a User experience expert, whereas content generation can be left under the realm of the programmer
- Easier to support different kinds of media for the same content. For example, the same content needs to be viewed differently depending upon a computer terminal, or a mobile phone or a printer. What is changing is only the CSS file rather than rendering a different content.

An example using this model is as follows.

```
<!DOCTYPE html PUBLIC "-//W3C//DTD XHTML 1.0 Transitional//EN"
"http://www.w3.org/TR/xhtml1/DTD/xhtml1-transitional.dtd">
<html xmlns="http://www.w3.org/1999/xhtml">
     <head><title> CSS Embedded Styling</title>
     <link rel=stylesheet href="myCSS1.css" TYPE="text/css">
```

```
    </head>
    <body>
    <p> This line leverages emdedded styling to color me</p>
    </body>
</html>
```

This example leverages an externally created CSS file (myCSS1.css). All styles can be defined in this file, thus separation of style with content is achieved. The style pertaining to the P tag will be applied.

As mentioned previously, there could be more than one CSS file declared for an HTML file. This is to allow for different sets of styles representing different sets of elements. If there are overlapping elements within the multiple CSS file definitions, the latest definitions that CSS encounters will be taken as the basis. However, these can be controlled to some extent by means of an "important" declaration. According to this, if a style is declared important (for instance as color:blue! important) then weightage is given to this definition irrespective of the order in which it occurs, provided it is not overridden by a similar statement later.

Having provision for more than one CSS file also adds to the advantage that different parts of UI work can be outsourced independently of the other (of course with some bit of communication!). Furthermore, it also allows different libraries to be imported into the application without having the botheration to merge the (style) files.

3.3 SAMPLE CSS FILE

Shown in Figure 3.2 is a sample CSS file that is generic. The CSS applies from top to bottom.

```
* { padding: 0; margin: 0; }

html, body, div, span, form, label, legend {
outline: 0; padding: 0;
background: #8CA3E6;
}

body {background: #092e20; color: #000; font: normal;}
body {
 font-family: Candara, Helvetica, sans-serif;
 font-size: 13px;
}
p {
padding: 2px;
border-style: solid;
border-width: 2px;
background-color: blue;
color: white;
font-family: arial,helvetica;
font-size: 11px;
font-weight: bold;
}
```

(Continued)

```
#wrapper {
 margin: 0 auto;
 width: 1000px;
}
#content {
 float:  right;
 width: 1068px;
 position: relative;
 color: #333;
 padding: 1px;
 border: 3px  double grey;
 margin: 0px 0px 0px 0px;
 background: transparent;
}
```

Fig. 3.2 *A snippet from a sample CSS file*

It is related to the HTML tags in the sense that the style definitions apply to a particular tag. For example the <body> tag is styled as per the body style definition described in the CSS file. Likewise, all content within <p> tags in the HTML file will follow that defined by the style within "p { …}" in the CSS file.

In addition to the tag, there could be classes or "id"s in the HTML file that can relate to the CSS style definitions. In an HTML page each "id" attribute is unique; however, there could be multiple elements in an HTML page that could have the same 'class' attribute.

3.4 SELECTORS

CSS rules (CSS Declarations) that are defined, are applied to individual HTML tags as per pattern matching rules. The patterns are defined in CSS as Selectors. They are many types of them, classified by their mode of application, that is, Styles that are defined are applied to a specific selection, identified by a Selector or group of Selectors. A simple selector is the Type Selector. For example, consider the following directive.

```
div {font-size: 1em;}
```

It matches all elements with <div> tag in the HTML form. After matching, it applies the style(s) indicated in the CSS Declaration block. In this case, a font size of 1 em is the style applied. This is the most straight-forward type of selector to understand. Now let us move on to the other types of selectors.

3.4.1.1 Class selectors All HTML tags can optionally have the class attribute associated with them. The value of the Class attribute can be anything that represents a class of tags. The web program can have any semantic (meaning) associated with the value (of the class attribute). As far as CSS is concerned, this value can be referenced to define a declaration. This is achieved by prefixing a dot (.) with the value. For example, consider the following HTML which is defined with a class attribute.

```
<tt class="warning">this is an error message … </tt>
```

The above (teletype) text is defined classified under warning. Assume that the CSS declaration is defined as below.

```
warning {color: red; font-weight: bold;}
```

Assuming that the HTML file references the CSS Link file, the above declaration instructs the browser to display all content specified with the class attribute named "warning" to appear red and in bold font.

Recall that there could be multiple tags in an HTML Page with the same value of class. Accordingly, in the example above, all elements with a class "warning" will appear in the format as defined above.

3.4.1.2 ID selectors This is similar to Class selectors but the difference is that it is applied using the ID attribute. Just like the dot prefix for class values, the character that connects the value of ID attribute in HTML and that in CSS is hash (#).

```
<div id="myhdg">
```

This is my text with a specific style defined by my ID

```
</div>
```

It is to be recalled that ID elements are unique to the document and hence appear only once in the HTML page. Assume the CSS Declaration as written below.

```
#myhdg {border 1px solid red; padding 40px;}
```

This follows that the element with an ID defined 'myhdg' is formatted as per definition.

3.4.1.3 Descendant selectors The individual Selector styles, discussed earlier in this section, apply to each selector element, but practically, it is useful to apply styles based on some combinations. For example consider the following definition.

```
div a { font-size: 1em;}
```

All <a> tagged elements in the context of <div> tags will be formatted as per the above definition. On a similar directive, but with a small variation here is another example.

```
div .divhdg {border 1px solid red; padding 40px;}}
```

The above definition formats all classes of elements (for any tag) with name "divhdg" in the context of a <div> tagged element.

```
div ~ a { font-size: 1em;}
```

The above style applies to all <a> tagged elements which are direct descendants of <div> tagged elements. This is an example of parent-child selector.

Sometimes, an attribute also becomes significant. An example will make it easier to explain. Consider the CSS Selector as below.

```
div a [href] {…}
```

The selector selects all anchor elements, with an HREF defined as attribute (within the context of a DIV element).

In all the above selector syntaxes, a comma operator in between the selectors will connote a different meaning. For example,

```
div, a { font-size: 1em;}
```

The above definition is meant to save typing and means that both <div> and <a> elements follow the defined style.

Likewise, a number of permutations & combinations of tags and classes can be used to come up with fine-tuned styles. It is to be noted that CSS styles apply in a hierarchical fashion aligned with the DOM's model of an HTML page.

3.4.1.4 Psuedo selectors There are some special contexts that act as selectors which may be then used to apply styles. Examples will make it clear, as we go through each of them.

3.4.1.4.1 First-child

It selects the first element within the parent. It is represented by :first-child. Similarly, there is another pseudo-selector called nth-child. It even accepts a parameter which could denote "even", "odd" or an equation of some order. In combination it is an amazing technique to get a table for instance with different colors for alternate rows or even alternate columns. The following example will make them clear. Notice the style shown in the file in a different color (Figure 3.3).

```
<?xml version="1.0" encoding="UTF-8"?>
<!DOCTYPE html PUBLIC "-//W3C//DTD XHTML 1.1//EN"
"http://www.w3.org/TR/xhtml11/DTD/xhtml11.dtd">

<html xmlns="http://www.w3.org/1999/xhtml" xml:lang="en">
<head>
<title>css-ps1</title>
<style type="text/css">

tr:nth-child(2n+1) {background-color: #F0E891; }

tr:first-child {background: #FEFE22;}
</style>
</head>

<body>
        <table border="solid">
        <tr>
```

```
            <th>FirstName</th>
            <th>LastName</th>
            <th>Department</th>
            <th>Join date</th>
            <th>Salary</th>
        </tr>

        <tr>
            <td>Smith</td>
            <td>Jones</td>
            <td>HR</td>
            <td>21/Jan/10</td>
            <td>200000</td>
        </tr>

        <tr>
            <td>Roger</td>
            <td>Smith</td>
            <td>Technical</td>
            <td>21/Jan/90</td>
            <td>190000</td>
        </tr>

        <tr>
            <td>Raman</td>
            <td>CV</td>
            <td>Technical</td>
            <td>21/Jan/99</td>
            <td>770000</td>
        </tr>

        <tr>
            <td>Alex</td>
            <td>Bell</td>
            <td>Telecom</td>
            <td>23/Jun/99</td>
            <td>670000</td>
        </tr>

        <tr>
            <td>Tanaka</td>
            <td>San</td>
            <td>Admin</td>
            <td>20/Jan/88</td>
            <td>550000</td>
        </tr>
        </table>
</body>
</html>
```

(*Continued*)

FirstName	LastName	Department	Join date	Salary
Smith	Jones	HR	21/Jan/10	200000
Roger	Smith	Technical	21/Jan/90	190000
Raman	CV	Technical	21/Jan/99	770000
Alex	Bell	Telecom	23/Jun/99	670000
Tanaka	San	Admin	20/Jan/88	550000

Fig. 3.3 *Demonstrating n^{th}-child and first-child*

The equation shown in the above example is (2n+1) which denotes even and odd entities. There are other possibilities—"odd", "even", and any number. Also note that the order of defining the style elements matter in this case since the header row of the table is displayed in a different color.

However, it is advised caution to test it out on all browsers uniformly.

3.4.1.4.2 Last-Child

This method selects the last tag of a parent. Otherwise, conceptually it is similar to the fist-child selector.

3.4.1.4.3 First-line/First-letter

It selects the first formatted line (or First letter) of a paragraph. It is mainly used for styling the first line/letter in a paragraph or in a title.

3.4.1.4.4 Hover

This is an event when the mouse (cursor) is held on top of the object (hovers around). As this occurs, a style change could be made to occur like for instance, changing the font color of the text, or creating a border on the (hovered) image, etc.

3.4.1.4.5 Active

A hyperlink is said to be active if it is clicked. It would apply for the duration of a mouse-click. This (pseudo) selector is used when it is required to customize the color elements (font color, background color) of an active link. It is defined after the hover pseudo selector is defined.

3.4.1.4.6 Focus

This selector selects elements that are the current focus of the form. It is used mainly for Form elements. It is related to the Hover pseudo selector, but then Hover is only for mouse, not for keyboard inputs.

```
input:focus { background-color:yellow; }
```

This style will select all focus elements of the "input" tag, that is, text boxes belonging to a form. As the focus changes from one element to the next, the background color changes to yellow, as per the above style.

3.4.1.4.7 Link

This selector selects all anchor elements where HREF attribute is defined.

```
a:link {color: #666;}
```

3.4.1.4.8 Visited

When links are visited at least once, they can be made to exibit a certain style like for instance changing their color.

```
table#edittable a:visited {
            font-weight:normal;
            color:#666;
            text-decoration: line-through;
}
```

The selector in this example selects all anchor elements within a table defined by name "editable" and which have been visited (i.e. clicked at least once by the user). The visited links as per the selector will have a style defined in the declaration block.

Observe in all the above examples that pseudo-selectors are defined with colon (:) as the separating character.

3.5 BOX MODEL

The Style properties that can be defined using CSS can be considered to be grouped into two categories—Layout properties and Formatting properties. To understand the layout properties, it (element) is best visualized as a (imaginary) rectangular area for display. It is represented in Figure 3.4.

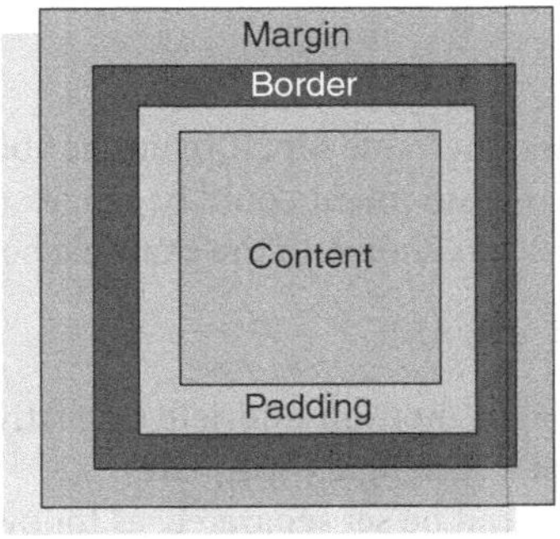

Fig. 3.4 *CSS box model*

3.5.1 Concept

CSS considers each element as a box. A piece of text (or any content), if displayed as-is, will not look appealing, so it is implicitly wrapped over layers. How these layers stack up together, is defined by the Box model, made up of the Content area, along with Padding, Border and Margin. The **Content** area could be a piece of text, an image or any of the content types. This area is surrounded by a transparent **Padding** layer, which is optional. The Border is again optional. If present, it is placed surrounding the Padding. Finally the Margin is applied over the Padding. Again the Margin is optional. The values for each of these optional elements can be fine tuned and configured as per each requirement, but overall the model serves as a template for CSS to process.

All Block elements and inline elements are treated as per the box model. As a result, Paragraph (<p>), Headings (<h1> through <h6>), lists (<li>), links, and other such elements are applied as per this concept.

A Block element is one which has line break. It is best understood by an example of such an element, which includes <p>, <h1>…<h6>, <ul>, <fieldset>, <div>, etc. Inline elements do not have line breaks in built in their display. For example, <strong >, <acronym>, <span> are inline elements.

Aside note

Three aspects to be noted in Block Vs Inline elements

Structure: Block elements are considered larger structures as compared to Inline elements. For instance, Block level elements can contain inline elements or other block elements. But Inline elements can contain either text or other inline elements.

Format: Block start with new lines; Inline elements do not.

Direction: The default direction (attribute dir) is "ltr" (Left to right). A Block element's dir attribute is either inherited or taken from the page default value. However, it is not inherited in an inline element.

Refer http://www.w3.org/TR/html4/struct/global.html for more details.

3.5.2 Padding

Padding is controlled by means of the "padding" style name. The simplest declaration looks like the example below.

```
{padding : 10px;}
```

Since padding is applied on all sides, the value set (10px in the above example) is applied to all 4 sides equally. Apart from pixel, the unit of measurement could be em, ex, pt, in, mm, cm or percentage.

Each side can also be individually set as shown in the example below.

```
{padding : 10px 12px 20px 15px;}
```

This setting corresponds to top, right, bottom and left respectively. The order of the sides is considered to move clockwise from top of a rectangle (or square).

Alternatively, padding for each side can be set separately as follows.

- padding-top
- padding-right
- padding-bottom
- padding-left

A similar concept can be applied to margin and border-width.

Thus the equation for the actual width and height are taken to be calculated as shown below.

Actual Width = definedWidth + padding-left + padding-right + border-left + border-right

Actual Height = definedHeight + padding-top + padding-bottom + border-top + border-bottom

When the border values or padding values are not explicitly defined, the browser takes the default values associated with them.

3.6 Float

In the context of CSS, a *Float* is used to control the flow of text around an element (or vice versa). It is not to be confused with the floating-point data types that are encountered in programming languages like Java.

Float in CSS can be set for any boxed element which is not positioned as absolute. For example an image may be floated around text. The *float* property can be given one of the three values —*left*, *right* or *none*, implying whether it floats (the element) to the left, right or not applying floating at all. If the float is applied to several elements in a sequence, it keeps following the rule (of right or left) as per the previous element, thus elements can be stacked sideways (as long as there is space).

```
<!DOCTYPE html PUBLIC "-//W3C//DTD XHTML 1.0 Transitional//EN"
"http://www.w3.org/TR/xhtml1/DTD/xhtml1-transitional.dtd">
<html xmlns="http://www.w3.org/1999/xhtml">
    <head><title> Float and Clear </title>

    </head>
    <body>

    <div id="wrapper" style="width:600px; border:solid;
height:600px;padding:10px;">
    <span> Demonstration about float </span>
    <image src="float2.jpg" alt="ship" style="float:right; padding:10px;
border:groove;"/>
    <p> The boundary of the display area is set by the DIV element in this
example with ID wrapper. Observe the content how it flows with the picture
element<AQ: Please correct for grammatical sense, suggestion: Observe the
content flow with the picture element OR Observe how the content flows
with the picture element. Please also update the accompanying image to
reflect this content and provide a new image.>. Just like the water which
flows freely around a ship, content should flow freely flow around the
image for a natural experience.

Float can be used not only with images but also for all (boxed) elements
that are not Absolutely positioned. They can position themselves towards
the right or left as indicated in the float property. If the picture
cannot be accommodated<AQ: Please update this spelling correction in the
accompanying image and provide the new image> within the width, it flows
downward.</p>
    </div>
    </body>
</html>
```

Demonstration about float

The boundary of the display area is set by the DIV element in this example with ID wrapper. Observe the content how it flows with the picture element. Just like the water which flows freely around a ship, content should flow freely around the image for a natural experience. Float can be used not only with images but also for all(boxed) elements that are not Absolutely positioned. They can position themselves towards the right or left as indicated in the float property. If the picture cannot be accommodated within the width, it flows downward.

The image referred to by the src property in the HTML listing should be present in the same directory.

What happens where there are exceptions arising when, for instance, the picture size extends beyond the size of the block (the DIV element with ID—*wrapper* in the example)? Examine the overflow:hidden directive in CSS. Experiment with different values for the height or width of the wrapper DIV.

3.6.1 Using Float and Clear

Many times it is required to arrange images on one side of the page, with content flowing around them. This can be accomplished using a combination of the *float* property and another property called *clear*, which can assume right, left, both or none.

```
<!DOCTYPE html PUBLIC "-//W3C//DTD XHTML 1.0 Transitional//EN"
"http://www.w3.org/TR/xhtml1/DTD/xhtml1-transitional.dtd">

<html xmlns="http://www.w3.org/1999/xhtml">
    <head><title> Float and Clear </title>
    </head>

    <body>
    <div id="wrapper" style="width:600px; border:solid;
height:400px;padding:10px;">
    <span> Demonstration about Float and Clear</span>

    <image src="float2.jpg" alt="ship" style="float:right; padding:10px;
border:groove;clear:right"/>

    <image src="float2.jpg" alt="ship" style="float:right; padding:10px;
border:groove; clear:right"/>
    <p>The boundary of the display area is set by the DIV element in this
example with ID wrapper. Observe the content how it flows with the
picture element. Just like the water which flows freely around a ship,
content should flow freely flow around the image for a natural experience.

Float can be used not only with images but also for all (boxed) elements
that are not Absolutely positioned. They can position themselves towards
the right or left
as indicated in the float property. If the picture cannot be accommodated
<AQ: Please update this spelling correction in the accompanying image and
provide the new image>within the width, it flows downward.</p>

    <p>Note how the images align towards the right side within the
wrapper DIV block</p>

    </div>
    </body>
</html>
```

Demonstration about Float and Clear

The boundary of the display area is set by the DIV element in this example with ID wrapper. Observe the content how it flows with the picture element. Just like the water which flows freely around a ship, content should flow freely around the image for a natural experience. Float can be used not only with images but also for all (boxed) elements that are not Absolutely positioned. They can position themselves towards the right or left as indicated in the float property. If the picture cannot be accommodated within the width, it flows downward.

Note how the images align towards the right side within the wrapper DIV block.

Aside note

Float and its related properties (like clear) are not implemented uniformly across all browsers, expecially the older versions of IE and Firefox. The situation has improved in the later versions, but there are many users still on the older versions. So it is advised caution to test across a cross section of browsers that are being targeted.

3.7 *Z*-Index

CSS uses *Z*-index to bring elements to the front or push them back, when there are overlapping elements. This is an important property that can be used for menus or other controls which require them to be brought forward. The example in Figure 3.5 will make it clear.

```
<?xml version="1.0" encoding="UTF-8"?>
<!DOCTYPE html PUBLIC "-//W3C//DTD XHTML 1.0 Strict//EN"
"http://www.w3.org/TR/xhtml1/DTD/xhtml1-strict.dtd">
<html xmlns="http://www.w3.org/1999/xhtml">
<head>
  <meta http-equiv="Content-Type" content="text/html;
  charset=UTF-8"/>
  <title>Z-Order</title>
  <style>
```

(*Continued*)

```
            #layer1 {
            position: absolute;
            left: 10px; top:300px;
            z-index: 1;
                background: #CC6666;
            color: white;
            font-size: 30pt;
            padding: 40px;
               font-family: sans-serif;
            border-style: ridge;
            border-width: 20px;
            border-color: #66CCFF;
            }
            #layer2 {
            position: absolute;
            left: 100px; top:200px;
            z-index: 0;
            color: blue;
                background: #CCCCFF;
            font-size: 30pt;
                font-family: sans-serif;
            padding: 20px;
            border-style: ridge;
            border-width: 20px;
            border-color: #FFAACC;
            }
            #layer3 {
            position: absolute;
            left:200px; top:70px;
            z-index: -1;
            color: blue;
                background: 00CCFF;
            font-size: 30pt;
                font-family: sans-serif;
            padding: 40px;
            border-style: ridge;
            border-width: 20px;
            border-color: #CD9575;
            }
</style>
</head>
<body>
        <h1>Demonstrate Stacking of Layers</h1>
        <div id="layer1">
            Top Layer ZIndex (1)
        </div>
        <div id="layer2">
            Intermediate layer ZIndex (0)
        </div>
```

```
        <div id="layer3">
            Innermost layer ZIndex (-1)
        </div>
</body>
</html>
```

Fig. 3.5 *Demonstrating z-index styles*

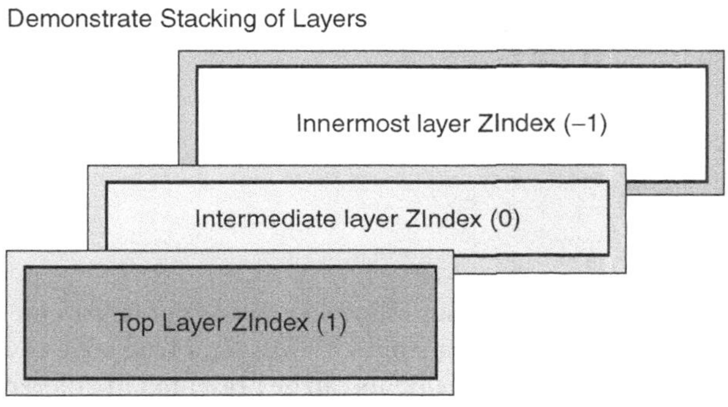

Fig. 3.6 *Stacked-up elements as per their ZIndex values*

The snapshot of the display in IE 8 is shown in Figure 3.6. Apart from noting ZIndex behavior, observe the way borders are constructed, to give a better look.

3.7.1 Websites

A website represents a set of web pages connected together by links. Essentially they are all HTML pages. Dynamic pages are HTML elements, generated by programs with inputs coming from databases or some dynamic source. These programs can reside in intermediate applications like Microsoft Share Point (also known as MOSS 2007 or Share Point 2010 or simply Share Point) or in some JSP (Java Server Pages). A site can consist of hundreds of web pages so they may become complicated if they are considered separately. Hence it is often examined for patterns or conversely, simplified to a set of patterns called templates, which can be leveraged by intermediate tools like Share Point.

A template represents a page structure. Using (one or even more) templates will not only conform to a uniform page layout but also help in standardizing elements, placement and choice of colors, thereby providing a uniform look & feel for a website. In marketing terminology, it reflects the brand of the company through its website.

Each part of the template structure can be considered to be made up of a DIV element. A simplified example is shown below.

```
<head>
<link rel="stylesheet" href="mystyle.css" type="text/css">
</head>
<body>
```

```
<div id="centre-section">
<div id="heading section"></div>
<div id="main section"></div>
<div id="footer"></div>
</div>
</body>
```

The reader is encouraged to try out creating the above files and trying them out using a browser. They can be typed in any text editor like vi (in Unix) or notepad in Windows. They may also be typed in through an IDE like Netbeans.

A CSS will be required to space the sections and provide the styles (mystyle.css).

```
#heading-section {
width: 800px;
height: 120px;
background-color: gray;
float: left;
}
```

A float directive is used to control the flow of an inline element as per its parent.

Multiple CSS files can be associated with a single HTML, in a true style of separation of concerns between content and style. Usually, different elements can be presented in different styles. Also, a plug-in or a library will optionally have a CSS definition to support UI elements, so this arrangement will be particularly convenient. However, it is to be noted that duplicate declarations across multiple CSS files, if any, will work using the latest definition.

3.8 BENEFITS OF CSS

Some of the benefits of using CSS are:

- offer more formatting choices as compared to HTML.
- CSS styles take up much less space than HTML's formatting options.
- promote standardized and centralized control of styles for a project or an organization.
- ability to separate Style from Content and Behaviour.
- promote first step towards unobtrusive JavaScript.

3.9 SUMMARY

This chapter started with the philosophy of CSS and their usages. We saw some of the ways in which CSS can be defined and how it can be connected with an HTML file. The concept of CSS selectors was explained with a few examples. Finally the advantages of CSS were also brought out.

EXERCISES

Q1. Using CSS, enlist the approach to format display of an HTMP page to suit a number of devices like mobile displays and printer output, apart from normal web displays.

Q2. Consider the following CSS definitions.

(a) p.myclass1 {color: red}

(b) p.myclass2 {color: blue}

(c) myclass3 {color: green}

Represent them in equivalent HTML inline styles.

Q3. Write a CSS rule to achieve the following:

(a) Set all headings (h1…h6) to Red font with all caps

(b) Set text color of all <p> elements to green

Q4. Consider this malformed piece of XHTML document as shown below. DOM is the document object model, which is the way tagged elements are organized (in a hierarchical fashion). What will be the resulting DOM fragment?

```
<!DOCTYPE html PUBLIC "-//W3C//DTD XHTML 1.0 Transitional//EN"
"http://www.w3.org/TR/xhtml1/DTD/xhtml1-transitional.dtd">
<html xmlns="http://www.w3.org/1999/xhtml">
<head><title> DOM Fragment </title> </head>
<body>
  <h1> write the DOM fragment for this HTML </h1>
</body>
  <p><i>this is in italics.
  <p><b>now in bold
  <p><i>back to italics (but the bold continues)
  <p><i>And again italics (here again)
</html>
```

Q5. Most websites make it easy to navigate between pages using a menu, which is generally shared as part of the header. A menu can be done by various means. Design a menu based on HTML and CSS.

Q6. If we can specify the width and height of an element, what happens if the area of the element is not large enough to contain the contents of the element? Give an example.

Q7. Examine the Float property of CSS. What are the ways it can be used?

Q8. How can we specify CSS if we want text to flow around a block or inline element like an image? Give an example.

Q9. What is a contextual selector in CSS?

Project Activities

Q10. (a) Imagine you are opening a virtual café selling a few varieties of coffee. The theme is social collaboration, that is, the idea of opening the virtual shop is for people to interact and collaborate with each other; in the process they buy coffee. How would you approach to create a simple website for the store? Start with a basic set of HTML pages. Come up with an overall CSS to present the view.

Q11. Do some research into the advanced features available in CSS3, as compared to CSS2.

Q12. Taking help from the web, create columnar layouts using HTML and CSS.

Caselet Activity

Q13. In the previous Caselet Activities of the café shop, how would you approach if the theme is "All About Coffee" (instead of collaboration)? What if the themes differ on a periodic basis? How would you change the layout and appearance of the website with minimal changes to code? How about leveraging different CSS files for each of the themes, with HTML almost remaining the same? Design a 2 or 3 columnar layout for the pages.

4

CLIENT-SIDE—BEHAVIOR

Chapter Objectives:

- ***Get to know the behavioural aspects of data***
- ***A peek into the history of Java Script***
- ***Learn Client side Java Script with examples including the language's object orientation***
- ***Understand DOM Structure***
- ***Know about DOM event handling***
- ***Get into some of the nuances of browser specific variations***
- ***Understand Ajax through an example***
- ***Get an idea of the concept of unobtrusive JavaScript, with reference to JQuery***

It is said that in a web application, Content is everything. If HTML is for **Content**, CSS is for **Style**, and then JavaScript is for **Behavior**. JavaScript is the basis for a lot of modern-age presentation oriented frameworks and tools, so it becomes a very important foundation for web development. What is being referred to here is the client side of JavaScript, which is the most popular—both in terms of its use in the client side as well as in terms of the server-side JavaScript, being the other variant.

4.1 JAVASCRIPT

As the name suggests, JavaScript is a scripting language. Though it is a scripting language, it is a far powerful technology for a web developer to ignore this language. One single component that has made the browser into a powerful application delivery system is JavaScript. Let's start with an understanding of what it is not, that will clear away a lot of myths.

- JavaScript is not Java. They are quite different, though both are object oriented languages. The reader is advised to refer to the Appendix on a short comparison between Java and JavaScript.
- JavaScript is a very powerful language. In fact there are two variants that are common—one is the client-side JavaScript which is to do with the Web Browser; the other is server-side JavaScript which is used to develop server side functionality. The chapter covers the client-side JavaScript, which is the most common.
- Despite being a scripting language, JavaScript is reasonably fast.
- JavaScript is not just used in/by browsers, it is also found in other applications like Flash, Mobiles and other applications.

4.2 A BIT OF HISTORY ABOUT JAVASCRIPT

JavaScript has its origins in 1995 from Netscape's Brendan Eich. It was initially called by the name LiveScript but renamed as JavaScript to probably capitalize on the rising popularity of Sun's Java. Since then, it has been a source of confusion about the name, since practically it is totally different from Java. Later in 1997, Netscape submitted the language to ECMA which is a European standards organization, for enhancements. The updated version was called ECMAScript. So sometimes it is also called by the same name. It underwent major enhancements regularly since then.

The running of JavaScript is dependent on a host environment, most notably the browser. Additionally, it can be found in other environments like Adobe's products, Widget engines, etc.

Several formal versions of JavaScript are as follows.

- 1.0: Netscape 2
- 1.1: Netscape 3 and Explorer 3 (not stable version)
- 1.2: Early Version 4 browsers
- 1.3: Later Version 4 browsers and Version 5 browsers
- 1.4: Not used in browsers, only on Netscape servers
- 1.5: Current version
- 2.0: Currently under development by Brendan Eich and others.

4.3 ORGANIZATION OF THE LANGUAGE

The language is organized as follows.

- JavaScript Core: This is built around a core set of objects like Array, Date, etc. and with a core set of language elements like operators, control structures and statements.
- Client-side Java Script (CSJS): This is built on JavaScript Core, with added functions on the client—namely controlling the browser and manipulating the object model followed by the browser (called the Document Object Model or DOM)
- Server-side Java Script (SSJS): This extends the JavaScript Core with added functionality pertaining to the server side, like accessing a database, sending e-mails, session management, etc. Server-side JavaScript is very powerful, based on object oriented programming. It is platform neutral as well.
- Since Java Script Core is the common piece in client-side JavaScript and server-side JavaScript, there are a lot of things that are common between them:

- Keywords, like new, throw, public and a lot more. These are used by JavaScript engine and cannot be used within the user-defined script.
- Statement syntax and grammar
- Rules for expressions, variables and literals
- Underlying object model structure (client-side and server-side JavaScript have different sets of predefined objects, though)
- Predefined objects and functions, such as such as Array, Date and Math

The most common mode of usage that is perceived is the client-side scripting, and is also simpler compared with server-side Java Script.

All browsers that support JavaScript will be able to run client side JavaScript code. The focus of this chapter is client-side JavaScript, which gives an overview of the language. The reader is free to refer other tutorials/material available freely on the web as it is very difficult to do justice to cover the entire [JavaScript] language within the confines of this chapter. It is felt that understanding JavaScript is very important in the context of web programming.

4.3.1 Basics of Client-side JavaScript

Client-side JavaScript extends JavaScript core with specialized functions to handle DOM manipulation. They are made available as JavaScript in a raw form, but a lot of them have been encapsulated and made available in libraries like jQuery.

4.4 AN EXAMPLE

It is said that a language like JavaScript is best learnt by examples but first things first—A JavaScript code is written as a text file and embedded as part of HTML. We have seen earlier that HTML supports extensibility intrinsically and we show an example of how it done.

Thus the steps to run JavaScript (on the client side) are as follows.

1. Write the program—Use any text editor, but given that a lot of IDEs support a web programming eco system, it is always better to use them. Use of an HTML editor will also help.
2. Embed the script within an HTML (XHTML) code
3. Invoke the HTML through a browser

Note that the above steps are not the only way to invoke a CS JavaScript. In fact, the above is just about OK for small snippets of the code, though best for demonstration purposes. Debugging is still a difficult exercise but not a concern when the size is small.

Let us look at a simple example of JavaScript code to begin with. Refer Figure 4.1, which demonstrates a random quote.

```
<html>
<head>
   <title> Sample Random Quotes </title>
</head>
```

(*Continued*)

```
5.
6.      <body>
7.          <script language="JavaScript">
8.              var idx;
9.              var quotes = Array('An Apple a day keeps the doctor away',
10.                  'Sweet are the ways of adversity',
11.                  'Practice unity in Thought, Word and Deed',
12.                  'Pick the flower when it is ready to be picked');
13.
14.             n = quotes.length;                    //get the size of the
                                                      //array
15.             idx = Math.floor(Math.random()*(n));  //restrict the range
                                                      //to size
16.             document.write(quotes[idx]);
17.         </script>
18.     </body>
19.     </html>
```

Fig. 4.1 *List a random quote*

Notes:

1. The client-side JavaScript code (shown in colored font above) is embedded in HTML within the <script> tag. Note the language option. However, the declaration about the language is strictly not necessary since the modern browsers detect JavaScript. In fact there are not too many options here (VBScript is another option but, being Microsoft's it is only supported by IE).
2. Math is an in-built library that JavaScript understands, as seen in line 15 of Figure 4.1. It supports functions like "random" which returns a random number in the range from 0 to 1 in decimal. Rarely do we directly use such a random fraction, so it is multiplied by a maximum number (n) to ensure we get it within the range 0 to n. Again since the number is a fraction, rounding it off could skew the result. Hence, it is further refined by rounding it off using floor, which is again a Math operation which rounds it off to the next lower integer. On the other hand Math.ceil rounds it off to the next higher number.
3. The resulting random number which is made to be within the range 0 to the size of the array is used as the index to output the quote randomly.
4. Notice the comments (starting with //) similar to C++ or Java.
5. Though use of semi-colons is optional, it is recommended to use them as a good practice.
6. document.write is a way to print output the specified string on the page. Document is the object which contains a method called write.
7. Invoke the saved (HTML) file from a browser (by File→Open in IE) and see the result.

In practice, document.write in JavaScript is to be avoided. Its usage overwrites the entire document's structure and hence throws the document object model out of gear. However, it is a quick and easy way to display variables or messages, and hence can be used for testing and practice purposes.

Given below is another way of writing the Factorials program in JavaScript—more interactive and more compliant to norms. However, be warned that much of the code will not make sense to a beginner.

```
<! DOCTYPE html PUBLIC “- //W3C//DTD XHTML 1.0 Strict//EN”
“http: //www. w3.org/TR/xhtml1/DTD/xhtml1- strict.dtd”>

<html>
<head> <title> Form Values </title> </head>
<body>
   <h1> Interactive Fact! </h1>
   <form name=“fact”>
      <table>
          <tr>
              <td> Enter a Number </td>
              <td> <input type=“text” id=“num” onchange=“Factorial();”>
              </td>
          </tr>
          <tr>
              <td> The Factorial of the number
              <td><span id=“factout”></span> </td>
          </tr>
      </table>
   </form>
   <script>
      function Factorial() {
               var n;
               n = document.fact.num.value;
               var factn = 1;
               for(i=1; i<=n; i++) {
                     factn = factn*i;
                }

                var fact = document.getElementById(“factout”);
                fact.innerHTML = factn;
      }
   </script>
</body>
</html>
```

Fig. 4.2 *Factorial–another view*

The JavaScript code is embedded within the Script tag and is seen interspersed with HTML as again observed in Figure 4.2. The function *Factorial()* is defined to be called from HTML (line 12) triggered on change of the value of text (with id of "num"). This kind of a trigger is termed event-driven, signifying a reaction to a response from the environment. In the *Factorial* function, the code in line 23 retrieves the number that was entered in the text box. The rest of the factorial calculation is similar to the previous example (Figure 4.1).

Take a look at another example (Figure 4.3), which demonstrates a similar kind of usage—an event driven behavioral (style) change. The event is mouse hovering on an object and the behavior is about changing of the color of the font.

```
<html>
  <body>
       <h1>MouseOver Demo</h1>
       <span id="me" onMouseOver="this.style.color='red'"
              onMouseOut="this.style.color='black'">
              Notice change in behaviour when the mouse hovers on me!
       </span>
  </body>
</html>
```

Fig. 4.3 *Trapping events*

The results are best observed when the script is run (on a browser). Note that the skeleton is still HTML and JavaScript is invoked (by the browser) through the *onMouseOver* and *onMouseOut* events. The statement following the event [onMouseOver="this.style.color='red'"] indicates the action that is performed. In this case, it is about manipulating the style. Instead of having a style statement, it could also call a (JavaScript) function.

```
<html>
      <script>
              function f1() {
                     alert("function called from f1");
              }
      </script>
      <body>
           <h1>MouseOver Demo 2</h1>
           <span id="mo" onMouseOver="f1()">
                  I will be alerted when the mouse is hovered on me!
           </span>
      </body>
</html>
```

Fig. 4.4 *Trapping events–2*

The reader need not get overly concerned if these snippets of code does not make sense at this point of time but is encouraged to try running this on a browser. While running, it is common for the browser to display warning similar to the one shown below (the example below is shown for IE).

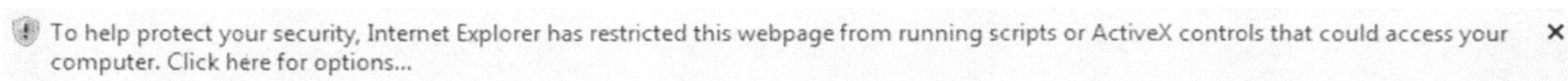

It is required to "allow blocked content" (by clicking on the message in the browser) so that the JavaScript code can be executed.

More on the aspects of the language is described in the subsequent sections.

4.5 DATA TYPES

It is thought that JavaScript lacks the rigor of other languages as compared to Java or C# because they are strongly typed. JavaScript is indeed not a strongly typed language so that makes it flexible and easier to code but on the flip side they are difficult to maintain because of the lack of typing. However, the client-side JavaScripts are shorter in size, and hence the rigor is actually not necessary thus benefiting in the overall context. Having said that, the types of values that JavaScript can handle, called Datatypes, can be thought of as being organized as follows.

- Primitive Datatypes
  - Numbers
  - Strings
  - Boolean
- Trivial Datatypes
  - NULL
  - Undefined (variable not declared is undefined, or a variable declared but not initialized)
- Reference/Composite Datatypes
  - Object
  - Ordered collection of values called an Array
  - Unordered collection
  - Function

Primitive datatypes are so called because they are atomic-level chunks—small and fixed size—of datatypes that are manipulated by JavaScript at the most granular level. Non-primitives that include array, objects and functions are composite data types containing arbitrary numbers of properties. These types are manipulated by *reference* whereas primitive data types are manipulated by *value*. Sometimes they (Composite types) are also called Reference types.

An interesting side note needs mention here. Consider the following snippet of code (Figure 4.5).

```
var x = 1;                //Declaration of variable x
var y = x;                //Declaration of y and assign the value of x
var x_arr = [11,22,33,44];

x = 9;
document.write(x);        //displays 9
```

(Continued)

```
document.write(y);                  //displays original value 1
var y_arr = x_arr;
document.write(x_arr);              //displays 11,22,33,44
x_arr[1] = 55;
document.write(x_arr);              //displays 11,55,33,44
document.write(y_arr);              //displays 11,55,33,44—note the changed
value
```

Fig. 4.5 *Primitive and reference types*

Observe the piece of code in Figure 4.5 and understand the difference in behavior between primitive and reference types. More on that is discussed in Section 4.7.3. Also, reference types do not have a fixed size, so that brings out a problem of orphaned references, which is solved by automatic garbage collectors.

Needless to say, numbers are the most basic of the types, but what is different than the rest of the languages (like Java/C#) is that it can represent both types of numbers—floating point as well as integer, so in effect a number is treated as a float or double, rather than an integer.

JavaScript does *not* have a void type. This aligns with being a loosely typed language. Every function must return a value, though. Default value is undefined.

4.5.1 Special Numbers

There is provision for special numbers like "+infinity" or "–infinity". The following are the special numbers.

- Infinity
- Number.POSITIVE_INFINITY
- Number.NEGATIVE_INFINITY
- NaN—stands for Not a Number when a number is divided by 0. It cannot be used for comparison. To check if a number is NaN, the built-in function, isNaN() is used, which returns true or false accordingly
- Number.MAX_VALUE which represents the largest number that can be handled
- Number.MIN_VALUE which represents the smallest number that can be handled

Strings store Unicode characters—can be represented within single or double quotes. There is no separate char type as seen in C or Java. In JavaScript a primitive type shows dual properties—the characteristics of a primitive type as well the characteristics of an object. This is achieved by means of a wrapper around each of the primitive data types, so we have Number, String and Boolean classes. Correspondingly for strings, there are a number of methods that are available. They are listed below:

- Length of the string as in s.length where s is the string.
- Position of a particular character (or set of characters) in a string as in s.indexOf('c')
- Substring as in s.substring(4,6)—extracts the characters from index 4 to 5. The index of the first character in a string s is 0, thus the 5th character is of index 4.
- The character in a string at a particular index is obtained using charAt(idx). In other words, the expression, c = s.charAt(0) will fetch the start character of the string s. Likewise the last character is obtained by s.charAt(s.length-1) provided s.length is greater than 0.

4.5.2 Boolean

As in other languages, a Boolean variable has two states—true or false. It is used to compare their values or conditionally execute statements as under:

```
If (someCondition) {
 ...   //enter this if block if the variable someCondition evaluates to true
}
```

How an expression or variable is evaluated true or false is slightly complicated. The below table summarizes the conditions on how they are evaluated.

If Variable or Expression is...	It Evaluates to...
Undefined—not assigned a value	False
Null	False
Boolean	Value of the variable
Number with value of 0 or NaaN	False
Number with non-zero value	True
String with a value	True
String which is empty	False
Object	true if present
Unknown variable—not declared	False

Thus to quote from one of O'Reily's talks on JavaScript:

In other words, zero, null, NaN, and the empty string are inherently false; everything else is inherently true.

```
var bin1 = new Boolean("abc"); //bin1 evaluates to true since the string
                               //is not empty
var bin2 = new Boolean("");    //bin2 evaluates to false since the string
                               //is empty
```

4.5.3 Constants

A constant value can be declared as below, signifying a read-only value.

```
const MONTH_PERSONDAYS = 20;
```

A constant value has a scope just as with other variables—local and global. However, it is best to treat constants universal and as such be used in a global context rather than local.

Though it is not compulsory for the variable name to be in capitals, it is normally the convention.

4.5.4 Typeof

```
Typeof() returns the type associated with the referred variable.
typeof null;               // object
typeof undefined;          // undefined
typeof undecl;             //undefined (variable is not declared)
typeof i;                  // number (variable i is a float or integer)
typeof b;                  // boolean; (b is a Boolean with value either
true or false)
typeof "abc";              // string
typeof {};                 // object
typeof function () {};     // function
typeof [];                 // object
```

A sample program to display various types is as follows:

```
<! DOCTYPE html PUBLIC "- //W3C//DTD XHTML 1.0 Strict//EN
"http: //www. w3.org/TR/xhtml1/DTD/xhtml1- strict.dtd">

<html>
<head>
  <title> variable types </title> </head>
<style type="text/css">
      * {font-family:sans-serif;}
</style>
<script type="text/javascript">
     function my_onload () {
     var defined;
     var n;
     var i = 10;
     var x;
     var y;

     n = "15";
     var so = new String;
     var sod = new String("Defined String");
     x = true;
     y = null;
     var myvarxx = null;
     disp("A variable not declared :" + "<b>" +
          typeof(myundefvar) + "</b>"); //a variable
                                        //undefined
     disp ("i is declared as " + "<b>" +
```

```
                typeof(i) + "</b>" + " (value " + i + ")");
            disp ("sod [declared new String] is " + "<b>" +
                typeof(sod) + "</b>" + "(value " + sod + ")");
            disp ("n is" + "<b>" +
                typeof(n) + "</b>" + "(value " + n + ")");
            disp ("'defined' is " + "<b>" +
                typeof(defined) + "</b>" + "(value " + defined +
")");
            disp ("so is" + "<b>" +
                typeof(so) + "</b>" + "(" + so + ")");
            disp ("sod is" + "<b>" +
              typeof(sod) + "</b>" + "(" + sod + ")");
            disp ("so.tos is" + "<b>" +
                typeof(so.tos) + "</b>" );
            disp ("disp is" + "<b>" + typeof(disp) + "</b>" );
            disp ("x is " + "<b>" + typeof(x) + "</b>" + "(value " + x
                  + ")");
            disp ("y is" + "<b>" + typeof(y) + "</b>" + "(value" + y +
                  ")");
            var yy = new fx(3);
            disp ("fx is" +  "<b>" + typeof(fx) + "</b>" );
            disp ("yy is" + "<b>" + typeof(yy) + "</b>" + "(value " +
                yy + ")");
        }

        function disp(msg) {
          c = document.getElementById("ans");
          c.innerHTML += msg + "<br />";
        }
        var fx = function(x) {
           var sq = function () { return x*x };
           return sq;
        }

    </script>
    <body onload="my_onload()">
        <h1>Check out various types in JavaScript</h1>
        <div id="ans"> </div>
    </body>
    </html>
```

Fig. 4.6 *Display of types*

```
Check out various types in JavaScript
A variable not declared :undefined
i is declared as number (value 10)
sod [declared new String] is object(value Defined String)
n is string(value 15)
'defined' is undefined(value undefined)
so is object()
sod is object(Defined String)
so.tos is undefined
disp is function
x is boolean(value true)
y is object(value null)
fx is function
yy is function(value function () { return x * x; })
```

Fig. 4.7 *Display of types–output*

The output of the program is shown in Figure 4.7. The reader is required to observe each line displayed and get an understanding of how JavaScript treats variables and their types. A word of caution—too much flexibility in types will make it difficult to debug.

4.6 CONVERSIONS

There are in-built ways to convert an object or a primitive into other primitive types. They are done through the methods toString() and valueOf(). In fact, all objects inherit the method toString from Object.prototype. By default, it returns "[object Object]". This is the reason you will see this output when you print the object. However, you can override the default behavior and it is easy as well.

Similarly valueOf() is another built-in function, with the same default value. Together, these functions are meant to return the most meaningful value belonging to String or Number or Boolean (Figure 4.8). For instance, the outputs (of either method) returned for an Array variable is a comma separated list of value.

Function parseInt() converts strings to number provided they are numeric or convertible to numeric with valueOf(). Similarly, parseFloat() converts strings to floats.For example, parseFloat("2.55") returns a float of value 2.55. These simple but important conversion functions are used with inputs from text box elements of a HTML page.

Note that the '+' operator is overloaded so it will be valid for Math operations as well for String operations. Sometimes this may be made to produce different results, as in the following example.

This is an example of a complex number of the form a+ib. By default, when the complex number (cn) is referred, it returns back with [object Object]. However, if the method toString is overridden, as shown in the above example, this method is invoked when the number cn is referred. It causes the toString method to output the number (3 + 4i in the example) to be printed in the desired form (a+ib). This is valid for String operations. Similarly, for Number operations, the valueOf() will be invoked.

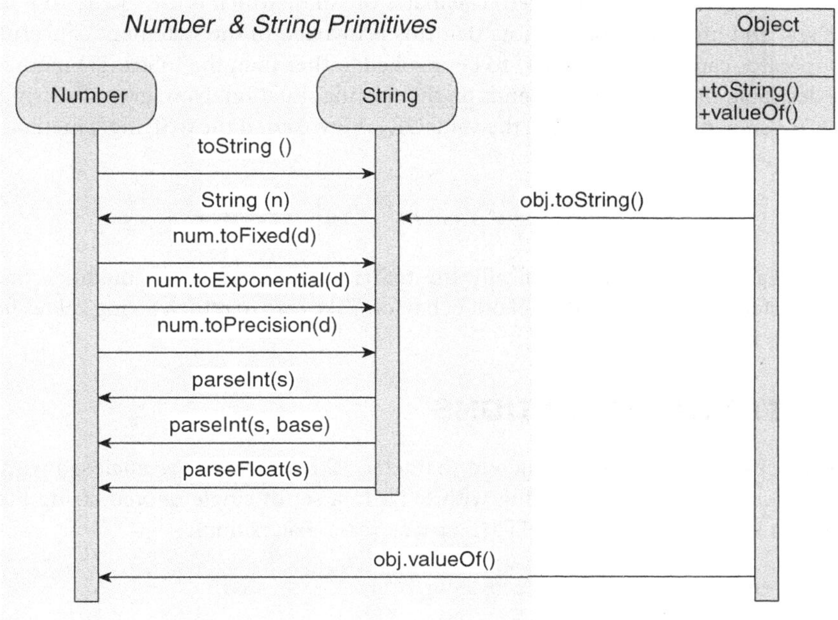

Fig. 4.8 *Display of types*

```
<!DOCTYPE html PUBLIC "- //W3C//DTD XHTML 1.0 Strict//EN"
"http: //www.w3.org/TR/xhtml1/DTD/xhtml1- strict.dtd">
<script type=text/JavaScript>
  function complex_number(r, i) {
    this.real = r;
    this.imaginary = i;

    this.toString = function() {
        return(this.real + "+" + this.imaginary + "i");
    }
    this.valueOf = function() {
       return(Math.sqrt(this.real * this.real + this.imaginary*this.
       imaginary));
    }
  }

  var cn = new complex_number(3,4);
  document.write(cn);                     //returns 3 + 4i
  document.write("<br></br>");
  document.write(cn + 0);                 //returns 5
</script>
```

Fig. 4.9 *Demonstrating overload operator (+) using a complex number representation*

The redefined function (which is overridden) calculates the value which is the square root of the sum of squares of the real and imaginary parts. Note that this is invoked in the statement concerning "cn + 0" since the "+" operator causes the toValue() to be invoked, rather than the toString() method. This may or may not be desirable since it totally depends on the specific situation. Now, even if a string follows the "+" (instead of 0 as shown in the example), the valueOf() is invoked. If the toString() method is required, specially state it as follows:

```
document.write(cn.toString() + "..."); //returns 3 + 4i...
```

It is a good idea to implement specifically the toString() and valueOf() methods on commonly reusable objects instead of relying on the default behavior. Take care to return String values for toString() and Number values for valueOf().

4.7 BASIC STRING OPERATIONS

Strings are sequences of zero or more Unicode characters. String literals are enclosed within single or double quotes. Since CSJS involves working with HTML, a set of single quoted string literals can be embedded within a set of double quoted HTML or vice versa. For example,

```
<a href="#" onClick="alert('continue')"> Click </a>
```

Strings are immutable in the sense that their values cannot be modified at a specific location. There is a charAt() method but nothing for setting a character at a specific location.

One of the most often used features pertaining to Strings is the concat operator. The '+' operator is used for this purpose, overloaded with the (same) arithmetic operator.

Some of the basic string operations are best seen with the example shown in Figure 4.10.

```
<!DOCTYPE html PUBLIC "- //W3C//DTD XHTML 1.0 Strict//EN"
"http: //www. w3.org/TR/xhtml1/DTD/xhtml1- strict.dtd">
<script type=text/JavaScript>
       a = "ABCDEFGHIJKLMNOPQRSTUVWXYZ";          //initialize the string
       disp ("str=" + a);
       disp ("------Now observe SLICE Operations--------");
       sect = a.slice(2,-6);
       disp ("str.slice(2,-6)=" + sect);      //CDEFGHIJKLMNOPQRST

       sect = a.slice(2,6);
       disp ("str.slice(2,6)=" + sect);       //CDEF

       sect = a.slice(2);
       disp ("str.slice(2)=" + sect);              //CDEFGHIJKLMNOPQRSTUVWXYZ

       sect = a.slice(-2);
       disp ("str.slice(-2)=" + sect);        //YZ
       disp ("<b>str is unchanged in all the above operations - check
       str = </b>" + a);
```

```
        disp ("----substr 3,6---------Start at position 3 for 6 positions");
        sect = a.substr(3,6);
        disp ("str.substr(3,6)=" + sect);          //DEFGHI

        sect = a.substr(2);
        disp ("str.substr(2)=" + sect);            //CDEFGHIJKLMNOPQRSTUVWXYZ

        disp ("----split ---------");
        sect = a.split("M");                       //ABCDEFGHIJKL,NOPQRSTUVWXYZ
        disp ("a=" + a);
        disp ("str.split('M')=" + sect);           //ABCDEFGHIJKL,NOPQRSTUVWXYZ

        function disp(msg) {
             document.write(msg, "<br>");
        }

</script>
```

Fig. 4.10. *A set of string operations*

The function, disp(), in Figure 4.10, function encapsulates the mode of display. We will look into the function declarations and usage later in this section. Here is the ouput.

```
str=ABCDEFGHIJKLMNOPQRSTUVWXYZ
------Now observe SLICE Operations--------
str.slice(2,-6)=CDEFGHIJKLMNOPQRST
str.slice(2,6)=CDEF
str.slice(2)=CDEFGHIJKLMNOPQRSTUVWXYZ
str.slice(-2)=YZ
str is unchanged in all the above operaions - check str =
ABCDEFGHIJKLMNOPQRSTUVWXYZ
----substr 3,6---------Start at position 3 for 6 positions
str.substr(3,6)=DEFGHI
str.substr(2)=CDEFGHIJKLMNOPQRSTUVWXYZ
----split ---------
a=ABCDEFGHIJKLMNOPQRSTUVWXYZ
str.split('M')=ABCDEFGHIJKL,NOPQRSTUVWXYZ
```

Fig. 4.11 *String operations-output*

As an extension to the interpretation of Strings mentioned in the previous section, examine the following code snippet and their expected surprise values.

```
var x = "45" - 5
//expect x to be 40 since it implicitly converts the string 45 into a Number
var x = "45" + 5
//expect x to be 455 since it retains the String flavor!
```

4.7.1 Other Common String Operations

The commonly used methods on a String object are summarized as follows:

Method/Property	Description
valueOf()	Returns the string literal that the String object is *wrapping*
Length	The property, not the method, with the length of the string literal
charAt(n)	Return a character or at a given position. Index starts from 0.
charCodeAt(n)	Return a character code at a given position. Index starts from 0.
indexOf (s)	Returns the starting position of the first occurrence of a substring
lastIndexOf (s)	Returns the starting position of the last occurrence of a substring
s.toLowerCase s.toUpperCase	Convert case
HTML Formatting methods • s.link(url) • s.strike • s.big • s.small • s.bold	Generate the HTML elements using the string s.

4.7.2 String Encoding for URIs

When an URI is sent across the network, there are some characters that cannot be sent in their normal (ASCII /UTF8 etc.) form. These characters will need to be converted to their HEX forms and then reconverted back to their original form.

There are a couple of related methods—`encodeURI` and `encodeURIComponent` to encode (also called escape) strings containing ASCII and non-ASCII characters. Using the backslash character is a means to escape characters but they work only with ASCII. To make a string safe for HTML it is necessary to properly encode them, which is why these methods are helpful.

Its inverse counterpart's methods are `decodeURI` and `decodeURIComponent` to convert them back to their original forms.

```
<html>
<head>
<title>Encode and Decode</title>
</head>
```

```
<body>
<script language="JavaScript" type="text/JavaScript">
    var uri = "http://www.abc.com/index?phrase='Vis-à-vis'"
    var e_uri = encodeURI(uri);
    alert(e_uri); //http://www.abc.com/index?phrase='Vis-%C3%A0-vis'
    var ec_uri = encodeURIComponent(uri);
    alert(ec_uri); //http%3A%2F%2Fwww.abc.
                   //com%2Findex%3Fphrase%3D'Vis-%C3%A0-vis'
    var d_uri = decodeURI(e_uri);
    alert(d_uri); //The original URI - http://www.abc.com/
                  //index?phrase='Vis-à-vis'
    var dc_uri = decodeURIComponent(ec_uri);
    alert(dc_uri); //The original URI - http://www.abc.com/
                   //index?phrase='Vis-à-vis'
</script>
</body>
</html>
```

Fig. 4.12 *Encode and decode*

There is another function in javascript which was available earlier (to convert) but was found inadequate for UNICODE. encodeURI supercedes escape function with additional capabilities. The encodeURIComponent (and decodeURIComponent) functions are an extension of encodeURI (and decodeURIComponent). The additional characters they handle include the following.

- `/ ? : @ & = + $`

4.7.3 Reference or Value

The preceding section indicated that primitive types are manipulated by value whereas non-primitive types are manipulated by reference. However, the distinction has to be made with respect to the type of operations—Copy, Parameter passing and Comparison. The following table summarizes the behavior.

Type	Copy	Parameter	Compare
Number	V	V	V
Boolean	V	V	V
String			V
Object	R	R	R

R = Reference; V = Value.

Figure 4.13 demonstrates the effect of calling by value.

```
<html>
<head>
<title>Calling by value</title>
</head>
```

(*Continued*)

```
<body>
<script language="JavaScript" type="text/JavaScript">
  var n = 2;

  disp("Before calling function, n=" + n); //n is 2

  change_param (n);
    disp("after calling function, n=" + n); //n remains 2

  function change_param (x) {
    x = x*2;
    disp("From function, x=" + x); //n is 4
  }

  function disp(msg) {
    document.write(msg, "<br>");
  }
</script>
</body>
</html>
```

Fig. 4.13 *The primitive (number) is called by value, so changes are not reflected back*

4.7.4 Regular Expressions

JavaScript supports regular expressions to process string formatting operations. There are two ways of creating a regular expression—one using RegExp and the other using a literal.

```
var sdPattern = new RegExp('[1-7]');        //using the RegExp object
var sdPattern = /[1-7]/;                    //using the literals option
sdPattern.test("8")                         //will return false
```

4.8 DATE OBJECT

A Date is an object in JavaScript. An instance is created using the Date() object.

```
var myDt = new Date();                     //returns current date
                                           //defined in the local
machine
var myDt = new Date(1926, 10, 23);         //pass date in the order—
                                           //year, month (0-11), day
```

Note that the month follows 0–11 rather than 1–12 convention. The time is optional. If it is required, pass additional parameters for hour, minutes, seconds and milliseconds.

```
<html xmlns="http://www.w3.org/1999/xhtml">
<head>
<meta http-equiv="Content-Type" content="text/html; charset=utf-8" />
<title>Basic Date</title>
</head>
    <title>Basic Date</title>
    <script>
```

```
    //This simple function gets the current date (& time), stores in a
    //variable
    //It then inserts into the Document object of the window.
    //While doing this it converts into a localized string
    function dateNow() {
            var myDt = new Date();
            document.write(myDt.toLocaleString());
    }
    </script>
</head>
<body>
The Date now is: <p> <script> dateNow(); </script> </p>
</html>
```

Fig. 4.14 *Date display*

The Date object has several get and set methods for getting and setting date components. The following is a list.

- d.getFullYear
- d.getMonth—returns an index between 0 and 11
- d.getHour
- getMinutes

4.8.1 A Note on Including JavaScript File

In the examples above, note that the HTML can be considered to have two sections, from a Javascript development point of view. The first section defines the Javascript function(s) and the second section executes it.

The first section (definition) is embedded between the <script> tags within the header of the HTML file. No (JavaScript) code execution happens here—it is just the definition that goes through. In the example above, the function, `dateNow()` is defined in the header. Likewise, there could be multiple functions that could be defined within this section. In the Body part of the HTML, the JavaScript function is executed at the required place. Here again, the calling happens within the <script> tag. If it is "called" without the <script> tag, there is no way the HTML can co-relate with the actual JavaScript function, so it just outputs the text that forms part of the calling function.

Now the reader could well have a question that if the function spans across several pages then it would be an unwieldy HTML file. Moreover, if functions will have to reused across several pages or applications, then the question becomes more compelling. Well, the alternative way to define a JavaScript is by including it (or them). Let us assume, for example, that the functions be defined in a JavaScript file (called myDate.js). The same can be included as in the following statement:

```
<script src="myDate.js"></script>
```

The single <script> statement with src attribute ensures that the functions within the JavaScript file are available for use. In fact, the src attribute can even take a URL as a parameter (that obviously points to a JavaScript file!). The rest of the usage remains the same as before.

This way of using JavaScript is one of the key enablers for unobtrusive JavaScript—considered as part of the best practices towards writing maintainable MVC code. This concept is covered in the later sections of this chapter. In summary the "src" type of usage has the following advantages.

- it is simpler to use
- promotes reuse of (JavaScript) functions
- easier maintenance
- enables caching by the browser, leading to faster page loads
- can also take an URL as an attribute, enabling libraries to be used

4.9 ARRAYS

Array is one of the non-primitive data types in JavaScript. Regular arrays, associated by an index, start with an index of 0. Associative arrays are indexed by Strings. Since JavaScript is a loosely typed language, the elements of an array need not belong to the same type. Thus, there can be a mix and match of numbers, arrays, objects, etc within an Array.

```
var arr = new Array();
var arr2 = ['a', 'b'];
```

4.9.1 Array Implementation Basics

There is no need to define a dimension for the Array as is commonly the requirement in other languages like C or C#. The way Arrays are implemented internally is that the elements are behaving as in a hash table. This means they are stored as name–value pairs. This type of implementation makes the job of the (JavaScript) programmer easier in terms of defining and manipulating them, but has the undesirable effect on performance.

The code sample in Figure 4.15 shows some of the basic characteristics of Array in JavaScript. Some of the pitfalls are also to be noted, for instance the length of the array when the third element (arr[3]) is initialized.

```
<!DOCTYPE html PUBLIC "- //W3C//DTD XHTML 1.0 Strict//EN"
"http: //www. w3.org/TR/xhtml1/DTD/xhtml1- strict.dtd">
<script type=text/JavaScript>
    arr1 = [11,22,-3,24,5];   //Declare and initialize a regular array
    arr2 = new Array(); //Declare an array this way as well
    arr3 = [1,'a',true,[11,22], {i:1}]; //See the different types in
    the same array

    arr2[2] = 23;             //initialize the 3rd element
    disp(arr2.length);        //check size of array = 3
    arr2['red'] = "Apple";    //associative array

    disp(arr2.length);        //size still remains the same!
    disp(arr2['red']);        //displays Apple
    function disp(msg) {
```

```
        document.write(msg, "<br>");
        }
    </script>
```

Fig. 4.15 *Example of array operations*

In these examples, note that the array (arr2) has different types of elements—an instance of Number and String are observed in this example. For instance the following declaration is also valid.

```
var arr3 = [1,' a', true, [11,22], {i:19}];
```

The array is a mixture of different types—number, string, Boolean, array and object (JSON).

For associative arrays the FOR loop will fetch all elements. For example observe the following snippet of JavaScript code.

```
var arr = new Array;
arr['red'] = 'APPLE';        //associative array
arr['blue'] = 'BERRY';
for (e in arr) {             //loop through to fetch each element e
alert(e + arr[e]);
//Two alerts as per number of elements producing outputs - redAPPLE &
//blueBERRY
}
```

The "FOR" loop demonstrates how to fetch each element of the (associative) array. The "in" operator works on associative arrays, fetching each element of the array (in the above example it is manifested in the variable "arr") in the element defined (as "e" in the above example). While the variable "e" will be the name of the associative index, arr[e] will contain its value.

This code will also work with the ordinal array.

4.9.2 Array and String Operations

- join()
- reverse()
- sort()—sort in alphabetical order by default
- concat()
- slice()—returns a subset
- Splice()—insert or remove elements from the array<title>Array Operations</title><html>

```
<html>
<head>
<title>Array Operations</title>
</head>
<body>
<script language="JavaScript" type="text/JavaScript">
      var arr1 = [11,22,-3,24,5]; //Declare and initialize a regular array
      var arr2 = new Array();     //Declare an array this way as well
```

(Continued)

```
    arr2[2] = 23;                //initialize the 3rd element
    disp(arr2.length);           //check size of array = 3
    arr2['red'] = "Apple";       //associative array

    disp(arr2.length);           //size still remains the same!
    disp(arr2['red']);

    b = arr1.join('/');
    disp(b);
    disp ("input array=["+ arr1 + "]");
    disp ("-----see how sort works (by default alphabetically) ------");
    arr1.sort();
    disp(arr1);

    disp("--see how sort can be manipulated by a function to perform
    numeric sort-");
    arr1.sort (function(a,b){ return a-b;});
    disp (arr1);
    disp ("---------------concat------");
    b = ['a','b',6];
    arr1.concat(b);
    disp(arr1.concat(b));
    disp ("-----splice (1,2) ---------------");
    disp (arr1);
    arr1.splice(1,2);
    disp (arr1);
    function disp(msg) {
    document.write(msg, "<br>");
    }
</script>
</body>
</html>
```

```
3
3
Apple
11/22/-3/24/5
input array=[11,22,-3,24,5]
-----see how sort works (by default alphabetically) ------
-3,11,22,24,5
--see how sort can be manipulated by a function to perform numeric sort-
-3,5,11,22,24
---------------concat------
-3,5,11,22,24,a,b,6
-----splice (1,2) ---------------
-3,5,11,22,24
-3,22,24
```

Fig. 4.16 *Array and string operations [output below]*

See Figure 4.16 for both code and the output. Some additional information about the method, splice, is necessary as there are multiple possibilities.

There are two things that Splice does—it returns the removed elements, if any, and will alter the array it is operating upon. For example, consider the following snippets of code.

```
var arr1 = [11,22,-3,24,5];        //Declare and initialize a regular array
alert (arr1);
alert(arr1.splice(0,2,'A').join(','));
//above statement displays 11,22 as these elements are returned back by
//splice
//These are 2 elements from position index of0, which is the first
argument //to Splice (i.e.) the 1st 2 elements.
//If there is none to be removed, then null is returned

alert(arr1);
//returns (A,-3,24,5) as it added the element A at index=0 after removing
//the elements as stated above.
```

Similarly, a negative index (instead of 0) in the splice method will operate from the reverse, instead of from the front.

The above descriptions on String and Array are meant to give an idea of the capabilities and the principles behind them. It is left to the reader to explore more on these topics by experimenting with negative indexes, overflowing index, etc.

4.10 VARIABLES AND FUNCTIONS

Here are some of the ways that variables and functions can be declared.

```
var n = 1;
function f1() {}                       //function statement
(function f2() {});                    //function expression
(function (f3) {} (param));            //function with parameter
```

At the outset it appears that functions in JavaScript are no different from functions in other programming contexts like C or C++ or Java. It is true that they are referred in the same context in the sense that a function is a block of code defined once but reused several times across. JavaScript also supports the concept of recursive functions. They are defined and invoked in much the same way as in other languages. However, there are stark differences in JavaScript which makes this language extremely powerful, which will be uncovered in this section.

4.10.1 Function Literals

JavaScript allows unmanned functions to be created. A function specified by a function literal can be stored in a variable and then invoked.

```
var square = function(n) {return n*n};
```

Calling square(3) for instance will return 9. Likewise, calling square(square(3)) will return 81. Thus it can be used as a convenient mnemonic to functions.

4.10.2 Function Arguments

Functions have an implicit variable inside their body called arguments, which is an array-like object holding all parameters passed to the function (Figure 4.17).

```
<html>
<head>
<title> Function Arguments </title>
</head>
<body>
        alert(product(2,3,4));
        alert(product(2,4,5,6,7,8);                    //same function called with 6
        arguments
        alert(product.call(this, 2,3,4));          //invoke function using call()
        function product() {
                var prod = 1;
                var nParams = arguments.length;  //get the size of the array-
                like object
                for (var i=0; i<nParams; i++) {
                prod = prod * arguments[i];          //assume all parameters are
                numeric!
                }
                return (prod);
        }
</body>
</html>
```

Fig. 4.17 *Function arguments*

Functions are objects too! They have methods like **call()** and **apply()**. This is illustrated in the example code above. The generic syntax of call is **func.call(obj, arg1, arg2...)** where the function (func) is executed in the context of obj. if the obj is not defined, the global object is assumed implicitly. The arguments to the functions are supplied thru arg1, arg2, etc., if any (Figure 4.18).

```
<html>
<head>
      <title> Using CALL </title>
</head>
<body>
<script>
      var title = "Mr.";
      var greet = function(name) {
              return ("Hello" + this.title + name);
      };
      alert(greet.call(this,"Ram")); //the default is 'this' object when
      null; returns Hello Mr.Ram
```

```
    var obj = {title: "Ms."};
    alert(greet.call(obj, "Rita")); //obj defines namespace containing
    title; returns Hello Ms.Rita
    </script>
</body>
</html>
```

Fig. 4.18 *Using call()*

The method apply() method is identical to call() except that it requires an array as the second parameter. The array can contain all the arguments that need to be passed to the function.

The arguments object also has an interesting property called callee signifying the calling function. However, this is not considered efficient and is best not to use it. It is also being deprecated in further releases of JavaScript though some of the browsers intend to support it to honor backward compatibility.

Note that if a function needs to be called then the brackets '()' are essential for a function. For example observe the following.

```
If (window.focus()) {
        //do something
}
```

This program tries to execute the focus operation on the window object. It assumes that the window object is available and if so tries to execute it. The loop is entered provided the object exists and it returns true on execution of the focus method.

```
If (window.focus) {
        //do something that is dependent on the window object
}
```

The above code checks for the presence of the window object (the only difference is the absence of opening and closing brackets in the focus function). It may be required to do something provided the browser supports the window object, for instance. This is often useful to check the existence of support for a method or an object.

4.10.3 Anonymous Functions

A static or a declarative function that is being commonly referred is created only once and used many times. Apart from this type of usage, JavaScript, perhaps uniquely, allows one to create a function dynamically. This is being called as an anonymous function as it can be assigned to a variable or even declared anonymously, which acts as a lambda expression.

JavaScript supports the concept of first-class functions because of its ability to support both storing these functions as data structures and variables and also supporting anonymous functions. Many of the languages like C# or Java support function pointers but not anonymous functions and hence does not provide true first-class support for functions. As a side information, the other languages that support first-class support include Ruby, Perl, PHP, and Lisp.

It has been seen earlier that a function is an object, just like String, Boolean and Array. So, imagine a Constructor is invoked for a Function object. The example of greet function above is a case in point.

```
function func_variable (arg1,…,argn) {
    function_body
}
```

The above function is equivalent to the generic format as shown below.

var func_variable = new Function(arg1,…, argn, function_body);

To invoke the function, func_variable(arg1,…,argn) can be used.

The way functions are treated as Objects in JavaScript throws open enormous possibilities that makes it powerful. For example, a function itself could be passed as an argument to a function.

If anonymous functions are not named, and since JavaScript supports recursion, how is it possible to call the function when it is declared anonymously? This is achieved by means of the callee property in the arguments object. As mentioned earlier, this is getting deprecated but it just suffices to know that there is a method to refer and hence call itself.

4.10.4 Inner Functions

In JavaScript, a function can be defined inside another. The concept of inner functions is not new. It was supported in legacy languages like pascal for instance. In C#, nested functions can be simulated. However, it is a feature that is supported in JavaScript and used quite often. These inner functions can access local variables defined within the outer function(s). The inner function can be defined to be global (without the var keyword) or local (with the var keyword). If it is in the global context, a closure is created and the function can be invoked from anywhere within the program. If it is local, then it can be invoked only with the context of the outer function.

4.10.5 Closures

A closure is a local stack frame for a function kept alive even after the function has returned. In other words, it is a function trace that is aware of its context at the time of invocation. Inner functions referring to local variables of its outer function are responsible for creating a closure. Contrast this with the behavior in most other languages like C where all local variables are not available after it comes out of a function because the stack frame is destroyed. Moreover, inner functions are peculiar to languages like JavaScript.

```
outerFunc = function () {
    innerFunc = function() {
    alert ("from inner…");
    }
}
outerFunc();
innerFunc();
//can also be called from here, since it is in global scope, as it is
//declared without the var keyword
```

```
<html>
<head>
   <title> global variables created thru function—basics of closure</title>
</head>
```

```
<body>
<script>
  try {
  document.writeln(msg1); //the msgs are not declared as of this moment
  document.writeln(msg2); //these portions of code will not be executed
  document.writeln(msg3); //it is a try-catch block
  }
  catch(err) {          //the error will be caught
  document.writeln(“From Error block; messages not yet available” +
                    “<br />”);
  }
  var initializeMessages = function () {
  msg1 = “This is created from a function”;
  msg2 = “Omitting the var keyword implies it is global”;
  msg3 = “See this magic! The messages are now available”
  }

  initializeMessages();
  try {
  document.writeln(msg1); //the msgs will now be available normally
  document.writeln(msg2);
  document.writeln(msg3);
  }
  catch(err) {
  document.writeln(“From Error block; not to reach!”);
  }
</script>
</body>
</html>
```

Fig. 4.19 *Concept of global variables created thru a function–basics of closure*

From the example in Figure 4.19 it follows that it is easy to create a closure condition. In fact, there may be situations where a closure can be accidently created. Care should be taken to ensure that the behavior is what is expected of the program.

Refer Figure 4.20. The demonstration program runs a set of counters which increments differently, thereby showing a simple case of closure. The functionality that this code attempts is to accept an initial value from the user, which then initializes two counters (one to increment 3 and the other to increment 5, every time the appropriate button is clicked). The counters run off a variable function which encapsulates the state of the function local variables, when it was called.

```
<! DOCTYPE html PUBLIC “- //W3C//DTD XHTML 1.0 Strict//EN”>
“http: //www.w3.org/TR/xhtml1/DTD/xhtml1- strict.dtd”>
<html>
<head>
<title></title>
```

(*Continued*)

```
    <meta http-equiv="Content-Type" content="text/html; charset=UTF-8">
    <style>
        .ctr3 {
                position: absolute;
                left: 120px; top:100px;
                z-index: 0;
                color: yellow;
                    background: black;
                font-size: 30pt;
                    font-family: "OCR A Extended";
                padding: 10px;
                border-style: ridge;
                border-width: 10px;
                border-color: #FEFE22;
                width: 50px;
         }
        .ctr5 {
                position: absolute;
                left: 10px; top:100px;
                z-index: 0;
                width: 50px;
                    background: black;
                color: yellow;
                font-size: 30pt;
                padding: 10px;
                    font-family: "OCR A Extended";
                border-style: ridge;
                border-width: 10px;
                border-color: #76FF7A;
         }
    </style>
    <script type="text/javascript">
      function runCounter(num) {  //set the context for a counter //function
      var localCtr = num;         //num is the initial value to start //with
      return function(ctr) {      //ctr is the incremental number
              localCtr += ctr;
              return(localCtr);
```

```
    }
    }
    function displayCtr(n) {
        var ctr;
        if (n == 5) {
                ctr = incrByFive(5);
                var res = document.getElementById("res5");
        }
        if (n == 3) {
                ctr = incrByThree(3);
                var res = document.getElementById("res3");
        }
        res.innerHTML = ctr;
    }

    function initCtr() {            //initialize the counter
        var start;
        var txtInput = startInput.value;
        start = parseInt(txtInput);
        if (isNaN(start)) {
        start = 0;
    }
    //Main purpose of this demo is in these variables (incrBy...)!
    //These are global variables
    incrByFive = runCounter(start);
    //returns a function for the counter. The valu, is passed when
    //the returned function is called
    incrByThree = runCounter(start);
    //this counter is independent of the other counter except for
    //initial value in this case
        document.getElementById("btn5").disabled = false;
        document.getElementById("btn3").disabled = false;
    }

    //Immediately on load of the page, diable the counter buttons as
    //they have to be initialized
   function onl() {
        document.getElementById("btn5").disabled = true;
        document.getElementById("btn3").disabled = true;
    }
    </script>
```

(Continued)

```
80.     </head>
81.     <body onload="onl()">
82.       <h2> Increment Multiple <span style="font-family: 'OCR A
          Extended';">Counters</span> using Closure </h2>
83.
84.       <input type="text" id="startInput" placeholder="Number?"
          value="0">
85.       <button onclick="initCtr()">Initialize</button>
86.       <button id="btn5" onclick="displayCtr(5)">Increment By 5</button>
87.       <button id="btn3" onclick="displayCtr(3)">Increment By 3</button>
88.       <div id="res3" class="ctr3">_</div>
89.       <div id="res5" class="ctr5">_</div>
90.     </body>
91      </html>
```

Fig. 4.20 *Increment multiple counters using closure*

The main HTML (body) is short—lines 81–90. Functions are attached to buttons on specific click events. Refer line numbers 85, 86 and 87. The Initialize button initializes the counters and sets the global variables for increment counters (lines 66 and 68). These functions are executed (lines 48, 52) when the event occurs (clicking of the appropriate buttons—btn5 or btn3).

Take a look at the (outer) function runCounter (line 38) which returns a function (which is the inner [anonymous] function—line 40). This returned (inner) function remembers the context in which it was called during the respective executions when the appropriate button is clicked.

Try out the program by clicking on initialize button and then trying out the counters. The function runCounter() is invoked with an initial value as the parameter. The initial value is set from the text box. Also notice how the data flows in from the text box into the JavaScript code.

Fig. 4.21 *Multiple counters–indicative output*

Lines 7–36 of the above code is for styling the output counter. This may be ignored for now as it is best understood after a study of CSS section. The functionality will work even without these style tags but will just look plain, instead of the boxes. See output in Figure 4.21.

```
<!DOCTYPE HTML PUBLIC "-//W3C//DTD HTML 4.01 Transitional//EN">
<html>
<head>
   <title></title>
   <meta http-equiv="Content-Type" content="text/html; charset=UTF-8">
</head>
<body>
   <h2> Increment same counter - Demo methods from a closure </h2>
   <input  type="text"  name="startInput"  placeholder="enter  a  number"
   value="0">
   <button onclick="f1()">Initialize</button>
   <button    onclick="alert(incrFuncs.incrByFive())">Increment    By    5
   </button>
   <button    onclick="alert(incrFuncs.incrByThree())">Increment    By    3
   </button>
   <script>
         function runCounter(num) {        //Initialize counter
            var localCtr = num;
            return {
               'incrByFive': function() { //Define function to increment by
5
                  localCtr += 5;
                  return(localCtr);
               },
               'incrByThree': function() {
                  localCtr += 3;
                  return(localCtr);
               }
            }
         }
         function f1() {
            var start;
            var txtInput = startInput.value;
            start = parseInt(txtInput);
            if (isNaN(start)) {
               start = 0;
         }
            incrFuncs = runCounter(start); //the object contains methods
                                           //for the counters required

         }
   </script>
</body>
</html>
```

Fig. 4.21 *Increment same counter–return function methods*

4.11 CLOSURE SCENARIOS

4.11.1 Simplify Scope

Other common Object-Oriented languages like C# have a concept of block scope. JavaScript does not. The scopes it can handle are either global or local within a function. This perceived simplicity on the other hand makes it clumsy to handle since variables are littered all over the place. Closures act as a means to simplify.

4.11.2 Return Methods from Functions

The idea is to encapsulate private logic and expose only certain, "public" methods. Take a variation of the above methods to implement a counter but with a difference—to reuse the same counter for both the increments. Also implement it by making a property of the returned function (in this case it is *incrFuncs*).

Take care to click on Initialize button to initialize the variables in the above example (Figure 4.21), the increment function can be generalized to increment by any number, instead of hard coding to 5 or 3. The return function will look like this below:

```
return {
'incr': function(x) {     //Define generic increment function
 localCtr += x;
 return(localCtr);
 }
 }                        //usage  incrFuncs.incr(5)  or  incrFuncs.incr(3)
                          //and so on...
```

Aside note

JavaScript can turn out to be a true Object-Oriented language since it supports info-hiding, inheritance and aggregation. But how does it support info-hiding as there is no concept of private, protected or public members?

By default any member is public. Properties or Methods defined **within** the Constructor are considered private. The principles of Closure are applied to implement these concepts.

In this connection, it is recommended to refer to views propounded by Douglas Crockford who is an authority on JavaScript. For more details refer to the website **http://www.crockford.com/javascript/private.html.**

4.12 SUMMARY OF WAYS TO USE A FUNCTION

Apart from a normal interpretation of function (as in other languages like C or pascal), functions are also used for the following:

- Methods
- Constructors
- Classes
- Module containers

4.12.1 Client-side Cookies

It may be pertinent to point out that writing on the client is forbidden, due to security issues. However, it is possible that small bits of information may be stored in a controlled manner, on the client side. This is possible in the form of a Cookie.

Cookies are not complete without their role in the server side. They are discussed in more detail on the server side in this book.

A Cookie is a piece of information stored in the client's machine. It is used in several contexts but the main reason is for a server to "remember" the client's specifics. Information is generally very small like storing a session-id or a username, etc., controlled by the server. In effect, a Cookie may be used as the bridge between the server side and the client side. In this context, on the client side, JavaScript is capable of creating and retrieving a Cookie. This support is provided by the browser. Controlling the option of accepting a Cookie is also left to the configuration of the browser as per user requirements.

Some example scenarios are included below, to aid the reader's understanding:

- Track first time visitors to the website/page and subsequent visits
- Store/Fetch user preferences
- Auto fill password

Cookie is a property of the Document object. A Cookie explicitly appears as a name–value pair. Implicitly, it has a number of other attributes related to its lifeline, accessibility and security aspects:

- Lifeline
  - Transient by default—lifetime for the browser session
  - Can be controlled by setting max-age attribute. The value is set in seconds (from creation). Any Cookie beyond the max-age is deleted by the browser.
- Accessibility
  - By default, accessible to the web page that created it and to other pages in the same directory or child directories
    - If for example, a web page www.abc.com/production creates the cookie, then it is also accessible to www.abc.com/production/operations but not accessible to www.abc.net for example.
  - To control the default behavior, the path attribute is specified. Setting the path to "/" in the previous example, any page can access the cookie.
  - Attribute called domain is set to include accessibility over the domain. For example if the domain is set to "abc.com" then the Cookie is made accessible to "examples.abc.com" as well as "exercises.abc.com".
- Security
  - By default, Cookies are sent insecurely (meaning normal mode) which is http
  - A cookie can be marked as secure, which means it is transmitted through a secure protocol like https.

An example of a simple Cookie handling script is in Figure 4.22A.

```
<!DOCTYPE html PUBLIC "-//W3C//DTD XHTML 1.0 Transitional//EN" "http://
www.w3.org/TR/xhtml1/DTD/xhtml1-strict.dtd">
<html xmlns="http://www.w3.org/1999/xhtml" dir="ltr">
<head>
    <title>JS Cookie</title>
    <script language=javascript type="text/javascript">
      function createCookie( ) {
          //Get name - abstracted to something from the Form element
          var name = document.nameform.myname.value;
          document.cookie = "myName=" + name; // Create the cookie
      }
      function fetchCookie(nm) {
          if (document.cookie != "") {

                var nms = document.cookie;
                writeData (nms);

          }

      }
      //define a easy function to write on to the DIV placeholder element
      function writeData(val) {
          e = document.getElementById("placeholder");
          e.innerHTML = val;

      }
    </script>
</head>
<body>
<!-A simple Form to accept the name -->
    <form method="post" class="form" name="nameform">
       Enter name: <input class="text" name="myname" type="text" />
       <input type="button" value="Sendcookie" onClick="createCookie()"/>
       <input type="button" value="FetchmyName" onClick="fetchCookie()"/>
    </form>
    <div id="placeholder"> </div>
</body>
</html>
```

Fig. 4.22A *Example cookie–create and fetch*

The program is run. With the sample value that is entered, the client program creates a cookie with name as "myName" and value as given by the user (in the example it is "CHOCookie"). This is created on clicking the Send Cookie button. The same is fetched and displayed when Fetch MyName button is clicked. The output is shown in Figure 4.22.B. The cookie can be displayed in the browser. In Firefox, the screen shot is shown in the same figure (Figure 4.22B).

Cookies on the client side are only half the story. More on Cookies are discussed in the server side chapter of this book.

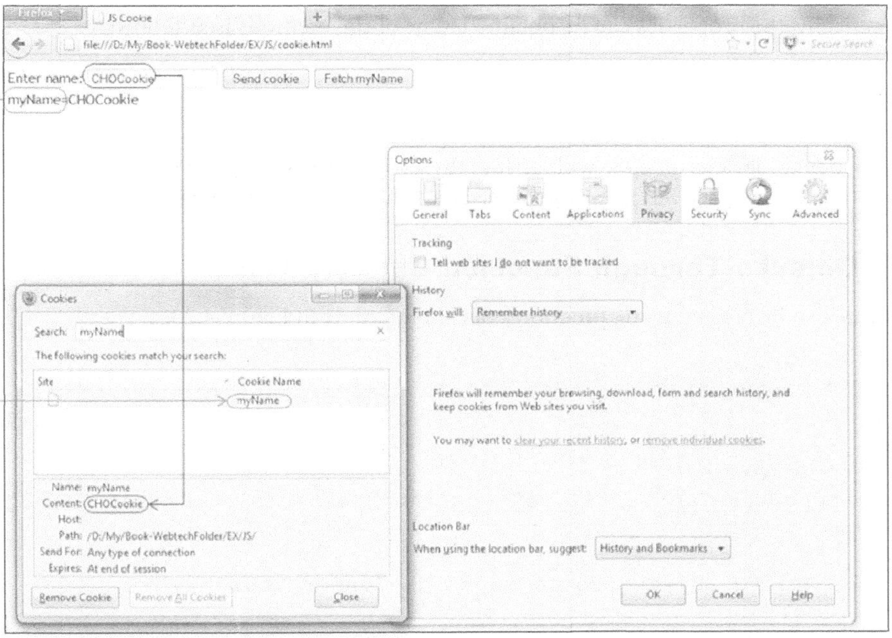

Fig. 4.22B *Example cookie ouput and appearing on Firefox browser*

4.13 THE CONCEPT OF CLASSES

JavaScript does *not* have a formal notation for Class. This makes it quite different from the other popular object-oriented languages like Java. However, realizing that JavaScript is a loosely typed language, this is hardly surprising! Notwithstanding this, it is still an object-oriented language. In languages like C++ or Java or C#, Classes are defined once and all objects are instantiations of the Class. In JavaScript, Classes can be *simulated* through the concept of objects and functions. An Object is a data structure that can (also) mimic a container containing attributes and methods. Methods can be implemented through functions. These properties can be dynamically added to the object at run time as well, which makes it different from the other popular object-oriented languages like C# or Java.

4.13.1 Creating Objects

Objects are created through the Object data type.

```
//Create a new object. Right now there are no properties defined.
    var Point = new Object;
    Point.x = 5;            //a property x is defined and initialized
    Point.y = 3;            //another property y is added
```

The above definition defines creation of an object instance. A new object can also be created using the {} syntax. For example the following statement is equivalent to the first statement:

```
var Point = {};
```

Programmatically, the properties can be obtained. One of the methods is as follows:

```
for (prop in Point) {
    alert (prop.toString());
}
```

The above snippet of JavaScript code will retrieve the two properties defined (x and y). Point[i] will fetch their values (5 and 3 respectively). For methods, attach functions to the objects.

4.13.2 Objects Through Function Constructors

An object can also be created using functions. See the example in Figure 4.23.

```
<!DOCTYPE HTML PUBLIC "-//W3C//DTD HTML 4.01 Transitional//EN">
<html>
<head>
<title></title>
<meta http-equiv="Content-Type" content="text/html; charset=UTF-8">
</head>
<body>
    <h2> Create Object from a function Constructor </h2>
    <script>
      function Point(x,y) {
        this.x = x;
        this.y = y;
        this.getCoordinates = function() {
          return ("(" + this.x + "," + this.y + ")");
        }
      }
      var p1 = new Point(4,8);     //instantiate a Point object
      var p2 = new Point(5,6);
      alert(p1.getCoordinates()); //output (4,8)
      alert(p2.getCoordinates()); //output (5,6)
    </script>
</body>
</html>
```

Fig. 4.23 *Create object* from *a function constructor*

The function (Point) is declared which acts as a constructor to a Class. Objects are instantiated using the new keyword as shown in the example above (Figure 4.23). The function method expects an object on which it acts or is applied. The keyword '**this**' specifies the object. The operator '**new**' creates a new object and passes it as '**this**' to the constructor (in this case the function Point). Not only that, it also enriches the object with a property called the constructor which points to the function that created it.

```
alert(p1.constructor);   //this will output the function constructor code
```

Note: If the **new** keyword is omitted from the initialization of variable **p1**, the default object that is associated with is the **Object**. Hence the constructor will point to the **Object** (function) rather than **Point** function.

4.13.3 Dynamic Addition of Methods—Prototype

In the examples so far, it has been seen that Objects were constructed according to the Constructor with a few attributes (or properties) and methods. In addition to these properties, an implicit or hidden property is also available. This is in the form of a link to prototype. New properties or methods can be added to the object's (Class) prototype.

For example in the above example, a new method can be added. Look at the code snippet below.

```
Point.prototype.resetXY = function(x,y) {
this.x = x;
this.y = y;
 }
```

Notice the way the new function (**resetXY**) has been added—to its **prototype** rather than to the object itself. The example shown in Figure 4.24 lists the code in full.

```
<!DOCTYPE HTML PUBLIC "-//W3C//DTD HTML 4.01 Transitional//EN">
<html>
<head>
<title></title>
<meta http-equiv="Content-Type" content="text/html; charset=UTF-8">
</head>
<body>
   <h2> Dynamic method addition </h2>
   <script>
         function Point(x,y) {
            this.x = x;
            this.y = y;
            this.getCoordinates = function() {
               return ("(" + this.x + "," + this.y + ")");
               }
         }
         var p1 = new Point(4,8);
         var p2 = new Point(5,6);
         alert(p1.getCoordinates()); //output (4,8)
         alert(p2.getCoordinates()); //output (5,6)

         Point.prototype.resetXY = function(x,y) { //add a method dynamically
            this.x = x;
            this.y = y;
         }
         p1.resetXY(8, 9); //invoke the method to change x, y
         alert ("p1 Co-ord are" + p1.getCoordinates()); //output (8,9)

         //loop through all properties in p1 object

         for(var p in p1) {
            alert(p.toString());
```

(Continued)

```
            if (p1.hasOwnProperty(p)) {
              document.writeln(p + "- own prop");
            } else {
              document.writeln(p + "- not own prop");
            }
          }
      </script>
    </body>
    </html>
```

Fig. 4.24 *An* HTML *file*

Each object has an implicit prototype property which can be enhanced as shown above. The **FOR** loop in the above code is the object iterator and lists out each property (both attributes and methods) of the object, **p1**. There is another interesting method—the **hasOwnProperty()** method of the property in question, applied to the object under consideration. If **true**, this implies that the property was originally defined in the Constructor function. If the concerned property (or method) was added later (like the **resetXY** method in the example) the **hasOwnProperty()** method returns **false**.

4.13.4 Inheritance

Inheritance in an object-oriented environment enables code reuse. There are two ways in which it is normally implemented in a language—Classical and Prototypical. Almost all object-oriented

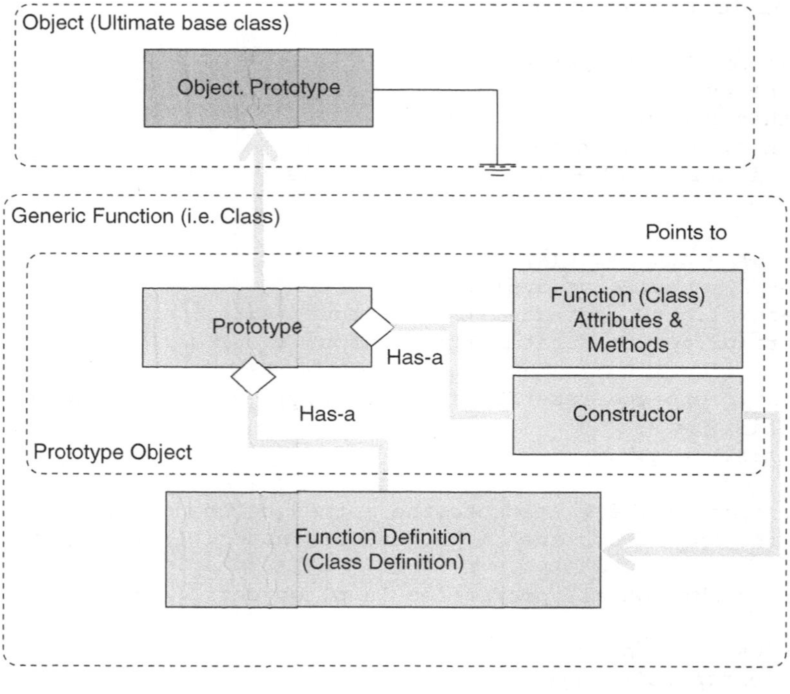

Fig. 4.25 *Overview of the Prototype object* and *inheritance*

languages fall in the former category (this includes C# and Java), while JavaScript follows a prototypical mode of inheritance. In fact, JavaScript is the only popular language that follows this model for inheritance.

When an object is created in JavaScript, a hidden property is implicitly created and made available in the form of a **prototype**. In fact, it inherits a chain of prototypes, terminating with the Object's prototype. A prototype is considered as a template for the object (similar to the concept of Classes) and is considered central to supporting JavaScript's object-oriented capabilities. Since inheritance is at the object level, it can be made dynamic.

A generic representation of an object is shown in Figure 4.25.

The above representation (Figure 4.25) shows that all Functions (which are used as Class objects) have the implicit property called the **prototype** which has the **constructor** as one its properties, implicitly. The **constructor** points back to the Function object. This is a generic representation shown above. A slightly specific representation consisting of an **Animal** function (class) is shown in an example code. From the **Animal** class, a **Dog** class is inherited as shown below in the diagram. Each such function or class is viewed as per the prototype and its constructor properties as shown in the figure. The inheritance ends with the Object class, which does not have any prototype further on (shown with the earth symbol), signifying the most generic of all classes (see Figure 4.26).

The code in Figure 4.27 demonstrates the usage of Functions as class templates, supplemented by using the prototypes. The example shows the concept of Animal class and a child Dog class. The Object is the topmost level in the hierarchy.

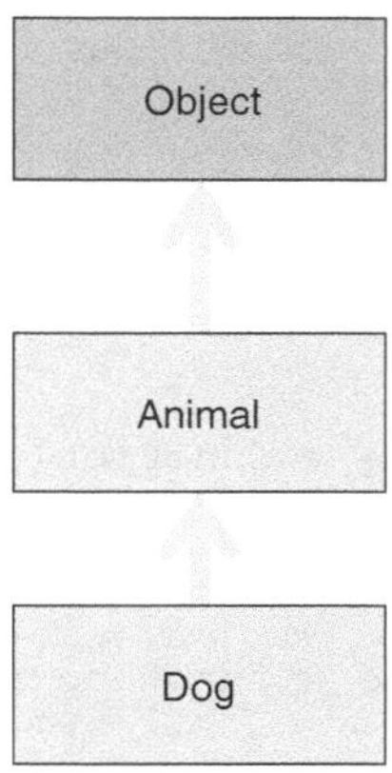

Fig. 4.26 *Example inheritance model*

A simplified program is shown in Figure 4.27:

```
<!DOCTYPE HTML PUBLIC "-//W3C//DTD HTML 4.01 Transitional//EN">
<html>
<head>
<title></title>
<meta http-equiv="Content-Type" content="text/html; charset=UTF-8">
```

(*Continued*)

```
<script>
  //construct a class for describing a generic Animal family. Set the
  //characteristics
  function Animal(family) {
    this.name = ‘noname’; //instance property of Animal class with
                          //value defaut
    this.family = family; //instance property initialized from
                          //parameter
    this.shout = ‘noshout’; //defalut value of the Shout variable
  };

  //example of class property which is a Constant applicable to all
  /Animal objects
  Animal.INHABITANTOF = ‘Earth’;

  //Dynamically supplement the class by defining these methods
  Animal.prototype.getFamily = function() { //Instance methods of the
                                            //class
    return (this.family);
  }
  Animal.prototype.setFamily = function(fam) {
    this.family = fam;
  }
  Animal.prototype.getName = function() {
    return (this.name);
  }
  Animal.prototype.setName = function(name) {
    this.name = name;
  }

/*Example of a Private variable for the function (class) for LE Expectancy.
This property can be accessed only thru setLE and then by getLE methods.
Just calling getLE (without setting it) will be invalid.
*/
  Animal.prototype.setLE = function(a) {
    this.getLE = function() {
    return a;
```

```
        }
    }

/* The toString() is meant to override the default; definition from Object’s prototype.
It demonstrates a different behavior which outputs the object in a readable fashion.
*/

    Animal.prototype.toString = function() {
      var str = ‘<b>Family: </b>’ + this.getFamily() + “;”;
      str = str + ‘<b>Name: </b>’ + this.getName() + “; <b>Shout: </b>” + this.shout;
      str = str + “;<b>Life Expectancy: </b>” + this.getLE() + “;<br></br>”;
      return (str);
    }
/* Now define a Dog function (class) with basic attributes, ( static properties).
Note that this definition need not mention about inheritance at this point.
This will later be inherited from Animal class.
*/
    function Dog (b) {
      this.breed = b;
    }
      Dog.prototype = new Animal;

      Dog.prototype.setBreed = function(b) {
      this.breed = b;
    }

/* Override the default behavior of the Object.toString method.
Note the way to get the string from the parent class (Animal) using call method.
*/
      Dog.prototype.toString = function() {
      var str = Animal.prototype.toString.call(this);
```

(*Continued*)

```
        str = str + "<b>Breed: </b>" + this.getBreed();
        return (str);
        }
    //define more properties and methods using its prototype
        Dog.prototype.getBreed = function() {
        return this.breed;
        }

      function onld() {
    //Define an instance of an Animal family.
    //Instantiate a wolf object and set some basic properties
        var wolf = new Animal('wolf');
        wolf.setName("ruffy");
        wolf.setLE(25); //set the life expentancy (LE) for wolf
        showMsg ("<u>Here are properties of the wolf Animal object just created</u>")
        showMsg(wolf); //invoke toString() of the Animal class

    //Now it is ready to to be instantiated
        var myDog = new Dog; //Dog derived from wolf Animal class
        myDog.setBreed('Labrador');
    /*Now inherit from Animal class wolf family. All Dog instances will be derived from wolf.
    This was the object that was created in the previous step. Automatically its prototype is used.
    */
        Dog.prototype = wolf;
    //Dog.prototype.constructor = Dog;

    //override the shout to a default value (bark) for all Dog objects
    //Dog.prototype.shout = 'bark';

    //typeof myDog will return Object

    /*
    Check out all properties/methods of the Dog class. Note the native properties and non-native properties.
```

```
Those defined within the Function are native and those supplemented thru the Prototype as well those
Inherited are shown as non-native. This will be useful to understand the concept better.
*/
      showMsg ("<u>Display properties of myDog object below</u>");
      for (var p in myDog) {
      if (myDog.hasOwnProperty(p)) {
      showMsg (p + "<b> is own defined</b>");
      } else {
      showMsg (p + " is supplemented/derived property ");
      }
      }

      myDog.setName("Julie");
      showMsg("----------------My Dog-------------");
      myDog.setLE(20);
      showMsg (myDog);
      Dog.prototype.shout = 'bark loudly';

      var myOtherDog = new Dog('Golden Retriever');
      myOtherDog.setName("Mojo");

/* Note that the LE (Life Expectancy) is not set for myOtherDog.
This means that the property will be inherited from wolf (which is 25 in this example)
*/

      showMsg("----------------My Other Dog-------------")
      showMsg(myOtherDog); //The toString method of Dog will be used here
      }

      function showMsg(msg) {
      msgdiv = document.getElementById("msg");
      msgdiv.innerHTML += msg + "<br />";
      }
```

(*Continued*)

```
        showMsg("================");
    </script>
</head>
<body onload="onld();">
    <h2> Inherited objects </h2>
    <div id="msg"></div>
</body>
</html>
```

Fig. 4.27 *Classes and inheritance*

Note how a private variable is simulated in Figure 4.27. In the example, the code for setting life expectancy is expressed as **setLE()**. The function implements a closure, returning a function called **getLE()**. There is no other way to get the variable—in fact it is not stored as any class variable but only through a function. This can also be defined in the body of the main constructor function for the class. A similar concept with private functions also hold good.

In **myOtherDog** object, the life expectancy variable is not set. However, the value is obtained from the parent object, in this case the **wolf** object where it was previously set to some value. This is, in fact, the default value set for all **Dog** objects. Any individual object like **myDog**, can override this value. However, the other property, **shout**, is valid for all objects of **Dog**. Changing this value will affect all objects (in this case **myDog** and **myOtherDog**) property for **shout**, no matter when the objects are instantiated. Take care of this behavior as sometimes it will lead to unintended consequences. It is left to the situation to handle the aspect that is required, but both these scenarios have been demonstrated here.

In summary, this is how variables and methods are treated:

- private variables are declared with the "var" keyword inside the object
- private functions are declared inline inside the object's constructor
- public properties are declared with this.variable
- public methods are defined by Classname.prototype.name from outside the object. This is similar for public properties
- static properties are defined by Classname.constant = value

At this point, it is worth mentioning about an operator that JavaScript provides called **instanceof**. It is used to check whether an object is an instance of a class. For instance, considering the above code example, the following will return true or false accordingly.

```
myDog instanceof Animal          //returns true
wolf instanceof Dog              //returns false
myDog instanceof Dog             //returns true
```

The output from the above code is handled by a general function called **showMsg** and is made just rudimentary for the sake of simplicity. It is hoped that the reader will understand that the focus is on

Inherited objects

Here are properties of the wolf Animal object just created

Family: wolf;**Name**: ruffy; **Shout**: noshout;**Life Expectancy**: 25;

Display properties of myDog object below

--getBreed is supplemented/derived property

--getName is supplemented/derived property

--getFamily is supplemented/derived property

--getLE is supplemented/derived property

--setLE is supplemented/derived property

--setName is supplemented/derived property

--shout is supplemented/derived property

--family is supplemented/derived property

--name is supplemented/derived property

--setFamily is supplemented/derived property

--breed **is own defined**

--setBreed is supplemented/derived property

---------------My Dog------------

Family: wolf;**Name**: Julie; **Shout**: bark;**Life Expectancy**: 20;

Breed: Labrador

---------------My Other Dog------------

Family: wolf;**Name**: Mojo; **Shout**: bark loudly;**Life Expectancy**: 25;

Breed: Golden Retriever

Fig. 4.28 *Output of the code demonstrating* inheritance

demonstrating the concept of inheritance and the prototype hierarchy, rather than on the UI. The output is shown in Figure 4.28.

The methods referenced in Figure 4.27 are not the only ways of achieving inheritance and object instantiations. There are other methods, and for reasons of efficiency and conforming to specific situations, it is fine to adapt to alternative ways. The above steps have been shown to drive a better understanding of the framework in which JavaScript's object model operates. Better readability of the code is many times preferred over abstruse code that might have better performance. Also, JavaScript 2, is moving towards Class based inheritance.

A lot of work on JavaScript has been conceptualized and pioneered by companies like Yahoo and Google. Besides, there are a lot of thought leaders like Douglas Crockford who have researched and created many libraries and functions that can be used. In fact, a lot of libraries exist that can be used straight away in a more simplified process. However, this is evolving and hence it makes sense to get educated about the latest versions in their respective websites that are updated quite frequently. A lot of these libraries are being used by applications emanating from these companies and are also generous enough to be made available to the general public for use. The reader is encouraged to innovate and bring up new applications using these libraries or otherwise.

4.14 EXECUTION CONTEXTS

Just like any other programming language, JavaScript also executes in a specific context. But in this case, it is slightly different because there could be multiple "global" contexts since each separate browser window (or a frame) in the client side defines its own specific global context. Some of these contexts can be linked as well. Knowledge of this behavior leads to an important security aspect which will be discussed later in this section.

4.15 DOM

The HTML document structure of any page is represented by the Document Object Model or DOM for short, specific to the page. It is the foundation for almost everything that JavaScript does on the client side. JavaScript has access to all elements of the DOM. Not only that, it can also manipulate the DOM, so that dynamism can be built at run time. HTML traversal leverages tag qualifiers like id and class.

4.15.1 The Bigger Picture of DOM

The Window object, as the name suggests, represents the objects present in the window. It is a key element housing the entire nodes like Document object, Navigator object, etc. This is the structure as implemented by any browser on a web page. However, the object hierarchy under the Document object is the most often used, and hence considered important. The structure is referred to as the DOM. It is different for different web pages, but the structure is always hierarchical. Moreover, the way it is organized is standardized across all browsers.

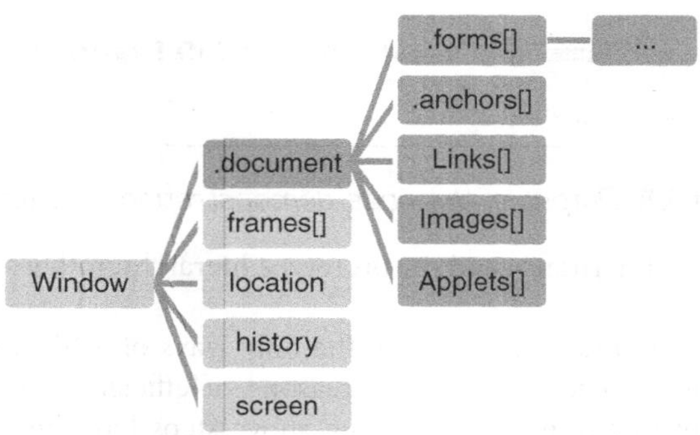

Fig. 4.29 *The bigger picture of DOM*

Figure 4.29 illustrates the super set of the DOM hierarchy. Note the darker shaded portions (subtree under the Document object) refer to the DOM.

4.15.2 Representing DOM

Consider the HTML shown in Figure 4.30.

```
<html>
<head>
    <title> DOM </title>
</head>
<body>
    <h1> DOM Structure </h1>
    <p id="txtID" class="stylish">
          This is my <b> first </b> Para
    </p>
    <p class="stylish">
          This is my second
    </p>
</body>
</html>
```

Fig. 4.30 *An HTML file*

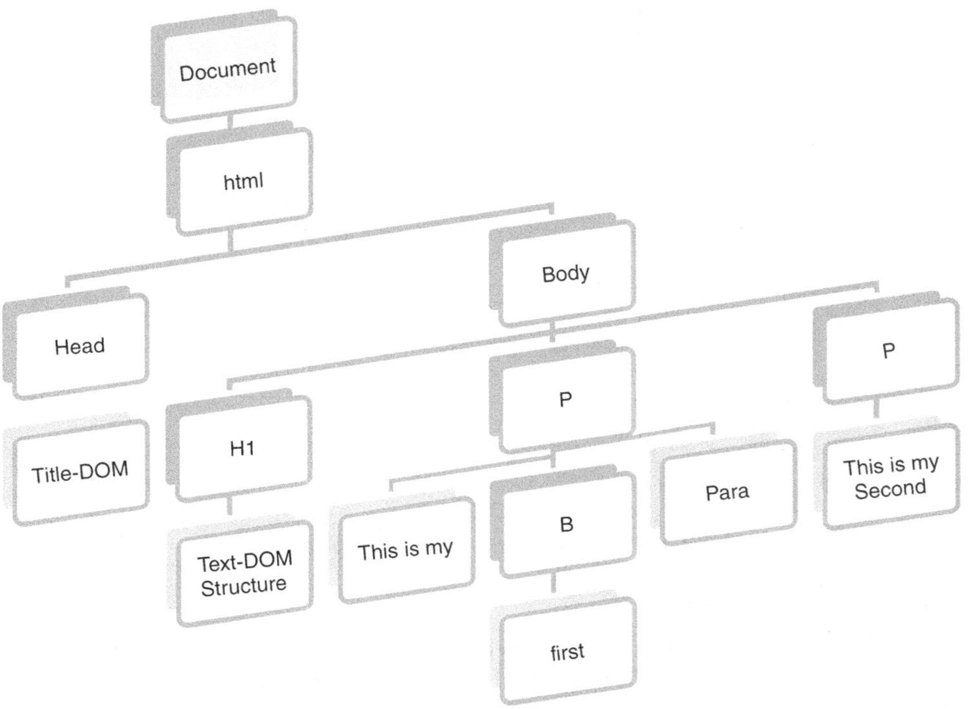

Fig. 4.31 *DOM representation of the HTML* document

The HTML page can be represented as a tree structure shown in Figure 4.31. Though this is supposed to be browser-independent, in practice, there could be small variations in the DOM structure followed by different browsers. However, the programmer who is writing the code to manipulate this structure and the elements, has to ensure that it works satisfactorily well in all browsers. JavaScript offers a few functions that peek into a browser's capabilities, so that it can be leveraged. A bit of special testing in all of the targeted browsers will also help in fixing gaps, if any. In fact, DOM manipulation is the most vulnerable area when it comes to browser compatibility. So care has to be taken accordingly.

Every Window object has a Document property accessed through window.document property. The HTML object is considered the root element for DOM.

Consider another example of an HTML document (Figure 4.32). The objective is to identify the anchor elements in the document. Note that the anchor element is identified by the <a> tag.

```
<!DOCTYPE HTML PUBLIC "-//W3C//DTD HTML 4.01 Transitional//EN"
"http://www.w3.org/TR/html4/loose.dtd">
<html xmlns="http://www.w3.org/1999/xhtml">
<head>
      <meta http-equiv="Content-Type" content="text/html;
      charset=utf-8" />
      <title>DOM</title>
</head>
  <script>
    function alertElements() {
      var elementATags = document.getElementsByTagName("a");
      for (var i = 0; i < elementATags.length ; i++)
      {
        alert("HREF of this anchor is:" + elementATags[i].href + "\n");
      }
    }
  </script>
<body onload="alertElements();">
  <h1>DOM</h1>
</body>
  <a href="#"> This section talks about the Anchor tag</a>
  <p></p>
  <a href="#"> The elements can be selected one by one </a>
  <p></p>
  <a href="#"> Observe as many alerts as the number of A elements </a>
</html>
```

Fig. 4.32 *Demonstrating a simple set of anchors*

4.15.3 DOM Traversal

The HTML page is arranged as an XML collection of elements—Links, Images, Tables, Forms, Text boxes, Drop downs, etc., in an arrangement called the DOM. The DOM is structured in the form of nodes in a hierarchical form. This is an exact reflection of the Strict XHTML format where, for instance, a start tag

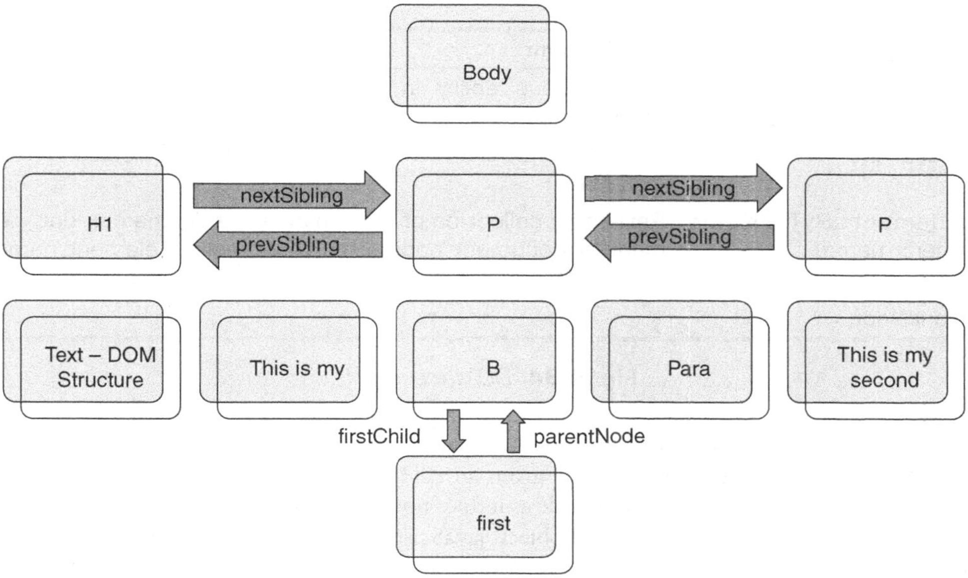

Fig. 4.33 *DOM traversal framework*

has to necessarily have an ending tag and so on. Each such node represents a unique object on the page. Then there are neighboring nodes but arranged in a definite order. Using these objects, JavaScript can get information about the nodes, travel to the next node, and also peek into its properties. The process of going after nodes in some sequence is termed DOM traversal. The idea is to navigate and make some changes to each part of the DOM during traversal. An example of a part of traversal is illustrated in Figure 4.33.

The DOM elements shown in Figure 4.33 are extracted from the same example shown previously. Only a subset is shown so as to show more clarity. Traversing from the first node H1 to next node P can be achieved by invoking the method nextSibling from H1. Conversely, from P, prevSibling will land on H1. That was about horizontal traversal. Vertical traversal is achieved by invoking firstChild or parentNode from the appropriate objects.

Figure 4.34 gives a summary of all methods useful for traversal.

Node Object.method	Description
N.childNodes	A collection of all text and element nodes of N. This is Read-only. Note the plural in the method name.
N.parentNode	A reference to the parent node (only one parent, obviously)
N.firstChild	The first entry in the childNodes collection if node is an element node or document node. (same as N.childNodes[0])
N.lastChild	The last entry in the childNodes collection if node is an element node or document node (N.childNodes[N.child-Notes.length minus 1])
N.nextSibling	next node on the same level

(Continued)

(*Continued*)

Node Object.method	Description
N.previousSibling	The previous entry in the childNodes collection of the parent node (read only)
offsetParent	The node that the element's offset can be calculated from (read only)
getElementsByTagName (element_name)	Returns a collection of all elements inside the current element or document node, with the specified element name. It returns an object with.0...n and.length properties
currentNode	

Fig. 4.34 *DOM traversal*

Looping through a DOM is a recursive process. Again refer the diagram—some conclusions can be drawn which will aid in visualizing the DOM given an HTML. The top level node is referred to as the *Document*, called the root node. It is a root node as it does not have a parent.node (which is null). Usually this is the starting point of the HTML DOM object. JavaScript makes it easy to access this node directly through the *document* object. It does have a Child node, called HTML node, accessible by the firstChild method.

```
var nHTML = document.childNodes[0];
```

HTML Node can also be accessed by document.firstChild.nHTML.nodeName property contains the name of the node which can be used to print the type of the node.

The Body node is obtained as the second child of the HTML element, the first child being the Head element.

```
var nBody = nHTML.childNodes[1];
```

Note that the HTML object is now used as the reference from which we obtain its second child.

A node's first child and last child are available in different methods, though they can be accessed by a single method itself or through the childNodes method. For example the lastChild can be accessed as firstChild[childNodes.length—1], but since it is rather unwieldy to use and the fact that they have to be accessed frequently, lastChild is a good alias to be used as a short cut.

```
var nHead = nHTML.childNodes[0];
//HTML element has 2 children–1st is Head, 2nd is Body element
var nTitle = nHead.firstChild; //Title is the only node
document.write(nTitle.nodeName);      // nodeName is Title
document.write(nTitle.text);   //text gives off the value–in this case
it is DOM

A <P> node can be accessed as under.

var nP = nBody.childNodes[1];

var PText = nP.firstChild.nodeValue;
```

Note that the value of the text in the (P) node can be retrieved using nodeValue method applied to its child. nodeName will output #Text, signifying it is a text element.

4.15.4 Accessing Nodes Directly

The above model of DOM traversal is useful but a bit cumbersome when a node is to be accessed directly. Furthermore, if the page is dynamically generated (which is true in almost all scenarios), it is extremely difficult to navigate and locate an element (node) precisely. So it is definitely required to access a node through some other means.

Recall that in HTML there are attributes declared to tags. Though the attributes are different for different tags, the id and class attributes are the most common ones that appear. This is being put to use while navigating. The value of an id attribute is unique within a page. Correspondingly, the method getElementById(idname) will fetch the node that contains the node identified by idname.

```
var nP = document.getElementById("txtID");
```

Note that the method is applied to the document object. While the above method fetches a single node (or none at all), it is possible to have methods that return multiple nodes. Take, for instance, fetching by means of class attributes or by means of tag names.

```
var allP = document.getElementsByTagName('P');
//returns 2 nodes as per example HTML
```

Note that the method name contains the plural of Elements as in getElementsByTagName, thus signifying that it could return more than one node. In the given example, it will return two nodes—the one that contains the id of txtID and the other that contains the text ("this is my second").

Similarly, the method getElementsByClass could return multiple nodes which has the given class name.

```
var allStylish = document.getElementsByClass('stylish'); //returns 2
nodes as per example
sz = allStylish.length;
for (i=0; i<sz; i++) {
     document.write("Stylish-" + allStylish.nodeName
}
```

The basic tools required for locating and traversing any part of the DOM has been discussed here. Do avoid hard-coding the code during traversal as pages could be dynamic. But the principle is the same.

4.15.5 Adding Dynamism—DOM Manipulation

So far, only navigating the elements and their nodes has been covered, in short how they chain together. But what about making a change to the HTML page? What about modifying the style or structure? How about adding new nodes, or elements in the page? In short how do we manipulate the contents of the page?

There are various methods to achieve this.

4.15.5.1 Changing text within nodes A node's nodeValue property gives off the value of the property in a text based node. To modify it, simply change the text and it gets reflected back on the page.

```
allP[i].childNodes[0].nodeValue = 'Now changed';
```

Likewise, the attributes associated with the text node can also be changed. This can be done using the setAttribute() method.

4.15.5.2 Adding new elements New elements can be created on the page (i.e. the document object) with the `document.createElement(tag)` method. This new element is first created like a pre-fabricated structure and then moved in place at the right location. Furthermore, when a new Element is created, it is empty. So, in parallel, a text node for instance needs to be created and attached to the previously created element. Style can also be (optionally) added, before it is put in place.

4.15.5.3 Replacing Elements Certain nodes can be replaced with new nodes to facilitate in-place modification of data within a form. This is true for child nodes especially `replaceChild` is used for this purpose. Actually replacing is done in two phases—preparation of the new node and then the replacement with the old one. For example, consider a simple P element replacement.

```
<!DOCTYPE HTML PUBLIC "-//W3C//DTD HTML 4.01 Transitional//EN">
<html>
<head>
  <title></title>
  <meta http-equiv="Content-Type" content="text/html; charset=UTF-8">
</head>
<body>
 <p id="anamika">This is the Current text</p>
    <button onclick="replacePText()">Replace</button>
 <script>
  function replacePText() {
    var newPElement = document.createElement("P");
    var txt = "This is the Replacement Text";
    var txtElement = document.createTextNode(txt);
    newPElement.appendChild(txtElement);
    //newPElement.innerHTML = txt;
    //An alternate and easier way is by using innerHTML!
    var currPElement = document.getElementById("anamika");
    var p = currPElement.parentNode;
    p.replaceChild(newPElement, currPElement);
  }
 </script>
</body>
</html>
```

Fig. 4.35 *Demonstrating a simple* replacement *operation*

The code example (Figure 4.35) shows how a simple operation of replacing text in a node is achieved. Note that the calls to various operations are not straightforward, though as a process it is simple. For larger operations it is cumbersome and warrants lengthy code. It is, therefore, advisable to have smaller functions to achieve the basic functionalities. However, it is strongly tied with the structure of the HTML file that is manipulated. Hence it is advisable to take care of a few things like hiding the implementation details and design a robust structure upfront so changes do not have a negative ripple effect.

(A) (B)

Fig. 4.36 (A) *Output of the replacement operation;* (B) *Output of the replacement operation after the button is clicked*

Even in the examples in Figure 4.36 (A) and (B) the verbose calls can be substituted by customized functions that can be called when required.

4.16 EVENT HANDLING

The concept of dynamic behavior can be achieved through a well-defined user event handling mechanism. Events refer to user actions like clicking of a button, mouse movement (up/down), change of values and on-load of a page. Each of these events can be recognized by JavaScript (though the browser), trigerring a callback that can be custom written in JavaScript.

The events happen in the objects within the DOM model as in the clicking of a button by a user. However, not all events are generated by users alone—the system also generates some events. Event handling has been one of the most challenging topics in JavaScript, since its implementation has changed over the years. Not surprisingly, its implementation is browser-dependent.

One of the ways event handlers can be defined is through attributes of an object. Not all events are applicable to all types of objects. For example, the 'onchange' event is applicable for text type of objects triggered when the value of the text changes. The most commonly used event based attributes are described in the following sub sections.

Table 4.1 is a list of such events.

Table 4.1 *Commonly used event based attributes*

Event	Description
onload	applies to page and image elements, immediately after they load
onunload	occurs after a page is unloaded or during transition of a page
onmouseover	occurs when the mouse movement occurs such that it is over the element
onmouseout	occurs when the mouse is moved out of the element
onmousedown	occurs when the mouse button is pressed down (on an element)
onmouseup	occurs when the mouse button is released (on an element)
onmousemove	occurs when the mouse moves
onfocus	occurs when the element receives focus
onblur	occurs when the element loses focus
click	when an element (button, text, etc) is clicked

(Continued)

Table 4.1 *(Continued)*

Event	Description
onsubmit	occurs when a Form is submitted
onchange	occurs when the selection value changes
onkeydown	

Events, in general, are mentioned as belonging to level-0 DOM, level-2 DOM or level-3 DOM. The level-0 model is based on the first implementation of event handling, which originated during the browser wars. Not surprisingly, there are multiple implementations—broadly two types—IE and the rest.

The level-2 DOM event model is a later implementation, but many browsers still support the older model. There are some major differences between the older event model and that of DOM Level-2.

- the newer model isn't as dependent on a specific event handler property
- multiple event handler functions can be registered on an object
- Instead of the event handler property, each object in Firefox has three methods:—
  - addEventListener: It registers the event listeners on the target
  - removeEventListener: Enables removal of the event listeners from the target
  - dispatchEvent: Enables sending the event to select listeners
- For Microsoft, the model follows a bit different upto IE8. IE9 follows level-3DOM. The three methods in IE are given below. In concept, it is similar to that for Firefox:
  - attachEvent
  - detachEvent
  - fireEvent

Event objects are dispatched to the target through a propagation path, which is hierarchical since the DOM is hierarchical. The event object must complete at least one phase in its path—Capture phase, Target phase and Bubbling phase. A phase can be skipped or stopped altogether.

The bubbling phase can be skipped by sending a value of false in the last parameter in addEventListener (Firefox). The propagation can be stopped by calling stopPropagation on the event.

The models are shown in the Figure 4.37.

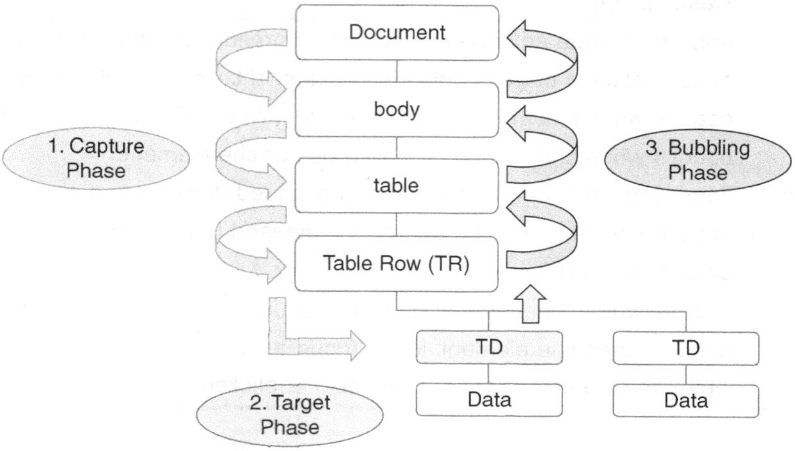

Fig. 4.37 *The event dispatch flow*

4.16.1 Event Onclick

This is applicable to all buttons and anchor elements, triggered when the user clicks on them. An example is given below.

```
<!DOCTYPE HTML PUBLIC "-//W3C//DTD HTML 4.01 Transitional//EN"
"http://www.w3.org/TR/html4/loose.dtd">
<html xmlns="http://www.w3.org/1999/xhtml">
<head>
  <meta http-equiv="Content-Type" content="text/html; charset=utf-8"/>
  <title>OnClick</title>
</head>
  <script>
    function alertMe(ele) {
      var Dt = new Date();
      alert("You clicked" + ele.id + "at" + Dt );
    }
  </script>
<body>
  <h1>Alert Me on Click </h1>
</body>
  <button id="OKButton" onclick="alertMe(this);">OK</button>
  <button id="CancelButton" onclick="alertMe(this);">Cancel</
  button><p></p>
</html>
```

Fig. 4.38 *Click event*

The OnClick event definition is done as part of the attribute "onclick" when the button (OKButton) is defined (shown above in a different color). Similarly, it is defined for another button (CancelButton). The function itself is defined in the header of the page.

Another point to observe is how the same function (alertMe) is used for either buttons (OK or Cancel).

4.16.2 Event Onchange

This is applicable when the value of text changes in text fields. Types of objects include <input>, <select> and <text-area>.

```
<html>
<head>
<meta http-equiv="Content-Type" content="text/html;
charset=utf-8" />
<title>On Click and Change</title>
```

(Continued)

```
</head>
  <script>
    function alertMe(ele) {
      var Dt = new Date();

      alert("You clicked" + ele.id + "at" + Dt );
    }
    function alertChange() {
      var a = document.getElementById("inp1");
      alert("Default Value: " + a.defaultValue + "; Changed:"
      + a.value);
    }
  </script>
<body>
  <h1>Alert Me on Click or Change </h1>
  <input id="inp1" onchange="alertChange();" value="ABC"></input>
  <button id="btnOK" onclick="alertMe(this);">Click</button><p>
  </p>
</body>
</html>
```

Fig. 4.39 *Change event*

In Figure 4.39 note the onchange attribute defined in the input text box, inp1. Any change in the value of the text box triggers the JavaScript function alertChange(). Refer to the definition of the function. It brings out the changed value as well as the default value.

4.16.3 Event Onload

There is a callback triggered just after the HTML page has been loaded. Page-load ensures all objects have been loaded and hence the complete DOM is available. Once this is made available, the system can optionally execute a set of customized functions. The attribute is generally defined as part of the "body" tag, but can be used as part of other tags as well.

When it is used as part of the frameset tag, it will apply just after the frame is loaded.

4.16.4 Mouse Events

The mouse events are onmousedown, onmouseup, onmouseover and onmouseout. The onmouseup and onmousedown are actually parts of the onclick attribute.

The onmouseover and onmouseout events are triggered when the mouse moves over an element or out of the element respectively.

4.16.5 Default Event Listeners

The browser provides a default listener that is applied after all the events on an element has been called. An example will provide better clarity—when a Submit button is clicked, there is a set of steps that the browser takes in terms of creating the query string and submitting as an HTTP request, as per the action attribute defined on the Form. Similarly, another example is the sequence of events that internally take place when the anchor href is clicked.

Default Listeners are applicable for some of the elements and for some of the events. They are not affected by stopPropagation, a call that was mentioned earlier.

```
<html>
<head>
<meta http-equiv="Content-Type" content="text/html; charset=utf-8" />
<title>Form Validation - Prevent Default</title>

<script>
/*
* Add the event listener, which enables validation, to the Form. alert
* Alternatively, the onsubmit event can be defined as part of the Form
*/
   function onld() {
      var f = document.getElementById("form1");
      f.addEventListener("submit",myvalidate,false);
   }
/*
* Validate the Form. Item is mandatory, rest of the fields are not.
* If validation fails, then prevent the default behaviour of Submit
* Else, it is normal - the action attribute in the Form element decides
* the next step. Normally (Form-Process) will be a Server side code,
* but it is dummy code in this case.
```

(Continued)

```
*/
    function myvalidate(e) {
      var itemvalue = document.getElementById("item").value.trim();
      if (itemvalue.length == 0) {
      alert ("Enter an item");
      e.preventDefault();
    }
      var qtyfld = document.getElementById("qty");  //validate qty for numeric
      var qtyvalue = qtyfld.value.trim();
      if (qtyvalue.length > 0) {
      if (isNaN(qtyvalue)) {
            alert ("Quantity should be numeric");
            qtyfld.select();
            e.preventDefault();
                 }
      }
      return;
    }
  </script>
  </head>
  <body onload="onld();">
    <h1>Item Form - Demo Prevent Default</h1>
    <form id="form1" action="Form-Process.html">
      <table id="tableId">
        <th>
            <td></td>
            <td></td>
        </th>
        <tr>
            <td> Item: </td>
            <td> <input id="item" type="text"> Try filling in / leave it blank</td>
        </tr>
        <tr>
            <td> Quantity: </td>
```

```
55              <td> <input id="qty" type="text"></td>
56          </tr>
57          <tr>
58              <td> Description: </td>
59              <td> <input id="desc" type="text"></td>
60          </tr>
61          <tr>
62              <td colspan="2"><button id="btnOK"
                type="submit">Submit</button></td>
63          </tr>
64        </table>
65      </form>
66    </body>
67    </html>
```

Fig. 4.40 *preventDefault code listing (for Firefox)*

The program in Figure 4.40 demonstrates not as much how a Form is validated but more on how preventDefault is applied to stop the browser's normal sequence of events, once the Form is submitted and found to be with validation errors. For this to be understood, take a look at line 43, where the Form is declared with an action attribute. This attribute is required to instruct the next step—in this case it is just another HTML file. In practice, this would most probably point to a Server code which will take the (valid) Form. At the very least, the (Form-Process) HTML file is shown below. There is nothing significant that can be found in the file in this current form, but that is fine as the focus of the demonstration code is not to show the processing part.

```
<html>
<head>
<meta http-equiv="Content-Type" content="text/html; charset=utf-8"/>
<title>Form-Process</title>
</head>
<body>
  <h1>Form - Item Process</h1>
  <h2> Item processing done here </h2>
</body>
</html>
```

Also take a look at the onload function, onld()—the Event is declared in line 41 and defined from line 11. The function (onld) adds the event listener to the Form (line 13).

```
f.addEventListener("submit",myvalidate,false);
```

It more or less translates into something like this—when the Form (defined by variable *f*) is submitted, intercept the submit process through the function (*myvalidate*) given. For now park aside the last parameter (*false*)—it will be explained later, but just to satisfy the curiosity in the reader, it is a boolean flag that signifies whether the event has to be Bubbling Up or Tricking Down.

As a side note, it is to be noticed that the Form validation that is defined in this example is only client-side validation, meaning there are no server-side checks like cross-referencing with a database or some kind of server processing to check validity. The client-side validation will generally be able to do checks like compliance to mandatory fields, numeric checks, format checks, etc. In the code for *myvalidate* (lines 22–38), note that whenever the validation fails, there is a call to preventDefault(). This is applied on the event object (for Firefox). It is required because otherwise the browser will go ahead and implement its next action sequence (as defined by the *action* attribute of the Form), even during error conditions. Not all event types can be canceled—there is a property called "cancellable" applied on the event object, which is true if it supports preventDefault.

Since it is not effective to produce screen shots of error conditions, the reader is encouraged to try out and verify for various conditions of the data. Error conditions include blank *Item* field, and Non-numeric *Quantity* field.

4.16.6 Browser Specific Challenges

The Prevent-Default code shown in Figure 4.40 will work on Firefox but not in IE. Here is an attempt to make the code browser independent. Only the changed functions are given below.

```
function onld() {
     var f = document.getElementById("form1");
     //browser specific code - check for the presence of function
     if (f.addEventListener) {
            f.addEventListener("submit",myvalidate,false); //Firefox
     } else if (f.attachEvent) {        //IE
            f.attachEvent("onsubmit", myvalidate);
     } else if (f.onclick) {
     f.onclick=clickMe;
     }
}
function myvalidate(e) {
     var itemvalue = document.getElementById("item").value;
     if (itemvalue.length == 0) {
            alert ("Enter an item");
     if (e.preventDefault) {
            e.preventDefault(); //Firefox
     } else {
            e.returnValue = false;     //for IE
            }
     }
     var qtyfld = document.getElementById("qty");
     var qtyvalue = qtyfld.value;
     if (qtyvalue.length > 0) {
     if (isNaN(qtyvalue)) {
            alert ("Quantity should be numeric");
            qtyfld.select();
            if (e.preventDefault) {
            e.preventDefault();
     } else {
            e.returnValue = false;
     }
```

```
            }
            }
            return true;
    }
```

The rest of the code remains the same.

4.16.7 Event Propagation

Sometimes it is tedious to define event handlers for all elements in a page, since there can be many tags handled. Also, it may be dynamic in nature, which could add to the complexity. Maintenance of these event handlers is yet another nightmare.

Fortunately, for events added through event handling DOM level-2, it is not necessary to define for all individual tags or elements, even if it is required to trap events for all of them.

Taking a common example of a Table set of tags, let us see how one definition of the event handler is enough to trap click of a mouse on any part of the table and getting their cell details.

```
<html lang="en">
<head title="Event Delegation">
<script>
/*
Add event on loading the page. Anywhere on the table element,
a click can be trapped
The event is registered on a parent element (table). The
target click element could be
multiple items - table, table header, table data, etc...
*/
  function addMyEvent() {
        var myID = document.getElementById('myTable1');
        addEvent (myID, 'click', myFunc); //add only 1 event,
        any browser
  }
//function implementing the event of clicking.
        var myFunc=function(e) {
//get hold of the traget object - different ways for IE
//and Firefox
        e = e || window.event; //IE
        var targetNode = e.target || e.srcElement; //Firefox

//take action when td is the target element. Can be
//tested for th or table itself
//if any other child is present within TD then they may
//also be trapped.
      if (targetNode.nodeName.toLowerCase() == 'td' ) {
```

(Continued)

```
        var myvalue = targetNode.innerText || targetNode.
        textContent;
        //cellIndex gives off the column number. For row number,
        //get from parent's rowIndex
        alert('Clicked table data at col ' + targetNode.cel-
        lIndex + ";row " +
        targetNode.parentNode.rowIndex + ";Value " + myvalue);
        }

    }

        //browser specific implementation of adding the event
        //handler
        function addEvent(elem, type, fn) {
          if (elem.attachEvent) {
          elem.attachEvent( 'on' + type, fn);
          return;
        }
        if (elem.addEventListener) {
          elem.addEventListener(type, fn, false );
          }
          return;
        }
</script>
</head>
<body onload="addMyEvent()">
        <h4 id="h4id">Table headers:</h4>
        <table border="5" id="myTable1">
          <tr>
            <th>Name</th>
            <th>Telephone</th>
            <th>mail</th>
          </tr>
          <tr>
            <td>Ram</td>
            <td>123-456-78</td>
            <td>ram@xyz.com</td>
```

```
            </tr>
            <tr>
                  <td>Shyam</td>
                  <td>123-123-12</td>
                  <td>shyam@abc.com</td>
            </tr>
            <tr>
                  <td>Amar</td>
                  <td>125-125-12</td>
                  <td>amar@abc.com</td>
            </tr>
         </table>
      </body>
   </html>
```

The output will display a table, and when clicked, will alert the message with the cell coordinates as shown in Figure 4.41.

Fig. 4.41 *Table click event co-ordinates*

4.16.8 Other Events

There are other types of events supported on the Web, without a mention of which the section on events is incomplete. However, a detailed study of the events is beyond the scope of the book, but it tries to give pointers to the reader for further reading.

Touch Events apply to touch-sensitive devices like Android. The events that make up Touch are touchstart, touchend, touchmove, touchcancel, etc.

Microsoft specific events (which work only on IE) include clipboard events (cut, beforecut, before-paste), Data binding events (afterupdate, beforeupdate, etc) and special mouse related events like drag-start, dragend, etc.

4.17 A SHOPPING CART TABLE SORT EXAMPLE

A shopping cart is a non-trivial utility that is a part of any eCommerce system. There are multiple implementations possible, in practice, each depending in turn on the domain or the items that are being sold. Essentially, it is represented by a table which contains the items that are shopped, a field for quantity and then a field for price. In practice there could be a few more columns for amounts, and a few extra methods (or operations) apart from adding/removing/modifying the items in the cart. For now, assume a very simple set of columns arranged in the form of a table. The point is to demonstrate the dynamic construction of elements of the cart, viz. the table header, its format and its rows (representing items).

Note that the table is generated dynamically within the function, initItems() and insertTableData(). They are implemented in a simplified way; in practice, this is expected to be more robust and more efficient. The elements are created first and then appended to the table.

```
<html>
<head>
  <meta http-equiv="Content-Type" content="text/html;
  charset=UTF-8">
  <title>Shopping Page</title>
</head>
<body>
  <h1>Example to re-arrange a Shopping Cart table</h1>
  <table id="scart" border="2" cellspacing="2" cellpadding="5">
  </table>
  <br />

 <button onclick="dispCart()">Initialize</button>
 <button onclick="colorRows()">Color Header Row</button>
 <button onclick="rearrange('sku')">Sort by Book</button>
 <button onclick="rearrange('qty')">Sort by Quantity</button>
 <button onclick="rearrange('price')">Sort by Price</button>
</body>
 <script>
     var items = []; //each row of the shopping cart
     var table; //DOM table object
    //displays the cart as a table. When empty, it initializes
    //with the seed data
```

```
        //The cart contains a set of books with a quantity and at
        //some price
     function dispCart() {
        table = document.getElementById("scart");

        if (table.firstChild == null ) { //if empty then initialize
        initItems();
        } else {
        replaceTableData(); //replace as opposed to add
        }
     }

   //Add items to the array which will will then be used to add to
   //the shopping cart table
     function addItems(s,q,p) {
        items[items.length] = {sku:s, qty:q, price:p};
     }

   //Initialize the table with the items as under. Right now it is
   //hard coded, but in reality
   //would originate from a database or some such source. Header
   //is also initialized
     function initItems() {
        addItems('Web Technologies',20,200);
        addItems('Software Engineering',2,100);
        addItems('Web Security',4,150);
        addItems('Algorithms',9,230);
        addItems('Systems Engineering',30,450);
        addItems('Image Processing',2,50);

   //Table header is created using TH elements.
   //The simple cart consists of 3 columns - Book, Quantity and
   //Price
        var hdrRow = document.createElement("TH");
        hdrRow.innerHTML = "Book";
        table.appendChild(hdrRow);

        hdrRow = document.createElement("TH");
```

(*Continued*)

```
        hdrRow.innerHTML = "Quantity";
        table.appendChild(hdrRow);

        hdrRow = document.createElement("TH");
        hdrRow.innerHTML = "Price";
        table.appendChild(hdrRow);

        //after the header row is created, data rows are to be handled
        insertTableData();
    }
    //Data in the table is replaced as per Items array. The array
    //contains in order the
    //shopping cart items.
    function replaceTableData() {
        table = document.getElementById('scart');
        //get the set of TR elements already existiing
        trs = table.getElementsByTagName("TR");
        node = trs[0].firstChild;

        for (var i=0; i<items.length; i++) {
        var item = items[i];
        //construct the whole TR set of elements
        var tr = document.createElement("TR");

        var td = document.createElement("TD");
        td.innerHTML = item.sku;
        tr.appendChild(td);

        td = document.createElement("TD");
        td.innerHTML = item.qty;
        tr.appendChild(td);

        td = document.createElement("TD");
        td.innerHTML = item.price;
        tr.appendChild(td);
        //Consider this TR set for replacement with the old node
```

```
      table.replaceChild(tr, trs[i]);
    }
  }

  function insertTableData() {
    table = document.getElementById('scart');

    for(var i=0; i<items.length; i++) {
    var item = items[i];
    //Create the TR representing the entire row
    var tr = document.createElement("TR");
    //Each row consists of TD (data) elements - as much as the
    //number of columns
    var td = document.createElement("TD");
    td.innerHTML = item.sku;
    tr.appendChild(td);

    td = document.createElement("TD");
    td.innerHTML = item.qty;
    tr.appendChild(td);

    td = document.createElement("TD");
    td.innerHTML = item.price;
    tr.appendChild(td);
    //finally add the TR set created above to the table. Likewise
    //do for all items
    table.appendChild(tr);
    }
  }

  function rearrange(sortFld) {
    //Sort
    //examine the sort function passed as a function argument.
    //it is supposed to return back either of 3 values on each
    //comparison pair
    //the return values are -1, 0 or 1 depending on the whether
    //the comparison is
```

(*Continued*)

```
      //smaller, equal or bigger
      items.sort(function(a,b){
      if (sortFld == 'sku') {
      x = a.sku;
      y = b.sku;
      } else if (sortFld == 'qty') {
      x = parseInt(a.qty);
      y = parseInt(b.qty);
      } else {
      x = parseFloat(a.price);
      y = parseFloat(b.price);
      }

      if (x > y) return 1;
      if (x < y) return -1;
      if (x == y) return 0;
      });
      dispCart();
    }

      //this function colors the header row. Useful for demonstrating
      //the style attributes than
      //can be changed.
    function colorRows() {
      table = document.getElementById('scart');
      //Get the header row of the table. It can be obtained by
      //many means like
      //getting the Table object and getting on to the first row.
      //Alternatively, consider as a collection of TH elements.
      hdrNodes = table.getElementsByTagName("TH");

       for(var i=0; i<hdrNodes.length; i++) {
      n = hdrNodes[i];
      n.style.backgroundColor = "pink";
      //Lets not assume sophisticated means of getting at a color!
      //Just hardcode for now...
    }
```

```
157
158         //Similarly, extend this concept to the data rows as well, (which
            //is left
159         //to the reader as an exercise!). Use a choice of alternative
            //colors to
160         //represent different shades for alternative rows.
161
162      }
163   </script>
164   </html>
```

Fig. 4.42 *Code listing to re-arrange shopping cart display*

First notice the body element (Figure 4.42 lines 7–15). This is indeed short when compared to the rest of the code. The display of the initial set of data is taken care by function initItems (starting from line 39). It inserts data into the table. Notice how the rows are added dynamically, though we could have just added these rows in a static way by directly writing the HTML as is seen in the previous examples. Just imagine that these set of data could come from a server which could potentially read the values from a database and populate the page accordingly. Furthermore, look at addItems (lines 33–35). The syntax on the RHS to initialize the set of values is aligned with a specific notation called JSON (Java Script Object Notation), appearing as name–value pairs. JSON has now become a standard data structure like XML and is picking up momentum to act as a substitute for XML. More discussion on this is given in later sections.

The initial set of data is populated by clicking on the Initialize button. After the Initialize button is clicked the screen appears as shown in Figure 4.43.

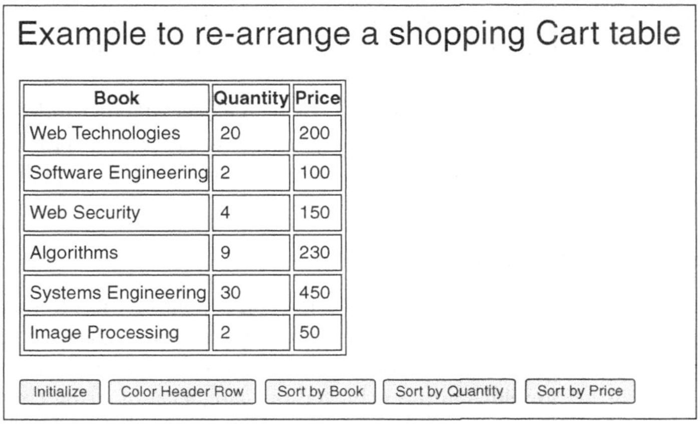

Fig. 4.43 *Screenshot from Mozilla–presorted list*

The button showing coloring in the header row demonstrates how attributes can be modified. In this case the style is modified to add color to the (header) element of the table. This also shows that styling can not only be done by CSS but also by JavaScript. Most of the styling elements that are available in CSS appear in JavaScript in CamelCase as a convention. Just remember that hyphens that appear in CSS styles (like background-color, font-family, etc.) are taboo in most languages since they are mistaken for a minus sign. Hence the convention is followed.

The screen-shot in Figure 4.44 is after 'Sort by Book' and 'Color Header Row' buttons are clicked.

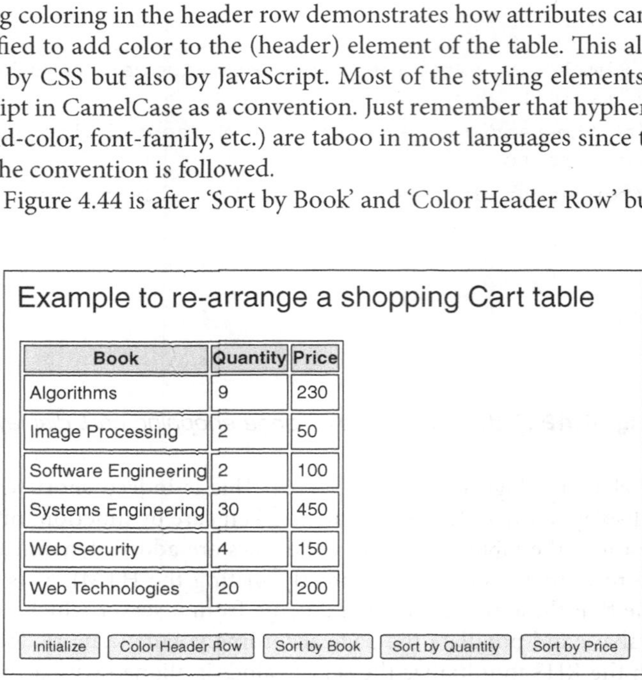

Fig. 4.44 *Screenshot from Mozilla–post-sorted and coloring*

The default sort behavior is overridden by enhancing it (line 117). By default sort assumes alphanumeric type. This is fine when sorting by Book, which is alphabetic but not desirable when sorting by Quantity or Price. Fortunately, the default sort behaviour can be enhanced to work on other types or even objects. For example there could also be a sort on complex numbers (of the type $ai + b$, where i = square root of −1), though I doubt if it really makes sense! The way it can be customized is for the function to return either of −1, 0 or +1 depending on the order that is required. See the example code for details.

Note that during modification of DOM elements (i.e. using *replaceChild* method—line 89), a fragment of the DOM (in the form of a node) is constructed just as a regular element. It is then used to replace the element, operated from its parent node. The functions shown in the example are in different colors to just add clarity and serve no other purpose.

4.17.1 Method InnerHTML

It is worth mentioning about this rather non-standard but a convenient method to manipulate DOM elements. This property of the DOM is also referenced in the example above. Usage of InnerHTML is used to simplify the process of retrieving as well as updating information of elements. This is used in function replaceTableData in Figure 4.42. Simplification is achieved by using a set of string characters to represent a chunk of elements, rather than by describing them through a set of methods like `appendChild` or `createElement`.

4.18 OVERALL OBSERVATIONS ABOUT DOM

DOM is one of the most complicated models, unfortunately, makes it difficult to program a browser. JavaScript has to handle the intricacies of the DOM API accordingly and consequently gets an unfavorable tag. An added effect, rather negative, is that it slows down the processing. Most of the time is spent in the DOM interface as compared to the other parts, but overall it will appear that JavaScript is slow. Despite its odds, it is an interesting API. In fact, its complexity is the genesis for modern frameworks and AJAX libraries. These do a lot to simplify the API. YUI from Yahoo is one of them.

4.19 AJAX WITH JAVASCRIPT

4.19.1 Ajax Introduction

All relevant examples above, where pages are shown, involve full-page updates, that is, a request is made by the client (browser), the server processes the request and sends the output (usually HTML). The client (again the browser) renders the HTML page. This way of posting a page will do well with processing a non-interactive web Form, but what about instances where is expected to be interactive? A key requirement of such a type of transaction (which could be very common) is to have the ability to fill up a partial page, consisting of a field or a set of fields in a Form, rather than the entire page. Now, this ability is natively present in a client-server (or even a desktop) model but is not that straightforward in a web model because of the inherent nature of interaction with the server. Ajax (Asynchronous JavaScript and XML) enables this feature by providing the ability to get small amounts of data from the Server asynchronously. Prior to Ajax, applications were designed to interact in lots with the server, thus reducing interactivity. Ajax is thereby the basic building block to developing Rich Internet/Interactive Applications (RIA).

Shown in Figure 4.45 (A/B) are typical interaction sequence diagrams for two identical web based scenarios—one as per the traditional way and the other using Ajax. They are represented in the form

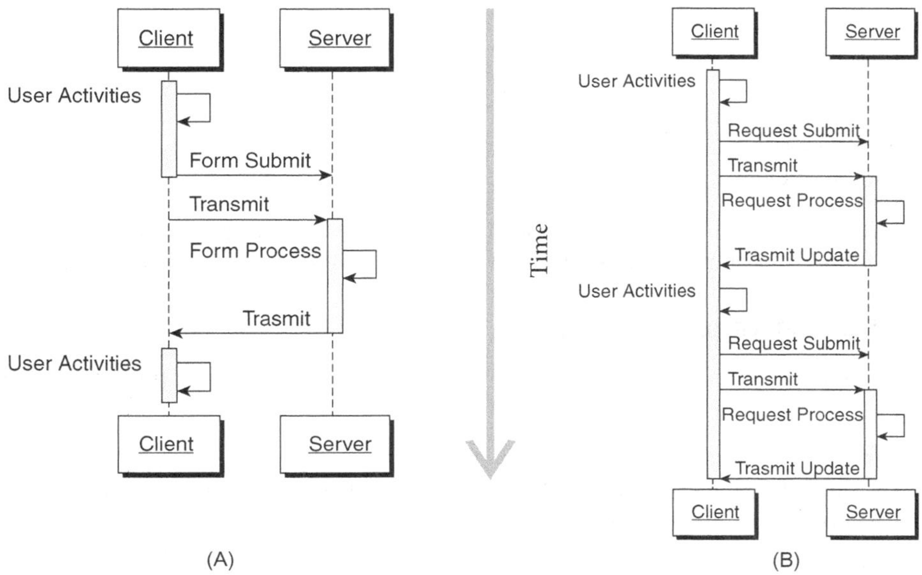

Fig. 4.45 (A) *A typical Sequence diagram for a traditional (non-Ajax) app;* (B) *A typical Sequence diagram using Ajax*

of a Sequence diagram—which is a standard way of representing a sequence of activities in UML. Time sequence is shown flowing top to bottom.

Notice that there is continuous user interaction (in the form of User Activities) in case of Ajax whereas the other way round, it is interrupted way of communication to the server. The client is typically a browser on the user's machine.

4.19.2 Scenarios

In summary, Ajax, which stands for Asynchronous JavaScript and XML, is a technique that allows partial web page updates, with information coming from a server. Imagine a scenario in which a user is trying to register on a social networking site like Facebook or Twitter, where it is required to enter a unique login name along with other information like address, gender, etc. The user has no idea if the login name that is entered is unique or duplicate since anyone can use the site and register himself/herself. A conventional application will wait until the user enters all the information and then check if the login name that was entered is unique or not by comparing the value against the database of users. Using Ajax, as soon as the user enters a login name in the text box, the system communicates with the server to check the uniqueness of the login name and then send back the result. If the login-name already exists, the user can then enter another name immediately. Similarly, data validation can be performed which can be corrected instantly. The technique can also be used to populate a set of dependent list boxes or make the entry form adaptive depending on the choices the user makes. Thus the application can respond to the user's needs and promote greater speed and interactivity, throwing open many possibilities.

A few of the earliest popular applications using Ajax has been Google mail, and Google maps.

4.19.3 Technology Components Required for Ajax

The major technology components required for Ajax are the following.

- JavaScript
- DOM
- CSS
- Server-side processing
- XMLHttpRequest Object

JavaScript, DOM and CSS have been covered already in this book. Server-side processing will be covered in subsequent sections. A brief overview of XMLHttpRequest is covered in the following section.

4.19.4 XMLHttpRequest Object

XMLHttpRequest is an object in JavaScript that enables AJAX. It has the following properties/methods associated.

- ResponseText
- readyState: Since the request is asynchronous, readyState helps in identifying the state of the request. The possible values are as follows:
  - 0 => The request is not yet initialized
  - 1 => Request has been set up
  - 2 => Request has been sent

    - 3 => Request is in process
    - 4 => Request is complete
- onReadyStateChanged

4.19.5 A Look at the Steps Involved

A detailed sequence of activities are shown and listed out in Figure 4.46.

- Step-0: A client event occurs
- Step-1: An XMLHttpRequest object is created
    - The XMLHttpRequest object is configured
- Step-2: The XMLHttpRequest object makes an async. Request
- Step-3a: Callback function is defined
- Step-3b: The callback function is registered
- Step-4: The server returns an XML document containing the result
- Step-4a: The XMLHttpRequest object calls the callback function and processes the result
- Step-4b: The HTML DOM is updated

4.19.6 Sample Ajax Code

The example demonstrates basic usage of Ajax using Javascript. For demo purposes, run this code and input a small text file to see the result. The text in the file will appear as soon as the text box is made to lose the focus.

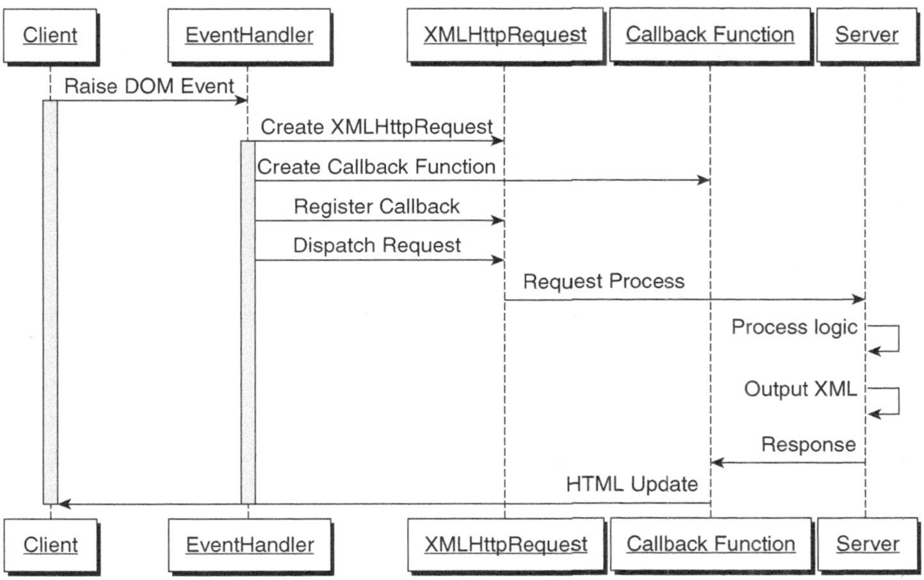

Fig. 4.46 *A detailed sequence diagram for an Ajax operation*

```
<html>
<head>
<script>
  var req = false;
  function processAjax() {
    var valFld = document.getElementById(“txtLocal”);
    var val = valFld.value;

        //Step-1 (example only for IE
        req = new ActiveXObject(“Microsoft.XMLHTTP”);

        //Step-2: Create an asynchronous request. The request will
        //upload a file
        //The filename is entered in the text box which is realized
        //in the “val” variable
        req.open(“GET”,val, true);

        //Steps 3a/b: Callback function is defined inline
        //(anonymously) and registered
        req.onreadystatechange = function() {
            if (req.readyState == 4) {
            //Step-4: Server returns data - add it to the response
            document.getElementById(“responseID”).innerHTML += “ Done”;
            document.getElementById(“responseID”).innerHTML += req.responseText;
            }
            if (req.readyState == 1) {
            document.getElementById(“responseID”).innerHTML = “Loading...”;
            }
            if (req.readyState == 2) {
            document.getElementById(“responseID”).innerHTML += “Loaded”;
            }
        }
       //Send data (null for GET)
       req.send(null);
  }
</script>
</head>
```

```
<body>
    <!-Define fields that accept values -->
    Local Text File Name: <input id="txtLocal"
    onchange="processAjax()"></input>
    Other Details...<input id="txtOther"></input>
    <div id="responseID">View Outputs: </div>
    <button id="btnSubmit">Submit</button>
</body>
</html>
```

Fig. 4.47 *Ajax code sample (without conventional server processing) on IE*

The reader is advised to check Ajax processing covered on the server side as well, since that will be the more standard way of usage. The above example is solely to demonstrate the client side capabilities, involving upload of a local file (entered in the txtLocal text box which is placed first in the page). In practice, instead of the val variable (defined as the second parameter in Open function) a URL can be given, which will point to a server side routine.

4.19.7 Ajax – Points of Caution

Ajax is definitely recommended to be used in a lot of scenarios while developing web applications. However, there are a few points to note when they are being used or designed:

- Using browser's Back button: A lot of internet users tend to use the back button of the browser to go the previous page they were in. This is fine with the traditional application, as the server reloads the previous page. However, when Ajax is used where a partial page is updated, the server has no idea of bringing out the partial page and hence refreshes the original page. This may not be what the user wanted. Designed well, this may not be that big an issue but could be bad as happened in Microsoft's "Windows Live" product.
- Browser inconsistencies: Different browsers adopt different ways of implementing Ajax functionality. Hence there will be differences in usage. This could lead to increasing the complexity of building Ajax based applications, but can be somewhat mitigated by use of Ajax based libraries.
- Search engines may not recognize the data updated through Ajax. This could be an issue with indexing which could possibly affect ranking, leading to lost pages on web search. However, this could be a non-issue in several cases since, generally, only UI is involved during Ajax calls.

4.20 JAVASCRIPT SECURITY

A web browser is a complex piece of software, and JavaScript is a powerful scripting language. It is no surprise that the intersection between these elements will be far too complex. On the flip side, it offers potential security holes. However, there are certain precautions that the language itself tries to provide.

The window object allows a lot of control to the JavaScript programmer.

4.20.1 File Handling and Execution

JavaScript cannot read files from the file server (except for cookies). Similarly, it cannot write any file into the file system (except through server-side programs). Likewise, it cannot execute any program in the file system.

4.20.2 Same Origin Policy

This security policy applies to client-side scripting (like JavaScript, Flash, etc). According to this policy, scripts running on a page can have access to other methods/properties available on the same site but not on other sites.

By Origin, it implies same values for Protocol, Domain-name and Port-number.

4.20.3 Pop-up Windows

Actually, a new window can be opened by issuing the window.open() method. JavaScript cannot open a window without the user's permission. Also, the program cannot open a window of abnormally small size.

There are some restrictions even on closing a window. It allows to automatically close only those windows which were created by the program earlier. Other windows will be asked for a conformation on close.

4.20.4 History

History of locations the user has visited is not made available. However, it can instruct the browser to jump back or forward any number of steps through the browser history.

4.20.5 Mail through a Form

Submitting a form to a mail address by JavaScript will necessarily ask the user's confirmation.

4.20.6 Server Restriction

If the window contains pages or frames from different servers, they cannot communicate with each other. This is to prevent a malicious user from accessing information on the other frameset.

Aside note

Cross Site Scripting (CSS—not to be confused with Cascading Style sheets), also abbreviated XSS, is a form of injection attack where a harmful script is injected into a trusted website. If it occurs, this often happens through the browser and can have access to private sources of information—typically Cookies, Sessions or Form data.

Refer **https://www.owasp.org/index.php/XSS** for details.

Harmful effects could ensue if the sources of data are not validated or escaped (this is a development issue). Go through the XSS Cheat Sheet on how to reduce vulnerability to XSS through contextual escaping.

4.21 CLOSING OBSERVATIONS ON JAVASCRIPT

Despite Javascript's complexity, it is powerful and is futuristic. Javascript is different from the other languages since it is predominantly popular as a means of browser implementation and the fact of the matter is that, the web is every where and so does the browser.

4.21.1 Client Side Compatibility

Client-side JavaScript depends on the web browser. Though there are W3C standards that define how a browser is to be implemented, in practice, there are variations. There are many variations of browsers—Microsoft's IE, Mozilla, Opera, Safari and newer additions like Google's Chrome.

Since each browser can have its own vision and styles for support of the language's features, it is sometimes hard to rely on a standardized approach, despite the tightening of standards. In order to mitigate this risk, use feature (object) detection as opposed to using browser detection or JavaScript version detection. This method is based on whether the object is known to the browser or not and accordingly executes the functions supported by the object. As a best practice, use them in the code.

Aside note

With the enormous increase in the power of browsers, more and more users are convinced that there could be minor differences in the way browsers render. Feature detection is therefore being increasingly used as the means to achieve **uniformity** in richer interfaces if the browser permits. This becomes more complicated when there is a combination of later versions - CSS3 and HTML5. How do we tackle this repetitively? An Open Source JavaScript library called "Modernizr" makes this job easy. Check out their website at **http://www.modernizr.com/**.

4.21.2 Unobtrusive JavaScript

Being unobtrusive is a characteristic that stands for being sort of inconspicuous or being low profile in the sense of functioning according to the circumstances at the same time aligning well with MVC (Model-View-Controller) pattern. This is used to imply the degree of hindrance because of the presence or absence of injecting a certain functionality—with low hindrance being unobtrusive. JavaScript, being powerful, has a side effect of being clumsy and hence difficult to maintain. So as part of a web application, how does it align with the objective of a pure MVC in terms of supporting the philosophy of separation of concerns? The separation of concerns promotes advantages of proper division of labor, easier maintenance and code reuse.

It may be recalled that the client side is predominantly about Style, Behavior and Content (that encapsulates Structure) of documents or web pages. The Structure has been taken care by HTML. With CSS, the Style is neatly separated from these components. However, with JavaScript, though it separates much of behavior, there are shades of mixing up Behavior with Structure. For example, take a look at the following style of code.

```
<p align="center">This is a mix of content and style </p>
```

Figure 4.48 represents the evolution and degrees of this concept.

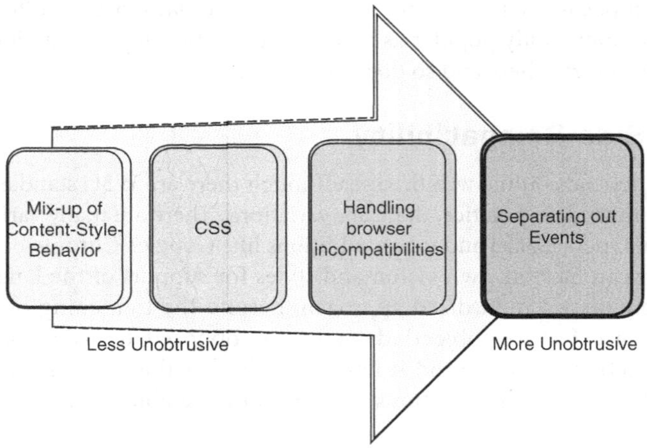

Fig. 4.48 *Degrees of Unobtrusiveness*

As mentioned in the chapter on CSS, when CSS was introduced, it brought about a change in terms of having all styles in one place. This also made the code compact and devoid of any style elements in HTML. It made the code compact because the style definitions are made only once (in the CSS file). It also made the code simpler because DOM traversal was left to CSS which was more efficient and standardized as well. However, the behavior elements still persisted in the code, but that had to do with JavaScript rather than on CSS. Consider the statement:

```
<a onclick="alert('hi')"> Click me and i will alert you</a>
```

The "onclick" behavior is attached to the HTML through JavaScript. The above is a trivial example of just performing an alert but complicated structures or procedures will be required in reality, which can be addressed by means of JavaScript functions. Nevertheless, this type of implementing event behavior is considered obtrusive since it does little to externalize JavaScript in the web programming ecosystem. Moreover, different browsers exhibit different kinds of behaviors with JavaScript. It is also easy to go a bit overboard with JavaScript and in the process creating different user experiences. Typical examples include drag/drop interfaces, Tree views, Grids, Sliders, Slideshow effects etc. But the questions that the web programmers need to ask are in terms of how does this work off different browsers, media devices (like mobiles included), without changing the underlying code; how can this work be outsourced well so that the JavaScript programs can be together in one source rather than spread about in different places.

When this aspect is also taken care (i.e. not mixing up Behavior and Structure), the layers of Style, Behavior and Structure can be neatly separated. This strategy forms the basis of Unobtrusive

JavaScript. The separation of Style, Behavior and Content Structure (on the client side) can be thought of as being on similar lines to the MVC (model-view-controller) representation that is practiced on the server side. The architecture of this strategy on the client side is represented simplistically as follows:

```
<HTML>
    <HEAD>
    [All Style Definitions—CSS]
    [All Behavior Definitions - JavaScript]
 </HEAD>
 <BODY>
    [All Structure Elements - HTML, JavaScript]
    </BODY>
</HTML>
```

In this representation, the technology enablers for each of these areas of separation are also mentioned. It is to be observed that JavaScript appears in two of the areas, which should be puzzling as to how can the objectives of Obstructive JavaScript be achieved. UI Kits based on JavaScript have come to the rescue. The most popular and effective among such toolkits has been JQuery. As with other toolkits, JQuery emphasizes on making it available and working on different browsers—which is one of the most significant challenges of JavaScript. But these are not the only two reasons for using toolkits. They improve the productivity by a large factor. DOM manipulation is made much concise and easier. In addition, JQuery, for instance, is available for use along with any server-side technology, like Java, MS.NET, Ruby on Rails, PHP, etc. So that makes learning the toolkit much more encompassing and more generic enough that can be studied, practiced and improved upon.

Aside note

JQuery is a library based on JavaScript. It is available for desktop as well as mobile applications. Refer www.jquery.com for details on the latest versions.

From a practical perspective, knowing the fundamentals of JavaScript is essential to understanding these toolkits, hence it is recommended to the reader to be familiar with JavaScript first, before getting up to date with toolkits like JQuery.

4.22 SUMMARY

This chapter dealt with a very important facet of client-side web programming—JavaScript. It is the basis for most of the client side frameworks—GWT, JQuery, YUI, etc. which are popular. It is also used in conjunction with popular server-side view frameworks like JSF or ASP.NET. Much of JavaScript can be learnt from examples like the ones presented in this chapter.

An important concept in JavaScript called Closures are about a function that remembers what happens around it. It is applicable when one function defines another function within it, that is, a case of one function defined inside another function.

Ajax, which forms the basis for rich UI on the web, was also explained with an example, albeit purely on the client side. The power of the language combined with the complexity of the browser throws up a lot of security challenges. These vulnerabilities were also covered. Finally, the importance of unobtrusive Javascript is highlighted.

EXERCISES

Q1. The onchange event defined in the example shows the original value when the program started. Intermediate changes are ignored altogether. Change the program to trap the intermediate values that can be shown as the old value (along with the changed value).

Q2. In the following HTML snippets, identify the DOM nodes.

a. <p> DOM Nodes </p>

b. <p> DOM <b>Nodes</b> </p>

Q3. Write a snippet of JavaScript code to find out the ID attributes for all <p> elements in a page?

Q4. Auto-Completion (of fields) is a feature wherein well-defined data such as email, city name or database based fields can be used to suggest as the user enters the first few characters in a text box. List out the approach how this may be implemented using Ajax.

Q5. As an added exercise, investigate options from jQuery on how the same feature (auto-complete) can be implemented.

Q6. Examine how closures can be used effectively in the context of events in HTML using JavaScript.

Q7. Write a JavaScript function to display the browser (along with version) that the user is using. Try the output with different browsers —IE, Netscape, Chrome, etc. Is the output consistent with different versions of the same browser?

Q8. Give some examples of how CSS can be used within JavaScript.

Q9. There are cases where it is required to display an image (or a document) with response to a question—useful to conduct online quiz, puzzles, etc. Demonstrate how this may be done using a combination of HTML, CSS, and JavaScript.
Hint: Enclose the text and image within 2 blocks of DIV and SPAN; Control the z-index in CSS accordingly. Use JavaScript's setTimeout() to fade in so that it appears gracefully.

Q10. State true or false. (3)

a. JavaScript is a simpler version of Java

b. JavaScript is a strongly typed language

c. JavaScript supports automatic type conversions

Q11. How is enumeration done in JavaScript? Explain with an example.

Q12. Explain the concept of classes in JavaScript. How are they implemented? Give examples for Constructors, Methods and Properties.

Q13. What are some of the areas in JavaScript where there are a lot of browser incompatibilities? How is this handled within JavaScript?

Q14. What will the following snippet of closure code result in, that is, what will the alert output show?

```
<script>
var g=1;
function addf(x) {
 var v = 5;
 return function addf2(y) {
return x+y+g+v;
}
}
g=3;
var add4 = addf(4);
v = 15;
var c = add4(8);
alert (c);
</script>
```

Q15. The following is a partial JavaScript code. Explain its output.

```
 var things = [1,2,3,4,5,6];
things.splice (3,0,4);
alert (things);
```

Extend the code to observe the output of splice and the effect it has on the variable. Splice behaves differently depending on the number of parameters as well as their values. Try out with different values for the parameters of splice.

Project Activities

Q16. Using HTML/CSS, JavaScript, implement a mechanism to accept values from the user (through a Form). While accepting values, perform validation to check if the fields are entered with the right types. For the example, include a numeric, alphanumeric, and also based on a pattern (like a phone number, etc.).

a. See if the field is empty for mandatory fields and thrown an error

b. Do not throw error if the field is empty for non-mandatory fields

c. Date fields are to checked if they are valid and in the proper format

d. Numeric fields are to be checked if they are indeed numeric and also belong to a certain range range. Otherwise throw an error.

e. Validate if an email address is in the proper format.

f. Tool tips to be shown if the mouse hovers on certain fields

Q17. In the above exercise on Form validation, it is required to identify if the field is mandatory or not. One way to do this flexibly is to place an asterisk (*) by the side of those fields, so that JavaScript will know and then carry out the validate functions part accordingly. What are the alternate ways of implementing this? Try this out for a sample Form.

Q18. Report the errors in both models—batch mode as well as instantaneously by the side of error fields.

Q19. In Exercises 16 and 17, add a bit of dynamism to the page. For example include a drop down box whose values depend on a previous text/select input value.

Q20. The last few sets of exercises relate to client-side validation in a web application. But any web application consists of a series of client side as well as server side validations. Without the need for knowing the details of server side, try to come up the pros and cons of client side validation and server side validation. Tabulate the results arranged in a 4 × 4 grid.

Caselet Activity

Q21. In continuation with the Caselet Activities in the previous chapters, design a client-side validation process for Form data using Ajax.

5

THE SERVER SIDE

Chapter Objectives:

- ***Understand the role of server-side technologies in the context of a web application***
- ***Bring out the concept of Servlets***
- ***Understand the Servlet life cycle and go through an example***
- ***Go through the concepts of State management and Cookies***
- ***Get used to JDBC connections—a basic persistence model***

Web programming broadly covers two aspects—the client side which runs on the user's local computer and the server side, which fetches data from databases, runs the business logic and processes them into a format that is understood by the client. Both of these aspects complement each other. Well, in most cases! For those where there is a possibility of doing the same thing in the client or in the server, my rule of thumb is to prefer the server side rather than the client.

5.1 A BROAD OUTLINE

A broad outline of the server-side section is given in Figure 5.1.

5.2 BEHIND THE SCENES

It can be realized that the client side is what is seen by the user but there are a lot of things that go on behind the scenes in a typical website or a web application (Figure 5.2).

Fundamentally, in this context, a server is software (which runs on a specific hardware or a set of hardware) that responds to queries or requests for documents, text, files or any other such resource, typically over the web. It typically follows the traditional client–server model. This section continues the study on web-based systems, focused on the server side—the components, how they have evolved and how they work.

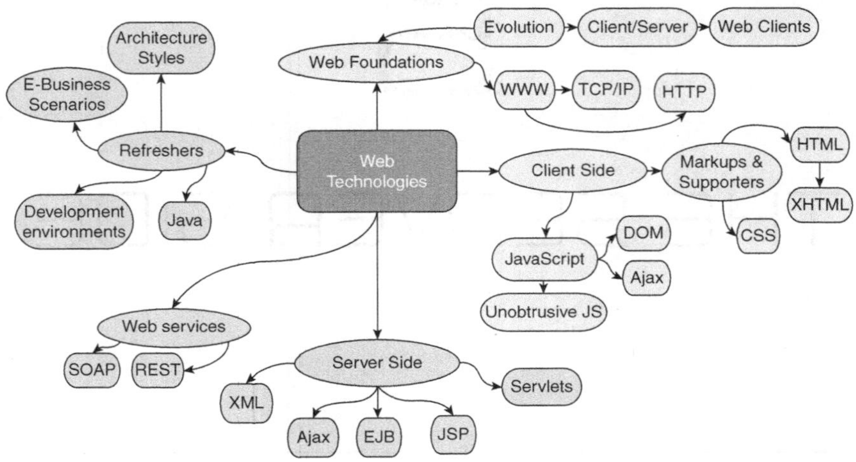

Fig. 5.1 *Broad outline of the server-side section*

Some examples of server-side programming languages are Java, C#, VB.NET, Ruby-on-Rails and PHP. Today's web is not the same as the web that was seen a few years back. What we had **seen** in the past is in fact now **experienced** in today's times. We enjoy websites that are rich in content and services that enable one to perform more tasks, with the advent of Web 2.0 and Web 3.0. However, the progress to Web 2.0 took more than a dozen years. Some of the important milestones and concepts related to server-side technologies are uncovered in the following sub-sections.

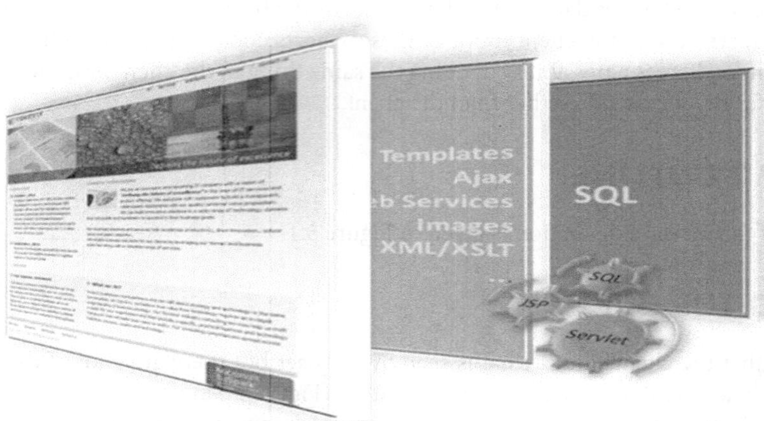

Fig. 5.2 *Components that work behind the* screen

5.3 CLIENT SIDE VS. SERVER SIDE

When developing web-based applications, it is required to understand the things that happen on the server side and those which happen on the client side. The website (or a web application) actually is thought to reside on the web server since a client request for a URL will lead to the server machine. The (web) server will process the request and load the corresponding page to the client's browser, which will then render the page. However, this is a very simplistic example. In reality, the information that is contained in the page(s) need to be processed or manipulated before it is rendered by the browser. This is what the server side does. It processes the information and leaves it to the client to render. Processing on the server side could involve interacting with a data layer, usually a relational database. The Client could not only be a browser but also a hand-held device or a mobile as well. A summary of the comparison follows.

Area	**Server Side**	**Client Side**
Technologies	Servlet, ASP.NET, JSF, ASPX, ASP	Client-side Javascript, Browser, JSF, HTML, CSS
Tools	JSP, JDBC, ADO.NET, ASP.NET, Rails	Ajax, RIA, Rich interfaces, Flash, JQuery
MVC	Database, Business logic	View
Trigger	Client side code triggering server side processing. However it is stateless so there is no active continuous connection	Server side code triggering client rendering. However it is stateless so there is no active continuous connection

5.4 TRANSFORMATION FROM STATIC TO DYNAMIC SITES

From a technology perspective, compared to the faster changing world of client-side technologies, the server-side technologies, largely pioneered by Java, has been changing relatively less fast. It has been mentioned that when the web first started, it had only static web pages. In addition, it was predominantly text based. The path from Static pages to Rich UI has taken the last decade and a half or so. Although the evolution did not happen in a structured way, it can be thought to be represented as shown in Figure 5.3.

After the introduction of HTML standards, the browser began to take shape that made dynamism possible. The client made requests to specific pages when the user clicked on links and then the server provided services to locate the specific page and render them.

The path of a simple GET request over HTTP sent from a client serviced by a web server is shown in Figure 5.4.

A classic web server from the legacy days handled just HTTP, but not dynamic content. Still there can be DHTML (Dynamic HTML) to exhibit some dynamic behavior but that is on the client side and not on the server side. As a result, before long, it was replaced by a technology on the server side which constructed the output HTML according to the needs and thus the dynamic responses were born. CGI was the first such technology to enable this. CGI stands for Common Gateway Interface, which is custom written in the form of scripts and is bolted on to a web server in the form of a pipe.

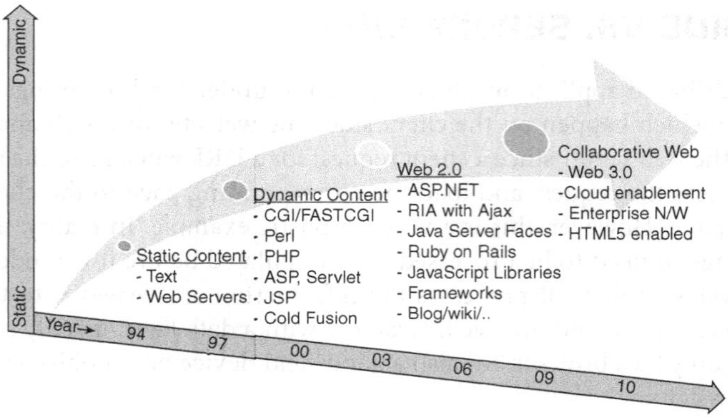

Fig. 5.3 *The evolution of the dynamic web–a server-side perspective*

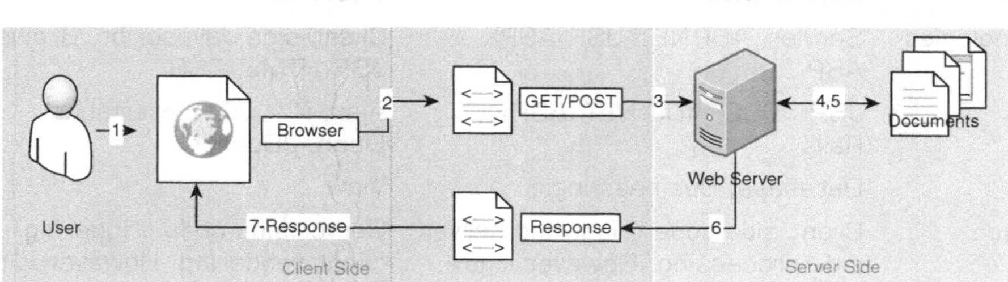

Fig. 5.4 *The role of a web server*

By pipe, it implies that the web server passes on certain information to the external program (the CGI) which performs the necessary tasks of fetching relevant data or files from the system processing into a format that is compatible with HTML. This processed HTML is sent to the user's browser. The diagram, shown in Figure 5.5 explains the sequence (numbered as shown) of activities that take place against a CGI request.

CGI Scripts can be written in many languages like C, C++, etc., but PERL has become the option of choice by programmers. However, using CGI will take extra resources for additional requests.

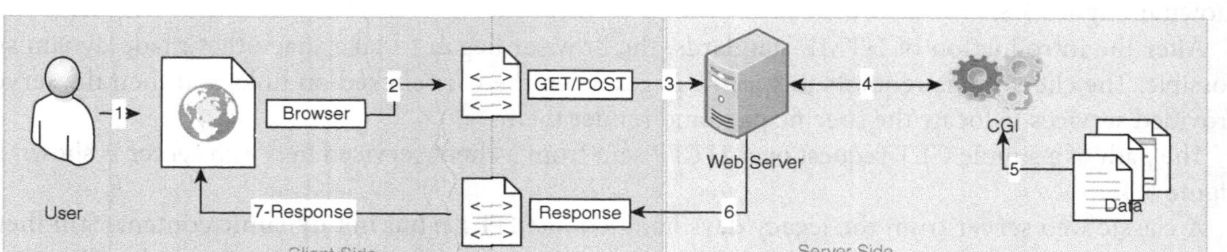

Fig. 5.5 *CGI along with a web server*

Moreover, the way CGI works is to spawn a different process for each request. Both these factors take quite a bit of memory and performance overheads. Hence it is neither scalable nor good in performance—both of which are vital to most modern web-based applications. Also, since CGI executes in a different process space, it is not able to communicate with the web server directly (e.g. for a logging process). Furthermore, security is a big concern as most CGI implementations used a kind of command line (shell) programs or scripts, which made the job easy for a hacker to intrude. Consequently, the CGI model is seldom used in serious kinds of newer applications and is replaced by newer technologies.

Meanwhile, an alternative was developed, called FastCGI, which works like CGI but spawns fewer processes. Scalability improved but not quite enough to match the increased demand for server processing, given that there were parallel advancements in making the UI richer. Furthermore, interaction even among the processes was found to be a challenge.

5.4.1 Embedded Server-side Scripts in HTML

During this time, Microsoft (as well as other companies) had come up with a technique for generating dynamic web content called Active Server Pages, or ASP. With ASP, an HTML page on the web server can contain snippets of embedded code in VBScript or JScript. This code is read and executed by the web server before it sends the page to the client. ASP was optimized for generating small portions of dynamic content.

The pattern that was observed during this time is simply to extend the capability of a web server. Retrospectively, the transition period saw the emergence of server side extensions, like server side includes (SSI).

SSI is a set of directives like include, echo, fsize, exec, if, etc, that are placed in an HTML pages, but evaluated on the server. The server part of the content comes from the server and hence the data can be dynamically generated. Unlike the model of CGI, a full blown program need not be written for getting dynamic information onto a page. SSI is useful when a small portion of the page (like date, a database field, a conditional execution, email functionality or such) is to be rendered dynamically from the server side and most of the remaining content being static. The format of the directives follows a generic syntax as given below.

```
<!-- # <tag> <RHS of the tag> -->
```

The identifier "<!--#" signals the server that it has to process the directives that span this and the ending tag which is "-->". They are shown in example above. <tag> is one of the directives like include, echo, exec, config, email, if, etc. <RHS of the tag> are the variables or statements that depend on the tag itself.

For example a header or footer on a web page can be accomplished by the #include directive which will have the file name like header.html.

```
<!--#include FILE="myheader.html"-->
```

A gist of the directives is shown below.

Directive	Description
Echo	Used to inserts value of variables—local as well as environment
Include	Inserts text of other documents in the server local directory—e.g. of header and footer
Fsize	size of a file that is specified
Exec	Used to execute an external program or a CGI program
flastmod	Refers to the last modification date/time
Config	Used for error messages, formats, etc

This section is not supposed to give the reader a tutorial approach to SSI but to just get an idea of what can be achieved by SSI and how it looks like.

There are many variations of server-side technology used by servers around the world. Generally, the extension that goes with the URL can give a peek into the sort of technology the site is using. Most web servers are configured such that it expects SSI files with an extension of SHT or SHTM .

Though the directives are sort of uniform, SSI implementation is left to the web server that supports them. Apache, IIS and lighttpd are among the web servers that support SSI.

Similar principles of server-side programs were adopted by Microsoft's ASP, first introduced around 1996, in which the server-side code is embedded in HTML. In this case the embedded code follows VBScript or JScript from the Microsoft stable. Support for ASP is natively provided by Microsoft's IIS, though there are other servers commercially available to support.

Server-side Javascript is made available by Netscape supported natively by their web servers.

Web server vendors (notably Microsoft and Netscape—in those times) came up with their APIs (ISAPI and NSAPI respectively) to solve some of these key challenges. However, they are termed proprietary as it leads to vendor lock-in.

On a generic note, it is simpler to write such parts of embedded server-side code in HTML. It is also more or less browser independent, which is good, but on the flip side there is some effort that is also involved in the configuration of the web server. Furthermore, for more elaborate processing, such a model like SSI or ASP cannot scale up and is, in fact, just a point solution for introducing dynamic content. These technologies are, in fact, seldom used for fresh development, although there are many sites operating on these older models that nevertheless need maintenance to keep them well oiled and running.

Though there are different technologies available to work on the server side, as also mentioned in the previous paragraphs, this book follows a particular stream of technology. While choosing this the main factors that play are its usage, support for a number of technologies under a single umbrella, availability as an Open source and its popularity. The Java EE environment fits in most of these criteria and hence has been chosen as a direction for web development in this book. At the same time, it is to be realized that the ideal case would be to be agnostic of the underlying technology. It is important for the reader to grasp the fundamentals, though the examples mostly refer to the stream provided by Java (EE). Furthermore, a larger number of third-party libraries and sources of information are available in the Java EE environment.

A quick Java refresher is included in the Appendix for those who wish to glance through the language. It should be equally effective if the examples followed Microsoft's DotNet or another open source environment like Ruby On Rails.

Aside note

The Java Community Process (JCP) is responsibile for the development of Java (www.jcp.org). They interact with the community technically through Java Specification Requests (JSRs), which are the descriptions of proposed and final specifications for the Java platform. At any one time there are numerous JSRs moving through the review and approval process. Refer **http://jcp.org/en/jsr/overview** for details. Readers may refer to visit these web sites which also encourages them to join their mailing list where members can even take part in reviews. There will be a mention of some of the relevant JSR's throughout this book.

5.5 JAVA SERVLETS

In the Java world, Servlet forms one of the most important topics in server-side architecture as it is the base for other related standardized technology such as JSP, JSTL, and also a host of frameworks like Spring, Struts, and JSF. These pieces of technology fit in well and offer a wide gamut of server-side programming environment.

Servlets extend the capabilities of a web server. They form part of a web application. The first Servlet specification was created by Sun. Servlet v.1.0 came out in June 1997. Version 2.3 onwards, the specification was developed under the Java Community. The examples and the explanation in this book will include relatively stabler versions. This is to facilitate the reader to understand the nuances of earlier versions. In fact, the current v.3.0 focuses on ease of development, by leveraging the newer developments in Java, such as support for Annotations and Generics.

Aside note

Servlets serve as the backbone of Java enterprise application. Servlet 3.0 is governed by a standard specification, JSR 315. A Servlet container is a software that loads, executes and unloads servlets and/or JSP. In other words, it is responsible for managing the Servlet's life cycle. The Container is a part of popular App Servers like JBoss or GlassFish.

Essentially, Servlets are Java classes, loaded dynamically on a Container within the JVM of the web server. They were not part of the core Java framework but formed a part of the Standard Java extension API, first coming out of Sun, now a part of Oracle. The web server should have support for a Servlet Container. Most of the web servers come with this support and includes Apache, JBOSS, Netscape FastTrack, Glassfish, etc.

Aside note

It is interesting to get an overview of the numerous projects under apache.org. *Tomcat* from Apache is a simple Open Source implementation of Java Servlet (& JSP). Visit http://tomcat.apache.org/index.html for details.

Functionally, Servlets operate very similarly to CGI scripts, however, since they are Java based, they can run multi-threaded and is also more platform independent. There are several advantages that a Servlet can offer in comparison with CGI.

- Performance is much better because Servlets execute within the address space of a web server. It is not necessary to create a separate process to handle each client request.
- Servlets are platform-independent because they are written in Java.
- Servlets are trusted.
- It is easily integrated with the other sets of functionality of Java class libraries, implying it can it can communicate with applets, databases, or other software via standard mechanisms like Sockets and RMI.

5.5.1 Servlet Creation and Lifecycle

A Servlet is implemented using the classes and interfaces as specified in the Servlet API. It consists of two packages—javax.servlet and javax.servlet.http. The former contains protocol-independent implementation while the latter is for HTTP. A Servlet program creates a Servlet by extending the standard interface implementations—either of **javax.servlet.GenericServlet** or **javax.servlet.http.HttpServlet**. The high level abstraction is shown in Figure 5.6.

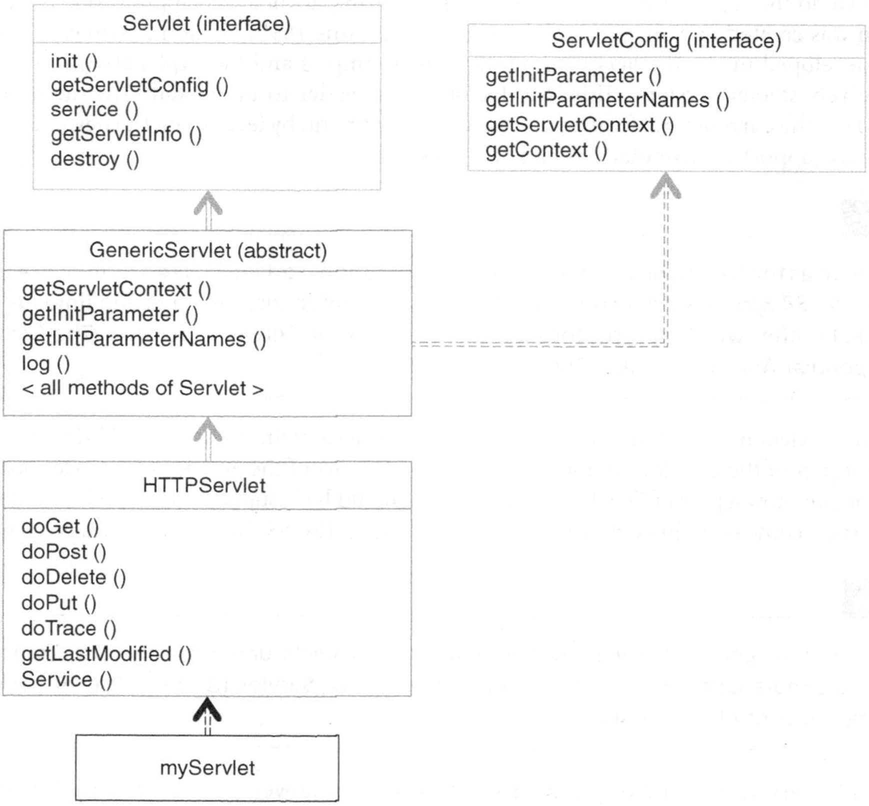

Fig. 5.6 *Abstraction of core servlet model*

The servlet interface is the core of the abstraction model of the Servlet API. All of the user program's servlets implement this interface by extending a class that implements the interface. The two classes delivered as part of the API that implement the Servlet interface are GenericServlet and HttpServlet. Practically, in a traditional web application, the `MyServlet` class (which represents the user program's implementation) extends `HTTPServlet` for leveraging the methods specific to HTTP and HTTPS protocols. It simplifies much of the common HTTP handling mechanisms like request/dispatch, cookies, session handling, etc. For non-HTTP applications, the program can extend from the GenericServlet class.

Note that the `HTTPServlet` class is abstract so all methods that are required, will need to be overridden.

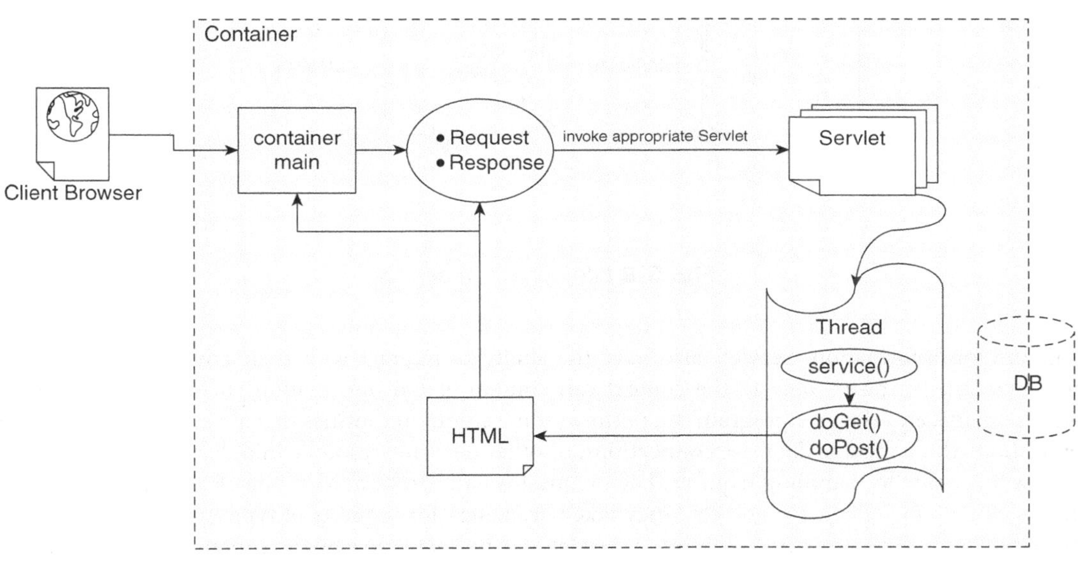

Fig. 5.7 *Overall flow of the* Servlet *request*

The container is a part of the application server (like Tomcat)Under the Tomcat root directory, the main things of interest are the `conf` directory, where configuration files are found; the `bin` directory where the scripts are found; and the `webapps` directory where servlets are installed by default. By default there is only one instance of Servlet running as defined in configuration file. Multiple requests are handled through multi-threading. But in cases where a single thread model is preferred then the Servlet container can be configured to invoke multiple instances of Servlet. The use of a Single Threaded model guarantees that only one Servlet thread will be active at a time.

5.5.2 Lifecycle of a Servlet

The Servlet container has the `main` function and is responsible for loading the Servlet. It has a well-defined lifecycle that defines how it is loaded, initialized, services and how it is taken out. Each of these functions can be controlled by the programmer using methods that the Servlet interface exposes—`init()`, `service()` and `destroy()`.

Refer Figure 5.8 which shows the lifecycle of a Servlet. Loading is done either during startup or when the request is first made. The container is responsible for loading (once) and instantiating (once or several times).

After it is instantiated, the container must perform the `init()` method before it is ready to accept requests from clients. It uses the `ServletConfig` interface to fetch the servlet's configuration information. Servlets also have the ability to interact with their environment through the `ServletContext` object. The context can contain global information such as email address, database name, etc. The user program can perform some common routines that are required for the web application. These include database connections, or other one time resource initializations.

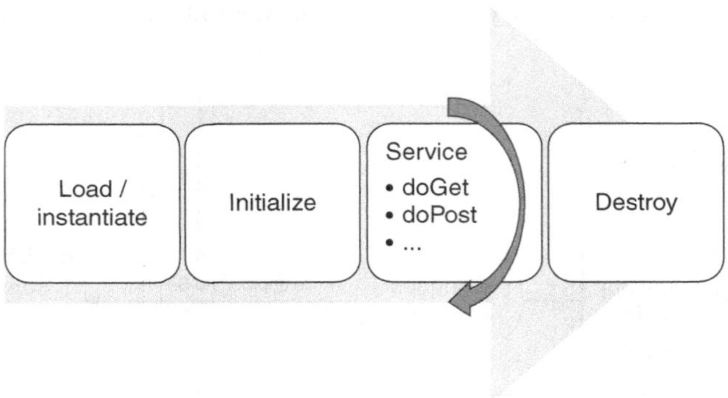

Fig. 5.8 *Life cycle of a servlet*

Now it is ready for handling requests. Each request is handled by at least one of the service methods such as `doGet()`, `doPost()`, etc. They take parameters for requests of type `ServletRequest` and output `ServletResponse` object. A Servlet may be kept active by the container for any amount of time. If it is required to be removed from service, either due to resource crunch or otherwise, the program calls the `destroy()` method. The cycle continues when a new request is received.

5.5.3 A Simple Servlet Example

Consider a simple example, other than the usual Hello World example, but just as simple. There is a counter that is initialized to some value (say 0) during the initialization phase. For every request that is handled by the Servlet, it increments the counter. This is used to display the result. While running the program, ensure that the browser actually does not run from the cache but actually executes it, so that the correct result is shown.

5.5.3.1 Prerequisites To try out the examples, it is necessary to use an IDE. The preference of choice is NetBeans, though any other IDE like Eclipse would just be as fine. Both of these are available as Open Source. The reader is encouraged to download the latest stable version of the IDE that is available. The examples have been tried out in NetBeans v.6.8. The reader is also expected to have a basic knowledge of core Java and concepts of Java SE (5 and above). However, a refresher on Java is included in the Appendix. The process of installation of Netbeans is highlighted in the Appendix.

5.5.4 An Intermediate Web Application Architecture

Just like any other learning exercise, it is useful to understand the global picture of the components that make up a web application. A typical web application in Java with Servlets and JSP as the significant components, is represented in the diagram (Fig. 5.9). In reality, today's web application does contain a lot more components. The purpose of this diagram is to introduce a simplified model as a first step towards learning the complete web architecture.

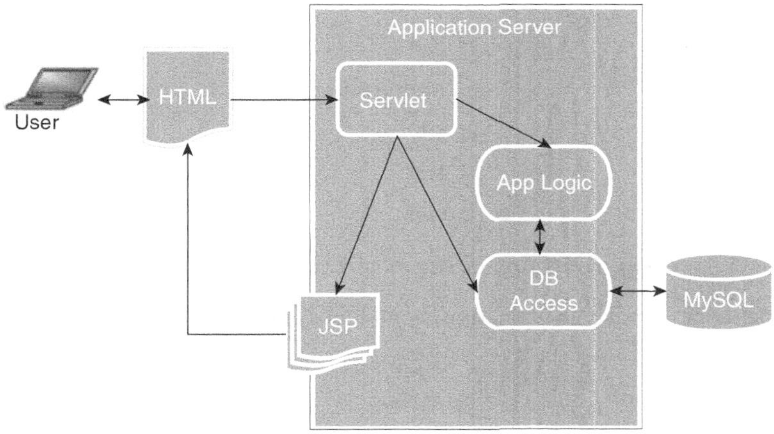

Fig. 5.9 *Simplified web application design*

The HTML file(s) as in Figure 5.9 signifies the client part of the application. Each step could potentially contain a static HTML page or a dynamic HTML page. It may have multiple Forms associated with the application, to include user inputs.

The HTML output that comes from the App server is generated from the JSP (as shown) or from a Servlet instead (not shown). In either case, it is the dynamic data that flows into the browser.

The DB Access component is responsible for the lifecycle of data that is used by the application. Most applications will require a database, but there may be situations where data need not be stored in a database. Some of the examples that follows will demonstrate accessing a database operation as well.

The Application logic will be the place where the processing occurs. It is possible to write the application in such a way that all components are written down in the same file, but that is not recommended. At the very least, it is required to split an application into these components, each acting as a layer within the application. Hence production applications are often architected in layers, the most popular one being the MVC2 (Model View Controller) pattern, which separates the application logically into these three layers—Model (for the database centric operations), View (presentation centric) and the Controller for tying these together in a definite sequence. More about this pattern will be found later in this book (refer Appendix on Architectural Styles). Now let us just consider a simple structure.

The Servlet acts as the controller that routes the incoming Forms (or Requests) to the appropriate modules as necessary. It then routes the output to the JSP for rendering it back to the browser that requested the service.

5.5.4.1 Configuration file As observed above, there are multiple components that form the application. During development, these are all individual program files, developed together by multiple people possibly at different locations around the world. Of course, for trivial applications and for training (like the ones shown in this book below) all of these can be developed under a single window. An IDE is required for this purpose to organize these files together. Fortunately, the IDE organizes these files in specific directories. See Figure 5.10 which shows a typical directory structure for a sample project. The name of the project is `FavConnectVanilla`. This was created through Netbeans 6.8.

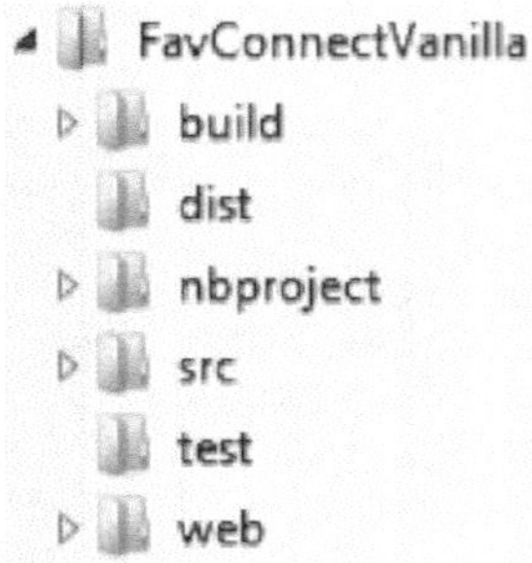

Fig. 5.10 *App directory structure–condensed*

If the directories are expanded, the resulting layout looks like the one shown in Figure 5.11.

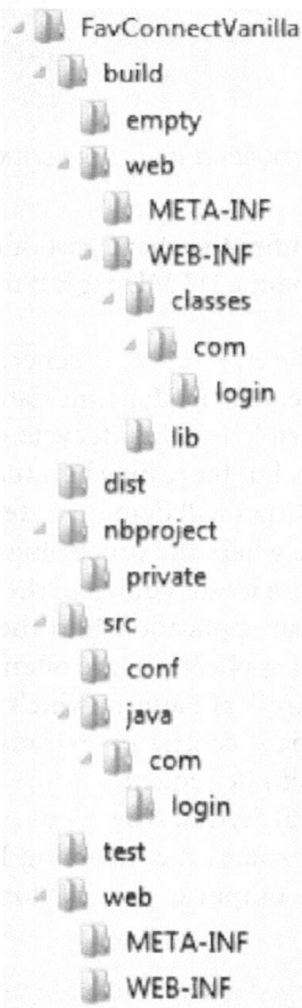

Fig. 5.11 *App directory structure–expanded*

Not only does it (IDE) organize the files, it also takes care of configuration files, required for building the application. Though database is the primary store for all data, there is a need to specify how the application should access the Database before it can access any of the data in the Database. For this, a configuration file is required. The file path should be a part of CLASS PATH environment variable that will be required to setup. The IDE takes care of setting this up, so that will not generally be an issue.

Shown in Figure 5.12 is a snapshot that is taken from configuration information that NetBeans uses to generate the configuration file. The Configuration file is in web.xml.

Initialization parameters (observe the section in Figure 5.12) can be (optionally) defined for the application, though in this example, there are no parameters. Parameters are defined as name–value pairs. Any such name–value pair can be included as part of the configuration information and then referenced in the Servlet code.

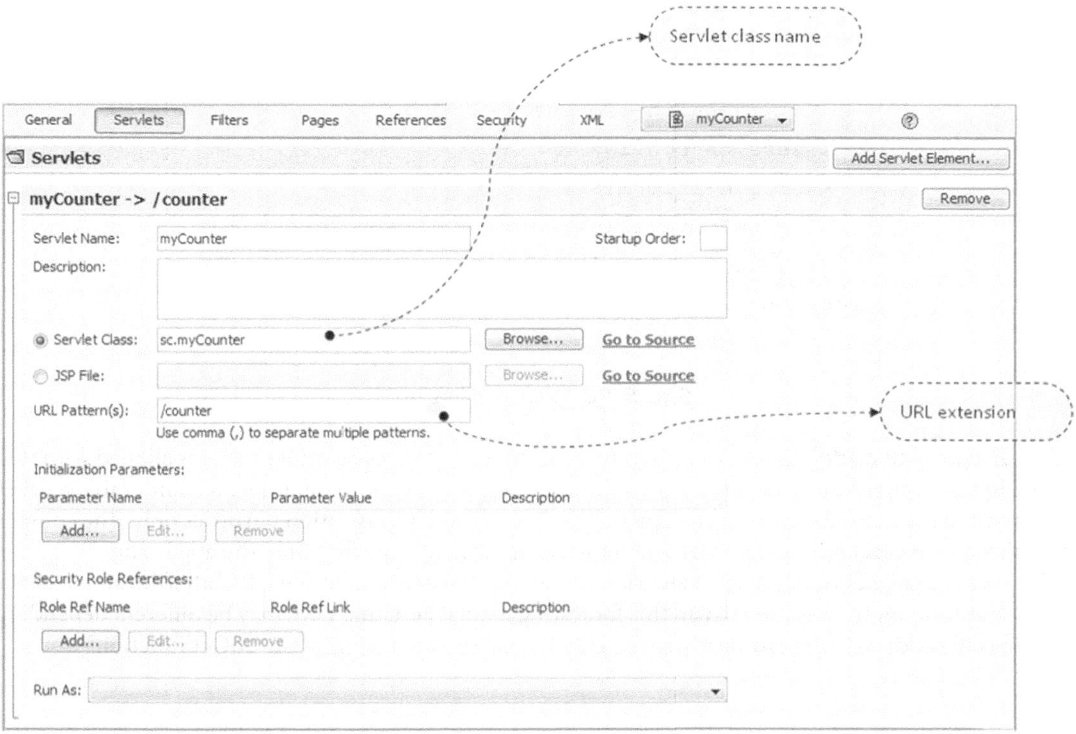

Fig. 5.12 *Web.xml configuration for a* SimpleCounter *example*

The corresponding web.xml listing is given below in Figure 5.13.

```
<?xml version="1.0" encoding="UTF-8"?>
<web-app  version="2.5"  xmlns="http://java.sun.com/xml/
ns/javaee"  xmlns:xsi="http://www.w3.org/2001/XMLSchema-
instance" xsi:schemaLocation="http://java.sun.com/xml/ns/
javaee http://java.sun.com/xml/ns/javaee/web-app_2_5.xsd">
```

(Continued)

```
<servlet>
    <servlet-name>myCounter</servlet-name>
    <servlet-class>sc.myCounter</servlet-class>
</servlet>
<servlet-mapping>
    <servlet-name>myCounter</servlet-name>
    <url-pattern>/counter</url-pattern>
</servlet-mapping>
<session-config>
    <session-timeout>
       30
    </session-timeout>
</session-config>
<welcome-file-list>
    <welcome-file>index.jsp</welcome-file>
</welcome-file-list>
</web-app>
```

Fig. 5.13 *Web.xml* listing

5.5.4.2 Servlet code The Servlet program is written as a Java class whose name is aligned with that defined in the configuration file. Figure 5.14 shows a sample code for maintaining a counter integer that can be used to track number of visits to a page. The code is for demonstration purposes only. The counter is initialized (Line: 22) once the servlet engine starts up, which is the first time the app is run.

The page is invoked as per the URL extension (Figure 5.12). For example, the URL http://localhost:8080/SimpleCounter/counter was used to run this for testing it out (the actual URL may be different depending on the specific address). The browser invokes a GET request which triggers the doGet function.

```
1.    package sc;
2.
3.    import java.io.IOException;
4.    import java.io.PrintWriter;
5.    import javax.servlet.ServletConfig;
6.    import javax.servlet.ServletException;
7.    import javax.servlet.http.HttpServlet;
8.    import javax.servlet.http.HttpServletRequest;
```

```
import javax.servlet.http.HttpServletResponse;

/*This is the Servlet class. Overrides the relevant methods of
the parent class. The init is performed once by the container
applicable for all requests, serviced by this Servlet.  Each
request in this case is handled by doGet, since there is no
separate form that gets in which in that case will require
doPost.  The function is just to simply increment a counter
and print it out. Ensure that the browser's options enable
running the program each time the screen is refreshed.
 */
public class myCounter extends HttpServlet {
    int counter;    //counter used for this process.

    //init() is  guaranteed to be called before the servlet
    //handles its first request
    @Override
public void init (ServletConfig config) throws ServletException
{
      super.init(config);

      //initialize to some default value - can also be set in
      //the definition rather on init() as well
      counter = 0;
}
protected void processRequest(HttpServletRequest request,
  HttpServletResponse response, String msg)
  throws ServletException, IOException {
response.setContentType("text/html;charset=UTF-8");
PrintWriter out = response.getWriter();
try {
          out.println("<html>");
          out.println("<head>");
          out.println("<title>Servlet myCounter</title>");
          out.println("</head>");
          out.println("<body>");
          out.println("<h1>Servlet myCounter at" +
            request.getContextPath () + "</h1>");
          out.println("</body>");
          out.println(msg);
```

(Continued)

```
            out.println("</html>");
        } finally {
            out.close();
        }
    }
/* This is the method that is most relevant in this example. The URL directs the control to this routine. There are no parameters that are passed through the URL in this case. The counter is incremented by 1. Note that the output is of type HTML and hence the entire page is to be constructed. For simplicity, it is implemented in the processRequest method.
 */
    @Override
    protected void doGet(HttpServletRequest request,
     HttpServletResponse response) throws ServletException,
     IOException {
        String msg = "";

        counter++;
       msg = "Counter is ".concat(Integer.toString(counter));
        processRequest(request, response, msg);
    }

    //this method is not used in this case
    @Override
    protected void doPost(HttpServletRequest request,
     HttpServletResponse response) throws ServletException,
     IOException {
        String msg="";
        processRequest(request, response, msg);
    }

    @Override
    public String getServletInfo() {
        return "Short description";
    }
}
```

Fig. 5.14 *Servlet Java code listing for* SimpleCounter *example*

Note that the function, `doGet`, is overridden; it is the method of interest as it has the code for processing the main logic. The counter is incremented as per line 51. The appropriate message to be used for display is constructed in line 52. The function processRequest handles the display of the message, and it is defined from line 24. Notice that the entire HTML is generated by this function. This includes setting up the Content-type and the various HTML open and end tags.

The output is given by the browser through the doGet Servlet code (line 52) and the function processRequest (lines 24–43).

Recall the notes on the servlet's lifecycle process and the overall flow in the preceding section. As the Servlet is invoked, it (the Servlet Engine) passes the control to service() method. This method determines the type of request—a GET or a POST. Correspondingly, it invokes the doGet() or doPost() method of the Servlet class, representing HTTP GET or HTTP POST respectively. In the case of raw HTTP GET, the parameters are attached to the URL as name value pairs (name=value&+) and extracted by parsing the parameter string. In the case of raw HTTP POST, the values of parameters are obtained as Form element values. However, in servlets, the parsing is done automatically and retrieved by means of getParameter(). The below table summarizes the scenarios of Get and Post.

doGet()	**doPost()**
Mirrors HTTP GET	Mirrors HTTP POST
Used to get a resource from the Server	Used to send (Post) Form data to Server
Parameters through the URL	Parameters through the Form
Length of parameters is limited	Unlimited length
Idempotent request—meaning the request can be safely repeated	Non-idempotent request—meaning the POST request cannot be fired multiple times without a (usually undesirable) side effect

In practice, support for Post and Get are similar and hence only one method is implemented, say doPost(). The same is invoked in doGet as shown in the following code snippet:

```
 public  void  doGet(HttpServletRequest  request,  HttpServletResponse
response)
 throws ServletException, IOException
 {
     doPost(request, response);
 }
```

If the client requires the server to respond to non-HTTP protocols, use the service() method.

5.6 EXAMPLE—READ ENVIRONMENT PARAMETERS

There are several environmental parameters that are available to the Servlet. Some of them are set by the programmer and the rest are available in the environment. Take a look at this program which prints out these variables.

First, let us see the parameters. There is something interesting—note the Inititalization Parameters.

The XML listing is shown below (Figure 5.16) for reference. Note the initial parameter set within the <init-param> set of tags (lines 6–9). The initial parameter is defined as name–value pairs; there can be many of them, but in this example there is only one defined (THEME:FORMAL).

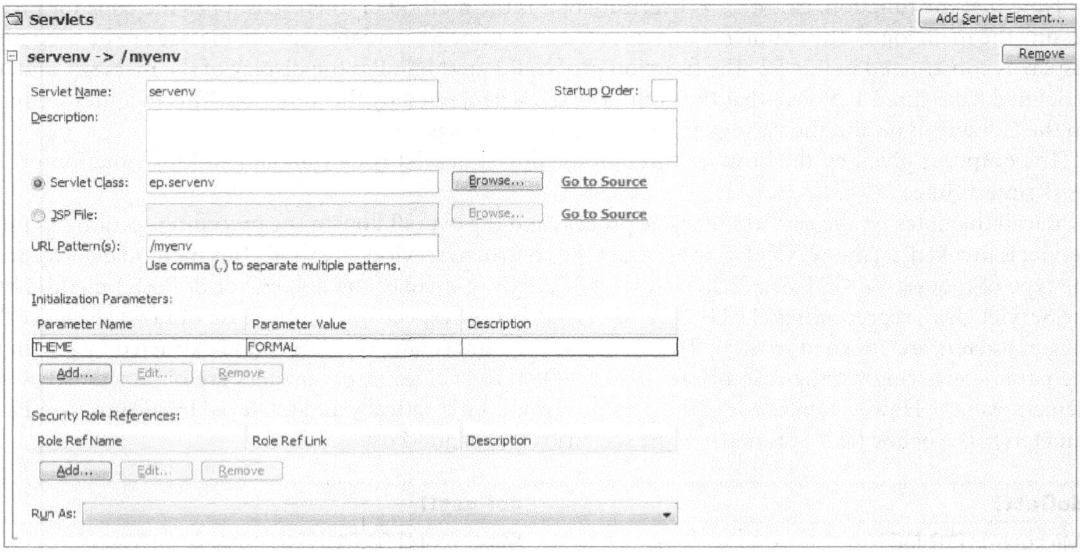

Fig. 5.15 *Web.xml configuration including an init parameter*

```
<?xml version="1.0" encoding="UTF-8"?>
<web-app version="2.5" xmlns="http://java.sun.com/xml/ns/javaee" xmlns:xsi="http://www.w3.org/2001/XMLSchema-instance" xsi:schemaLocation="http://java.sun.com/xml/ns/javaee http://java.sun.com/xml/ns/javaee/web-app_2_5.xsd">
    <servlet>
        <servlet-name>servenv</servlet-name>
        <servlet-class>ep.servenv</servlet-class>
        <init-param>
            <param-name>THEME</param-name>
            <param-value>FORMAL</param-value>
        </init-param>
    </servlet>
    <servlet-mapping>
        <servlet-name>servenv</servlet-name>
        <url-pattern>/myenv</url-pattern>
    </servlet-mapping>
    <session-config>
        <session-timeout>
          30
        </session-timeout>
    </session-config>
```

```
20.         <welcome-file-list>
21.             <welcome-file>index.jsp</welcome-file>
22.         </welcome-file-list>
23.     </web-app>
```

Fig. 5.16 *Web.xml file (myEnv)*

The entry point is determined by the Welcome-file tags in the Deployment Descriptor (Web.XML), when the user has not specified a filename in the URL (refer line 21 in the web.XML listing). There can be multiple welcome-file tags signifying the order of preference. Being the entry point, an HTML file is expected, however, the welcome-file specifies index.jsp. Suffice to know that the JSP file can be treated like an HTML file. See the listing below.

```
1.      <%@page contentType="text/html" pageEncoding="UTF-8"%>
2.      <!DOCTYPE HTML PUBLIC "-//W3C//DTD HTML 4.01 Transitional//
        EN"
3.      "http://www.w3.org/TR/html4/loose.dtd">
4.      <html>
5.      <head>
6.        <meta http-equiv="Content-Type" content="text/html;
          charset=UTF-8">
7.        <title>JSP Page</title>
8.      </head>
9.      <body>
10.       <h1> Know my Environment </h1>
11.         <form method="POST" action="myenv">
12.           <input type="submit" value="Click to know more" >
13.         </form>
14.     </body>
15.     </html>
```

Fig. 5.17 *Index.jsp for myEnv*

For all practical purposes treat this file like an HTML, though the extension is jsp. There is a Form element and then a button, which on submit, is defined to invoke the Servlet. This is achieved by the action attribute (see line 11). The attribute specifies the name of the URL, which in this example points to myenv. Checking back on the web.xml file (lines 11–14—Servlet-Mapping tag), the URL pattern, myenv, points to the Servlet name (which happens to be servenv). This mapping facilitates changing the name of a Servlet without bothering to tinker with web.xml.

A listing of serenv is shown below. Note that the doPost method is invoked instead of doGet since the Form is submitted using POST method. Refer code from line 40 onwards for the details.

```
package ep;

import java.util.Enumeration;
import java.io.IOException;
import java.io.PrintWriter;
import javax.servlet.ServletException;
import javax.servlet.http.HttpServlet;
import javax.servlet.http.HttpServletRequest;
import javax.servlet.http.HttpServletResponse;

public class servenv extends HttpServlet {

protected void processRequest(HttpServletRequest request,
HttpServletResponse response, String msg)
    throws ServletException, IOException {
        response.setContentType(“text/html;charset=UTF-8”);
        PrintWriter out = response.getWriter();
        try {
            out.println(“<html>”);
            out.println(“<head>”);
            out.println(“<title>Servlet plan</title>”);
            out.println(“</head>”);
            out.println(“<body>”);
            out.println(“<h1>Servlet to fetch Environment
            variables</h1>”);
            out.println(msg);
            out.println(“</body>”);
            out.println(“</html>”);

        } finally {
            out.close();
        }
}

    @Override
    protected void doGet(HttpServletRequest request,
      HttpServletResponse response) throws ServletException,
      IOException {
        String msg=null;
```

```
            processRequest(request, response, msg);
        }
    // method that is invoked is POST
        @Override
        protected void doPost(HttpServletRequest request,
         HttpServletResponse  response)  throws  ServletException,
          IOException {
            String p, msg = “”;
            p = getParams(request);
            msg = msg.concat(p + “</br>”);
            //end get server params
            response.setContentType(“text/html”);
            processRequest(request, response, msg);
        }

        @Override
        public String getServletInfo() {
            return “Short description”;
        }
        //Programmer-defined method to get some of the parameters
        public String getParams(HttpServletRequest req) {
            String params;
            String tmp;
            params = “”;
            String nl = “<br></br>”;    //new line

            //Get the Servlet version that is being used.
            params = params.concat(“Servlet Version=” +
                     getServletContext().getMajorVersion() + “.” +
                     getServletContext().getMinorVersion()) + nl;
                       //HTTP Protocol and then the Port
            params = params.concat(“Protocol=” + req.getProtocol())
            + nl;
            params  =  params.concat(“Port=”  +  req.getServerPort())
            + nl;
            //Request method (Post or Get)
            params = params.concat(“ReqMethod=” + req.getMethod())
            + nl;
            //Relative Path of the Servlet
            params = params.concat(“PathInfo=” + req.getPa-
            thInfo()) + nl;
```

(Continued)

```
                params = params.concat("PathTranslated=" + req.get-
                PathTranslated()) + nl;
                params = params.concat("ScriptName=" + req.getServ-
                letPath())+ nl;
                params = params.concat("RemoteHost=" + req.get-
                RemoteHost()) + nl;
                params = params.concat("Context Path=" + req.getCon-
                textPath()) + nl;

               // initialization parameters of the Servlet are defined
               // in web.xml
                params += "<u>Here are initial parameters from the
                Servlet:</u>" + nl;
                Enumeration enum1 = getInitParameterNames();
                while (enum1.hasMoreElements()) {
                    String name = (String) enum1.nextElement();
                    params = params.concat(name + ": " +
                    getInitParameter(name));
                }

                return(params);
            }
    }
```

Fig. 5.18 *Environment parameters*

The meat of the code is in *getParams* function. For a reader with knowledge of basics of Java, it is not hard to find out the APIs for getting the environment parameters.

Run the above app and check the results. An indicative output is presented in Figure 5.19.

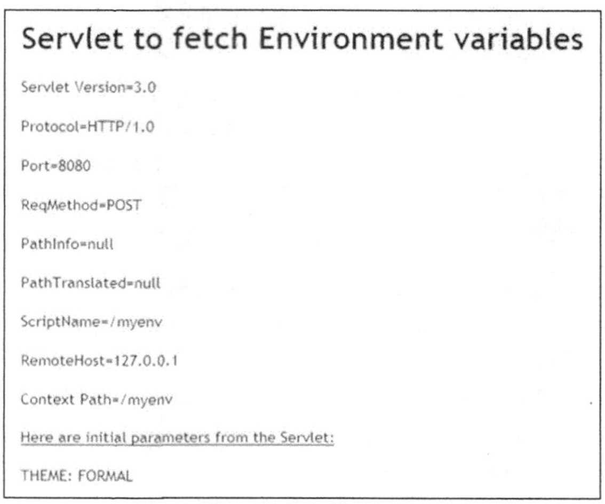

Fig. 5.19 *Output*

All Servlet programs suffer from the drawback that code appears unstructured since view and logic both are mixed up. It is indeed the case. MVC is achieved with the use of other technologies like JSP, and is further enhanced with the use of frameworks like Spring. In fact, real life examples seldom follow the structures demonstrated here, but the path towards the higher goal is by a good understanding of the basics. The point of these examples is to drive towards better understanding of the capabilities of servlets accordingly.

5.7 ACCESSING PARAMETER DATA

It has been seen earlier that in a GET request, the request parameters are given from the Query string. The Query string is the data following the question mark(?) on the URL. It is possible to include multiple parameters in the Query string, and they are separated by the ampersand (&) character. For example, consider the following URL.

```
http://www.abc.com?name1=val1&name2=val2
```

The Query string contains two parameters—`name1` and `name2` with values `val1` and `val2` respectively.

For a request submitted with a POST method, the request parameters are taken from both the query string and the posted data. The posted data is available in the body of the request, generally encoded. Irrespective of POST or GET, the methods that are used to get parameters from the URL string are as follows:

- getQueryString()—returns URL encoded query string
- getParameterNames—returns all parameters in enum
- getParameter(nm)—returns URL encoded value of nm
- getParameterValues(nm)—all values of nm (URL encoded)

5.7.1 Sharing Data Through Servlet Context

All Servlets in an application belong to one Servlet context. It has been seen earlier that the ServletContext has provision for initializing data through web.xml, which can be retrieved within any Servlet program (of the application). There are also ways to define them at run time and to retrieve them. In this context, there are three common methods for a Servlet to share data with another, belonging to `ServletContext`.

- getAttribute
- setAttribute
- removeAttribute

Their names are self explanatory. They are primarily intended to be used with the RequestDispatcher. This is an object that is used to forward a request from one servlet to another.

Aside note

Both ServletConfig and ServletContext belong to the Servlet API. ServletConfig are String name-value pairs available to all users invoking the Servlet, that is, a "get" returns the same value available to all users within the servlet.

The ServletContext is available to all users but is global and hence shared within the application, often referred to as the application context.

5.7.2 Trip Pooling Example

These concepts can be best learnt from an example. Consider a scenario to implement a trip pooling system where a user submits his requirement of travelling from point A to point B. The requirement for the system is to find out if there is someone else already planning to travel in the same route. In other words, find if there is a match with another person travelling on the same route (source-destination pair). The matching program will print accordingly. If a match is found, the information about the match (in the form of name and contact) will be displayed, so that they can perhaps car pool together and save the environment plus costs. Though it makes more sense to make this facility available on both mobile as well as a normal browser-based application, assume for now that this is to be made available only on the latter.

The organization of the modules is represented in the following diagram.

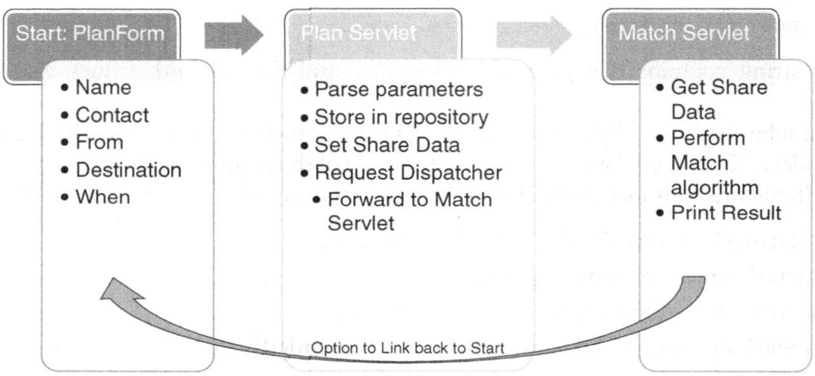

Fig. 5.20 *Organization of the simple trip example* program

The entry point is through a user interface abstracted through `index.jsp`. The set of files are organized automatically by the IDE, which otherwise will be a cumbersome process, as the reader may well realize. The organization and build process is not touched upon in this book since, with an IDE, they are relatively straightforward. The process of installing an IDE is highlighted in the Appendix.

```
<?xml version="1.0" encoding="UTF-8"?>
<web-app version="2.5" xmlns="http://java.sun.com/xml/ns/
javaee" xmlns:xsi="http://www.w3.org/2001/XMLSchema-instance"
xsi:schemaLocation="http://java.sun.com/xml/ns/javaee http://
java.sun.com/xml/ns/javaee/web-app_2_5.xsd">
    <servlet>
        <servlet-name>plan</servlet-name>
        <servlet-class>plan</servlet-class>
        <init-param>
```

```
                <param-name>test</param-name>
                <param-value>TEST</param-value>
            </init-param>
            </servlet>
        <servlet>
            <servlet-name>match</servlet-name>
            <servlet-class>match</servlet-class>
        </servlet>
        <servlet-mapping>
            <servlet-name>plan</servlet-name>
            <url-pattern>/plan</url-pattern>
        </servlet-mapping>
        <servlet-mapping>
            <servlet-name>match</servlet-name>
            <url-pattern>/match</url-pattern>
        </servlet-mapping>
        <session-config>
            <session-timeout>
               30
            </session-timeout>
        </session-config>
        <welcome-file-list>
            <welcome-file>planForm.html</welcome-file>
            </welcome-file-list>
        </web-app>
```

Fig. 5.21 *Trip*

The XML listing in Figure 5.21 provides a snapshot of the structure of the web application. Entry point is PlanForm.html. Its listing is given in Figure 5.22.

```
<!DOCTYPE html PUBLIC "-//W3C//DTD XHTML 1.0 Strict//EN" "http://www.w3.org/TR/xhtml1/DTD/xhtml1-strict.dtd">
<html xmlns="http://www.w3.org/1999/xhtml">
<head>
   <title></title>
```

(Continued)

```
        <meta http-equiv=“Content-Type” content=“text/html; charset=UTF-8” />
    </head>
    <body>
        <h1> Trip Match Advisory </h1>
        <form method=“POST” action=“plan”>
            Enter your Name: <input type=“text” name=“name”> </input>
            Your contact: <input type=“text” name=“contact”> </input>
            <p></p>
            From :
            <select name=“from” size=“1”>
                <option value=“BLR”> Bangalore </option>
                <option value=“SPN”> Prashanthi </option>
                <option value=“MAA”> Chennai </option>
                <option value=“MYS”> Mysore </option>
            </select>
            <p></p>
            Destination :
            <select name=“dest” size=“1”>
                <option value=“SPN”> Prashanthi </option>
                <option value=“BLR”> Bangalore </option>
                <option value=“MAA”> Chennai </option>
                <option value=“MYS”> Mysore </option>
            </select>
            <p></p>
            When: <input type=“text” name=“when”> </input>
            <p></p>
            <input type=“submit”>
        </form>
    </body>
</html>
```

Fig. 5.22 *Trip web.xml*

The Form gets input of the required data from the user. Accordingly, the user inputs the name of the person requesting the trip, and a basic contact number. Information about locations—From and To (destination) are also required. The `index.jsp` code (Figure 5.22) is just HTML.

Notice (line 9) the action when the Submit button is clicked. The URL value is "plan", which translates to Servlet, also named the same. The Plan Servlet takes over. Its listing is given in Figure 5.23.

```
import java.io.*;
import javax.servlet.*;
import javax.servlet.http.HttpServlet;
import javax.servlet.http.HttpServletRequest;
import javax.servlet.http.HttpServletResponse;

public class plan extends HttpServlet {
   int count;
   static String[] trips = new String[100];
   static String[] names = new String[100];
   static int nTrips = 0;

public void init (ServletConfig config) throws ServletException {
      super.init(config);
   }

protected void doGet(HttpServletRequest request,
HttpServletResponse response)
      throws ServletException, IOException {
            doPost(request, response);
      }

      protected void doPost(HttpServletRequest request,
      HttpServletResponse response)
      throws ServletException, IOException {
            String msg = "";
            String p;
            String trip = "";
            String pc = "";      //person with contact
            String match = "";

            response.setContentType("text/html");

            //Get the Name parameter from Form
```

(Continued)

```
p = request.getParameter(“name”);

          String name = p;     //store this name
          msg = msg.concat(p);
             //There are 5 parameters from the Form - name, contact,
             //from, dest, and when
             //Get these one by one thru getParameter
          pc = p;
          p = request.getParameter(“contact”);
          pc = pc.concat(“@” + p);

          msg = msg.concat(“ plans to travel from ”);
          p = request.getParameter(“from”);
          msg = msg.concat(p);

          trip = trip.concat(p);

          //Get the Destination
          msg = msg.concat(“ to ”);
          p = request.getParameter(“dest”);
          String dest = p;
          msg = msg.concat(p);

          msg = msg.concat(“ during ”);
          p = request.getParameter(“when”);
          msg = msg.concat(p);

             /*the trip contains the FROM already. Now cat with
               DEST
             Idea is to (later) compare the trip with trip of
             someone else
             */
          trip = trip.concat(dest);
          trips[nTrips] = trip;
          names[nTrips] = pc;
          //update the number of trips in memory
          nTrips += 1;
          msg = msg.concat(“</br>”);
```

```
68.
69.             msg = msg.concat(“</br>”);
70.
71.     //Prepare the context - this area can be shared with other
        //parts of the app
72.             //Name-Value pairs are used while sharing
73.             ServletContext shareArea = getServletContext();
74.             shareArea.setAttribute(“alltrips”, trips);
75.             shareArea.setAttribute(“allnames”, names);
76.             shareArea.setAttribute(“ntrips”, nTrips);
77.             shareArea.setAttribute(“thistrip”, trip);
78.             shareArea.setAttribute(“thisname”, pc);
79.
80.             //Pass on control to another Servlet called “match”
81.             String addr = “/match”;
82.             RequestDispatcher di = request.getRequestDispatcher(addr);
83.             di.forward(request,response);
84.         }
85.
86.         public String getServletInfo() {
87.             return “Short description”;
88.         }// </editor-fold>
89.     }
90.
```

Fig. 5.23 *Plan.java*

The first part of the code deals with storing the Form values locally, through `getParameter` (around line 40). The name is stored along with contact information, so the comparison is made accordingly.

The example demonstrates the concept of storing a set of variables that are shared across different programs in the context of the application (line 73). It also demonstrates the action of forwarding the control to a different servlet (line 82) in the same Servlet Context. The `forward` method belongs to the `RequestDispatcher` (RD) object, which receives request from a client and enables sending to another resource (Servlet/ JSP/HTML). It is created by the Servlet container. There are two ways to get the RD object:

- one is through the Servlet Context and the other is through Servlet Request. The Servlet Request method (shown in line 82) allows you to use a path argument as the destination that is relative to the current resource (/match).
- The Servlet Context getRequestDispatcher method is used for specifying the destination path relative to the application root.

The *forward* is used when a resource (JSP/Servlet/HTML) does some preliminary processing and transfers control to perform business logic in another resource (possibly a Servlet) or shares the results with another resource (JSP/Servlet). A `Forward` request happens internally on the server side, that is, the client has no idea of the forward. Hence no history is maintained, and the back button of the browser will be ignorant of the `forward`. While doing the `forward` operation, the response should not be flushed, otherwise, the operation will throw an exception (IllegalStateException).

The control is forwarded to the Servlet called "match" in the example. The Match Servlet is shown in Figure 5.24.

```
import java.io.*;

import javax.servlet.*;
import javax.servlet.http.HttpServlet;
import javax.servlet.http.HttpServletRequest;
import javax.servlet.http.HttpServletResponse;

public class match extends HttpServlet {
  static String[] trips = new String[100];
  static String[] names = new String[100];
  static int nTrips = 0;


  public void init (ServletConfig config) throws ServletException {
    super.init(config);
  }

  protected void processRequest(HttpServletRequest request, HttpServletResponse response, String msg)
    throws ServletException, IOException {
      response.setContentType(“text/html;charset=UTF-8”);
      PrintWriter out = response.getWriter();
      try {
          // TODO output your page here
          out.println(“<html>”);
          out.println(“<head>”);
          out.println(“<title>Servlet match</title>”);
          out.println(“</head>”);
          out.println(“<body>”);
```

```
            out.println("<h1>Servlet Match at " + request.get-
            ContextPath () + "</h1>");
            out.println(msg);
            out.println("</body>");
            out.println("</html>");
        } finally {
            out.close();
        }
    }

        protected void doGet(HttpServletRequest
        request, HttpServletResponse response)
    throws ServletException, IOException {
        String msg = "From Match </br>";

        processRequest(request, response, msg);
    }

        protected void doPost(HttpServletRequest request,
        HttpServletResponse response)
    throws ServletException, IOException {
        String msg = "";

        //Recall the context that was shared from the Plan
       //Servlet.
        ServletContext shareArea = getServletContext();

        /* After getting the Servlet Context object, get the
           values against the name-value pairs.
         * Refer the same Name in the name-value pairs defined
           in the Plan context.
         * Get all trips and names in the list. A Database is
           not used here since
         * it is yet to be covered. For simplifying things, the
           list is stored
         * in memory only.
        */
    this.trips = (String[]) shareArea.getAttribute("alltrips");
    this.names = (String[]) shareArea.getAttribute("allnames");
     this.nTrips = (Integer) shareArea.getAttribute("ntrips");

```

(*Continued*)

```
        //The requestor name and trip are required to compare...
    String thistrip = (String) shareArea.getAttribute(“thistrip”);
    String thisname = (String) shareArea.getAttribute(“thisname”);

        //string together the trips for display. All trips in
        //memory are taken.
        String mm = “”;
        for (int i=0; i<nTrips; i++) {
            mm = mm + “/” + trips[i];
        }
        //this display is done solely for checking out.
        msg = “All Trips Reference: ” + mm + “</br>”;
        //Do the actual Match
        String match = getMatchInfo(thistrip, thisname);
        msg = msg.concat(“Match Result: ” + match);
        processRequest(request, response, msg);
    }

    public String getServletInfo() {
        return “Short description”;
    }

    /* Match logic routine. If a database was used to store the
       entries (instead
     * of in-memory), a select ... where clause would do
       instead.
    */
    public String getMatchInfo(String trip, String thisname) {
        String match = “”;  //output string
        int i = 0;
        String nm = “”;
        String tr;
        String alltrips = “”;

        for(i=0; i<nTrips; i++){
            nm = names[i];
            tr = trips[i];
```

```
96.                 if (tr.equals(trip)) {
97.                     if (!thisname.equals(nm)) {
98.                         match = match.concat(nm) + "/";
99.                     }
100.                }
101.                alltrips = alltrips + "/" + tr;
102.            }
103.
104.            if (match.isEmpty()) {
105.                match = "No Match";
106.            } else {
107.                match = "Successful - " + thisname + ", check with
                    " + match;
108.            }
109.            return match;
110.        }
111.    }
```

Fig. 5.24 *Match.java*

Line 50 shows how the share area is re-claimed in this servlet. The globally available information about all the trips (lines 58–60) as well as the currently sought information (lines 63–64) is obtained. The function `getMatchInfo` (from line 86) implements the logic of finding the match. The match is generated in the form of a return string, which is used to display the result. Function `processRequest` (from line 18) generates the HTML.

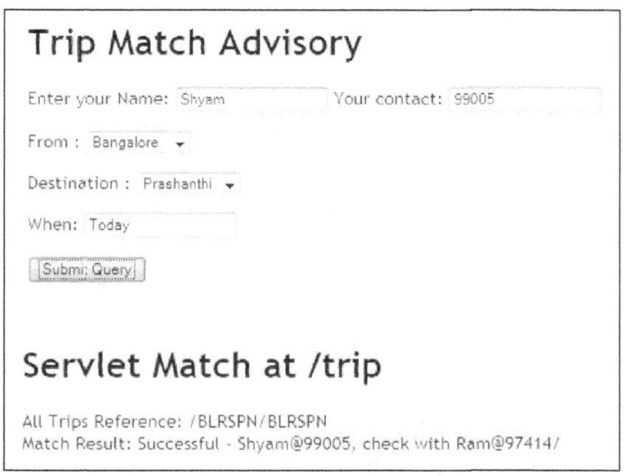

Fig. 5.25 *Trip input form and output*

Run the program in your favorite browser and try out with various combinations. The input form along with an indicative output is shown in Figure 5.25.

5.7.3 Thread Safety

The Servlet environment supports multi-threading, so there is an element of multi-threading in the code, though it is not used explicitly by the developer. Concurrent requests for a servlet are made possible by spawning different threads. The methods responsible are `doGet` and `doPost`. Care should be taken when instance variables are used.

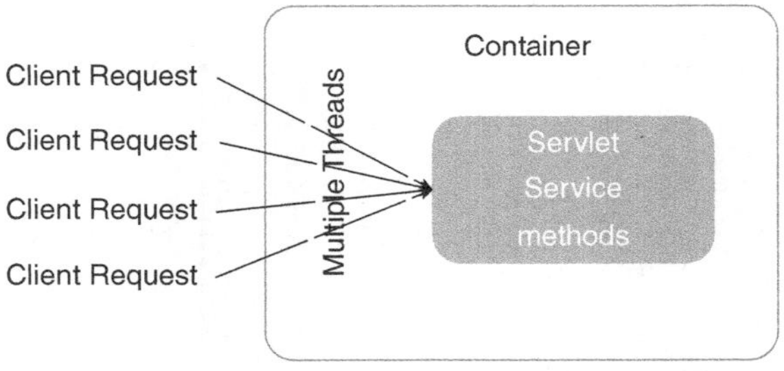

Fig. 5.26 *Multi-threaded*

Each `doGet` or `doPost` on a servlet (Figure 5.26) is running a separate thread. So data saved on a class instance variable or a local file is to be approached with caution. For example consider the following snippets of code (this is slightly different from the examples).

```
public class match extends HttpServlet {
  String[] trips = new String[100];          //Some instance variables
  String[] names = new String[100];
  int nTrips = 0;
  ...
    protected  void  doPost(HttpServletRequest  req,  HttpServletResponse
    resp)
    throws ServletException, IOException {

        ...
        //Do the actual Match
        String match = getMatchInfo(thistrip, thisname);
  ...
    public String getMatchInfo(String trip, String thisname) {
        //USE trips, names...
  ...
 }
 ...
}
```

The above code is not thread-safe since, for instance, if two threads are executed in parallel, they may not have the same value of instance variables (trips, etc). Whether this may or may not be desirable to have is dependent on the application requirement. In this example, it may perhaps be acceptable to have this as these variables are found to be application-wide. However, adequate care should be taken when executing such a code.

An alternative is to avoid instance variables in the Servlet class. This implies two possible alternatives—using class variables (by using static) or passing these variables as parameters to the (MatchInfo) function. This way, each thread can be considered to have its own variable.

Another alternative is to use full synchronization. This is achieved through the Single Thread model (STM), by implementing javax.servlet.SingleThreadModel. Thus the class declaration could be as follows:

```
public class match extends HttpServlet implements SingleThreadModel {
...
}
```

The Servlet container will then guarantee that only one thread will execute the service() method at a time.

A third alternative is to synchronize manually, which actually amounts to local or partial synchronization since only a code block is synchronized.

5.8 STATE MANAGEMENT

It is well known that the HTTP protocol to communicate with servers is actually a stateless protocol. This is good enough for point interactions, but what about an entire transaction? For example visualize the shopping cart scenario or airline reservation scenario. To complete one transaction, the user internally may have to connect and communicate with a server (or different servers) over a period of time. The question is how to achieve this over a stateless mechanism where each time is a different connection.

The problem is about how the server manages to connect pieces of information from each request that makes the transaction. This in turn translates into the problem of how the server (Servlet) identifies the multiple clients when they come back (i.e. abstracting each request which is a part of the larger transaction). Session management is all about how state is managed in a set of related transactions.

Given that the IP address is not a viable option to identify clients in this case, there are primarily three ways of identifying clients—Cookies, URL Rewriting and Hidden form fields. Once identified, objects can then be stored as object–value or name–value pairs within a named session, which can be shared across servers. For example, the shopping cart can leverage a session to coordinate a set of Servlets each doing a specific task where, one of the Servlets adds items to the cart, another Servlet displays it and yet another one calculates the price and so on.

Cookies and URL Rewriting are supported by the Servlet specification, while the method through the Hidden form field is application specific.

Sessions are created using the HttpSession object, which is a data container. The object itself is created through getSession() on the request object. The following are the methods of HttpSession:

- `getAttribute`(nameString) which gets the object that is associated with the nameString
- `setAttribute`(nameString, object) which binds the object with the nameString
- `getAttributeNames()` which returns an Enumeration of all nameStrings bound to the session
- `removeAttribute`(nameString) which removes the object associated with nameString

Another way of looking at a session is to consider it a means to save in-process (run time) data for a servlet. It may be realized that there are 3 different ways a Servlet can store its in-process data—the Request object, the Servlet Context and a Session. The examples that cover the first two ways have been seen earlier in this section. It is now time to look at the Session way!

5.8.1 Example—Session Basics

Imagine an example app in which sessions are created and then values are attributed or bound to them. What is shown is a generic case, but this could be translated into practical ideas like creating a shopping cart or initiating a funds transfer request. The beginning action-clicks from a client will trigger the creation of a session and it is to be viewed in this context. **Remember that there will be only one session for the user (per transaction) that will be active at a single point of time.**

An HTML file is designed to provide controls to the user in terms of Initializing with a new session, adding or binding some information to the session and printing the summary of sessions with values (Figure 5.27).

```
<%@page contentType="text/html" pageEncoding="UTF-8"%>
<!DOCTYPE HTML PUBLIC "-//W3C//DTD HTML 4.01 Transitional//EN"
"http://www.w3.org/TR/html4/loose.dtd">
<html>
<head>
<meta http-equiv="Content-Type" content="text/html; charset=UTF-8">
<title>Session</title>
</head>
<body>
    <h2>Sessions History</h2>
    <form action="<%=response.encodeURL("router")%>" method="GET">
        Enter Info:
        <input type="text" name="info" />w
        <input type="submit" name="clicker" value="NewSession" />
        <input type="submit" name="clicker" value="AddInfo" />
        <input type="submit" name="clicker" value="PrintInfo" />
    </form>
</body>
</html>
```

Fig. 5.27 *HTML (index.jsp) to demo session basics*

Let us also suppose that there is a Servlet for performing each of these tasks. To provide proper control, we have a router which is invoked upon Submit of the form. The router in turn dispatches the appropriate Servlet to perform the task (Figure 5.28).

```
package abc;

import java.io.IOException;
import java.io.PrintWriter;
import javax.servlet.RequestDispatcher;
import javax.servlet.ServletException;
import javax.servlet.http.HttpServlet;
import javax.servlet.http.HttpServletRequest;
import javax.servlet.http.HttpServletResponse;
```

```
public class router extends HttpServlet {
  @Override
  protected void doGet(HttpServletRequest request, HttpServletResponse
response)
     throws ServletException, IOException {
         String opt;
         String addr=“”;
         opt = request.getParameter(“clicker”);
         if (opt.equals(“NewSession”)) {
             addr = “makesession”;
         } else if (opt.equals(“AddInfo”)) {
             addr = “addinfo”;
         } else if (opt.equals(“PrintInfo”)) {
             addr = “printInfo”;
         }
         RequestDispatcher di = request.getRequestDispatcher(addr);
         di.forward(request,response);
     }
```

Fig. 5.28 *Router to dispatch the* appropriate *Servlet*

Servlet `makesession` is responsible for creating a Session. Just after creating the new session, it binds some information to the Servlet. This information is in the form of an object called *UserInfo*. Just for this example it contains two strings—an ID and a user entered information. If a new session is explicitly requested, it invalidates the old session. Before invalidating, the program is designed to use the existing attribute (UserInfo) as the starting point, should the session continue to be active.

```
package abc;

public class UserInfo {
  private String[] id = new String[100];
  private String[] name = new String[100];
  private int n = 0;
  public UserInfo() {
  }
  public String getId(int i) {
      return (this.id[i]);
  }
  public String getName(int i) {
      return (this.name[i]);
  }
  public void addInfo(String id, String nm) {
      this.id[this.n] = id;
      this.name[this.n] = nm;
      this.n++;
  }
```

(Continued)

```
    public int getNumberItems() {
        return this.n;
    }
}
```

Fig. 5.29 *UserInfo class definition*

The `UserInfo` class (Figure 5.29) is used to demonstrate how an object structure can be shared within a session. The class contains an array of id-name pairs with the id field representing session-id and the name field representing a user value (input from the info text box from Figure 5.27). Though the name ID connotes something unique, in this particular example (Figure 5.30), it is not supposed to be.

```
package abc;

import java.io.IOException;
import java.io.PrintWriter;
import javax.servlet.RequestDispatcher;
import javax.servlet.ServletException;
import javax.servlet.http.HttpServlet;
import javax.servlet.http.HttpServletRequest;
import javax.servlet.http.HttpServletResponse;
import javax.servlet.http.HttpSession;

public class makesession extends HttpServlet {
protected void processRequest(HttpServletRequest request,
HttpServletResponse response, String msg)
    throws ServletException, IOException {
        response.setContentType(“text/html;charset=UTF-8”);
        PrintWriter out = response.getWriter();
        try {
            out.println(“<html>”);
            out.println(“<head>”);
            out.println(“<title>Servlet getsess</title>”);
            out.println(“</head>”);
            out.println(“<body>”);
            out.println(“<h1>Servlet getsess at ” +
                    request.getContextPath () + “</h1>”);
            out.println(“<p>” + msg + “</p>”);
            out.println(“<form action='index.jsp' method='GET'>
            <input type='submit' name='submiT2' value='Click'
            /> </form>”);
            out.println(“</body>”);
            out.println(“</html>”);

        } finally {
            out.close();
```

```
            }
        }

    @Override
    protected void doGet(HttpServletRequest request,
    HttpServletResponse response)
      throws ServletException, IOException {
          String msg="";
          HttpSession sess=null;
          String sessid= null, nm = "";
          UserInfo info = new UserInfo();
          UserInfo t;
          String opt;
          String addr="";

          //Get the session if it already exists. If not create
          //one in variable sess
          sess = request.getSession();
          if (!sess.isNew()) {//if session was already existing
              t = (UserInfo) sess.getAttribute("userinfo");
              if (t != null) {
                  info = t;
              }
              //Now destroy this session and create a new one
              sess.invalidate();
              sess = request.getSession();//create a new session
              sess.setMaxInactiveInterval(100); //session termi
                                                //nates in n seconds
          }
          sess.setAttribute("userinfo", info);
          addr = "addinfo";
          RequestDispatcher di = request.getRequestDispatcher(addr);
          di.forward(request,response);
      }

    @Override
    protected void doPost(HttpServletRequest request,
    HttpServletResponse response)
      throws ServletException, IOException {
          String msg = "";
          processRequest(request, response, msg);
      }

    @Override
    public String getServletInfo() {
```

(Continued)

```
73.             return "Short description";
74.         }
75.     }
```

Fig. 5.30 *Servlet makesession*

The `getSession()` method (line 47) on the Request object simplifies the action of creating a session. This is handled entirely by the container (Tomcat's or JBOSS's container for instance). Note that the method operates on the Request object, which rightly implies that the session pertains to the requestor client, and not to someone else. The `getSession` method takes a Boolean as a parameter. By default it is taken to be true, which implies that a session will be created if it does not already exist. It is to be noted that an `HttpSession` object is unique for one user session. Since HTTP is stateless, sessions are to be maintained, if they are to be associated with multiple requests. The `getSession()` method handled by the Servlet Container takes care of not just the creation of a session, but also creation of a cookie in the first instance of the session request. In case Cookies are disabled, URL Rewriting can be used.

The details of Cookies and URL Rewriting will be dealt with in the subsequent sub-sections.

The method for getting a session (i.e. the active session) is also the same—`getSession()`. It returns the session object in either case. To disable creation of a new session, call the `getSession` method with a parameter of value `false`, that is, `getSession(false)` will not forcibly create a new session. If there was no session, it will return null value. To reiterate, by default the parameter to `getSession()` is considered true (which is practically convenient), so sessions are forcibly created.

The method `isNew()` goes along with the *`getSession`* method. It returns *true* if the session has just been created, otherwise it returns false.

A Session can get inactive in two ways through a program.

- It times out—the default time-out is set in web.xml through <session-timeout> tag, but can be overridden by code (for the specific session) in the form of `setMaxInactiveInterval`. The parameter to the method takes a number which represents the seconds for which it is to be active. If this number is 0, the session is immediately invalidated. If the number is -1 the session is kept until the browser terminates.
- The program can invoke `session.invalidate()` which make it permanently inactive.

Notice how an object (`UserInfo`) is set as an attribute to the activated session. After inactivation, all attributes attached to the session will no longer be available through the session object because the session itself is inactivated. Other than inactivating programmatically, a session can get inactivated automatically when the browser is closed or when the system hangs.

Play around with the program by including test Scenarios with the following:

- Set a value in the text box and Initiate a new session
- Add additional info by entering something in the text box and clicking on Addinfo button
- Wait for the session to get timed out (in the example set to 100ms)
- Check information summary by clicking the PrintInfo button

The `addInfo` Servlet takes care of adding information to the existing `UserInfo` object (Figure 5.31).

```
package abc;

import java.io.IOException;
import java.io.PrintWriter;
import javax.servlet.ServletException;
import javax.servlet.http.HttpServlet;
import javax.servlet.http.HttpServletRequest;
import javax.servlet.http.HttpServletResponse;
import javax.servlet.http.HttpSession;

public class addinfo extends HttpServlet {

    protected void processRequest(HttpServletRequest request,
    HttpServletResponse response, String msg)
    throws ServletException, IOException {
        response.setContentType("text/html;charset=UTF-8");
        PrintWriter out = response.getWriter();
        try {
            out.println("<html>");
            out.println("<head>");
            out.println("<title>Servlet getsess</title>");
            out.println("</head>");
            out.println("<body>");
            out.println("<h1>Servlet getsess at " +
            request.getContextPath () + "</h1>");
            out.println("<p>" + msg + "</p>");
            out.println("<form action=" + response.
            encodeURL("index.jsp") + " method='GET'> <input
            type='submit' name='submit' value='Return' />
            </form>");
            out.println("</body>");
            out.println("</html>");
        } finally {
            out.close();
        }
    }

protected void doGet(HttpServletRequest request,
HttpServletResponse response)
    throws ServletException, IOException {
```

(Continued)

```
            String nm = null;
            String msg = “</br>”;

            HttpSession sess=null;
            String sessid= null;
            String pc = “None”;
            String thisID;
            UserInfo info;

            nm = request.getParameter(“info”);  //info from the form

            sess = request.getSession(false);
            if (sess == null) {
                msg = msg + “No active session present”;
            } else {
                info = (UserInfo) sess.getAttribute(“userinfo”);
                if (info == null) {
                    msg += “User Info not found” + “<br />”;
                } else {
                    thisID = sess.getId();
                    info.addInfo(thisID, nm);
                    msg += “Added :” + nm + “; ” +
                    info.getId(info.getNumberItems()-1);
                }
            }
            processRequest(request, response, msg);
        }

        protected void doPost(HttpServletRequest request,
        HttpServletResponse response)
        throws ServletException, IOException {
            String msg = “”;
            processRequest(request, response, msg);
        }

        /*
        * Returns a short description of the servlet.
        */
```

```
71.        public String getServletInfo() {
72.            return "Short description";
73.        }// </editor-fold>
74.
75.    }
```

Fig. 5.31 *AddInfo.java*

AddInfo is meant to demonstrate getting Session data from the session. Line 50 shows the typecasted information.

PrintInfo Servlet is responsible for rendering the information log, based on the inputs. It prints out details based on UserInfo class (Figure 5.32).

```
package abc;

import java.io.IOException;
import java.io.PrintWriter;
import java.util.Date;
import javax.servlet.ServletException;
import javax.servlet.http.HttpServlet;
import javax.servlet.http.HttpServletRequest;
import javax.servlet.http.HttpServletResponse;
import javax.servlet.http.HttpSession;

public class printInfo extends HttpServlet {
    protected void processRequest(HttpServletRequest request,
HttpServletResponse response, String msg)
        throws ServletException, IOException {
            response.setContentType("text/html;charset=UTF-8");
            PrintWriter out = response.getWriter();
            try {
                out.println("<html>");
                out.println("<head>");
                out.println("<title>Servlet getsess</title>");
                out.println("</head>");
                out.println("<body>");
                out.println("<h1>Servlet getsess at " + request.get-
                ContextPath () + "</h1>");
                out.println("<p>" + msg + "</p>");
```

(Continued)

```
    //out.println(“<form  action=‘index.jsp’  method=‘GET’>  <input
    type=‘submit’ name=‘submit2’ value=‘Click’ /> </form>”);
    out.println(“<form action=” + response.encodeURL(“index.jsp”) + “
    method=‘GET’> <input type=‘submit’ name=‘submit2’ value=‘Return’
    /> </form>”);
                out.println(“</body>”);
                out.println(“</html>”);

            } finally {
                out.close();
            }
        }

        @Override
        protected void doGet(HttpServletRequest request,
        HttpServletResponse response)
        throws ServletException, IOException {
            String msg = “”;
            UserInfo info;
            HttpSession sess=null;
            String nl = “<br></br>”;

            sess = request.getSession(false);
            if (sess == null) {
                msg = msg + “No Active Session!”;
            } else {
                info = (UserInfo) sess.getAttribute(“userinfo”);
                if (info == null) {
                    msg += “Empty” + nl;
                } else {
                    int n = info.getNumberItems();
                    for (int i=0; i<n; i++) {
                        msg = msg + “SessID=” + info.getId(i) +
                        “, Info=” + info.getName(i) + nl;
                    }
                }
                //Print extra info about current active session
                msg += “<u>Now some data about the active session
                </u>” + nl;
                msg += “Active Session ID=” + sess.getId() + nl;
                Date dt = new Date(sess.getCreationTime());
                msg += “Active Session Created time =” +
                dt.toString() + nl;
                dt = new Date(sess.getLastAccessedTime());
```

```
                    msg += "Active Session Last accessed time =" +
                    dt.toString() + nl;
                    msg += "Active Session Max inactive interval =" +
                    sess.getMaxInactiveInterval() + nl;
                }
                processRequest(request, response, msg);
            }

            @Override
            protected void doPost(HttpServletRequest request,
            HttpServletResponse response)
            throws ServletException, IOException {
                String msg="";
                processRequest(request, response, msg);
            }

            @Override
            public String getServletInfo() {
                return "Short description";
            }// </editor-fold>

        }
```

Fig. 5.32 *PrintInfo servlet*

The above example will work provided Cookies are enabled on the browser. It was mentioned earlier in this section that the Servlet container manages session information to be shared among the transactions using session id. This single id is enough to share among sessions between the client and server. The `id` could represent a whole lot of information behind it, like a shopping cart or the money transfer set of operations forming a transaction. The question now translates to how this `id` is shared between each operation (instead of how information is transferred)?

It has been mentioned in this section that the `getSession()` method is used to create a session. However, that is just half the story—the container takes care of not just creating the session but also the response mechanism through cookies. This is done automatically by the Container.

The actions that are implicitly done behind the scenes are shown in (Figure 5.33). On a higher level of observation, this will work well, but what about a situation when Cookies have been disabled in the browser? If Cookies are disabled, `getSession` will always return a new session, but that may not be desirable. Encoding the URL is an alternative solution to this. The process of encoding URL is called URL Rewriting in which the Session ID is passed through the URL, instead of the Cookie. But for this to work, all the URLs will have to be encoded. This means that a parameter in the form of a session id is added to the parameter list and passed through the URL. It is achieved as in the following statement:

```
Out.println("<a href=" + Response.encodeURL('<URL String>') + ">Click
</a>");
```

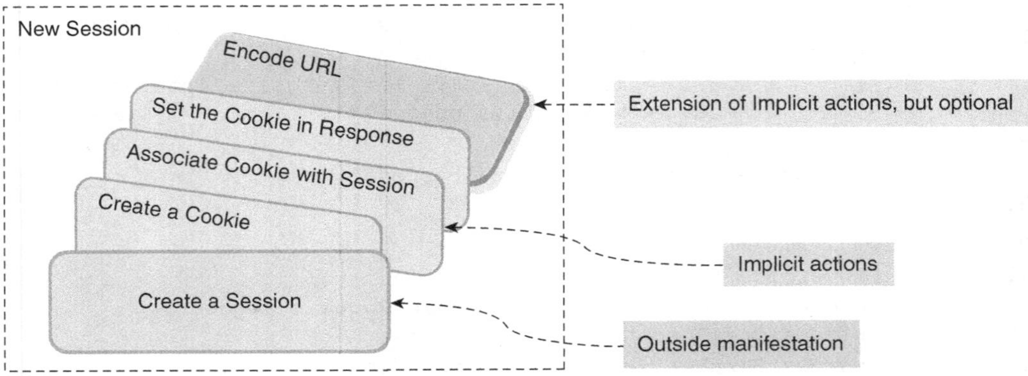

Fig. 5.33 *What happens behind creation of a session?*

For instance while the link is clicked, it will append a parameter something like JSESSIONID=<session id> to the URL. The name of the parameter is immaterial since this is handled by the Container. Each Container might implement a different name, so hard coding this value will not work.

The encoding process is followed for all URL definitions including forwarding requests. The example set of programs can be modified as shown in Figure 5.34–5.36 (corresponds to line 25 of Figure 5.31).

```
//out.println("<form action='index.jsp' method='GET'> <input
type='submit' name='submit2' value='Click' /> </form>");
//Above line is substituted by the following line
out.println("<form action=" + response.encodeURL("index.jsp") +
" method='GET'> <input type='submit' name='submit2' value='Click' />
</form>");
```

Fig. 5.34 *Changes to printInfo.java*

```
//Note that encodeURL is applied to response object and passed with the
//URL, represented by addr
RequestDispatcher di = request.getRequestDispatcher(response.
encodeURL(addr));
```

Fig. 5.35 *Changes to router.java*

```
//Note that the response object is available in the JSP file
<form action="<%=response.encodeURL("router")%>" method="GET">
```

Fig. 5.36 *Changes to index.jsp*

It is advised to modify the code and try running it by deliberately turning Cookies *off/on* and seeing the difference in the URL. When Cookies are on, the Cookie is created in the local machine and Session ID is not included in the URL. When Cookies are turned off (disabled), the URL encoding takes over where the URL includes the Session ID.

5.8.2 Cookies

The concept of Cookies was discussed in the client-side section of this book (Chapter 5, Section 5.12.1). The present section attempts to discuss the the server–side concept. Their usage is complete only when they are used on both the Client and the Server sides, though it appears that the Server side alone is the one using it.

Cookies were originally started to help in Session management like in the previous example. It was first introduced by Netscape and soon became a standard in all popular browsers. However, it can be extended for other purposes as well. Essentially, a Cookie is a name–value pair which is persisted across sessions, or over a period of time. The Cookie that has persisted in the client, is used to share values between the client and the server. This is the most common way for servers to remember clients. For example, if a site remembers the client's login name or fills up a form then most probably there is a set of Cookies that work behind the scenes. In fact, its presence is not normally known to the user explicitly. By default, Cookies are only visible to the server that created them.

A server creates a new Cookie by the following method.

```
Cookie myCookie = new Cookie("name", "value");
```

The name, once set, cannot be changed but the value can be changed using `setValue` method. A comment can be set to this Cookie through the `setComment` method while the same can be retrieved through `getComment`. The Cookie, by default, has a domain, in the form of the web address (as specified by RFC 2109). The method `getDomain` on the Cookie object returns the string representing the domain name. By default, a Cookie is (programmatically) visible only to the server which created it. The Cookie is also only visible if it is active. Its shelf life can be controlled programmatically through `setMaxAge`(seconds) method. If the value is set to a negative value, it will expire upon closing the browser. If the value is set to 0, the browser deletes it immediately. Once set (other than 0), it can be retrieved through `getMaxAge` or changed by invoking the `setMaxAge` again, if it still exists. The Cookie is persisted in the client machine and can be seen through browser settings. The (relative) path of the Cookie can be set using `setPath`.

The name–value pair in the form of myCookie can be written to the client as follows.

```
response.addCookie (myCookie);
```

Many such Cookies can be added. To retrieve the Cookies, `getCookies()` is applied on the `request` object. The method returns an array of Cookies and the required name can be filtered out through a loop. There is no method for retrieving a Cookie with a specific name!

From a business perspective, Cookies are to be viewed as something that will aid the process and not something that can be relied upon. Consider the following factors that are practically possible:

- Cookies can be disabled on the browser at the option of the user.
- Cookies store relatively small amount of information.
- The number of Cookies that can be stored is also limited.
- Cookies can expire.
- Cookies can be deleted by the user (through the browser) at any time. So an application should not be critically dependent on Cookie information.

It is suggested to weigh these aspects on how to use Cookies and how much to depend on Cookies for the application to work. Where security is a primary concern, it is better to avoid Cookies as bits of information might be available on the client. However, on the brighter side, it is simpler to use, and there are an increasing number of websites or applications that insist on the availability of Cookies, i.e., force users to enable Cookies on the browser. For example, Gmail insists on enabling them, so also banking applets like Citibank's. As long as the information stored (on the client) is not critical or vulnerable to security risks, it is considered good to use them.

The Servlet API has exposed all Cookie operations through three classes: `HttpServletRequest`, `HttpServletResponse` and `Cookie`.

5.8.2.1 Cookie usage scenarios for added convenience Cookies can offer a lot of convenience to an end user. Here are some of scenarios that typically can use a Cookie.

- Identifying a repeat-user in a site. Applications could include remembering user preferences on a online eCommerce site for a user's shopping cart
- Auto-filling a Form
- Remembering login and password information for a site
- and a host of other scenarios...

It is said that Cookies are considered to be insecure, but it is an exaggerated statement. A Cookie is just a piece of information (a name-value pair) placed in a client's disk—it is not used for executing or interpreting, so it cannot be a carrier of virus. It also does not occupy any significant disk space, as the number of Cookies and the storage for each Cookie is itself limited. However, they can be a source of intrusion or a threat to privacy. By remembering a user's preferences or their choices, they can provide subtle clues into a person's personal information. Also, sometimes, advertisers, in their eagerness to promote their products, could cause irritation in form of too many pop-up windows.

Aside note

Use your judgement to create Cookies. There are a few guidelines that are being proposed for its usage, which includes privacy concerns. Take care of the degree of intrusiveness that a Cookie intends to introduce.

5.8.2.2 Cookie example This example demonstrates adding Cookies through server-side code. A Cookie is added generally without any direct intervention from the user. Most popularly it is used to store Session ID. Though storing Session ID is trivial (meaning it takes very little space and is hence an ideal candidate for a Cookie), the amount of information it points to, could be enormous—both in terms of quantity of data as well as its significance. The way information is shared between client and server is that the client stores the index of the session (session-id), while data it points to is stored in the server. Irrespective of where the data is stored, it is useful to get additional information about the session, over its properties like *Domain*, *Path*, etc. to enable sharing of information between different Servlets or even between servers.

```
<!DOCTYPE HTML PUBLIC "-//W3C//DTD HTML 4.01 Transitional//EN">
<html>
```

```
      <head>
      <title></title>
      <meta http-equiv=“Content-Type” content=“text/html;
      charset=UTF-8”>
      <script>
         var req = false;
         function processAjax() {

              var f = document.getElementById(“form1”);
             //browser specific code - check for the presence of
             //function

             if (f.addEventListener) {
             f.addEventListener(“submit”,myvalidate,false);
                                                   //Firefox

             } else if (f.attachEvent) {     //IE

             f.attachEvent(“onsubmit”, myvalidate);

       }

             var cksdiv = document.getElementById(“cks”);

             //Step-1 (create the ajax request obj)
             if (window.ActiveXObject) {
                req = new ActiveXObject(“Microsoft.XMLHTTP”);
             } else if (window.XMLHttpRequest) {
                req = new XMLHttpRequest();
             }
             //Step-2: Create an asynchronous request.
             if (req != null) {
                 req.open(“GET”,“getck”, true);
                 //Steps 3a/b: Callback function is defined
                 //(anonymously) and registered
              req.onreadystatechange = function() {
                 if (req.readyState == 4) {
                    //Step-4: Server returns data -
                    //add it to the response
                    cksdiv.innerHTML = req.responseText;
```

(*Continued*)

```
                    }
                    if (req.readyState == 1) {
                    cksdiv.innerHTML = "<b>Loading...
                    </b>";
                    }
                    if (req.readyState == 2) {
                    cksdiv.innerHTML = "Loaded";
                       }
                     }
                        //Send data (null for GET)
                        req.send(null);
                    }
                }
      function myvalidate(e) {
    var cknamx = document.getElementById("cknam").value;
    if (cknamx.length == 0)  {
            alert ("Cookie name cannot be blank");
            if (e.preventDefault) {
                 e.preventDefault();
                                              //Firefox
            } else {
                 e.returnValue = false;
                                              //for IE
                                      //e.cancelBubble = true;
                 }
            }
                    var cktim = document.getElementById("cktim").
                    value;
      if (cktim.length > 0) {
             if (isNaN(cktim)) {
                 alert ("Timeout should be a number");
                 }
             }
      }
       </script>
      </head>
      <body onload="processAjax();">
       <H2>Getting a taste of Cookies</H2>
       <p style="border:ridge; width:430px; padding:2px;">
```

```
            Cookies are normally set by the system backend,
68      without direct user interference. However for demo purposes,
        let us try to enter through the front door.
69          </p>
70          <form id="form1" method="POST" action="ckset">
71              <table>
72                  <tr>
73                      <td>Enter Cookie Name:</td>
74                      <td><input type="text" name="cknam"> </input>
                        </td>
75                  </tr>
76                  <tr>
77                      <td>Cookie Value :</td>
78                      <td><input type="text" name="ckval"> </input>
                        </td>
79                  </tr>
80                  <tr>
81                      <td>Cookie Lifespan (seconds):</td>
82                      <td><input type="text" name="cktim" value="10">
                        </input></td>
83                  </tr>
                    <tr><td colspan="2">

84                  <button type="submit">Store Cookie</button>

                    </td></tr>
85              </table>
86          </form>
87          <div id="cks"></div>
88         </body>
89        </html>
```

Fig. 5.37 *Demo–EnterCK.html–enter Cookie details*

The entry point is a Form (code in Figure 5.37) which accepts values for a Cookie. Normally Cookies are created internally without much direct interaction with the user. However, for demo purposes, assume that Cookies are given by user and stored in the client system. The Form design in IE is shown in Figure 5.38.

The above code shows a combination of JavaScript (Client side) and use of Ajax. The significant part of the HTML body tag starts from line 66. Event handlers are defined in two places:

- The first definition is *"Onload"* of the Body (Figure 5.37, line 65), which defines the Ajax operations (*processAjax*) needed for displaying the current set of Cookies that are valid. The function first defines another event handler for the Form (discussed below in the next point). Then it creates the Ajax request (lines 21–25). Here the URL points to another Servlet, *getck* (Figure 5.37, line 28), responsible for getting the cookies that are existing on the client. This is explained in Figure 5.39. The anonymous function from line 30 shows how it handles the state of the asynchronous request.

- The second event handler is defined as part of onload, through the function myvalidate. It handles the client side validation of the Form. It checks the presence of the Cookie name (mandatory). It also checks if the timeout is numeric or not.
- The list of Cookies (if any) is placed in the *div* element, *cks*, corresponding to line 87 in the code. The screen shot is shown below in Figure 5.38 where the user can enter any Cookie name, a Value and a timeout number. It may be recalled that a name–value pair can be taken to represent the name and value of the cookie to aid in meaningful entries.
- Before invoking this program, there are a few things that need to be set on the browser.
- It is advised to enable cookies on the browser. In Firefox 5.0, it is done by navigating through the Options. The *Enable JavaScript* check box is in the *Content* tab.
- Use IE or Firefox
- Disable use of browser cache. In IE (ver.8), it is done by navigating to Internet Options and clicking on the Settings button. In "check for newer versions of stored pages", select the option which allows each time a web page is visited.

The Servlet *ckset* is invoked as per the action attribute of the Form (Figure 5.37, line 70). The code for *ckset* is shown below in Figure 5.39. The *doPost* method is the most relevant method of the Servlet. In a nutshell, it does a couple of things—one it creates the cookie and two, it sets a session.

The process of creating a cookie is simple. A Cookie object is instantiated (Figure 5.39, line 50) along with its name and value. Cookie names are case sensitive. If the name already exists, it will not create a

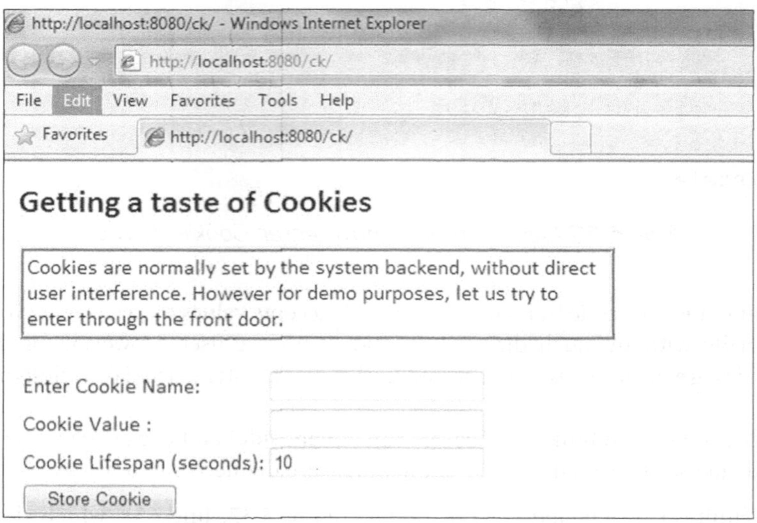

Fig. 5.38 *Cookie details form*

fresh one but its value will be overwritten. Other properties of the cookie object may be optionally initialized. For instance, line 51 shows how to set a cookie's life span.

Finally, the addCookie method is invoked on the Servlet's response object for the cookie to get added on the client's system.

The session part of the code is from line 58 (Figure 5.39). This part is independent of the Cookie's and so there is no sequence or no dependency on each other. This is included in the demo only to show a couple of interesting things.

- As soon as the new session is added, a Cookie is automatically added. The name of the cookie is dependent on the specifics of the implementation of the Servlet container. For GlassFish it is JSESSIONID. For others it might just be SESSIONID, but that should not matter.
- A session can be made to set and get attributes, just similar to the operations on the Servlet Context that was addressed earlier in this chapter. Setting of an attribute is shown in line 65. The attribute name in the example is "msg". Not only string types, even objects can be a part of the attributes.

After the cookie is added, the control is redirected to the entry Form (*enterck.html*). The added cookie can instantly be seen in the display.

There are other properties which could be set (not shown in the code):

- public void Cookie.setDomain(String): It specifies a domain restriction constraint in the servers that should see a cookie. By default, cookies are returned only to the host that saved them. This can be overridden by specifying a domain name using this call, which instructs the browser to return Cookies to other hosts within the same domain. The domain name should follow the formats as shown below.
- For non-country domains, it must begin with a dot and must contain two dots. Example, if the domain is set as ".abc.com", it matches www.abc.com and x.abc.com but not y.x.abc.com.
- For country domains, it should again start with a dot and should contain three dots.
- public void Cookie.setPath(String): The Cookie can be visible to all paths under the directory it was set.
- Public void Cookie.setValue(String): setValue assigns a value to the Cookie object. It has certain restriction on characters that could be a part of the value. It should not include whitespace, slash, question mark, quotes, brackets and semicolons

```
1.        Package module_a;
2.
3.        import java.io.IOException;
4.        import java.io.PrintWriter;
5.        import javax.servlet.ServletException;
6.        import javax.servlet.http.Cookie;
7.       import javax.servlet.http.HttpServlet;
8         import javax.servlet.http.HttpServletRequest;
9         import javax.servlet.http.HttpServletResponse;
```

(Continued)

```
import javax.servlet.http.HttpSession;

public class ckset extends HttpServlet {
    protected void processRequest(HttpServletRequest request,
HttpServletResponse response)
        throws ServletException, IOException {
        response.setContentType("text/html;charset=UTF-8");
        PrintWriter out = response.getWriter();
        try {
            // TODO output your page here
        } finally {
            out.close();
        }
    }

    protected void doGet(HttpServletRequest request,
    HttpServletResponse response)
    throws ServletException, IOException {
        processRequest(request, response);
    }

    protected void doPost(HttpServletRequest request,
    HttpServletResponse response)
    throws ServletException, IOException {
        String cknam, ckval;
        int cktim;
        Cookie usrCk;

        String msg="</br>";

        //Get Cookie name and Value Form values.
        //Timeout value is fetched in the try-catch block.

        cknam = request.getParameter("cknam");
        ckval = request.getParameter("ckval");

        //Let us try to create the cookie
        try {
          //Ensure that non-numeric value is caught and ignored
```

```
            cktim = Integer.parseInt(request.getParameter("cktim"));
                //Cookie names have certain constraints - no spaces, no special characters, etc
                //Catch anything that it does not like, and ignore it!
                if (cknam.trim().length() > 0) {
                    usrCk = new Cookie (cknam, ckval);
                    usrCk.setMaxAge(cktim);
                    response.addCookie(usrCk);
                }
        } catch (Throwable e) {
                msg = "Error: " + e;
        }

        /*
         * Two things to note here - one is the way a Cookie is automatically added
         * the other is using it as a means to transfer a server information.
         */
        HttpSession sess;
        sess = request.getSession(); //add session if it does not exist
        //Set some value in the session.
        sess.setAttribute("msg", msg);
        //this info (msg) can be used to display by retreiving
        //the session from the client
        //One way to acheive is to use a JSP (not shown in this
        //example)
        response.sendRedirect("enterck.html");   //back to where
                                                 //i came from
    }

    public String getServletInfo() {
        return "Short description";
    }// </editor-fold>
}
```

Fig. 5.39 *Servlet to add Cookie–ckSet.java*

The cookies are displayed as per the following program (*getck.java*—Figure 5.40). Cookies are retrieved from a request object through `getCookies()` method. It returns an array of Cookies. There is no call for separately retrieving them given name or such parameter. If a specific cookie is required to be fetched, it has to be done by individually comparing their names. Besides, there are other properties like Domain which could be helpful.

```
package module_a;

import java.io.IOException;
import java.io.PrintWriter;
import javax.servlet.ServletException;
import javax.servlet.http.Cookie;
import javax.servlet.http.HttpServlet;
import javax.servlet.http.HttpServletRequest;
import javax.servlet.http.HttpServletResponse;

public class getck extends HttpServlet {
    protected void processRequest(HttpServletRequest request, HttpServletResponse response, String msg)
    throws ServletException, IOException {
        response.setContentType(“text/html;charset=UTF-8”);
        //response.setContentType(“text/xml”);
        PrintWriter out = response.getWriter();
        try {
            // TODO output your page here
            out.println(“<html>”);
            out.println(“<head>”);
            out.println(“<title>Servlet getck</title>”);
            out.println(“</head>”);
            out.println(“<body>”);
            out.println(msg);
            out.println(“</body>”);
            out.println(“</html>”);
        } finally {
            out.close();
        }
    }
```

```
        protected void doGet(HttpServletRequest request,
        HttpServletResponse response)
        throws ServletException, IOException {
            Cookie[] cks;
            String nm;
            String msg="</br>";

            cks = request.getCookies();
            if (cks != null) {
                for (int i=0; i<cks.length; i++) {
                    msg = msg + "(" + (i+1) + "/" + cks.length + ") "
                    + cks[i].getName() + " => " + cks[i].getValue();
                    msg = msg + "</br>";
                }
            }
            processRequest(request, response, msg);
        }

        protected void doPost(HttpServletRequest request,
        HttpServletResponse response)
        throws ServletException, IOException {
            String msg="";
            processRequest(request, response, msg);
        }

        public String getServletInfo() {
            return "Short description";
        }// </editor-fold>

    }
```

Fig. 5.40 *Servlet to get cookies–getck.java*

The output of *getck.java* is fed into the Ajax request object (Figure 5.37, line 33), which is displayed as part of the *enterck.html* routine, so this appears as output that is continuously displayed.

For this to work properly on the browser, Cache has to be turned off, that is, refresh from server option should be checked on. Different browsers have different ways of doing it. In IE-8, it is under *Tools→Internet Options→Browser History settings.* The option related to "Check for newer versions of stored pages" should be set to "Every time I visit the page". This implies that the Cache is not be used as a means to display the pages, but should be got from the server, all the time. This will have an impact on performance of the browser, so it may be a good idea to reset it whatever is required, after the demo.

One observation in the output is that the Cookie, JSESSIONID, is displayed, though the user has not entered it. Also the value of this Cookie is prone to change from time to time.

This Cookie is a result of the call to create a session (Figure 5.39, line 63). It is created automatically by the Servlet Container when the new session is established.

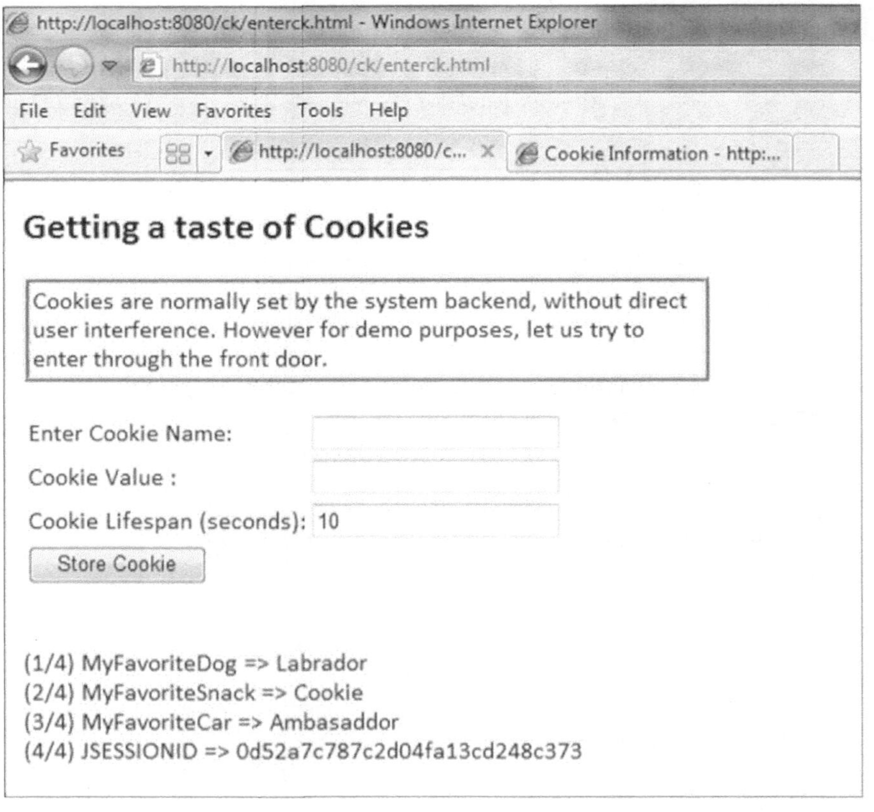

Fig. 5.41 *Cookie details displayed*

After creating the Cookies, it is advised to check the same in the browser. Accessing Cookie information is different in each browser, but is not very difficult to find it out. In IE, the output of Cookies information in Figure 5.41 is shown through a Developer Tool that is an add-on to IE-8. The tool is useful in debugging JavaScript, HTML and CSS on the client side.

NAME	MyFavoriteSnack
VALUE	Cookie
DOMAIN	
PATH	/
EXPIRES	At the end of the Session

NAME	MyFavoriteDog
VALUE	Labrador
DOMAIN	
PATH	/
EXPIRES	At the end of the Session

NAME	MyFavoriteCar
VALUE	Ambasaddor
DOMAIN	
PATH	/
EXPIRES	At the end of the Session

Fig. 5.42 *Check Cookie details in the browser (IE-8)*

Aside note

The newer version, HTML5, offers a concept called web storage, available as two objects—*sessionStorage* and *localStorage*. These are promising alternatives to Cookies, which suffer from a few drawbacks–related to the size of storage, performance and the need for multiple transactions from different windows by the same user.
The code for handling Cookies could be written such that if *localStorage* is available, then leverage it, otherwise fall back on the traditional Cookies method. This will offer better Ajax response turn-around (irrespective of whether Cookies are used or not). For information on the new specifications, check out **http://dev.w3.org/html5/webstorage/ for details.**

5.9 EVENT DRIVEN TRACKING

An application can be interacted through three objects—the Servlet Context, Request and Session objects. Any change in state of an object is manifested as an event which is handled through listeners. In general, a listener is something that will alert the program, on the occurrence of an event. Conceptually, it is similar to the click of a button or moving the mouse as interjected by a VB program. In this context, there are a few events that are applicable. In the case of a session, it can be tracked through certain events in its lifetime. These events can be trapped and the callback function executed. It helps the system do specific tasks like session or request logging or setting up database operations during initialization or releasing a service, or cleaning up during termination. The following are such events and the associated listeners.

5.9.1 Listeners and Events

Listeners are a part of the standard Servlet API. They give a greater control of the application by trapping events with the Request, Context and Session objects.

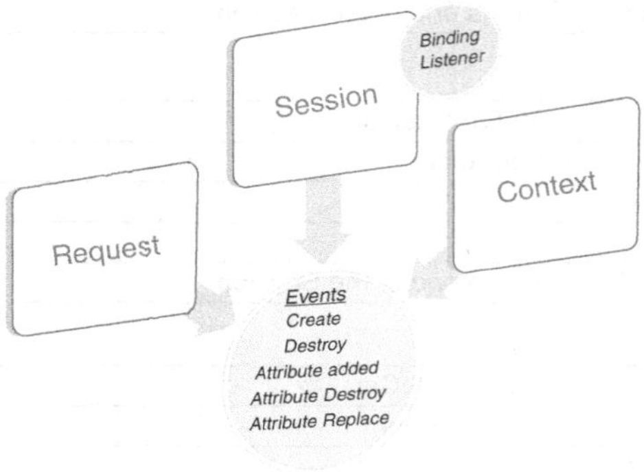

Fig. 5.43 *Understanding listeners–from object's perspective*

Figure 5.43 represents the event model from the object's perspective. Viewed in another way, from the event's perspective, it can be represented as follows:

- Create/Destroy
- Attributes
- Binding

Event	Object	Example of Application Scenarios
Creating a Session	Implements HttpSessionListener Method—sessionCreated (e)	Counter for concurrent users, that is, number of active sessions. They require to be configured in the web.xml (Deployment Descriptor)
Destroying a Session	Implements HttpSessionListener Method—sessionDestroyed (e)	
Attribute added to the session	Implements HttpSessionAttributeListener Method—attributeAdded(e)	Initialization or cleanup routine associated with the object. Use e.getName and e.getValue to get the name and value respectively.
Attribute removed	Implements HttpSessionAttributeListener Method—attributeRemoved(e)	
Attribute replaced	Implements HttpSessionAttributeListener Method—attributeReplaced(e)	
Value Bound	HttpSessionBindingListener Method—valueBound(e)	Also triggered when the session is established. No need for configuring in web.xml.

Value Unbound	HttpSessionBindingListener Method—valueUnbound(e)	Also triggered when the session invalidates or time out. No need for configuring in web.xml.
Migrated to another server	HttpSessionActivationListener Method—sessionDidActivate	Attribute moved to another VM and the possibility of re-initializing or clean-up routines. Not used often since it deals with internal workings of the Servlet. When the session is moved to another JVM it needs to be Serializable.
Activated in another server	HttpSessionActivationListener Method—sessionWillPassivate	
Servlet Context ready for servicing	contextInitialized	
App about to be shut down	contextDestroyed	
Attribute added	attributeAdded	
Attribute removed	attributeRemoved	
Attribute replaced	attributeReplaced	

Fig. 5.44 *Session related event classes*

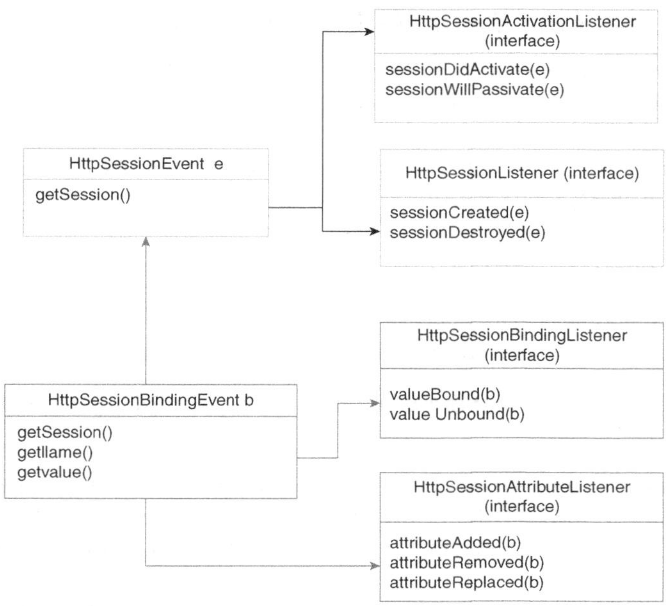

Fig. 5.45 *Organization of the session-based* events

For distributed environments, the JSP or Servlet specifications support the 2 methods—*sessionDidActivate* and *sessionWillPassivate*. If the container migrates the session to a different JVM for purposes like load balancing or failover, the listener responds to these events. Session passivation event occurs when they are about to be passivated. The Activate event is invoked by the listener when the object has been migrated to another JVM (Figures 5.44 and 5.45).

5.9.2 Steps

Writing a listener-based class is relatively straightforward. The steps are highlighted in Figure 5.46.

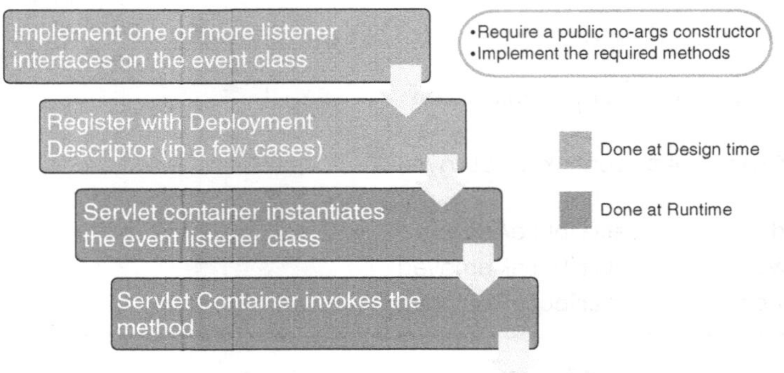

Fig. 5.46 *Listener–an idea of the basic steps and* flow *of control*

5.9.3 Session Tracking Example (FavConnect)

Consider an example of a module to help connect like-minded people with similar interest groups. Here, the user submits his/her choice of interest and comes to know who else in the ecosystem is having a similar set of interests.

It consists of a login procedure, an interest capture facility which is used to match with like-minded people. A user logs in when internally the system creates a session and initializes an object called UserInfo, which is then bound to the session. The user types in his/her favorite item against a category. The program validates the input and searches for another user with the same item of interest, which is displayed to the user.

The purpose of this module is to highlight the process of creating a session, a means to track some of events (implementing valueUnbound) through listeners, a Database operation and a simple JSP.

5.9.3.1 FavConnect—Organization of modules The organization of the FavConnect module is represented by Figure 5.47.

5.9.3.2 FavConnect—Login.JSP *Login.jsp* is the entry point. For now, consider a JSP as a special kind of Servlet, but similar to an HTML file in style and behavior. Internally, a JSP file is converted into a Servlet but that is encapsulated so well by the container that the programmer need not be concerned about how it is achieved.

The code shown in Figure 5.48 is the code for a simplified login form. In practice there will be links for "forgot password" and so on, but letu keep it simple enough and focused to enable understand the bare essentials of how it works.

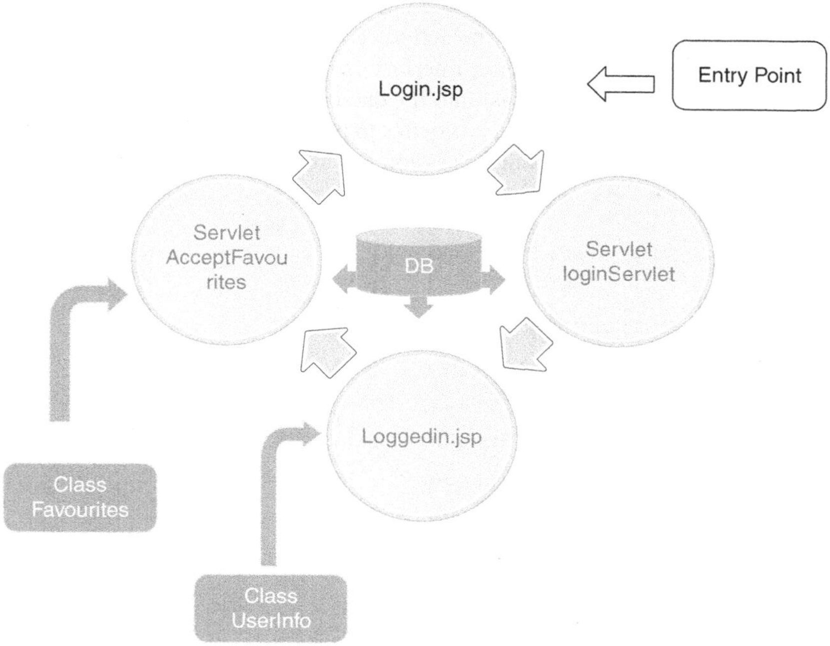

Fig. 5.47 *FavConnect*

Login.jsp is the entry point. It throws up a simple form to capture user login and password. It then leads to the Servlet called LoginServlet which is responsible for logging in and creating the session.

```
<%@page contentType="text/html" pageEncoding="UTF-8"%>
<!DOCTYPE HTML PUBLIC "-//W3C//DTD HTML 4.01 Transitional//EN"
"http://www.w3.org/TR/html4/loose.dtd">

<html>
<head>
   <meta http-equiv="Content-Type" content="text/html; charset=UTF-8">
   <title>JSP Page</title>
</head>
<body>
    <h2>Login</h2>
        <form action=<%=response.encodeURL("LoginServlet")%> >
            Username: <input type="text" name="username"/>  <br/>
            Password: <input type="text" name="password" /> <br/>
            <input type="submit" value="submit" />
        </form>
</body>
</html>
```

Fig. 5.48 *Login.jsp*

5.9.3.3 Login Servlet If the Save button was clicked in the earlier form, the savFav method is invoked. If the Accept button was invoked, the actions correspond to holding the information in the session. When the session expires, the listener interface invokes the valueUnbound method, which in this case saves the information (in Favourites) into the database. Contrary to that given in this example, it is to be remembered that as a best practice, it is better to programmatically control the life of a session (through invalidate()) rather than force wait for session timeout (Figures 5.49 and 5.50).

```
package com.login;

import java.io.IOException;
import java.io.PrintWriter;
import javax.servlet.ServletException;
import javax.servlet.http.HttpServlet;
import javax.servlet.http.HttpServletRequest;
import javax.servlet.http.HttpServletResponse;
import javax.servlet.http.HttpSession;

public class LoginServlet extends HttpServlet {
    //this method is not relevant here—can be used for testing and
    //debugging
    protected void processRequest(String msg, HttpServletRequest
    request,
    HttpServletResponse response)
        throws ServletException, IOException {
          response.setContentType(“text/html;charset=UTF-8”);
          PrintWriter out = response.getWriter();
          try {
              out.println(“<html>”);
              out.println(“<head>”);
              out.println(“<title>Servlet LoginServlet</title>”);
              out.println(“</head>”);
              out.println(“<body>”);
              out.println(“<h1>Servlet LoginServlet at ” + request.get-
              ContextPath () + “</h1>”);
              out.println(msg);
              out.println(“</body>”);
              out.println(“</html>”);
          } finally {
```

```
            out.close();
        }
    }

    /* From the login form, check user credentials and log him in.
       Open the session, Initialize the user object and attach the
       user object to the session and
       redirect the response to LoggedIn.JSP , if login is successful.
       Otherwise, redirect to the home page (Login.jsp)
    */
     @Override
     protected void doGet(HttpServletRequest request,
     HttpServletResponse response)
     throws ServletException, IOException {
         HttpSession sess;
         String uname, pwd;
         int numOfFavs;
         String msg = "<br></br>";
         try {
             //Get parameters from the login form
             uname = request.getParameter("username");
             pwd = request.getParameter("password");
            //Make ready the object meant for storing user information
             UserInfo usr = new UserInfo();
             usr.setLogname(uname);
             usr.setPassword(pwd);
             //Check the login process in UserInfo class definition.
              //It returns the status of the login in the state variable
              //of the class
             usr.tryLoggingIn();

             if (usr.getState()) {   //If successfully logged in
                 sess = request.getSession(true); //Create a session
                 in any case
                     //Set a timeout suitably to test the valueUn
                     //bound listener interface.
                     //The interface is implemented
```

(Continued)

```
                        //as part of the Favourites class so it is defined
                        //in that class definition
                    sess.setMaxInactiveInterval(60*1);
                    msg += uname + " Successfully logged in";
                    //Get the number of Favorites for this user object
                    numOfFavs = usr.getNumFavourites();
                    usr.setNum(numOfFavs);

                    //Attach the User object to the session
                    sess.setAttribute("user", usr);
                    response.sendRedirect(response.encodeRedirectURL("LoggedIn.jsp"));
                } else {    //i.e. if login was unsuccessful
                    response.sendRedirect(response.encodeRedirectURL("Login.jsp"));
                }
            }
            catch (Throwable theException) {
                System.out.println(theException);
            }
        }

        @Override
        protectedvoiddoPost(HttpServletRequest request, HttpServletResponse response)
        throws ServletException, IOException {
            String msg="";
            processRequest(msg, request, response);
        }

        @Override
        public String getServletInfo() {
            return "Short description";
        }
    }
```

Fig. 5.49 *LoginServlet*

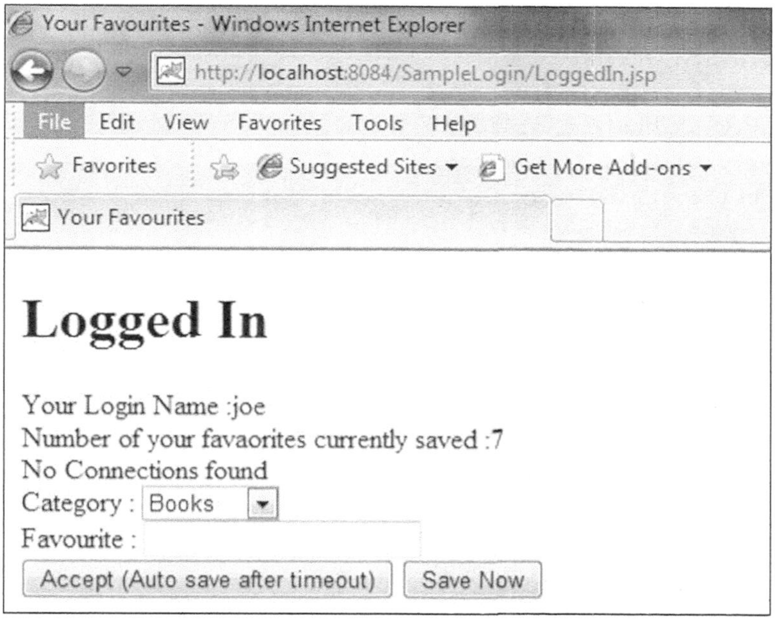

Fig. 5.50 *Displays the result and accepts new items*

5.9.3.4 Database access It is worth mentioning an important aspect of server-side programming—the means to access database data for reading and writing. The details are included in a later section titled Database Connection manager, in this chapter.

5.9.3.5 User information The user information class is structured as follows: essentially, the Favourites class structures the data into category and an item. The Matching method handles the process of finding users with similar interests. Though this process is simplified to make this example brief, it can be made to search with greater vigor and intelligence (Figure 5.51).

```
package com.login;

import java.sql.Connection;
import java.sql.ResultSet;
import java.sql.Statement;
import java.util.ArrayList;

public class UserInfo {
    private String logname;
```

(Continued)

```
    private String password;
    private String name;
    private int numFavs;
    private boolean state;
    private ArrayList match;
    public String msg;

    private Connection DBConnection;
    ResultSet rs;

    public UserInfo() {

    }
    public UserInfo(String lname, String pwd) {
        this.logname = lname;
        this.password = pwd;
    }
    public String getName() {
        return (name);
    }
    public void setNum(int n) {
        this.numFavs = n;
    }
    public int getNum() {
        return this.numFavs;
    }
    public void setName (String s) {
        name = s;
    }
    public String getPassword() {
        return (password);
    }
    public void setPassword(String s) {
        password = s;
    }
    public String getLogname() {
        return (logname);
    }
```

```
        public void setLogname(String s) {
            logname = s;
        }
        public boolean getState() {
            return (state);
        }
        public void setState(boolean st) {
            state = st;
        }
        public void setMsg(String s) {
            msg = s;
        }
        public void setMatch(ArrayList a) {
            this.match = a;
        }
        public ArrayList getMatch() {
            return this.match;
        }

        public void tryLoggingIn() {
            Statement st = null;
            int numOfFavs=0;
            String msg="";

            if (this.logname == null) {
                return;
            }
            String qry = "SELECT * FROM users WHERE username='" + this.
            logname + "'" +
          " AND password='" + this.password + "'";
            try {
                DBConnection = ConnMgr.getConnection();
                st = (Statement) DBConnection.createStatement();
                this.rs = st.executeQuery(qry);
                boolean more = this.rs.next();
                if (!more) {
                    this.setState(false);
                    //msg = "";
```

(*Continued*)

```
            }
            else {
                String email = this.rs.getString(“email”);
                String passwd = this.rs.getString(“password”);
                this.setName(email);
                this.setState(true);
                //numOfFavs = this.getNumFavourites();
                //this.setNum(numOfFavs);
            }
            return;
        }
        catch (Exception e) {
            System.out.println(“Login failed ” + e);
        }
        finally {
            if (this.rs != null) {
                try { this.rs.close(); }
                catch (Exception e) { this.rs = null; }
            }
            if (st != null) {
                try { st.close(); }
                catch(Exception e) {st = null;}
            }
            if (DBConnection != null) {
                try { DBConnection.close(); }
                catch(Exception e) {}
            }
        }
    }
    public int getNumFavourites() {
        int num = 0;
        Statement st = null;
        boolean more;

        String qry = “SELECT COUNT(*) AS cnt FROM Favourites WHERE owner=’” + this.logname + “’”;
        try {
            DBConnection = ConnMgr.getConnection();
            st = (Statement) this.DBConnection.createStatement();
```

```
            rs = st.executeQuery(qry);
            more = rs.next();
            if (!more) {
                num = 0;
            }
            else {
                num = rs.getInt("cnt");
            }
            return(num);
        }
        catch (Exception e) {
            return (-1);
        } finally {
            if (this.rs != null) {
                try { this.rs.close(); }
                catch (Exception e) { this.rs = null; }
            }
            if (st != null) {
                try { st.close(); }
                catch(Exception e) {st = null;}
            }
            if (DBConnection != null) {
                try { DBConnection.close(); }
                catch(Exception e) {}
            }
        }
    }
}
```

Fig. 5.51 *UserInfo.java*

An implementation of the *Favorites* class is shown in Figure 5.52.

```
package com.login;

import java.sql.Connection;
import java.sql.ResultSet;
```

(Continued)

```
import java.sql.SQLException;
import java.sql.Statement;
import java.util.ArrayList;
import javax.servlet.http.HttpSessionBindingEvent;
import javax.servlet.http.HttpSessionBindingListener;
import javax.servlet.http.HttpSessionEvent;
import javax.servlet.http.HttpSessionListener;

/*
 * Class to store all the aspects pertaining to an user's favou-
   rites, organized by category.
*/
public class Favourites implements HttpSessionListener,
    HttpSessionBindingListener {
    private String category;
    private String favItem;
      private String owner;
      private String status;

      private Connection DBConnection;
      ResultSet rs;

      public Favourites(String c, String f) {
          this.category = c;
          this.favItem = f;
      }
      public void setCategory(String s) {
          this.category = s;
      }
      public String getCategory() {
          return this.category;
      }
      public String getFavItem() {
          return this.favItem;
      }
      public String getUserName() {
          //fetch owner, then retrieve record from users table
          //where owner is known
          return "Under Dev - Name";
```

```
    }

    public String getOwner() {
        return this.owner;
    }
    public String getStatus() {
        return this.status;
    }
    public void setStatus(String s) {
        this.status = s;
    }
    public void setOwner(String s) {
        this.owner = s;
    }
    /* Method to persist the item in the Database. An item is
       saved if there is no duplicate
       for the same item and
      category for the user (owner). The item is associated
      with an owner.
  */
    public Boolean saveFav() {
        Statement st=null;
        int n;

        String cat = this.getCategory();
        String owner = this.getOwner();
        String favitem = this.getFavItem();
        String status = this.getStatus();

        String qry = "INSERT INTO Favourites (item, category,
        owner, status)
        VALUES ("
                + "'" + favitem + "',"
                + "'" + cat + "',"
                + "'" + owner + "',"
                + "'" + status + "'"
                + ")";
        try {
            DBConnection = ConnMgr.getConnection();
```

(*Continued*)

```
                String qry2 = “SELECT ITEM FROM Favourites WHERE CATEGORY = ‘” + cat
                + “‘AND ITEM=’” + favitem + “‘ AND OWNER=’” + owner + “’”;
                st = (Statement) DBConnection.createStatement();
                rs = st.executeQuery(qry2);
                if (rs.next()) {
                    this.setStatus(“EXISTS”);
                    return false;
                }
                n = st.executeUpdate(qry);
                if (n > 0) {
                    this.setStatus(“SAVED”);
                    return true;
                } else {
                    return false;
                }
            } catch (SQLException e) {
                //log.error(e);
                return false;
            } finally {
                try {
                    st.close();
                    DBConnection.close();
                    return true;
                } catch (Exception e) {
                    return false;
                }
            }
        }
        /*
         * Finds other owners (users) who have the same category and item of interest
         * Return an array of strings refering the owner (user). For simplicity each array item
         * is a string rather than a user object. Other information about the user like his contact number, etc
         * can be likewise returned (if objects are used)
        */
        public ArrayList findMatch() {
            int num = 0;
```

```
            Statement st = null;
            boolean more;
            ArrayList match = new ArrayList();
            //Very simple match! It is encouraged to make this
            //robust and more intelligent.
            String qry = “SELECT DISTINCT owner FROM Favourites
            WHERE owner <> ‘” +
            this.owner + “’” +
               “ AND category = ‘” + this.getCategory() + “’” +
                “ AND item LIKE ‘” + this.getFavItem() + “’”;
            try {
                DBConnection = ConnMgr.getConnection();
                st = (Statement) this.DBConnection
                .createStatement();
                rs = st.executeQuery(qry);
                more = rs.next();
                if (more) {
                    while(more) {
                        match.add(rs.getString(“owner”));
                        num++;
                        rs.next();
                    }
                }
            } catch (Exception e) {
            } finally {
                if (this.rs != null) {
                    try { this.rs.close(); }
                    catch (Exception e) { this.rs = null; }
                }
                if (st != null) {
                    try { st.close(); }
                    catch(Exception e) {st = null;}
                }
                if (DBConnection != null) {
                    try { DBConnection.close(); }
                    catch(Exception e) {}
                }
            }
```

(Continued)

```
            return (match);
        }
        public void sessionCreated(HttpSessionEvent e) {

        }
        public void sessionDestroyed (HttpSessionEvent e) {

        }
        public void valueBound (HttpSessionBindingEvent e) {
            //System.out.println("Session attribute Bound: [" +
            //e.getName() + "] value [" + e.getValue() + "]");
        }

         /* An attribute gets off the session when the session
            terminates or the attribute is taken out
            by the program. In this case, it is used to save the
            object if the status is seen as AUTO.
            It is not required to save an already saved item.
    */

        public void valueUnbound (HttpSessionBindingEvent e) {
            if (this.getStatus().equals("AUTO")) {
                this.saveFav();
            }

        }
    }
```

Fig. 5.52 *Favourites class (model)*

There are two ways of transferring control from a Servlet to a JSP or for that matter another Servlet. They are the *Forward* method and *Redirect* method. The *Forward* is through the *RequestDispatcher* object.

```
RequestDispatcher rd = request.getRequestDispatcher("/LoggedIn.jsp");
rd.forward(request, response);
```

The forward (in the above example the transfer is to Loggedin.JSP) is effected internally with the *Request* and *Response* object intact. What this implies is that the client does not know of this transfer of control. Any attributes set in the Servlet code is made available in the forwarded module (through the getAttribute method).

Another form of transferring control is through the Redirect method is through the response object.

Aside note

> The include method of dispatcher object includes the output of the (included) servlet. This is different from forward method where the contoil is transferred to the (forwarded) servlet. The forwarded or included object can be a servlet or JSP.

```
Response.sendRedirect("/LoggedIn.jsp");
```

Here again the control of transferred to the destination, but this time it is through the URL. The client is aware of the redirect (which could have implications on back buttons), in fact the client builds a new request and sends it to the server. The client's history will be correspondingly updated.

```
package com.login;
import java.io.IOException;
import java.io.PrintWriter;
import java.util.ArrayList;
import javax.servlet.RequestDispatcher;
import javax.servlet.ServletException;
import javax.servlet.http.HttpServlet;
import javax.servlet.http.HttpServletRequest;
import javax.servlet.http.HttpServletResponse;
import javax.servlet.http.HttpSession;

public class AcceptFavourites extends HttpServlet {
    protected void processRequest(String msg, HttpServletRequest
    request, HttpServletResponse response)
    throws ServletException, IOException {
        response.setContentType("text/html;charset=UTF-8");
        PrintWriter out = response.getWriter();
        try {
            out.println("<html>");
            out.println("<head>");
            out.println("<title>Servlet Accept Favourites</title>");
            out.println("</head>");
            out.println("<body>");
            out.println("<h1>Servlet LoginServlet at " + request.get-
            ContextPath () + "</h1>");
            out.println(msg);
            out.println("</body>");
            out.println("</html>");
        } finally {
            out.close();
        }
    }

    @Override
```

(*Continued*)

```
protected void doGet(HttpServletRequest request, HttpServletResponse
response)
throws ServletException, IOException {
    String msg="";
    processRequest(msg, request, response);
}

@Override
protectedvoiddoPost(HttpServletRequest request, HttpServletResponse
response)
throws ServletException, IOException {
    String msg = "<br />";
    String info, owner;
    String[] cats;
    String nl="<br />";
    HttpSession sess;
    UserInfo usr;
    Favourites fav;
    String opt;
    boolean bflag = true;
    ArrayList match = null;

    opt = request.getParameter("clicker");

    cats = request.getParameterValues("category");
    info = request.getParameter("info");

    sess = request.getSession(false);
    if (sess == null) {
        msg += "No active session";
        bflag = false;
    } else {
        usr = (UserInfo) sess.getAttribute("user");
        if (usr == null) {
            response.sendRedirect(response.encodeRedirectURL("Login.
            jsp"));
        }
        owner = usr.getLogname();

        fav = new Favourites(cats[0], info);
        fav.setOwner(owner);

        sess.setAttribute("FAV", fav);

      if (opt.equalsIgnoreCase("save now")) { //Save button clicked
            fav.setStatus("SAVE");
            if (fav.saveFav()) {
                usr.setNum(usr.getNumFavourites());
                match = fav.findMatch();
                if (!match.isEmpty()) {
```

```
                    msg += "User[s] with similar interest (" +
                    cats[0] + "/" + info + ") " + "as yours :";
                    for (int i = 0; i < match.size(); i++) {
                        msg += "<b>" + match.get(i) + "</b>/";
                    }
                }
            } else {
                fav.setStatus("NOT SAVED");
                msg += "NOT SAVED" + nl;
            }
        } else {
         fav.setStatus("AUTO");  //to be saved when session expires
                                 //and if it lasts until then
            msg += "Set for AUTO - will be saved after session
            expires if it lasts until then";
        }
        usr.setMsg(msg);
        usr.setMatch(match);
        request.setAttribute("msg", msg);
        request.setAttribute("item", info);
        request.setAttribute("category", cats[0]);
    }
    if (bflag) {
        RequestDispatcher rd = request.getRequestDispatcher("/
        LoggedIn.jsp");                   //RD can also be invoked
                                          // from getServletContext()
        rd.forward(request, response);
    } else {
        request.setAttribute("msg", "Session timed out. Please
        login again");
        RequestDispatcher rd = request.getRequestDispatcher("/
        Login.jsp");
        rd.forward(request, response);
    }
}

@Override
public String getServletInfo() {
    return "Short description";
}
}
```

Fig. 5.53 *AcceptFavourites.java*

The logged in JSP displays a logged in page and a form to collect the favorites' information. There are clickable buttons for saving the information into the database or just accepting the information. The choice of categories is hard coded for simplifying the code, but a better way is to extract it from a file (Figure 5.53 and 5.54).

Fig. 5.54 *Displays the result along with* matched *items*

```
<%@page contentType="text/html" pageEncoding="UTF-8"%>
<!DOCTYPE HTML PUBLIC "-//W3C//DTD HTML 4.01 Transitional//EN"
"http://www.w3.org/TR/html4/loose.dtd">
<html>
<head>
<meta http-equiv="Content-Type" content="text/html; charset=UTF-8">
<title>Your Favourites</title>
<%@page  import="java.util.ArrayList" %>
</head>
<body>
     <h1>Logged In</h1>
        <jsp:scriptlet>
            HttpSession mySess = request.getSession(false);
            com.login.UserInfo  usr  =  (com.login.UserInfo)  mySess.
            getAttribute("user");
        </jsp:scriptlet>
         Your Login Name :<%= usr.getLogname() %> <br />
         Number of your favaorites currently saved :<%= usr.getNum()
         %> <br />
         <% if (usr.msg != null) { %> <%= usr.msg %> <%}%> <br />

         <form method="POST" action=<%=response.encodeURL("AcceptFavo
         urites")%>>
```

```
            Category :
             <select name="category" size="1">
               <option value="BOOK"> Books </option>
               <option value="CARTOON"> Cartoons </option>
               <option value="LEADER"> Leaders </option>
             </select>
             <br />
            Favourite : <input type="text" name="info" > </input>
             <br />
             <input  type="submit"  name="clicker"  value="Accept  (Auto
             save after timeout)" />
             <input type="submit" name="clicker" value="Save Now" >
         </form>
</body>
</html>
```

Fig. 5.55 *LoggedIn.jsp*

5.9.3.6 Database connection manager It is assumed that the reader is familiar with databases. If not, it is recommended to get equipped with a reasonable knowledge of any relational database like MS-SQL Server, Oracle or MySQL. There is probably no dynamic website that does not use a database. SQL is used to handle the database through JDBC.

5.9.3.6.1 Connection Object

To submit an SQL statement to a database, first there has to be a connection made to the specific database. An object called the *connection object* is created. Among the various methods, the *getConnection* method is popular.

The DB connection is handled by the Connection Manager using JDBC. It stands for Java DB Connectivity, and is the industry standard for connecting Java with any relational based structure (which includes RDBMS and Spreadsheets or Flat files). It is implemented as a SQL Level API that enables executing SQL scripts and retrieves the results. JDBC itself consists of a number of interfaces. This is shown in the Figure 5.56.

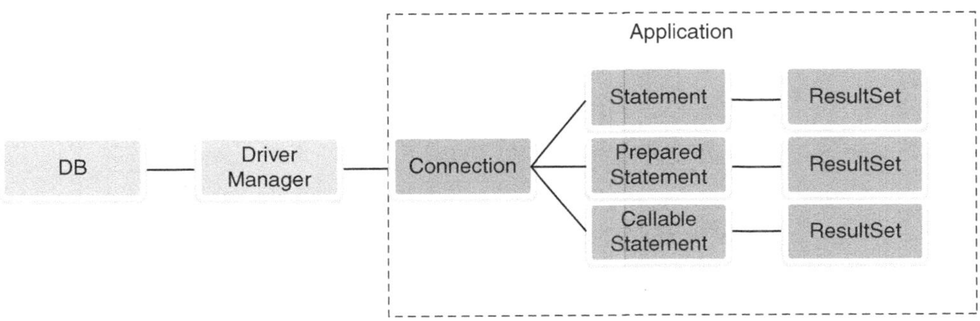

Fig. 5.56 *JDBC API structure*

The JDBC API set of interfaces, structured as shown in the Figure 5.56 is found in the package, java.sql. This package also includes implementations from 3rd party vendors like Oracle, mySQL, etc.

Take a look at the Connection manager code (Figure 5.57). The first step is to load the specific driver (line 14—mysql driver) in memory. It registers the DriverManager class with the specified database driver. It is then used to open a database connection (line 16).

```
1.   package com.login;
2.
3.   import java.sql.Connection;
4.   import java.sql.DriverManager;
5.   import java.sql.SQLException;
6.
7.   public class ConnMgr {
8.       static Connection conn;
9.       static String url;
10.
11.      public static Connection getConnection() {
12.          try {
13.              String url = "jdbc:mysql://localhost:3306/myDB";
14.              Class.forName("com.mysql.jdbc.Driver");
15.              try {
16.                  conn = DriverManager.getConnection(url, "root",
                     "root");
17.              }
18.              catch (SQLException e) {
19.                  e.printStackTrace();
20.              }
21.          }
22.          catch (ClassNotFoundException e) {
23.              System.out.println(e);
24.          }
25.          return (conn);
26.      }
27.  }
```

Fig. 5.57 *Connection manager* (ConnMgr.*java*)

Connection is a static Java class. The connection is made specific to the environment. Change the URL and port number, as required, for the connection. To interact with the database, the returned Connection object is used. Refer Figure 5.52, which is the code for Favourites.java. It is the model (MVC model) implementation of Favourites class. Thereafter, it is purely based on SQL.

Line 76 from Figure 5.52 shows the connection object that is obtained from the Connection Manager. The Connection Manager implementation is shown in Figure 5.58. To connect to a database, it is required to load the appropriate driver and then request for a connection object. The Class.forName (line 14) will load the driver and register it with the Driver Manager. Notice that the access to database (line 16) will require a username and a password, which are hard-coded in this example. This should ideally come through a configuration file and with the password encrypted.

Instead of using the Driver Manager to connect to a database, there is a more elegant way of getting a handle to the Database connection and that is using Data Source. It used JNDI to read into the application context. The advantage is better portability of the connection object.

5.9.3.6.2 Prepared Statements

A Prepared Statement enables pre-compilation of the query. THe SQL statement is parsed and kept for reuse, thereby improving performance albeit marginally. Parameters are supplied dynamically in place of "?" character(s) in the query. This is also a means to guard against SQL Injection attacks.

As an example, consider the following statement:

```
PreparedStatement  st  =  connectionObject.prepareStatement  ("SELECT
itemname FROM items WHERE id = ?");
```

Here the statement prepares the SQL Query. Before executing the query, the parameters should be supplied.

```
st.setString(1,"ABC001");
```

The setString accepts the parameters (1 for the first parameter), the value being BB001. Internally the query is translated as follows.

```
SELECT itemname FROM items WHERE id="ABC001";
```

The query is executed as in the following line of code.

```
ResultSet rs = st.executeQuery();
```

Aside note

There are various types of jdbc drivers as follows:

- Type 1: JDBC-ODBC Bridge driver (Bridge)
- Type 2: Native-API/partly Java driver (Native)
- Type 3: Java driver (Middleware)
- Type 4: Java/Native driver (Pure)

5.9.3.7 Data model used in the example A (SQL) Statement is created (line 78), which is then executed. The results are in the form of rows, which could return 0, 1 or multiple rows. Hence, it is iterated in a loop (Figure 5.52, lines 81–84) to access data.

The example database contains two tables that are of relevance. They are "users" and "favourites" as described in the screen shot in Figure 5.58. The database that is used for the example is mySQL.

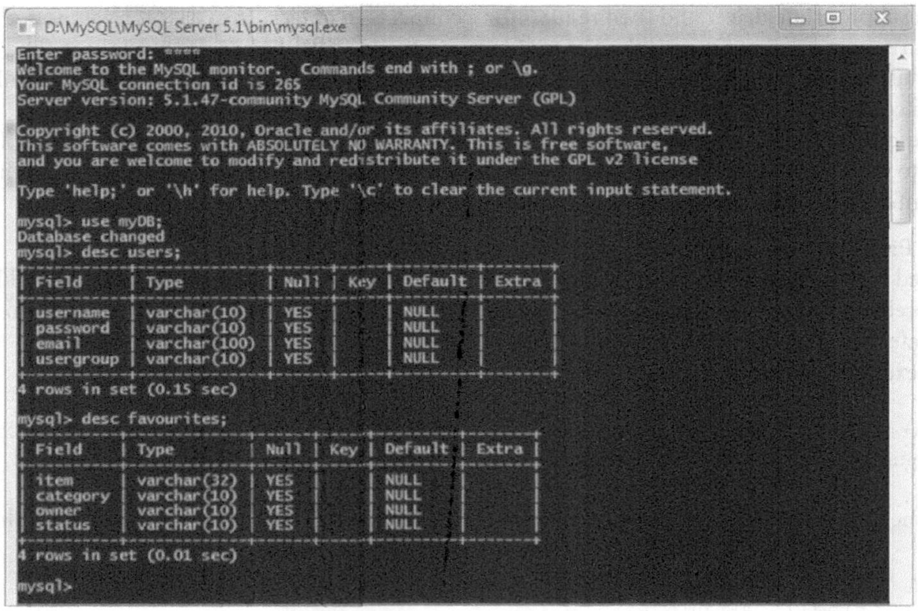

Fig. 5.58 *Table structures used in the example*

5.9.4 Attribute Scopes

Servlet is by default multi-threaded. Care has to be taken when the attributes are set (through setAttribute). Consequently, it is important to understand the nature of the scope in which they are set (and read). The scopes are handled by these methods:

- setAttribute(String, Object)
- getAttribute(String)
- removeAttribute(String)
- getAttributeNames()

There are three scopes that are normally encountered are as follows:

- Context through the servletContext interface
- Session through HttpSession interface
- Request through servletRequest interface

The Scopes differ in the accessibility governed by their respective lifecycles.

5.9.4.1 Context Everyone in the application has access to objects set in the application context. It can be defined during deployment (web.xml) or also set during the lifetime of the context. Since it operates over the life of the context, it will be destroyed when the server goes down or the application is shut down. Examples where it could be used are global application constants, or Database connection names, Common Email addresses, etc.

```
contx = getServletContext();
synchronized(contx) {
contx.setAttribute("REGION", "APAC");
}
```

These variables can be accessed in some other part of the program or in some other Servlet or JSP or even in listener contexts (through getAttribute).

Since the impact of context variables is global, care has to be taken to use it with caution. For instance if they are used to just set and get variables between Servlets, it is possible that these values could be altered by some other thread, satisfying some other request from the same or some other user.

5.9.4.2 Session attributes The usage has been seen in the example on FavConnect. The attributes share the same lifecycle as that of the session. It is specific to a particular user logged in, but if the same user opens up another window in the same client, then chances are that the session attribute variables could be garbled. Hence, care should be taken accordingly. A synchronized block on the session variable will be helpful.

5.9.4.3 Request A request pertains directly to a specific servlet request or to its listeners. Since the life of a request is short and specific to a particular request, it is thread-safe. No other possibility exists that could garble the attribute values set in a request. The example of getting the Form variables from a JSP (HTML) has been seen in the FavConnect example.

5.10 SUMMARY

We have seen the importance of server side in a typical dynamic web application. In the Java world, the concept of server side has been introduced through Servlet technology which has its own lifecyle, supported within the context of the Servlet container as part of an application server. Servlets can act as the Controller in an MVC application. We have also seen how they can react to events (listeners), work in a session and leverage Cookies within an application.

EXERCISES

Q1. Name some of the practical ways which *Init()* can be useful in the context of a Servlet.

Q2. Examine the differences between GenericServlet and HttpServlet.

Q3. What are the differences between Request attribute and Request parameter?

Q4. What are the ways to create a session?

Q5. Discuss the ways to transfer control from one Servlet to another.

Q6. There are three scopes in a Servlet-based application—Context, Session and Request. Describe the following aspects of each scope:

a. Accessibility
b. Life cycle
c. Example of Scenarios that are applicable
d. Garbage collection strategy

Q7. What are different ways of maintaining sessions through Servlet?

Q8. What are the ways in which cookies are useful in a server-side application? Explain with examples.

Q9. Create a HTML code along with a Servlet to display the list of the first *n* Factorial numbers. Accept the value of *n* from the user. Display the result as a bulleted list. Remember not to have large values of *n* as it is a memory-intensive operation. Implement a cut-off value of *n* while accepting values.

Q10. What are the precautions that need to be taken to make a Servlet thread-safe?

Q11. Why do you think the Single Thread Model of Servlet is not used and now deprecated?

Q12. If you want to trap an event (for writing a callback procedure)and if an attribute in a web application context has been added or removed, what is the listener interface that can be used?

Q13. If it is required to know how many concurrent users are there in an application, which is the type of listener interface that can be used?

Q14. Imagine that Servlets are deployed on multiple clusters. Enumerate some of the issues that the developer needs to take, to ensure that integrity of data is maintained.

Q15. Transferring control from one servlet to another (or to a JSP) is achieved by two different methods—`sendRedirect()` or `forward()`. What is the difference between these two methods?

Q16. A Servlet can be used as the Controller in an MVC model application. Write a Servlet filter that logs all accesses that it serviced. Include information on the visitor (IP, etc), URL, when request was received, where it was directed to and the time taken to respond.

Q17. Enumerate the steps to develop an Ajax operation.

Project Activities

Q18. There is a reference to SQL injection attacks in the section on Prepared Statements. Investigate the nature of this vulnerability and the measures that should be taken to prevent the attack. Prepare a report.

Q19. Research into the concept of transactions during database updates (Creates, Updates, Deletes—CUD). Come up with a code snippet for simplified transaction handling for a fund transfer scenario.

Q20. Refer to the Trip example (Figure 5.20). What are the steps to make this program into a usable application. Some clues towards adding new functionality are given below:

a. Login functionality with user profile: for example the user's contact details can be brought in automatically.
b. Combine client-side validation along with server-side validation in the input Form. Feel free to come up with your own formats for use.
c. Additional JSP file to display the Match results (you may have to probably wait until the next chapter on JSP!)
d. Try to rewrite the application so that it can be used through a mobile.

Caselet Activity

Q21. To continue the caselet from the previous chapters, now we are ready to work on the backend activities, vital to the functioning of the application. We can make it as complex as possible like for a fully functional eCommerce site/app. For experimental purposes, let us make it much simpler. Consider the following set of activities to continue with the development.

a. Create a broad set of Requirements

b. Design the data model , which is about determining the tables that are required and the relationships between them

c. Design a few backend processes:

   i. Accept a user registration form

   ii. Update items into the product list (catalog). Example items in the products catalog include Coffee mugs, Beans variety, T-shirts, etc.

d. Design a system to dynamically update contents of the website. How does a Content Management System fit in this scenario?

6

JSP

> *Chapter Objectives:*
> - ***Enable understanding of the View part of an application through JSP***
> - ***Understand the working of JSP***
> - ***Get a peek into JSP Standard Tag Library***
> - ***Go through examples involving JSP and Custom tag library***

It has been seen so far that Servlets provide the dynamism that is required for a web application. They are efficient to execute, powerful and can flexibly manipulate HTML. There are all the ingredients for a good server side environment. However, on skimming the surface, it can be observed that the code looks awful. There is too much of mixing or intertwining of presentation and business logic. Changing one of them to perhaps suit changing business needs, becomes a costly affair or at worst impossible. Furthermore, if the same business logic is reused across multiple places or if the same data is to be viewed in different ways, then code reuse becomes difficult.

6.1 A BETTER WAY

Rather than focusing on the data with presentation methods supplementing it, there should be a better way to present dynamic data. Imagine the inverse way—with presentation (view) as the focus and then the processing logic supplementing it (the view), rather than the other way round. This is the core approach to JSP. JSP standing for Java Server Pages, enables mixing of HTML code with content that is dynamically generated by server code, like Servlet. While Servlets have HTML-like syntax embedded within Java code, the JSP has java-like code embedded within HTML. By now the reader would have realized that embedding HTML within the server side, like in Servlets, forces the creation of creative stuff in the form of dynamic web pages onto the programmers. JSP changes all that.

6.2 WHY JSP?

If Servlets do their job well enough, what is the need for another piece of technology like JSP? How is it warranted? Let's examine some aspects of the web application written with just Servlets, that is, without JSP.

- It is difficult to embed HTML code using print statements like writeln, within Servlets. Not only it is tedious to write, it is also difficult to debug.
- It is also difficult to change the business logic, should the business model change.
- Writing HTML in the above style also has a drawback that standard HTML tools that are normally available to the programmer as aids to productivity, will not be useful. These tools include the likes of an IDE, an HTML editor or the HTML Validator.
- If it is required to produce a different kind of output (presentation) for the same process logic, it is difficult to implement the same without violating the DRY principle. DRY in web programming context stands for Don't Repeat Yourself which promotes leaner code by reusing code within the application.
- Intertwining presentation logic and business logic within a program does not align with the concept of outsourcing. Presentation is best done by the UI expert while the business logic is best done by the developer.

One of the most critical factors that JSP enables is this: the process of creative UI design can be done by a separate set of people as the focus of JSP is HTML, which in turn implies that it is more for web UI (web designers and developers). JSP was thus the beginning of the pure MVC 2 model, facilitating separation of concerns between View and the rest of the Model/Controller. So typically the Servlet serves as the controller and the JSP as the View.

In effect the benefits of the JSP are that the language facilitates a UI designer to design HTML screens with dynamism built in through Java scriptlets, accessing the attributes that a Servlet makes them ready.

JSP has also given rise to a lot of extensions in the form of tag libraries (both standard and custom) and a lot of frameworks like Struts and Spring. It is interesting to note that this in turn has led to reuse of components. Thus a study of the basic form (which is JSP) will be most useful.

6.3 A BRIEF HISTORY AND BACKGROUND

Led by Oracle (Sun), the JSP has grown to be a standard, endorsed by industry leaders. It is a key component of the java EE. As of EE6, JSP 2.2 is in use, along with expression Language 2.2 and Standard Tag Library (STL) 1.2. It is closely tied to the Servlet (2.5) specifications since a JSP in internally transformed into a Servlet. It is recommended that the reader consult the latest specification of the mentioned technologies under Java EE.

6.4 OVERVIEW

A JSP file is written as HTML. It gets converted to a Servlet. The process (of conversion) is done entirely internally, so it does not matter to an end-user, but definitely is of interest to the developer.

A JSP page runs on a JSP container, just like a Servlet runs on a Servlet container. The Servlet container normally doubles up as a JSP container as well. For instance Tomcat is a Servlet/JSP container.

When a JSP page is requested by the user, the container handles the action as follows.

- First time (by any user for the JSP page)
  - Translate: Automatically translate the JSP code (i.e. the file/page) into a Java class. As in a Servlet, this class implements the *javax.servlet.Servlet* interface. Finer details like the name of the (generated) class depend on the container (Tomcat, JBOSS, Apache, GlassFish, etc.) but the name is immaterial to the developer.
  - Compile: Assuming the translation is successful, the JSP container compiles the implementation class, and then proceeds with the normal Servlet lifecycle.
  - If the translation is unsuccessful, then it implies that the JSP page contains syntax errors and will need to be corrected. Logically, the sequence goes back to the Translate Step.
- For subsequent requests for the same JSP page, the JSP container checks if the JSP page has been modified since the last time it was translated. If so, the container (re)starts the Translate sequence to perform the above steps.

It follows that the first time a JSP Page is invoked, it does take a longer time than the subsequent requests because it involves translation and compilation. For Production environments, there are a few ways to solve this issue:

- Configure the application so that all JSP pages will be called (so that they will be translated and compiled) when the application starts, rather than wait for the first requests.
- Precompile the JSP pages and deploy them as servlets.

JSP comes with an API that comprises three packages. However, when working with JSP, you do not often work directly with this API. Instead, you will work with classes and interfaces in the Servlet API.

Aside note

JSP 2.2 specification can be downloaded from the oracle site through JSR 245. Just like any other spec document, it is lengthy, use it as a reference and glossary.

6.5 JSP LIFECYCLE

It is reiterated that a JSP is converted into a Servlet, so in many aspects they share similar life cycles (Figure 6.1).

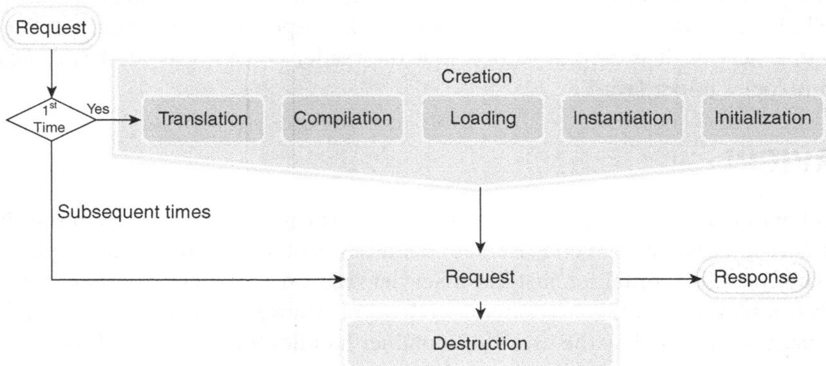

Fig. 6.1 *JSP lifecycle*

However, they share different names. The initialization corresponds to `jspInit();` Service corresponds to `jspService();` and the destruction to `jspDestroy()`. The JSP is translated into a Servlet and compiled the first time it is changed/created. Subsequently, it is ready for requests.

6.5.1 JSP Service Methods

As mentioned earlier, a JSP script is translated into Servlet code and then compiled into a Java Servlet class. The methods that a custom Servlet overrides are its Service methods. A JSP page body translates into Service methods of Servlet. However, in a Servlet we also have the *init* and *destroy* methods for writing initialization and cleaning up code. How do you override these methods in a JSP page?

In a JSP page you have two similar methods: jspInit. This method is similar to the init method in Servlet. jspInit is invoked when the JSP page is initialized. One difference is jspInit does

6.6 ELEMENTS IN A JSP PAGE

A JSP can be considered to be a higher level abstraction of a Servlet since JSP's are converted into Servlets. So, it follows that things that can be accomplished by a Servlet can also be done by JSP. However, JSP contains HTML and is fundamentally in the form of an HTML page – in fact it is referred to as a JSP page. A JSP page contains static elements and dynamic elements. The static elements form the HTML, WML (Wireless Markup Language) or XML and the dynamic elements in Java scriptlets. The JSP elements are in between the <% and %> tags. The following are the tags that are used.

6.6.1 Declarations

JSP Declarations are used to declare members of the (servlet) class. This applies to methods as well as variables. It is declared in between the "<%!" tag and the end tag "%>" (without the quotes).

```
<%! String itemname = "None"; %>
```

This declaration will cause an instance variable of type String to be defined in the servlet class. Notice the semi colon at the end of the line – signifying that it is not an expression. Consider a different example – a code snippet as shown below.

```
<%!
          Public void jspInit() {
String AdminEmail = getServletconfig.getInitParameter("AdminEmail");
//code for overriding the method...
...
          }
%>
```

The above declaration snippet overrides the jspInit() method

6.6.2 Directives

Directives in the form of <%@page ... %> for importing classes and <%@ include ...%> for including a header file, etc. By default the include type is HTML but for others include a contentType attribute. A set of accepted content types include text, video, etc. A full listing of the types (and sub types) are found in http://www.iana.org/assignments/media-types/.

6.6.3 Scriptlets

Scriptlets in embedded within <% ... %> tags. These are used for retrieving attributes from the Session, Context or Request scopes.

6.6.4 Expressions

Expression embedded within <%= and %> tags. It is used to display the value outputted from the expression. These standards are followed throughout the web community, whatever be the programming environment.

6.6.5 Transfer Control

Transfer control to another web component as below

```
<jsp:forward page="homepage.jsp" >
          <jsp:param name="param1" value="value1" />
</jsp:forward>
```

6.7 IMPLICIT JSP OBJECTS

In a Servlet, there are objects available for the programmer but they have to be initialized specifically. For example, to get a session object, the HttpSession's getSession method is invoked in the Servlet. But in a JSP these objects are available by default. They help the content to be dynamic. The objects are named below. Their methods can be accessed directly using the respective objects.

Object	Description
application	This is the context object (javax.servlet.ServletContext). The context is commonly referred to as the application's environment in which the JSP executes.
Config	Initialization information for the page's Servlet. (javax.servlet.ServletConfig)
Exception	Used along with the error directive as in <%@ page errPage="file_name" %> This is available from an error page if it occurs
Out	The output stream (javax.servlet.jsp.JspWriter)
Page	JSP page's servlet processing the current request
pageContext	The context for the JSP page to manage the scoped attributes and tag handlers
Request	The Request object (ServletRequest)
Response	The Response object (ServletResponse)
Session	Session object (HttpSession) available in the request

The jspWriter object is similar to PrintWriter.

6.8 JSP OBJECT SCOPES

There are four levels of scope that determines the visibility of attributes bound to it. Any object's visibility can be controlled by putting them in the appropriate scope (Figure 6.2).

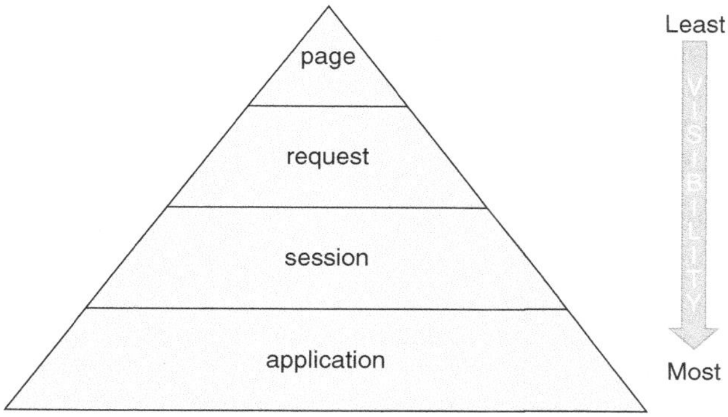

Fig. 6.2 *JSP scopes*

6.9 FAVCONNECT EXAMPLE MODIFIED

The example of FavConnect is shown in Figure 6.47 while discussing Servlets. The output was rather raw. Now let us consider a formatted output using JSP. The *LoggedIn.JSP* program can be modified to show the connections in a more palatable format as shown below. The code is just for showing the connections.

```
<%@page contentType="text/html" pageEncoding="UTF-8"%>
<!DOCTYPE HTML PUBLIC "-//W3C//DTD HTML 4.01 Transitional//EN"
"http://www.w3.org/TR/html4/loose.dtd">
<html>
<head>
  <meta http-equiv="Content-Type" content="text/html; charset=UTF-8">
  <title>Connect with your Favorites on the table!</title>
  <%@page  import="java.util.ArrayList" %>
</head>
<body>
  <h1>Logged In</h1>
  <jsp:scriptlet>
    HttpSession mySess = request.getSession(false);
    com.login.UserInfo  usr  =  (com.login.UserInfo)  mySess.getAttribute("user");
  </jsp:scriptlet>
    Your Login Name :<%= usr.getLogname() %> <br />
    Number of your favorites currently saved :<%= usr.getNum() %> <br />
    <%
    String msg = "";
    ArrayList match = usr.getMatch();
```

(*Continued*)

```
22.         if (match != null) {
23.           for (int i=0; i<match.size(); i++) {
24.           msg += “<b>” + match.get(i) + “</b>/”;
25.           }
26.         }
27.         %>
28.       <jsp:include page=“dispItems.jsp” />
29.         <form method=“POST”
              action=<%=response.encodeURL(“AcceptFavourites”)%>>
30.             Category :
31.             <select name=“category” size=“1”>
32.               <option value=“BOOK”> Books </option>
33.               <option value=“CARTOON”> Cartoons </option>
34.               <option value=“LEADER”> Leaders </option>
35.             </select>
36.             <br />
37.               Favorite : <input type=“text” name=“info” > </input>
38.             <br />
39.               <input type=“submit” name=“clicker”
                  value=“Accept (Auto save after timeout)” />
40.               <input type=“submit” name=“clicker” value=“Save Now” >
41.         </form>
42.       </body>
43.       </html>
```

Fig. 6.3 *LoggedIn.jsp*

It is to be observed that the JSP code shown in Figure 6.3 can be included by the statement as shown below.

```
<jsp:include page=“dispItems.jsp” />
```

This appears in line 28 of Figure 6.3. The output produced by the included code will be put in place at the location of the include directive. The include directive can also appear as in the following line.

```
<%@ include file=“dispItems.jsp” %>
```

Both formats are accepted, but the include directive (<%@...) is literally included pre-runtime, as opposed to the <jsp:include... happening at runtime, which implies that the response object is substituted at the given place.

The JSP code is given in Figure 6.4. This replaces the raw display that was output from the previous example. The dispItems.jsp takes care of handling the output in a better way by using a tabular display. The table, row and data elements (table, TR, TD) are responsible for formatting the output which is enclosed within <%= and %> tags.

The concept of include file in JSP can be extended to accommodate scenarios like providing a common header section, footer area, etc in a page.

```
<%@page contentType=“text/html” pageEncoding=“UTF-8”%>
<!DOCTYPE HTML PUBLIC “-//W3C//DTD HTML 4.01 Transitional//EN”
“http://www.w3.org/TR/html4/loose.dtd”>
<html>
<head>
  <meta http-equiv=“Content-Type” content=“text/html; charset=UTF-8”>
  <title>Match Results</title>

  <%@page  import=“java.util.ArrayList” %>
</head>
<body>
  <jsp:scriptlet>
    HttpSession mySess = request.getSession(false);
    com.login.UserInfo usr = (com.login.UserInfo) mySess.getAttribute(“user”);
  </jsp:scriptlet>
  <%
    String msg = “”;
    ArrayList match = usr.getMatch();
      if (match != null && !match.isEmpty()) { %>
        <h4>Match Connections</h4>
        <table id=“scart” border=“2” cellspacing=“2” cellpadding=“5”>
          <th> Category </th>
          <th> Item </th>
          <th> Connections </th>
          <%
          for (int i=0; i<match.size(); i++) { %>
          <tr>
            <td><%=(String) request.getAttribute(“category”)%></td>
            <td> <%= (String) request.getAttribute(“item”) %></td>
            <td>Check with :<%= match.get(i) %></td>
          </tr>
          <% } %>
        </table>
          <% } else { %>
          No Connections found
```

(*Continued*)

```
                    <% } %>
        </body>
        </html>
```

Fig. 6.4 *dispItems.jsp*

The modified output is displayed as below.

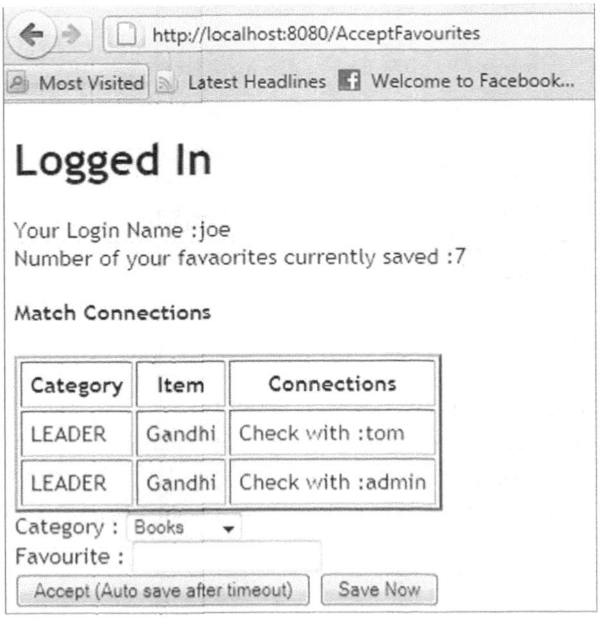

Fig. 6.5 *Displays the result along with matched items*

6.10 JSP TAGS

The reader can observe the syntax of JSP which is just like any other web framework like ruby on rails or ASP.NET. In short, barring Comments, the JSP syntax can be considered to fall into the following types:

- Declarations
- Directives
- Expressions
- Scriptlets
- Actions

Each of these types are differentiated in the representation by means of tags. The code, consisting of a line or a group of lines, is embedded within each pair of tags (just similar to any HTML). For example a comment is embedded between <%-- and --%>.

6.10.1 Declarations

Declarations are used to define variables, when the page is loaded. It internally declares them in the servlet class that is generated.

```
<%! String msg=null; %>
```

The above statement declares a variable, msg. It is to be noted that this is not the only way or place to declare a variable. It can also happen as part of scriptlets for instance.

Declarations can also be done for methods. For instance, overriding *jspInit()* can be achieved through declaration for a method.

6.10.2 Directives

A *Directive* is a means to pass on special instructions. A JSP page Directive provides information to the JSP Engine (in Servlet Container), about the page. There are three types of Directives – *Page*, *include* and *taglib*. Directives start with "<%@" sign.

- Page for defining attributes about the page like character encoding, content type, etc. They can be of the following
  - Import – used to import a class to the page.
    - <% @page import="java.util", "..." %>
  - Session – it is a Boolean value specifying if the page participates in a session or not. By default it is true.
    - <%@ page session="false" %>
  - Error Page – Exception handling for a JSP page can be separated into another JSP.
    - <%@ page errorPage="myJSPException.jsp" %>
    - Within the myJSPException.jsp file, there is a special (page) directive attribute (called isErrorPage) that can be set to true to indicate that the page is an error exception page rather than otherwise. By default it is false.
  - <%@ page isErrorPage="true" %>
    - An example of exception handling code is included in the this section below
  - Language – This attribute specifies the language used by the JSP page; it supports only the value of "java" which is also the default.
    - <%@ page language="java" %>
  - Extends – It is to be recalled that a JSP is actually translated to Servlet code. The Extends attribute specifies the super class of the generated Servlet.
  - Buffer – specifies the minimum buffer size that will be sent to the client when flushed
  - Auto flush – by default it is set true.

- Include directive defines a piece of common code that is added to a page
  - <jsp:include page="dispItems.jsp" />
- Taglib directive defines tag libraries that are available to the JSP. There are two types of tags – Standard tags and Custom tags. An example of a taglib is shown below.
  - <%@taglib uri="RandomTFD" prefix="tfd" %>

6.11 JSP EXCEPTIONS

Exceptions in JSP can be handled by a special page. There is an object called Exception which is set by the container (only on the JSP Exception page). The JSP Exception page is marked by a directive as shown below.

```
<%@page isErrorPage="true" %>
```

An example will make it clear. Consider a Form which accepts a PIN value as the password. The HTML is shown in Figure 6.6.

```
<%@page contentType="text/html" pageEncoding="UTF-8"%>
<!DOCTYPE HTML PUBLIC "-//W3C//DTD HTML 4.01 Transitional//EN"
"http://www.w3.org/TR/html4/loose.dtd">
<html>
<head>
  <meta http-equiv="Content-Type" content="text/html;
  charset=UTF-8">
  <title>JSP Page</title>
</head>
<body>
      <h2>PIN</h2>
        <!-- PIN is expected to be numeric so if the user types in non-
        numeric it can be made to throw an error.
        However, triggering the error is thru another JSP. -->
        <form action=<%=response.encodeURL("validateAndShow.jsp")%> >
          Username: <input type="text" name="username"/><br/>
          Numeric PIN: <input type="text" name="pin" /><br/>
          <input type="submit" value="submit" />
        </form>
</body>
</html>
```

Fig. 6.6 *A sample index.jsp with exception through JSP*

Index.jsp captures the form data and hands it over to *validateAndShow.jsp*. The code shown in Figure 6.7 is written in a way to experiment with invalid data. In this case a non-numeric data on the PIN field will wrest control on to the error file which takes care of throwing the exceptions. It is to be noted that, with the development of Ajax and other utilities, this is no longer the best way to trap errors, but just to show the Exception feature in JSP.

```
<%@page contentType="text/html" pageEncoding="UTF-8"%>
<!DOCTYPE HTML PUBLIC "-//W3C//DTD HTML 4.01 Transitional//EN"
"http://www.w3.org/TR/html4/loose.dtd">

<%@page errorPage="myJSPException.jsp" %>
<!-- Include the JSP Error handler above -->

<html>
<head>
  <meta http-equiv="Content-Type" content="text/html;
  charset=UTF-8">
<title>JSP Page</title>
</head>
<body>
  <h1>Display PIN</h1>
  User: <%= request.getParameter("username") %>
  <!-- Get the Form parameter by name. The PIN is expected to be
       numeric.
  An exception is thrown if it is otherwise, deliberately it is
  written such. -->
  <%
     int pin = Integer.parseInt(request.getParameter("pin"));
  %>
     PIN typed is <%= pin %>
</body>
</html>
```

Fig. 6.7 *ValidateAndShow.jsp—Sample exception through JSP*

The page displayed in Figure 6.8 is the exception handler for the *validate And Show page*. The error message is displayed in the object called "exception". Note that this is not the only way to handle exceptions. They can be trapped in the main page itself, but as a good practice it is beneficial to separate the job of handling exceptions.

```
<%@page contentType="text/html" pageEncoding="UTF-8"%>
<!DOCTYPE HTML PUBLIC "-//W3C//DTD HTML 4.01 Transitional//EN"
"http://www.w3.org/TR/html4/loose.dtd">
<%@page isErrorPage="true" %>
<!--The above line declares that this page is for exceptions. Control
will come to this page if there is an exception -->
```

(*Continued*)

```
<html>
<head>
    <meta http-equiv="Content-Type" content="text/html; charset=UTF-8">
    <title>JSP Error Page</title>
</head>
<body>
     <%-- Exception is available in the object appropriately called by
          the same name. The font control is
          just like any normal HTML - in this case the error message will
          be reported in red. --%>
     <font color="red">
          <%= exception.toString() %> <br>
     </font>
          <!-- Control passed back to the main form -->
          <form action=<%=response.encodeURL("index.jsp")%> >
              <input type="submit" value="Click" />
          </form>
</body>
</html>
```

Fig. 6.8 *myJSPException.JSP—Sample exception through JSP*

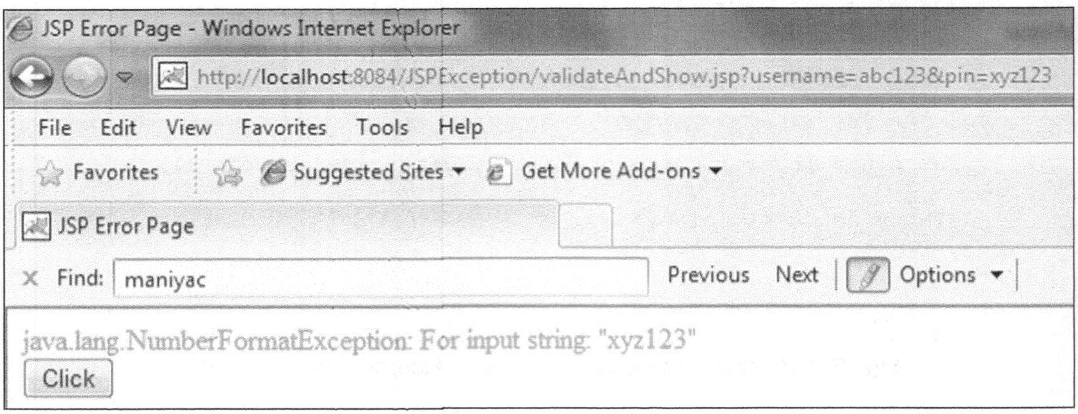

Fig. 6.9 *On exception for a PIN entered as xyz123*

The error message is displayed as shown in Figure 6.9.

6.11.1 Expressions

An expression is based on a java code snippet that displays a value in the page. The expression is embedded within <%= and %> tags. The equal-to sign included in the tag (<%=) represents the expression that implies displaying out. If the equal-to sign is omitted, it is not an error only it is not printed. In fact, it then becomes a Scriptlet.

```
<%= request.getParameter("username") %>
```

6.11.2 Scriptlet

Scriptlets are java code executed when the page is accessed. They are embedded within <% and %> tags of the JSP page.

```
<%
     String uname = request.getParameter("username");
     String msg = "this is a sample message";
%>
```

The scriptlet can span multiple lines or even a single line. Conditional or iterative loops can be included as part of this, perhaps mixed with expressions, taking care not to embed expressions within scriptlets. In case it is required to display certain intermediate variables in a scriptlet, it is a common practice to terminate the scriptlet (with a %> tag), include the expression and then resume the scriptlet (with a fresh <% … %> tag).

Though these features are included in the language, it is strongly recommended to maintain strict separation of concerns, conforming to the MVC architecture. In other words, care should be taken not to misuse the facility to include too much of business logic within the JSP fragments.

6.11.3 Actions

JSP actions are instructions to control the behaviour. Standard JSP actions include the following.

- *jsp:forward:* The request is forwarded to a different page.
- *jsp:include:* The response of the included page is embedded in the current response
- *jsp:param:* This is used to define parameters that are passed to the to the new JSP page, applicable when referenced through forward or include
- *jsp:useBean:* Defines the Java beans class that are referenced
- *jsp:setProperty*
- *jsp:getProperty*
- *jsp:plugin:* indicates that browser will execute applet or bean

They have attributes namely id, scope, type and class.

6.12 EXPRESSION LANGUAGE (EL)

JSP EL (Expression Language) was added to JSP 2.0 Specifications makes it easier to get values of variables, as opposed to complex scripting which would have been otherwise necessary. An example of EL is shown below, which gets the property of the emp object.

```
${emp.name}
```

EL looks like Java but they have lot of differences. In fact, EL can be used to access Java objects without little knowledge of Java. Its predominant usage is through implicit objects that are available. They are mentioned as follows:

- pageContext
- Standard Scopes

    - pageScope
    - requestScope
    - sessionScope
    - applicationScope
- param
- paramvalues
- header
- headerValues
- cookie
- initParam

6.13 JSP STANDARD TAG LIBRARY

JSP has five standard tag libraries. The core library is called by the same name, generally prefixed with a "c". Rest of the standard libraries are specialized in its own way.

Area	Subfunction	Prefix
Core	General	c
	Control	
	Navigation management	
	Iteration	
XML	Core	x
	Flow control	
	Transformation	
I18N	Locale	fmt
	Message formatting	
	Number and date formatting	
Database	SQL	sql
Functions	Collection length	fn
	String manipulation	

The Core library is organized as follows.

- General purpose scripting
    - Examples include c:out, c:set, c:catch
- Conditional/Control
    - Examples include c:if, c:choose, etc
- Iteration
    - Examples include c:forEach, c:forTokens.
- Navigation
    - Examples include c:url, c:redirect, c:import

6.14 A JSP EXAMPLE

There are various ways to fetch and set information through JSP. Let us consider an example which highlights various ways to retrieve information.

```
<%@page contentType=“text/html” pageEncoding=“UTF-8”%>
<!DOCTYPE HTML PUBLIC “-//W3C//DTD HTML 4.01 Transitional//EN”
“http://www.w3.org/TR/html4/loose.dtd”>

<html xmlns=“http://www.w3.org/1999/xhtml”>
<head>
  <meta http-equiv=“Content-Type” content=“text/html;
  charset=UTF-8” />
  <title>User Login</title>
</head>
<body>
   <h2>Login</h2>
     <form action=<%=response.encodeURL(“LoginServlet”)%>
     method=“POST” >
       Username: <input type=“text” name=“usrnm” />
       <input type=“hidden” name=“pwd” />
       <button type=“submit”>Get Me Details</button>
     </form>
</body>
</html>
```

Fig. 6.10 *UserBee - Index.jsp—Form to accept user name*

It accepts a user name for which to snoop into. The control passes on to LoginServlet (line-12). Let's take a look into that Servlet.

```
1.     protected void doPost(HttpServletRequest request,
       HttpServletResponse response)
2.          throws ServletException, IOException {
3.               HttpSession sess;
4.               response.setContentType(“text/html”);
5.               try {
6.                    UsrBean usr = new UsrBean();
7.                    String usrnm = request.getParameter(“usrnm”);
8.                    usr.setLogname(usrnm);
9.                    usr.setPassword(request.getParameter(“pwd”));
10.                   usr = UserDAO.login(usr);
11.
12.                   if (usr.getState()) {
13.                        sess = request.getSession(true);
14.                        sess.setAttribute(“currUser”, usr);
15.                        response.sendRedirect (“userLogged.jsp”);
16.                   } else {
17.                        response.sendRedirect(“index.jsp”);
18.                   }
19.
20.              }
21.              catch (Throwable theException) {
22.                   System.out.println(theException);
23.              }
24.         }
```

Fig. 6.11 *UserBee—doPost method of LoginServlet.java*

Only the doPost method is included in the code listing shown in Figure 6.11, since other methods are not used. Nothing unusual about the code listing except that there is a reference to a Java Class (line 6), which is a Java Bean class. A Java Bean is a plain java class conforming to some conventions or rules as listed as follows:

- The class should have a no-argument constructor. This is to facilitate the JSP to instantiate automatically.
- The class should have setter and getter methods for each instance variable.

Java Beans encourage reusability and component based design. The JavaBeans specification defines a bean as "*a reusable software component that can be manipulated visually in a builder tool*". Usually they are graphical UI elements like Swing or AWT components. As a corollary it implies that the Java Bean could also refer to something that exists as a third party component. In the example, a Java Bean is created and used internally. The bean class (UsrBean) is listed in Figure 6.12. The reader may note that Java Beans and Enterprise Java Beans (EJB) are completely different. A note on EJB is included in the next section.

```
package usrpkg;

public class UsrBean {
    private String logname;
    private String password;
    private String name;
    private String email;
    private int role;

    private boolean state;

    public String getName() {
        return (this.name);
    }
    public void setName (String s) {
        this.name = s;
    }
    public String getPassword() {
        return (this.password);
    }
    public void setPassword(String s) {
        this.password = s;
    }
    public String getLogname() {
        return (this.logname);
    }
    public void setLogname(String s) {
        this.logname = s;
    }
    public String getEmail() {
        return (this.email);
    }
```

(*Continued*)

```
    public void setEmail(String s) {
        this.email = s;
    }
    public int getRole() {
        return (this.role);
    }
    public void setRole(int i) {
        this.role = i;
    }

    public boolean getState() {
        return (state);
    }
    public void setState(boolean st) {
        state = st;
    }

}
```

Fig. 6.12 *UsrBee—UserDAO.java*

The getter and setter methods are defined. Observe the naming convention followed. Unlike in the example shown in Figure 6.51, this class does not have the Model (database) methods. The code shown here (Figure 6.12) keeps the class as simple as possible. However there should be model method defined somewhere as there is going to be some persistence (saving into a storage like a file system of most commonly a database). This is indeed in a separate class (UserDAO.java), shown in Figure 6.13, signifying the Data Access Object.

```
package usrpkg;

import java.sql.*;

public class UserDAO {
    static Connection conn = null;
    static ResultSet rs = null;
    public static UsrBean login(UsrBean b) {
        Statement st = null;
        String usr = b.getLogname();
        String pwd = b.getPassword();
```

```

            String qry = “SELECT * FROM users WHERE username=’” +
            usr + “’”;
            try {
                conn = ConnMgr.getMyConnection();
                st = (Statement) conn.createStatement();
                rs = st.executeQuery(qry);
                boolean more = rs.next();
                if (!more) {
                    b.setState(false);
                }
                else {
                    b.setName(rs.getString(“username”));
                    b.setEmail(rs.getString(“email”));
                    b.setRole(rs.getInt(“role”));
                    b.setPassword(rs.getString(“password”));
                    b.setState(true);
                }
            }
            catch (Exception e) {
                System.out.println(“Login failed” + e);
            }
            finally {
                if (rs != null) {
                    try { rs.close(); }
                    catch (Exception e) { rs = null; }
                }
                if (st != null) {
                    try { st.close(); }
                    catch(Exception e) {st = null;}
                }
                if (conn != null) {
                    try { conn.close(); }
                    catch(Exception e) {}
                }
            }
            return b;
        }
    }
```

Fig. 6.13 *UsrBee—userLogged.jsp*

The Connection Manager (Line 15 – ConnMgr object) is implemented exactly the same as in the Favourites example (Figure 6.58). It is not being repeated here.

From the objective of this demonstration example, the most important code listing follows in Figure 6.14. Contrary to its looks, the code is simple to understand. The same set of information is obtained in different ways.The output is available in a session context (Figure 6.11, line 14) on an attribute named currUser. This is all the JSP code need to know.

Since Java Beans wis also used as a means to display, the declaration (line 6) instantiates the object in the JSP's context.

```
1.  <%@page contentType=“text/html” pageEncoding=“UTF-8”%>
2.  <!DOCTYPE HTML PUBLIC “-//W3C//DTD HTML 4.01 Transitional//EN”
3.  “http://www.w3.org/TR/html4/loose.dtd”>
4.  <%@page contentType=“text/html” import=“usrpkg.UsrBean” %>
5.  <%@ taglib prefix=“c” uri=“http://java.sun.com/jsp/jstl/core”
    %>
6.  <jsp:useBean id=“currUser” class=“usrpkg.UsrBean” scope=
    “session” ></jsp:useBean>
7.  <html>
8.  <head>
9.  <meta http-equiv=“Content-Type” content=“text/html;
    charset=UTF-8”>
10. <title>JSP Info fetch</title>
11. </head>
12. <body>
13.     <h2>Same Information from different JSP sources</h2>
14.     <% String s = ((usrpkg.UsrBean)
           session.getAttribute(“currUser”)).getName(); %>
15.     <% String p = ((usrpkg.UsrBean)
           session.getAttribute(“currUser”)).getPassword(); %>
16.
17.     <blockquote>
18.         <h3>
19.             Using Scripting
20.         </h3>
21.         <% usrpkg.UsrBean b = (usrpkg.UsrBean) session.
              getAttribute(“currUser”); %>
22.           User name:  <%= b.getLogname() %> <br />
23.           Sh! Password: <%= b.getPassword() %> <br />
24.           Email: <%= b.getEmail() %> <br />
25.           Role : <%= b.getRole() %> <br />
```

```
          </blockquote>
        <blockquote>
          <h3>
             Using Java Bean actions
          </h3>
            User name: <jsp:getProperty name=“currUser”
            property=“logname”></jsp:getProperty>
            <br />
            Sh! Password: <jsp:getProperty name=“currUser”
            property=“password”></jsp:getProperty> <br />
            EMail: <jsp:getProperty name=“currUser”
            property=“email”></jsp:getProperty>
            <br />
            Role : <jsp:getProperty name=“currUser” property=“role”>
            </jsp:getProperty>
            <br />
            <br />
            </blockquote>

            <blockquote>
          <h3>
             Using JSP EL
          </h3>
            User Name: ${sessionScope.currUser.logname} <br />
            Sh! Password: ${sessionScope.currUser.password} <br />
            EMail: ${sessionScope.currUser.email} <br />
            Role : ${sessionScope.currUser.role} <br />
            <br />
          </blockquote>
            <blockquote>
            <h3>
               Using JSP Standard Tag Library
            </h3>
            User  Name:  <c:out  value=“${sessionScope.currUser.
            logname}” /> <br />
            Password:<c:outvalue=“${sessionScope.currUser.password}”
            default=“None”/>
            <br />
            EMail:  <c:out  value=“${sessionScope.currUser.email}”
            default=“No Email!” />
            <br />
            Role : <c:out value=“${sessionScope.currUser.role}” />
            <br />
```

(*Continued*)

```
                <br />
            </blockquote>
    </body>
    </html>
```

Fig. 6.14 *UsrBee—userLogged.jsp*

An indicative output is shown in Figure 6.15.

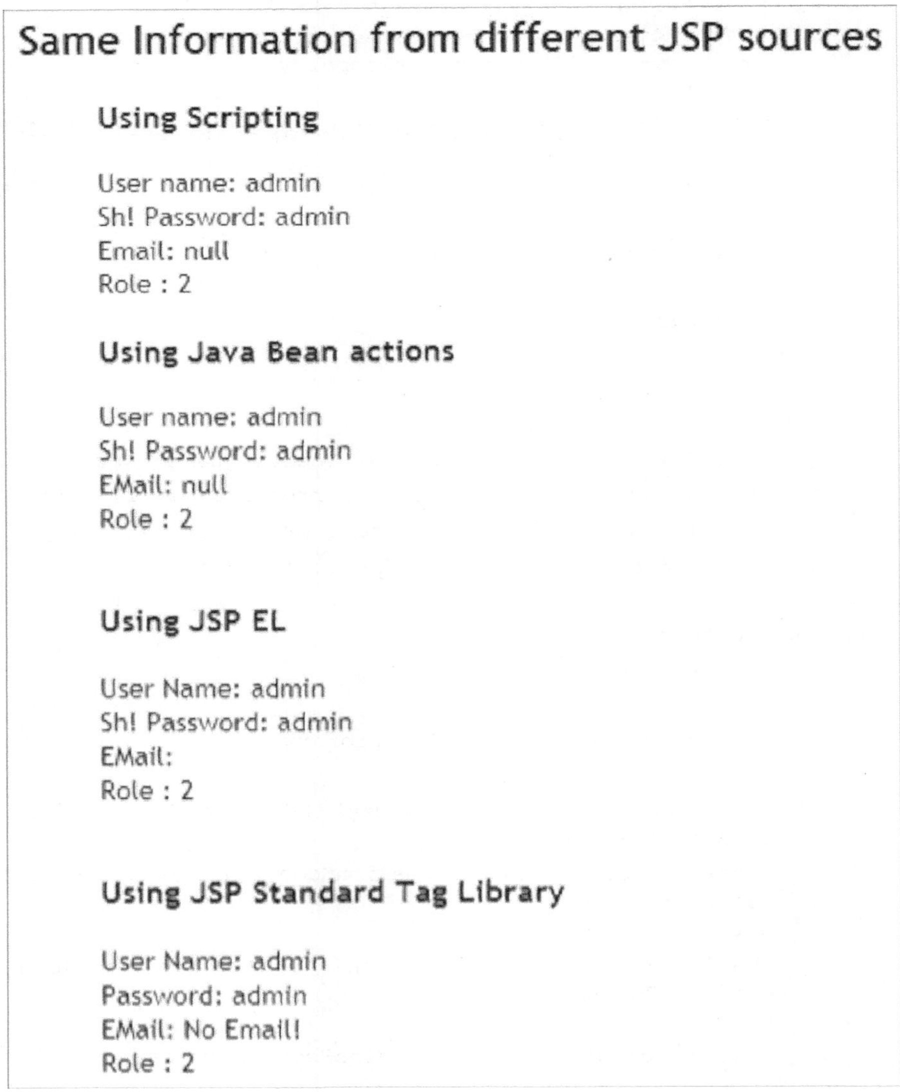

Fig. 6.15 *UserBee–Indicative output*

6.15 CUSTOM TAG LIBRARY

A tag in the context of JSP signifies a lot of abstraction – a piece of recurring function that works behind the scenes, an architecture that promotes separation of concerns. When standard tags may not suit every occasion, there are situations where this model is put to use for customized needs. This is where custom tag libraries are positioned.

Designers or Developers can create their tags to be used in JSP. Consider for instance a requirement where a randomized thought-for-the-day is to be shown.

```
1.  <%@page contentType=“text/html” pageEncoding=“UTF-8”%>
2.  <!DOCTYPE HTML PUBLIC “-//W3C//DTD HTML 4.01 Transitional//EN”
3.  “http://www.w3.org/TR/html4/loose.dtd”>
4.  <%@taglib uri=“RandomTFD” prefix=“tfd” %>
5.  <html>
6.  <head>
7.  <meta http-equiv=“Content-Type” content=“text/html;
    charset=UTF-8”>
8.  <title>TFD</title>
9.  </head>
10. <body>
11.    <h1>Thought For the Day</h1>
12.    <tfd:fetch category=“General” />
13.       General: <%= pageContext.getAttribute(“TFD”) %>
14.
15.     <tfd:fetch category=“Inspire” />
16.     <br />Inspire: <%= pageContext.getAttribute(“TFD”) %>
17. </body>
18. </html>
```

Fig. 6.16 *Index.jsp–TFD*

Figure 6.10 shows the main display page that will show the TFD (Thought for the day). Refreshing the page will show a different set of them. For the sake of demonstrating arguments to calls, the example considers two types of quotes belonging to ‘Inspire’ and ‘General’ categories.

Observe that the JSP is simple enough. That is the intent (for a tag library) – in making the presentation simple enough for a UI designer or someone who need not know the programming complexities of Java. The quotes (TFD) are displayed from lines 12 through 16 only. The tag library is declared in line 4. According to this definition, the URI representing the Java Class is RandomTFD.

There is a configuration file called a Tag Library Descriptor, an understanding of which is extremely vital. The file is listed in Figure 6.11.

```
<?xml version=“1.0” encoding=“UTF-8”?>
<taglib version=“2.1” xmlns=“http://java.sun.com/xml/ns/javaee” xmlns:xsi=“http://www.w3.org/2001/XMLSchema-instance” xsi:schemaLocation=“http://java.sun.com/xml/ns/javaee http://java.sun.com/xml/ns/javaee/web-jsptaglibrary_2_1.xsd”>
  <tlib-version>1.0</tlib-version>
  <short-name>fetch</short-name>
  <uri>RandomTFD</uri>

  <tag>
    <name>fetch</name>
    <tag-class>base.randomTFD</tag-class>
    <body-content>empty</body-content>
    <attribute>
        <name>category</name>
        <required>true</required>
        <rtexprvalue></rtexprvalue>
    </attribute>
  </tag>
</taglib>
```

Fig. 6.17 *fetch.tld*

The TLD is an XML file (with ".tld" extension), which contains information about the library and each tag in the library. A pictorial representation is shown in Figure 6.12.

Note the relationship between the TLD and the JSP file and how they connect with each other.

There are 3 different units that comprise a custom tag library. They are summarized as follows:

- JSP File
  - imports tag library (URL),
- Define tag prefix to use tag
- TLD – Tag Library Descriptor
  - XML specifying tag name, attributes, tag handler class
  - Under WEB-INF
- Tag handler class
  - A Java Class
  - Overriding doTag() extending the SimpleTag interface specifying output

We have seen the example on JSP and TLD files. The Tag handler implementation follows next. See Figure 6.13.

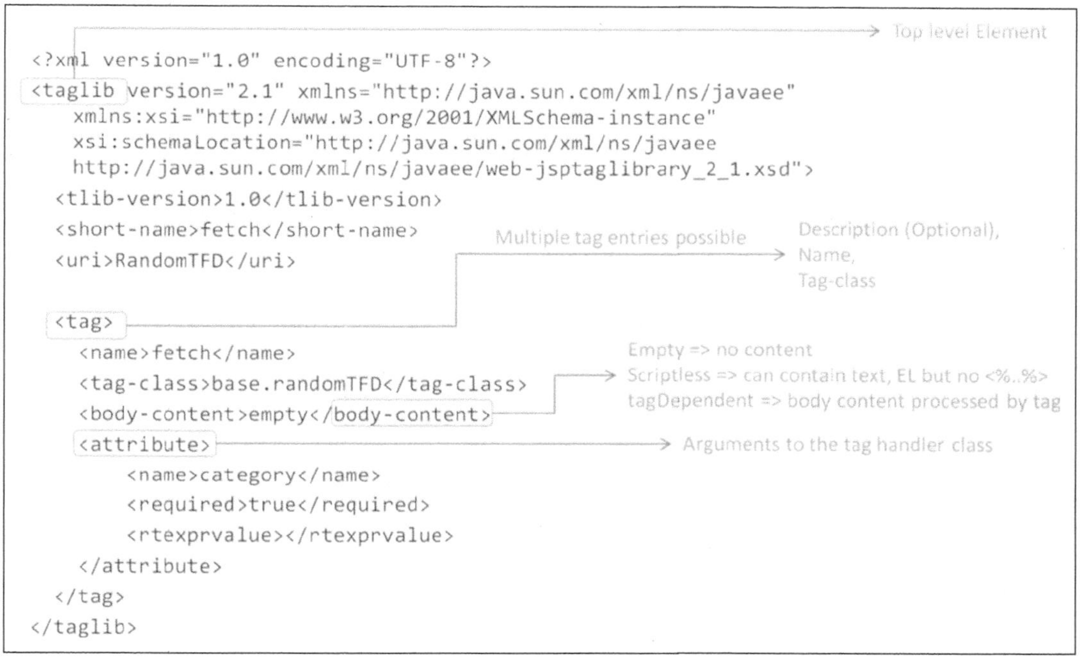

Fig. 6.18 *TLD description*

```java
package base;
/*Demonstrate use of a Custom tag library
  Refer the JSP code as well as the tag library descriptor (TLD).
  Code outputs a random Thought for the Day as String.
  The TFD is in 2 categories (General and Inspirational) to
  demonstrate use of parameter in JSP
 */
import javax.servlet.jsp.JspException;
import javax.servlet.jsp.tagext.SimpleTagSupport;
import java.util.Random;
import javax.servlet.jsp.PageContext;

public class randomTFD extends SimpleTagSupport {
    String Category;
    /* Store data in internal memory instead of in DB (for simplicity) */
    static String[] TFD_General = {
                                   "An apple a day keeps the doctor away",
```

(*Continued*)

```
                                  "Be good, see good, do good",
                                  "Start early, finish the game",
                                  "Love all Serve all",
                                  "Lead kindly light"};
        static String[] TFD_Inspire = {
                              "Allow Your Own Inner Light to Guide You",
                              "Be strong enough to at least try",
                              "Feel the calmness on a quiet sunny day",
                               "Say hello to strangers and enjoy the people
    you know"};
        @Override
        public void doTag() throws JspException {

            PageContext pc = (PageContext) getJspContext();
            if (Category.equals("General")) {
                int r = new Random().nextInt(TFD_General.length);
                pc.setAttribute("TFD", TFD_General[r]);
            } else {
                if (Category.equalsIgnoreCase("Inspire")) {
                    int r = new Random().nextInt(TFD_Inspire.length);
                    pc.setAttribute("TFD", TFD_Inspire[r]);
                } else {
                 pc.setAttribute("TFD", "Ask for General or Inspire");
                }
            }
        }
        //parameters to the function!
        public void setCategory (String s){
            this.Category = s;
        }
}
```

Fig. 6.19 *RandomTFD.java*

6.16 JSP AND EQUIVALENT TECHNOLOGIES

There are a number of technologies that come under the umbrella of the web. However, to bring a practical learning effort to fruition, there has to be a focus on one specific technology set. Accordingly, this book focuses on learning the fundamentals of web technologies in Java environment. The decision stems from (Java and related frameworks) being available on Open Source as well as being the most popular and comprehensive among web development environments today. Microsoft.NET offers an equivalent set of technologies for web development and they are equally powerful. It does not do justice to cover both these technologies in one single book within one academic session.

Aside note

Take a guess at the number of users and developers of Java. It is interesting to take a look at the timeline of Java. Refer the website at http://oracle.com.edgesuite.net/timeline/java.

As a web architect, it is advisable to get exposure or even work on multiple environments because ultimately it is a business solution that is being sought – not a technology solution. These environments are only instruments to achieve the goal. So, readers are encouraged to take on multiple skills and be agnostic about technology, when they arrive at a solution. In this context, it is relevant to mention about other programming environments similar to JSP that are available. For instance in the Microsoft environment, ASP was the language that was introduced much earlier, now referred to as "classic ASP". ASP stands for Active Server Pages and the files created for ASP have the same extension. ASP files contain Jscript code and VBScript which are understood by the server (typically IIS – Internet Information Server) to generate dynamic web pages. So conceptually they are similar to JSP, but on an implementation level, they are totally different.

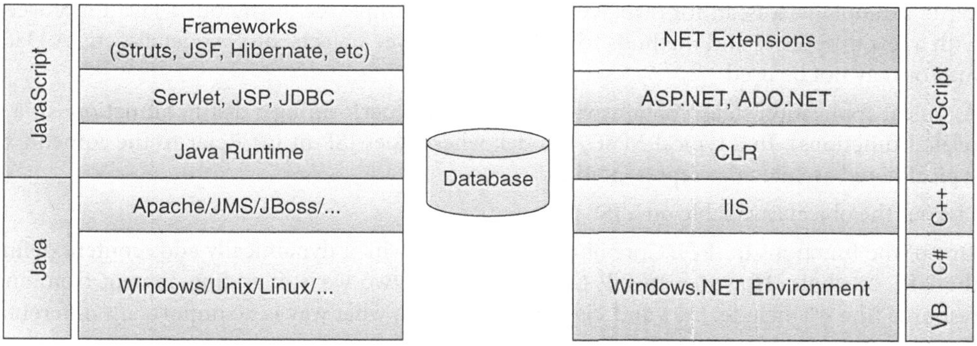

Fig. 6.20 *Equivalent Microsoft stack*

The diagram (Fig. 6.20) shows the equivalent layers in the Microsoft stack on the right side. The layers on the extreme ends indicate the programming languages that are supported on either of the stacks. It is seen that Microsoft supports multiple languages whereas the Java stack supports uniformly, Java as the programming language. On the other hand, the underlying Operating System in the case of MS stack is just Windows whereas in the Java stack, multiple operating systems are supported – in fact the only requirement is the availability of a JVM. Returning back to ASP, it supports predominantly two programming languages – VBScript and Jscript. The scripting syntax is quite similar to that followed in a JSP program (usage of "<%...%>"). It may be noted that ASP is getting obsolete since the ability to separate strictly into Model, View and Controller code is limited, leading to higher maintenance efforts. (this is the reason it is not shown as part of the MS stack in the diagram). As such, Microsoft has come up with a much more advanced technology in the form of ASP.NET.

By comparison, ASP.NET offers a much better web application framework as compared to ASP. It supports a wider number of programming languages (C#, VB.NET, J#, etc.) and also good web services capability. In ASP.NET, the code is compiled rather than scripted (as in the classic ASP model). Similar to JSP, ASP.NET provides a mechanism to combine server side code, database access, HTML and Java Script to create dynamic and rich content. To cover the details of this technology will warrant a separate book by itself, but the concepts are similar to that in the Java environment.

6.17 SUMMARY

An introduction to JSP and how it fits into the overall view part of an application was discussed in the beginning of this chapter. The example brought out the advantage that JSP holds over doing the same in Servlet. In fact, Servlets can act as the Controller while JSP can act as the View in an ideal application implementing the MVC pattern. The chapter also highlighted the usage of standardized libraries and how it can enhance by provisioning for custom tag libraries. A note on other equivalent technologies available, sets the tone for the importance to have multiple skills towards offering technology-agnostic solutions to business problems.

EXERCISES

Q1. Bring out the advantages of JSP.

Q2. Write a simple Java Bean for displaying details of an Employee. Bring out a Java Employee class with a few properties and methods to add new employee objects, display details, etc. A Database may or may not be used.

Q3. A typical application stack contains various tiers, each performing a distinct function (or a set of related functions). In a typical MVC2 model, where does JSP fit in? Refer to the Appendix on a typical tiered architecture representation.

Q4. List out the objects available on a JSP page.

Q5. One of the functions in JSTL Core library is c:import which dynamically adds content defined in the URL attribute. However, in JSP, there are already two ways of adding content from another resource (the <%include…%> and <jsp:include…/>. In what way is <c:import .../> different from the other two.

Q6. Using jsp:include demonstrate how dynamic content can be achieved. For instance, write an example to customize a value from the main JSP that modifies a string to be displayed in the called (i.e. included) JSP file.

Q7. Implement a simple error handler in which it should redirect to an error page in the event an error occurs. Clue: Use JSP's isErrorPage directive and errorPage. Extend the demonstration to land into different pages depending on the error status code (404, or even program exceptions).

Q8. We all would have played dice to play games like Snakes & Ladders or such. Write a JSP based web application to simulate rolling of a dice. Recall that a dice has six faces numbered 1–6. Use an appropriate Tag Library as you realize that this will be a part of a larger set of games.

Q9. Bring out a comparison chart between Java Servlets/JSP and Microsoft ASP.NET development environments.

Project Activity

Q10. Read through the basics of JSF (Java Server Faces) – the technology for server side presentation layer, which is a better substitute for JSP. Prepare a report on your observations about their comparison.

Caselet Activity

Q11. To continue with the Caselet, create a User Bean for the User Registration process.

7

THE BUSINESS LAYER—EJB FUNDAMENTALS

> ***Chapter Objectives:***
>
> - ***Introducing the concept of layering***
> - ***How EJB helps in layering applications***
> - ***Understanding the persistence framework***
> - ***Going through a few examples***

So far, we have covered a facet of web applications development which included the simple or not too-complex sort of scenarios. However, enterprise applications are characterized by the presence of rich interfaces, large number of components, persistence mechanisms, need for fail-safe transactions mechanism, message queues, server/database clustering, and many such combinations.

At a high level, this calls for an engineering approach involving distributed systems and the need for a layered architecture. Development of complex enterprise applications with these characteristics will introduce a good amount of system complexity and volume. Fortunately, they can be abstracted into a set of patterns having common functionalities, which translates into something like this—a kind of user interface aligned with a business process (business logic layer) and a data model, and saving data into a database (persistence).

Enterprise JavaBeans is a server-side platform that is provided by the Java Enterprise (Java EE 5 onwards) to enable distributed computing. In the context of web layering, it is primarily meant to hold the business logic layer, supported by some sort of persistence layer.

7.1 LAYERING

The concept of layering is not new in the context of the application or systems architecture. We have seen earlier about the OSI model and the networking layers. It is also widely present in the traditional industries.

It is critical for the potential web architect (or designer) to understand layering. To understand the concept, it will be useful to draw a parallel in some of the other industries or situations that we commonly encounter. Take, for instance, the music system. Broadly, we have two kinds of music systems—an integrated system where all devices are available in a single box, includes a set of speakers, CD drives, MP3 player, radio, a built-in amplifier, etc. The other kind of a music system is of the plug-in type where all of these components are available to be connected and played. The former can be thought of as belonging to a traditional, non-layered architecture and the latter can be thought of as belonging to a layered architecture.

Both of them are identical with respect to performance in all respects, so there is practically no difference in effects, power consumption and operations. So where is the difference? It is not a simple answer, but can be abstracted in terms of flexibility and simplicity.

Imagine if the music system is being played regularly as in a restaurant. It is good for a start but what happens if the restaurant expands? Perhaps the speakers may not be powerful enough. An additional set of speakers might do, but the amplifier may not catch up with the need for increased load. It may be that impedance matching could also be an issue. To complicate matters, what if the CD player fails suddenly? Also, how will it be compliant with newer types of players (USB drives, Blu-ray and yet other

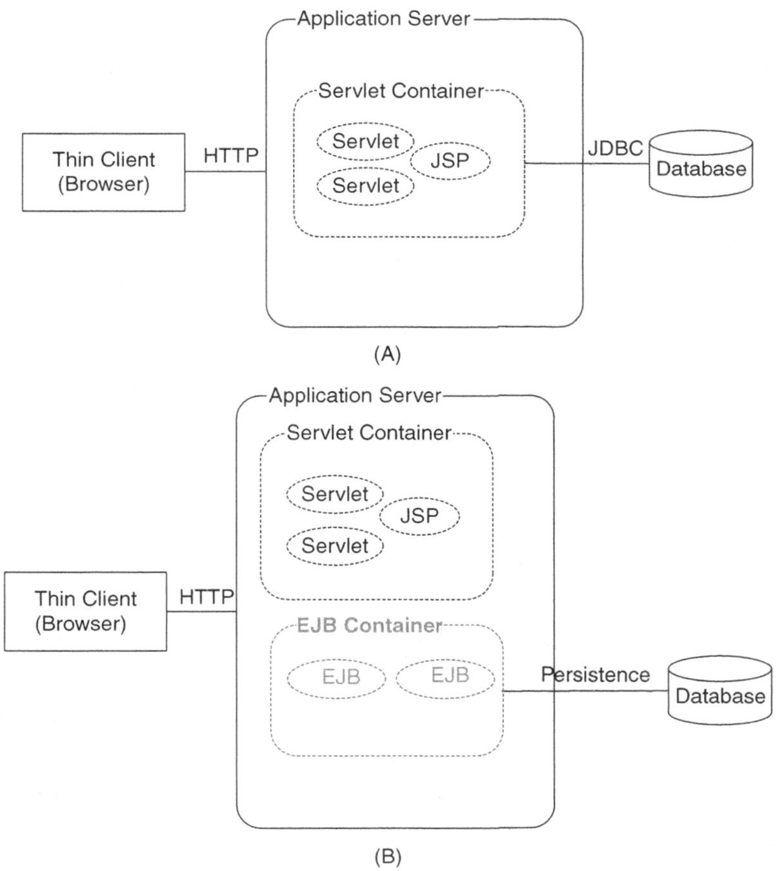

Fig. 7.1 *Layering without EJB (A) with EJB (B)*

technologies to come)? For a music system this may sound a bit trivial but for a full fledged system, these are all the engineering practices that make a system sound.

Rather than replacing the expensive system altogether, all of these issues can be adequately addressed by a well-layered architecture. Re-engineering or replacing just the set of components that need attention, are all that is required. For instance, adding a Blu-ray player to the system is as easy as buying the component and plugging it in. If a component fails, it may not affect the other components (unless of course it is one of the critical components!).

The example mentioned above is valid in a typical web application. It may be realized that business models are seldom static, so there will be situations that will require replacing or re-engineering a component. The IT system that supports it has to align and catch up with the changes in business. Furthermore, each of these components has its own lifecycle and they could have different half-lives. Layering supports the concept of breaking down a complex application into components that can be managed better. It also supports plugging in the components that are best suited for the application. With the advent of SaaS models, part of the components can also leverage the cloud as part of the application. Above all, it promotes best of breed and a neater split in skill sets needed to develop and manage the components.

The logical design of an enterprise application is usually layered into blocks called tiers. Thus there are three tier and four tier applications that are common. Layering and multi-tiering of an application are synonymous. Any single layer is responsible for a single set of related functions. These functions can actually be referred to as roles within an organization, responsible for a specific function (or a set of related ones).

EJB promotes better separation of data layer within the application. This also helps the application to be independent of the underlying database.

7.2 WITH SERVLETS

With this introduction, how are Servlets and EJB's placed? Table 7.1 attempts to uncover this idea.

Table 7.1

	EJB	**Servlet**
Web positioning layer (tier)	More towards backend, but broad based	More towards presentation
Primary responsibility	Persistence	Request–response mechanism
Nature of functionality	Encapsulate data	Expose data (present)
Enabler	Enterprise capability	Multi-threading capability
Enterprise concerns	Scalability,transactions, load-balancing,component based model (promoting reusability)	Can act as the controller (C in MVC) in the application
Tier	Three or more tier architecture	Two or three tier architecture
Development complexity	Complex	Simpler

Nature of application	Requirement for heavy middleware (distributed computing, transactions management, persistence, etc.)	Presentation centric, low or medium complexity in backend
Underlying programming Environment	Java (EE) with EJB container	Java with Servlet container

It clearly shows that though there is overlapping functionality in Servlels and EJBs, they could complement each other. However, the choice of whether the designer wants to use EJB or not in the application, rests predominantly on the nature of the application (stated in the table). Otherwise, using EJB will be an overhead, if the requirement is not justified.

7.3 EJB VERSIONS

EJB has progressed through many versions since it was first introduced as EJB 1.0 and then progressed into EJB2. Currently, the version is called EJB3, which is a lot different from EJB 2.0 in terms of functionality and architecture. Historically, EJB1.0 was unusable to an extent that EJBs were discontinued to be used. EJB2 served some good purpose but was far from simple to use. However, the new avatar in the form of EJB3 is not to be missed as it greatly enhanced ease of use and applicability. This section emphasizes EJB3.

7.4 USAGE SCENARIOS

Imagine situations where you need to implement a component that can be accessed by multiple applications like for instance a credit card checking application. Imagine another application which is transaction-intensive like consumer banking or an online shopping cart. EJB can be used in these situations.

7.5 EJB COMPONENTS

Just as Servlets run in a Servlet Container, EJBs run in an EJB container. The container itself could be either standalone or a part of an (Java EE) Application server. There are three types of EJBs—Session Beans, Entity Beans and Message driven Beans. A *Bean,* in general EJB parlance, is a component, but different from *Java Beans.* They are classified into these categories as per their specific functionalities they intend to achieve. Session Beans and Message driven Beans drive business logic (in slightly different ways) and Entity Beans manage persistence. Persistence can be achieved in different ways, but Java uses JPA (Java Persistence API) to deal with persistence, through the *EntityManager* interface. Most EJB containers contain a pluggable persistence mechanism, so practically JPA abstracts a persistence provider that is behind. EJB containers are included as part of a heavy weight application server like JBoss or Glassfish.

Aside note

EJB3 offers a simpler programming model as compared to its earlier versions. Many of the features in EJB3 are similar to certain modules of Spring and Hibernate, some of the popular frameworks in ORM.

7.5.1 Session Beans

Session Bean, as the name hints, is a (EJ) Bean that is used to write business logic (which is, of course, a natural thing to do for a Bean!) that has to maintain state information. Many situations in business require a series of steps to complete. This is valid much in both complex process as the order-to-cash cycle or even in smaller processes like an online shopping facility. The common requirement thread that runs across (from a Session Bean standpoint) is that a conversational state needs to be maintained. We have seen this situation when session management was discussed as part of the section on Servlets. The difference here is that here the concept is extended to be persistent. In the example of the shopping cart, the user's online shopping process can span over an extended amount of time and the application is expected to retain the work-in-process shopping cart for better user experience, throughout the process.

Session beans are of two types—Stateless and Stateful. Both can be invoked directly by client interactions. Stateful Beans are useful when a conversational state is to be preserved as in a workflow or in a process like the online shopping cart.

Stateless Beans, on the other hand, perform a single operation for a client that need not maintain conversational state. An operation in a Stateless bean is completed in a single method call. With an application server, it need not be instantiated each time it is required—it can be taken from an already preconfigured pool of Stateless Beans. Examples of Session Beans include searching for an item, adding an item to a cart, etc.

7.5.2 Message Driven Beans

Message driven Beans (MDBs) are also used to write business logic, but unlike Session beans, do not interact directly with the user (client). They are in fact trigerred by messages sent to a messaging server (like MQ Series, MS BizTalk, etc). So all the Client does is send a message and check for return messages through callbacks since the messages sent through the messaging queue asynchronous. MDB use cases include applications where async processing will be required but need fail-safe operation. An example is a situation where a Purchase Order need to be trigerred whenever the stock runs out in an online store. Likewise, inventory update during online sales can be done using MDB.

7.5.3 Entity Beans

Entity Beans model the persistence part of the application. The persistence in EJB3 is handled by the JPA, which is based on object relational mapping (ORM). While Session beans and MDB can be thought to encapsulate a *process*, an Entity Bean can be thought to encapsulate an *object*, also referred to as an *entity*. Simply put, ORM is the process of mapping the data stored in object model (implementing by classes) to relational model in a database (specifically a RDBMS). This is made possible through serialization and achieved by JDBC. However, EJB3's Entity Beans relieve the developer from these cumbersome tasks.

The ORM framework is available through a number of sources like Hibernate and TopLink, all following the architecture of JPA, thus keeping the developer agnostic of the underlying ORM engine. For now, it is enough to understand about JPA and its components namely:

- Entity Manager API which abstracts the common Database operations for CRUD (Create, Read, Update & Delete)
- Java Persistence Query Language (JPQL) – a SQL-like language for manipulating data
- Meta data for configuring the program with the Persistence mechanism

7.6 LIFECYCLE OF AN EJ BEAN

The EJB container manages the lifecyle of a bean. The EJB container itself is in most cases a part of the Application Container, though it could be separate. For simplicity let us assume they are available in the same application server. Glassfish Java EE compliant Application Server comes with a Web Server, a Servlet container, an EJB container and a JPA provider.

The lifecycle depends on the type of the Bean. Let us consider the case for Stateless Session Bean, Stateful Session Bean and a Message driven Bean. Their states can simply be represented in Figure 7.2.

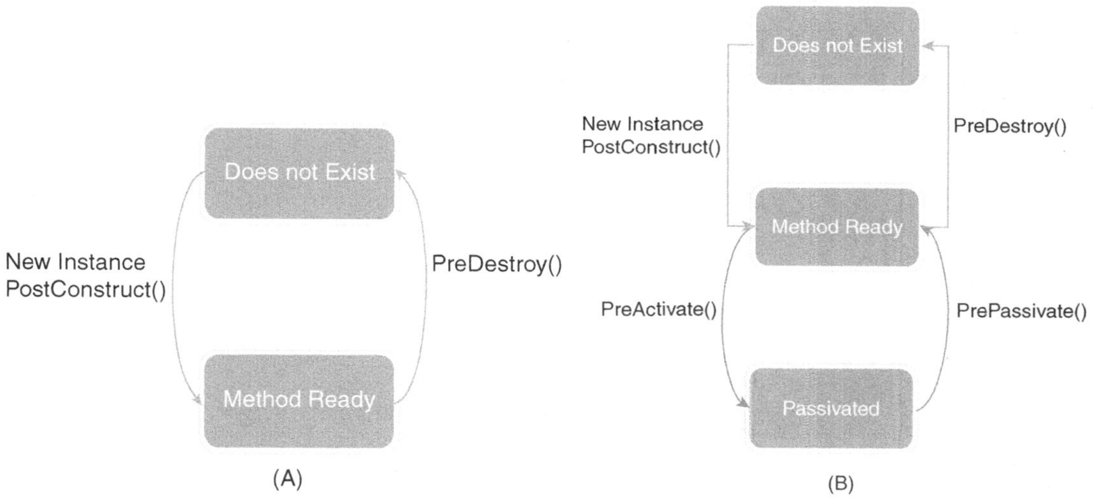

Fig. 7.2 *(A) Stateless session bean (B) Stateful session bean*

Since the lifecyle is managed by the container, it offers the developer a few channels to interact in the form of callback functions. These callbacks are shown in Figure 7.2 alongside the arrows that point to the possible States. The lifecyle of an Entity Bean is similar to that of the Stateless Bean, except that it is pooled for better performance.

Aside note

Dependency Injection allows an application to collaborate with services rendered by the container (which is part of the App Server). There are notes available on the web and the article specifically at *http://www.theserverside.com/news/1321158/A-beginners-guide-to-Dependency-Injection* has been found to be useful.

The lifecyle of a bean starts when a bean instance is created. However, it is not to be created using the usual "new" operator. It is instead created through a reference to the bean. A reference is obtained by either of two means—using JNDI lookup or using dependency injection. Both concepts are vast by themselves, but an introduction to JNDI is included in the Appendix (Section 12). Dependency injection, simply put, is a design pattern which helps in promoting loose coupling between components by using callback mechanisms to collaborate with the container to achieve better control over processes.

With help of APIs (for JNDI) and annotations (for DI), the process of doing it is simple. The container can inject the following types of resources into the bean.

- @EJB
- @PersistentContext
- @Resource
- @WebServiceRef

For instance, consider the following annotation in Java.

```
@EJB
Private X2BizLocal x2;
```

The code creates the reference to the bean (X2BizLocal) and instantiates in the variable x2. Refer to the example in the subsequent section.

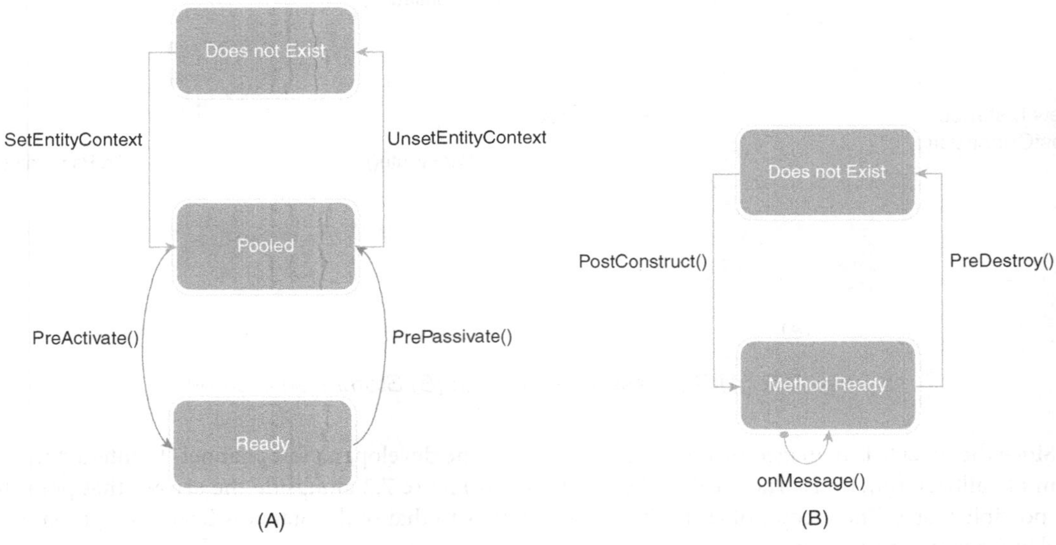

Fig. 7.3 *(A) Entity Bean (B) MDB*

A Stateful Session Bean (or an Entity Bean) can be caused to passivate (by the container) when the idll time for a bean instance expires or when the memory limit (on the JVM) has been reached. It is to be borne in mind that Stateful Session Beans take a much bigger overhead in resources, so it should be used with care. However, this is not to say that their use is to discouraged.

It is also possible to interact with Beans through interceptors. While lifecycle callbacks handle EJB life cycle events, Interceptors handle business methods events (during Invoke). interceptors enable aspect oriented programming (AOP), according to which, any horizontal functionality (also called cross-cutting concerns) can be neatly implemented. An example of such a functionality is Logging or checking for credentials. Many of these features are available in a variety of ways in modern frameworks like Rails. In Java EE, there are annotations which easily create these functions. For example, consider this piece of code:

```
Public class X2Biz implements X2BizLocal {
     //attach the interceptor
     @Interceptors(myLogger.class)
public void addItem(String item, int quant) {
            items.put(item, quant);
     }
}
Public class myLogger {
     ...
     @AroundInvoke
     Public
}
```

The following points can be summarized about the best usage of Beans:

- Choose the type (Stateless, Stateful, Entity or MDB) carefully.
- Use them in combination.
- While using Stateful session beans, optimize on the size of the bean class. Sometimes it is better to use an ID to point to a whole employee record, for instance, instead of storing all the fields.
- Use interceptors for horizontal functions to leverage Aspect Oriented Programming.

7.7 A SHOPPING CART—SIMPLIFIED EXAMPLE

Consider a Bean shopping cart which lists out a set of beans (of the eating variety!) for the user to order items and store in a shopping cart. Though production-ready implementations of shopping cart handles complex scenarios, lets us abstract into a simple set of beans to demonstrate a local interface and how business logic is defined and applied.

```
package abc.com;

import java.util.Map;
import javax.ejb.Local;
/*An EJB can have multiple interfaces on how they may be exposed
to the outside world
 This is a case of a Local interface (as opposed to Remote) */
@Local
public interface X2BizLocal {
    Map getItems();
    void addItem(String item, int quant);
    void removeItem(String item);
```

(Continued)

```
    void clearItems();
}
```

Fig. 7.4 *X2BizLocal.java–The EJB business interface*

The business interface is listed out in the code shown in Figure 7.4. The interfaces are implemented in the Bean class.

```
package abc.com;
import java.util.HashMap;
import java.util.Map;
import javax.annotation.PostConstruct;
import javax.ejb.Remove;
import javax.ejb.Stateful;

@Stateful
public class X2Biz implements X2BizLocal {
    private Map items;
    @PostConstruct
    private void initialize() {
        items = new HashMap();
    }
    @Override
    public Map getItems() {
        return items;
    }
    @Override
    public void addItem(String item, int quant) {
        items.put(item, quant);
    }
    @Override
    public void removeItem(String item) {
        items.remove(item);
    }
    @Remove
    @Override
    public void clearItems() {
        items.clear();
    }
}
```

Fig. 7.5 *X2Biz.java–The EJB business interface logic*

A few Java annotations observed in the code listing (Figures 7.4 and 7.5), are explained as below:

- @Stateful: this annotation signifies to the container that this is a Stateful Session Bean. It helps to avoid session management, which otherwise would be essential. The use of such annotations has been made possible since Java 5. However, this concept is valid in any web programming environment. The other alternative is Stateless, which means the container automatically will provide Bean services like concurrency control, thread safety, pooling or transaction management.
- @local: This tells the container that the session bean can be accessed via the local interface, that is, within the same JVM. The other option is to use @remote, which allows access to Beans via the network using remote method invocation (RMI). The @webservice annotation allows non-java applications to access the bean.

The home page is shown in Figure 7.6.

```
<%@page contentType="text/html" pageEncoding="UTF-8"%>
<!DOCTYPE html>
<html>
<head>
  <meta http-equiv="Content-Type" content="text/html; charset=UTF-8">
<title>Cart</title>
  <link href="styles/expCSS.css" rel="stylesheet" type="text/css"/>
</head>
<body>
   <form action="X2Servlet" method="POST">
      <table>
          <tr>
             <td>Item</td>
             <td>Item Name</td>
             <td>Quantity</td>
          </tr>
          <tr>
             <td><img src="images/beansGreen.jpg" width="50"
                    height="50" alt="Green Beans"></td>
             <td><label  id="item1" style="border: none;">
                    Green Beans</label></td>
             <td width="40px"><input type="text" name="Green Beans"
                    size="5"  ></td>
          </tr>
          <tr>
             <td><img src="images/beansBaked.jpg" width="50"
                    height="50" alt="Green Beans"></td>
```

(Continued)

```
                <td><label type="text" name="item2" style="border: none;">Baked Beans</label></td>
            <td width="40px"><input type="text" name="Baked Beans" size="5"  ></td>
            </tr>
            <tr>
                <td width="50px"><img src="images/beansFava.jpg" width="50" height="50" alt="Green Beans"></td>
            <td><label type="text" name="item3" style="border: none;">Fava Beans</label></td>
                <td width="40px"><input type="text" name="Fava Beans" size="5"  ></td>
            </tr>
            <tr>
                <td width="50px"><img src="images/beansKid.jpg" width="50" height="50" alt="Green Beans"></td>
                <td><label  type="text"  name="item4"  style="border: none;">Kidney Beans</label></td>
                <td width="40px"><input type="text" name="Kidney Beans" size="5"  ></td>
            </tr>
            <tr>
                <td colspan="3"><button type="submit">Add to Cart</button></td>
            </tr>
        </table>
      </form>
    </body>
</html>
```

Fig. 7.6 *index.jsp*

The Servlet code is shown in Figure 7.7.

```
package abc.in;

import java.io.IOException;
import java.util.Enumeration;
import java.util.Map;
import javax.ejb.EJB;
```

```
import javax.servlet.RequestDispatcher;
import javax.servlet.ServletException;
import javax.servlet.http.HttpServlet;
import javax.servlet.http.HttpServletRequest;
import javax.servlet.http.HttpServletResponse;

public class X2Servlet extends HttpServlet {

    @EJB
    private abc.com.X2BizLocal X2;

    @Override
    protected void doGet(HttpServletRequest request,
HttpServletResponse response)
            throws ServletException, IOException {
        doPost(request,response);
    }

    @Override
  protected void doPost(HttpServletRequest request, HttpServletResponse
response)
            throws ServletException, IOException {
        String item;
        int qty;
        String x="";
        Enumeration e = request.getParameterNames();
        while (e.hasMoreElements()) {
            item = (String) e.nextElement();
            qty = 0;
            try {
                qty = Integer.parseInt(request.getParameter(item));
            } catch (Exception ex) {
                qty = 0;
            }
            if (qty > 0) {
                //after reading the Item from the user, add this to
                //the cart
                X2.addItem(item, qty);
            } else if (qty < 0) {
                //X2.removeItem(item);
```

(*Continued*)

```
                X2.clearItems();
            }
        }
        //Get the current cart items in a Map. Order of items will not
        //be preserved in a Map!
        Map items = X2.getItems();
          //Bundle them in a Request object for use in JSP that is
          //forwarded to
        request.setAttribute("myItems", items);

        //Forward the request to another view for displaying
         RequestDispatcher rd = request.getRequestDispatcher("showX2.jsp");
        rd.forward(request, response);
    }

    @Override
    public String getServletInfo() {
        return "Short description";
    }
}
```

Fig. 7.7 *Servlet*

The display is achieved through showX2.jsp as shown in Figure 7.8.

```
<%@page import="java.util.Iterator"%>
<%@page import="java.util.Map"%>
<%@page contentType="text/html" pageEncoding="UTF-8"%>

<!DOCTYPE html>
<html>
    <head>
      <meta http-equiv="Content-Type" content="text/html;charset=UTF-8" />
      <title>Show Cart</title>
      <link href="styles/expCSS.css" rel="stylesheet"type="text/css" />
    </head>
```

```
    <body>
        <% Map items = (Map) request.getAttribute("myItems");
         Iterator items_it = items.entrySet().iterator();
        %>
        <!--Include the initial page for new items -->
        <table class="" style="border:solid; padding: 20px; ">
            <tr>
                <td align="center"><h2>Order</h2></td>
                <td align="center" width="250px"><h2>Cart</h2></td>
            </tr>
            <tr>
                <td><jsp:include page="index.jsp" /></td>
                <td align="center">
                    <!-- Table within another -->
                    <table border="solid">
                        <thead>
                        <tr>
                            <td align="center"><b>Item</b></td>
                            <td align="center"><b>Quantity</b></td>
                        </tr>
                        </thead>
                        <% while (items_it.hasNext()) { %>
                        <% Map.Entry m = (Map.Entry) items_it.next(); %>
                            <tr>
                                <td><%= m.getKey() %></td>
                                <td><%= m.getValue() %></td>
                            </tr>
                        <% } %>
                    </table>
                </td>
            </tr>
        </table>
    </body>
</html>
```

Fig. 7.8 *showX2.jsp*

The application needs to be compiled with the appropriate libraries, specific to the app server.

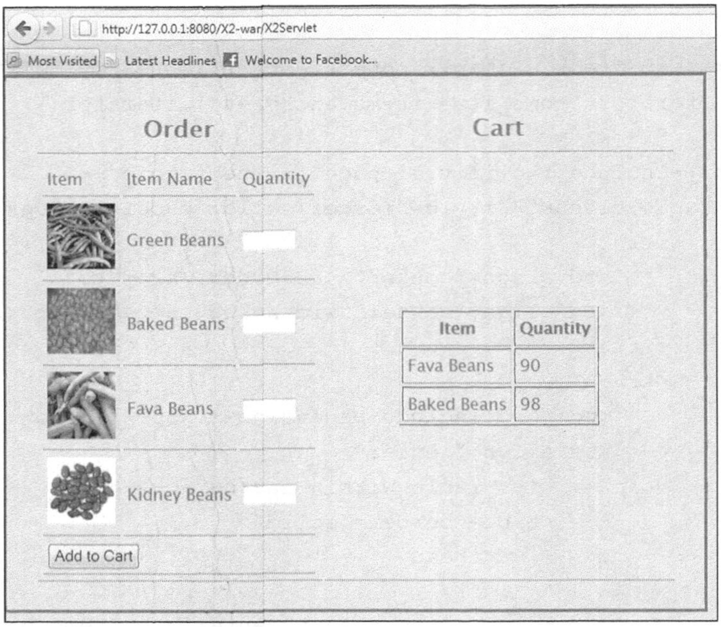

Fig. 7.9 *Indicative output (with CSS for styling)*

7.8 SUMMARY

The current version EJB3 has undergone many avatars before its present state today. EJB3 has been found to be far usable and adopted by many programmers. In fact it manifested as part of JPA (Java Persistence API) which is generic enough. It is being increasingly realized that there is now a good alternative to using ORM frameworks like Hibernate and even certain modules of Spring that JPA attempts to implement. The examples bring out the ease of backend design. Using annotations, it is much closer to a POJO, which has been the driving force behind the increased adoption of this technology by web designers and programmers.

EXERCISES

Q1. Explain the parameters that you would consider while choosing the role of EJB in an application.

Q2. Bring out a layering model for an application that uses EJB.

Q3. List out the Annotations available in Java, with respect to EJB3.

Q4. What are the advantages of using Annotations as opposed to defining Configurations (in the context of EJB3)?

Q5. Elaborate the salient aspects of JPA.

Q6. Bring out the advantages of using POJO-like classes in the context of EJB. What is the alternative?

Q7. What are the common functionalities that JPA brings out?Discuss the role of JNDI in an EJB based application.

Q8. Discuss the role of JNDI in an EJB based application.

Project Activity

Q9. EJB container is a part of app servers like Glassfish, JBOSS and Websphere. Select 2 of these - one from the Open Source community and another from regular licensed software. Gather information on the kind of security features that are available on the Containers from an EJB standpoint. Organize the security concerns in terms of Principal (Identification), Authentication, Authorization and data hiding.

Caselet Activity

Q10. For the online ordering module of the Caselet activity, create a shopping cart on EJB3.

8

XML

Chapter Objectives:

- ***What is XML?***
- ***Why is XML used?***
- ***Understand in what ways can XML data be manipulated***
- ***Seek alternatives to XML***

8.1 INTRODUCTION

The web is enabling users to talk to applications. But, an equally important facet is on how applications talk to other applications. When they communicate, what is one single format that is popularly used, irrespective of whatever be the content that is being exchanged? The answer to this is XML which stands for Extensible Markup Language. It is a standardized form of data to store, manipulate and transport over the internet. Though XML is a single format, there are different forms that can be used. For example purchase orders can be communicated in B2B over XML. Applications themselves use XML in exchanging configuration information, for instance. The most common usage of XML is XHTML, which has been mentioned in the chapter on Web Essentials.

8.2 THE NEED

We have observed that standardization improves connectivity between applications, paving the way for people to collaborate. HTTP defines the standard format of communication. HTML/CSS defines the standard way of handling content. But content itself is made of data. Isn't there a means of a standardized structure for data? XML attempts to standardize the definition, validation and sharing of data across applications.

Most of the Client's Requests are serviced by the Server, but it is well streamlined when the content is structured as in the case of data from a database table. However, this should not be a condition to enable sharing of information. In reality, much of the content is unstructured or semi-structured at best. Even for structured content there are multiple possibilities for content's structure because, for instance, each table in a database could follow a different structure. The only way to deal with it is through meta data which operates at a level higher than data. In fact, on the other hand, even a seemingly unstructured content like a letter can be considered as having a definite structure as in address element, title element, body of the letter, signature, etc.

It is in the best interests of an application to bring as much data as possible to semi-structured or fully structured state. Even a news item can be thought of as having a semi-structure if it is viewed as consisting of headline, a date, location and content. For example a letter can be structured in XML is shown in Figure 8.1.

Any letter knowingly or unknown to us, follows the above structure. By having it in the above structure, the application can process it more intelligently by say, processing the <to> tag, checking for an email address and routing the letter to the mail server. It can check for spelling mistakes in the <body> content and/or translating into a different language and so on. Additionally, using the above structure, it is also possible to convert into a normal language based letter.

Another example of XML tries to describe the BOM (Bill of Materials) of a ball point pen.

```
<?xml version="1.0" encoding="ISO-8859-1"?>
<ballpen>
<brand> Parker </brand>
<penBody>
<quantity> 1 </quantity>
<material> steel </material>
<color> blue </color>
</penBody>
<refill> blue </refill>
<refill> black </refill>
<lid type="press fit"> Blue </lid>
</ballpen>
```

This definition can make sense to a system that procures the individual components and assembles them. In this case assembly is perhaps a trivial operation, though. At a glance it is seen that the pen is made of steel, blue in color and comes with two refills of blue and black colors. The lid is blue in color with a press fit design. The idea is to lend structure to an otherwise plain set of words (just like the last two sentences) which can be manipulated. This way, the system that generates this XML (or the system that consumes this XML) ensures that the values are valid, at least with respect to the tags and attributes, if not more.

```
<letter>
 <to> recipient address </to>
<from> sender address </from>
<body>
    Content goes here
</body>
</letter>
```

Fig. 8.1 *Semi-structured data appearing as XML*

This is what XML is meant for—handling data—not just data from databases but also different kinds of data. It could also serve as a universal data translator, passing (and also translating) data from one application to another. Furthermore, XML is used widely as part of web applications development. XML is a part of W3C recommendation since 1998.

In summary, the reasons why XML scores well as a means of data interchange are as follows:

- They are Standardized including support from W3C and many vendors.
- XML is Simple to use—both human readable and machine readable.
- XML is Expandable—implying that a structure is not cast in stone. It can be enhanced without affecting the applications that already use them
- XML is Open and self-describing.

8.3 XML BUILDING BLOCKS

The fundamental building blocks of XML are Tags (Elements), Attributes and Namespaces. Like HTML, it is also derived from SGML. Tags have content between them (start and end tags). Attributes describe about the Tag, without having to add additional tags! For example, type is an attribute with value of CDMA.

```
<mobile type="CDMA">
<provider>Reliance</provider>
 </mobile>
```

Namespaces define the domain. They are important because they avoid name collisions, given the fact that XML definitions can be developed independently. For example, if some entity called JAVA is being defined through XML, it could refer to a definition pertaining to the programming language Java or to an island called Java. Namespaces come to the rescue to identify the relevant "Java" that is required.

They may not be required to be defined (implies default namespace) for small and less formal situations. But for standard situations like WSDL definitions for SOAP, or XHTML, a formal namespace will be required. Industry standard namespaces that are relevant to designers and developers include the following:

- XML Schema: http://www.w3.org/2001/XMLSchema
- SOAP: http://schemas.xmlsoap.org/wsdl/soap/
- XHTML: http://www.w3.org/1999/xhtml
- WSDL: http://schemas.xmlsoap.org/wsdl/

Observe that the namespace is defined by means of an URI. They appear with a prefix attribute called `xmlns`, standing for XML namespace. These URIs appear as a unique identifier only, there is no access involved.

The partial declaration in Figure 8.2 of XML is for a SOAP web service. It shows the various namespaces in the form of many `xmlns` attribute declarations used in the document. When there are multiple of them defined, one of them is considered default. Definitions without any namespace prefix belong to the default namespace (as long as it lies within the parent element where the default is defined).

```
<?xml version="1.0" encoding="UTF-8"?>
<definitions name="priceServe"
    targetNamespace="..."                                  → Default Namespace
    xmlns=http://schemas.xmlsoap.org/wsdl/
    xmlns:soap=http://schemas.xmlsoap.org/wsdl/soap/
    xmlns:tns="..."
                                                           → Namespace prefix
    xmlns:xsd="http://www.w3.org/2001/XMLSchema">
    ...
    <message name="getPrice"> <item="upc001" type="xsd:number"/> </message>
    ...

</definitions>
```

Fig. 8.2 *Namespaces and prefix*

The others with prefix can be considered to override the default namespace. For example the type attribute overrides the default to belong to the XSD namespace.

The namespace URI is used to identify the namespace uniquely, it is not siginifcant in the sense that the URI is not used to navigate into it.

8.4 HOW IT WORKS

An HTML or XHTML uses tags to describe the way content is to be displayed. It is recalled that, for instance, <h1> tag is used to display the content, within the start and end tags, as a top heading. XML is similar but it is obvious that tags may not be universally standard semantically. In the example shown in Figure 8.1, the tag "<to>", is not a standard representation because it could mean differently in different contexts. It is left to the application to make sense out of it from a semantic perspective. The term Semantic refers to the meaning of the tags—programmatically it implies that appropriate actions should be defined.

Based on its broad framework of message structure, an XML may be specific to an application that is being developed or used, or it could also be specific to an industry or domain. An example of a domain specific XML (which may be called a standard for that industry) includes Chemical Markup Language (CML), Production Markup Language (PRODML), Open Exchange data Format (OpenXDF), etc. There are even XML definitions in music called MusicXML. XML is also used in developing applications like for instance WSDL (Web Services Definition Language). Practically, there is no limitation in terms of usage or applicability in domains as long as there is a structure and a following to become an industry standard. An application-specific XML is some structure that is created and understood by the application.

So apart from the structure, it can be deduced that there should be something like a meta data about the structure. This is referred to in two ways—DTD (data type definition) or XSD (XML Schema Definition), which will be discussed in later sections.

8.4.1 Basic Structure

Figure 8.3 shows an sample XML file.

```
1.  <?xml version="1.0" encoding="ISO-8859-1"?>
2.  <?xml-stylesheet type="text/xsl" href="trip.xsl"?>
3.  <trip>
4.   <request>
5.     <name>Ram@88990</name>
6.     <from>BLR</from>
7.     <to>PTP</to>
8.     <when>01JAN2012 13:00</when>
9.   </request>
10.  <results>
11.  <match>
12.        <name>Shyam@99000</name>
13.        <when>01JAN2010 13:30</when>
14.  </match>
15.  <match>
16.        <name>Mike@79200</name>
17.        <when>01JAN2012 15:30</when>
18.  </match>
19.  </results>
20. </trip>
```

Fig. 8.3 *Trip XML*

The header line (Line-1) specifies the XML declaration along with the version number and character encoding format that is used.

8.5 CHARACTERISTICS

- An XML document should be well formed, with a root element.
- XML tags are case sensitive.
- Many times, attributes can be substituted by elements and is in fact a good practice to follow. The thumb rule is that whenever metadata is to be represented, choose attribute instead of element. Examples of metadata include ID, type information, path etc., though it is dependent on the semantics. The majority of the representation is data (or properties) for which element is chosen over attribute.
- XML is extensible.
- An XML document's format can be extended without causing existing format to crash. For example, if elements are added to an existing XML structure, parsing will still work off the old elements and go ahead with (existing) functionality.

8.6 SCENARIOS FOR HANDLING XML

XML, in a web application, performs one or more roles in terms of creating or consuming XML documents. They are summarized in Figure 8.4.

Any web application that handles XML will have to do with one or more of the aspects shown in Figure 8.4. There are APIs and tools that are open and generic to handle them.

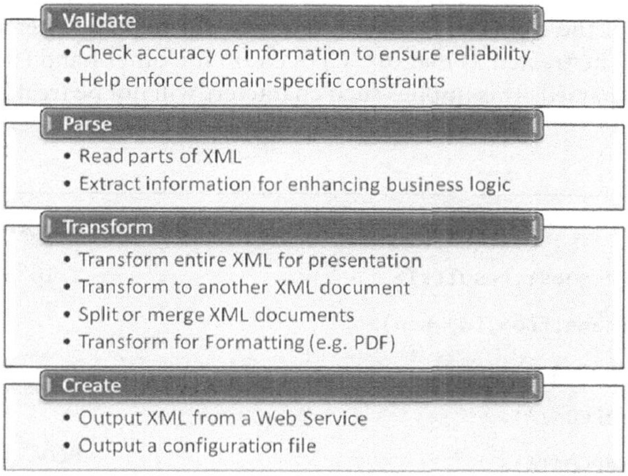

Fig. 8.4 *Handling XML*

8.7 VALID XML DOCUMENT

An XML document is supposed to be a Valid XML, if, in addition to being well formed, it also conforms to its semantics that it is supposed to convey. The rules, as per its semantics, are governed by a set of legal building blocks called the Document Type Definition, abbreviated as DTD. It is specific to the XML in the sense that any XML document which describes it is governed by the same DTD.

8.7.1 DTD

In other words, DTD specifies what the rules are, that govern the specific XML. All items that we see around us have a structure. A book has a structure (TOC, Chapters, Paragraph, etc), a magazine has a structure (Headline, Article, picture, etc); and so also an Invoice, a Purchase Order, and the tons of document that are processed in our daily lives and business transactions. This structure is equally important in the context of XML.

It is to be realized that XHTML is also a special case of XML and that it has its own structure. The following header statement may be recalled.

```
<!DOCTYPE html PUBLIC “-//W3C//DTD XHTML 1.0 Transitional//EN”
“http://www.w3.org/TR/xhtml1/DTD/xhtml1-transitional.dtd”>
```

The browser recognizes this structure uniquely.

But the point is DTD is not just for standard definitions but also for specific ones where an independent set of people agree to follow a convention. For example study the following DTD (as per Figure 8.5) for the XML shown in Figure 8.3.

The elements in the XML (Figure 8.3) conform to the DTD shown in Figure 8.5. For example Element results, could contain more than one match which is indicated by a plus sign. Instead of a plus sign, if it were an asterix (*) sign, it would have meant zero or more occurrences of match element (rather than one1 or more occurrences as in a plus sign). A question mark (?) sign would have meant zero or one occurrence of the element. PCDATA refers to Parsed Character Data implying that the text (within the tags) will be treated as markup. CDATA on the other hand (not shown in the Fig.) is character data that is not parsed. This implies such characters will not be treated as markup and hence will not be expanded.

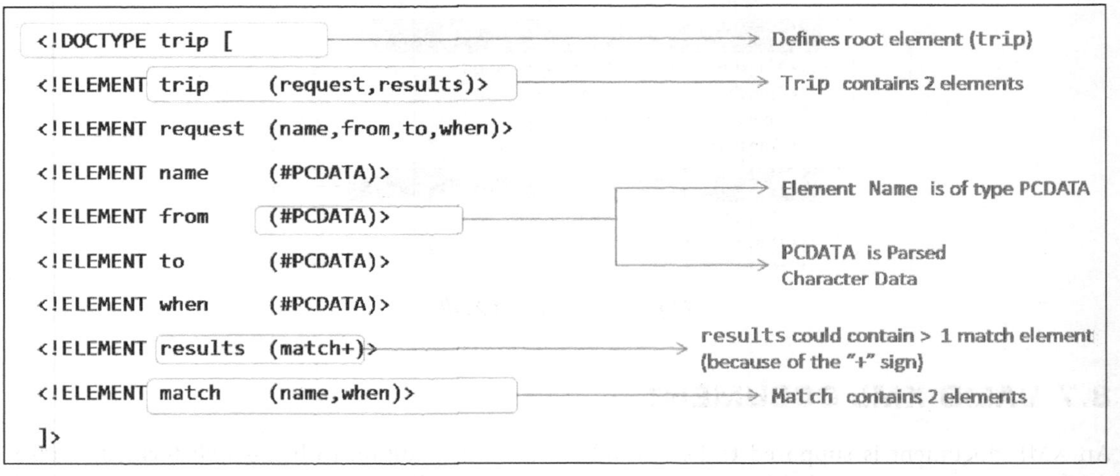

Fig. 8.5 *DTD*

The full XML file listing is in Figure 8.6 for convenience.

```
<?xml version=”1.0” encoding=”ISO-8859-1”?>
<!DOCTYPE trip [
<!ELEMENT trip (request,results)>
<!ELEMENT request (name,from,to,when)>
<!ELEMENT name        (#PCDATA)>
<!ELEMENT from        (#PCDATA)>
<!ELEMENT to  (#PCDATA)>
<!ELEMENT when        (#PCDATA)>
<!ELEMENT results (match+)>
<!ELEMENT match (name,when)>
 ]>
<?xml-stylesheet type=”text/xsl” href=”trip.xsl”?>
<trip>
```

```
  <request>
    <name>Ram@88990</name>
    <from>BLR</from>
    <to>PTP</to>
    <when>01JAN2012 13:00</when>
  </request>
  <results>
  <match>
         <name>Shyam@99000</name>
         <when>01JAN2012 13:30</when>
  </match>
  <match>
         <name>Mike@79200</name>
         <when>01JAN2012 15:30</when>
         </match>
  </results>
</trip>
```

Fig. 8.6 *XML with DTD listing–trip example*

The DTD capabilities shown in the examples in this chapter are just samples. There are many other formats and rules that exist for the DTD.

The DTD file can be inline within the XML or referenced from the XML. When the DTD (external) file is referenced within the XML, the declarative is as follows:

```
<!DOCTYPE trip SYSTEM "trip.dtd">
```

Here, trip is the name of the XML root element and trip.dtd is the name of the DTD file that is being referenced.

8.7.2 XSD—Schema

The DTD is not itself written in XML. What offers an XML based, alternative to DTD, is XML Schema or XSD (XML Schema Definition). It succeeds DTD and is a preferred alternative to describing XML data. One of the greatest capabilities XML Schema brings is its support for data types. DTD supports 10 datatypes; XML Schemas supports more than 44 datatypes. XML Schemas also support more sophisticated element structures.

XSD is thus an XML representation of an XML structure. It is a text file with an extension of xsd, written in a special Schema language.

A portion of the Schema is shown in Figure 8.7 for the same XML file shown in Figure 8.3. Each of the Schema elements has a prefix XS, which maps to the suffix defined in the Namespace declaration. Any name could be used as the prefix as long as it is uniquely identified in the document.

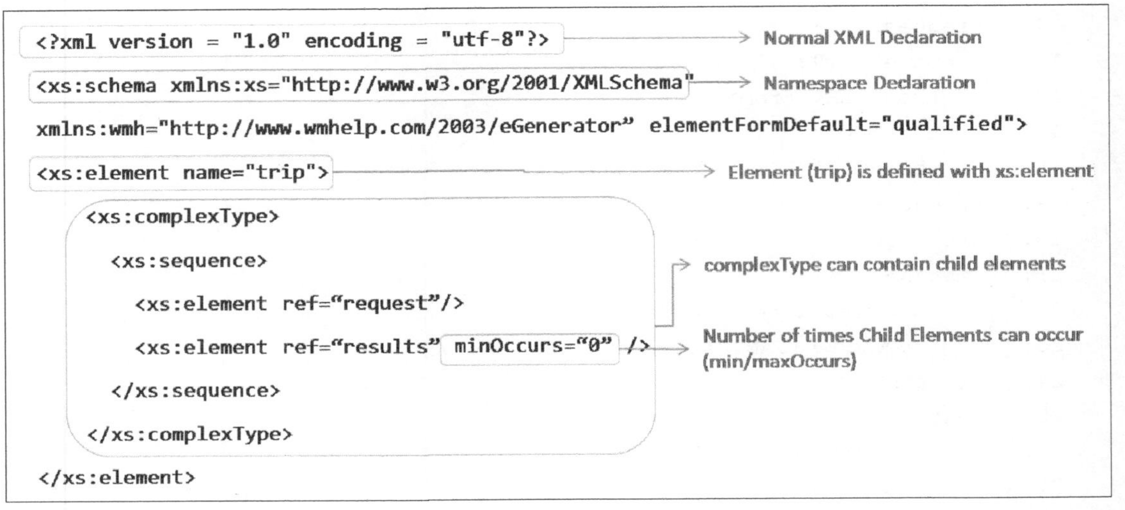

Fig. 8.7 *A snippet of XSD*

8.7.2.1 XSD advantages The following are the points favoring XSD as opposed to DTD:

- Support for enhanced data types. XSD supports more than 40 data types. There is provision for user defined types as well
- Valid value range possible to be defined in XSD
- XSD is written in XML, so there is no need for a special parser
- It follows (since it is written in XML itself) that there is namespace support
- It is more aligned with the concept of extensibility, in the sense that any enhancements need not alter the current structure, thus honoring older versions of data.

8.8 XML TRANSFORMATIONS—XSL

XML is pure data—the information in an XML document does not contain information about how it is to be presented. Frequently, a lot of situations are encountered which requires transforming a document from one format (of XML) to another format (of XML). The transformed XML is functionally enhanced by means of a format that could be used for storage or presentation. Sometimes the transformation will be necessary to communicate across two different systems as part of EDI (Electronic Data Interchange). Thus it is useful for a few B2B operations.

The XML Stylesheet Language (XSL) is a standard that helps in transforming XML data. It consists of the following components:

- XSLT (XSL Transformation)
- XPATH
- XSLFO (XSL Formatting Objects)

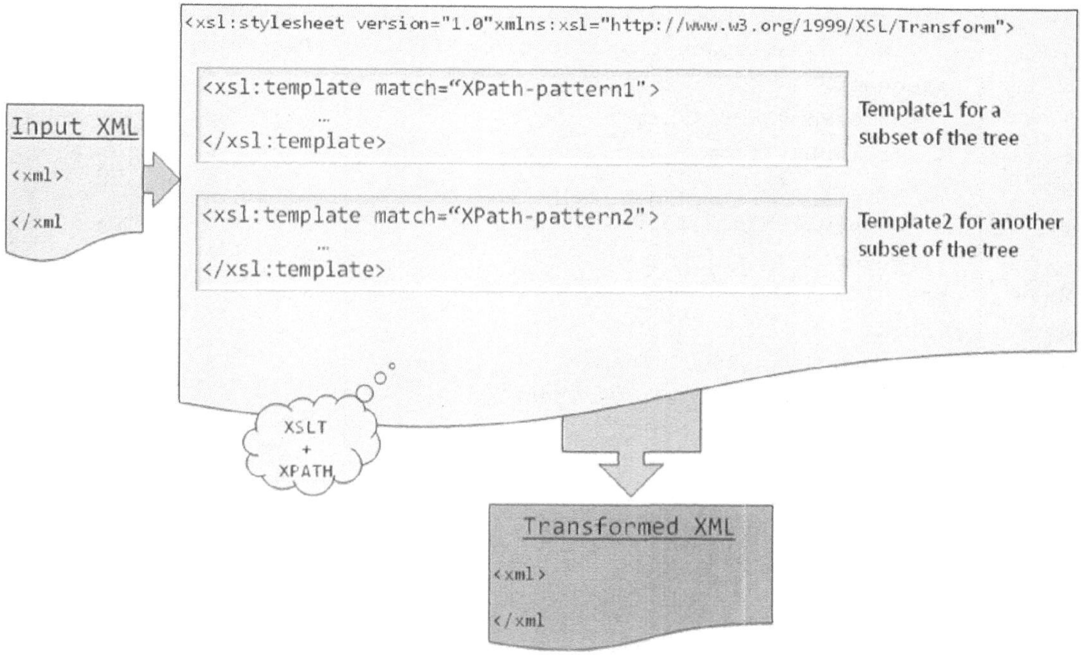

Fig. 8.8 *XML transformation process*

The working of XSL is shown in Figure 8.8.

8.8.1 XSLT

An XSLT stylesheet is an XML document that specifies *how* an XML is transformed. The elements are defined as per the XSLT vocabulary, to describe the transformation. The vocabulary is defined in the header of the XSLT Document as in the following example.

```
<xsl:stylesheet version="1.0" xmlns:xsl=http://www.w3.org/1999/XSL/
Transform>
```

An example of a transformation can make this clear. Consider the XML as shown in the Figure 8.6. Imagine that this is the output from a part of an application in which it delivers an XML document containing details of a trip. The output document contains two parts—the request (`<request>` tag) trip details and zero or one or more matches (<results> tag), signifying other people planning the same trip—useful for car pooling or for parts of a social networking application. Actually the functionality is a reference to the Trip Match advisory (Figure 6.20) example in the section on Servlets, but with output in XML.

```
<?xml version="1.0" encoding="ISO-8859-1"?>

<?xml-stylesheet type="text/xsl" href="trip.xsl"?>
```

(Continued)

```
4.    <trip xmlns:xsi="http://www.w3.org/2001/XMLSchema-instance"
5.          xsi:noNamespaceSchemaLocation="file:///[PathTo Trip.xsd]">
6.      <request>
7.        <name>Ram@88990</name>
8.        <from>BLR</from>
9.        <to>PTP</to>
10.       <when>01JAN2012 13:00</when>
11.     </request>
12.     <results>
13.    <match>
14.        <name>Shyam@99000</name>
15.        <when>01JAN2012 13:30</when>
16.    </match>
17.    <match>
18.        <name>Mike@79200</name>
19.        <when>01JAN2012 15:30</when>
20.    </match>
21.     </results>
22.    </trip>
```

Fig. 8.9 *Input XML (trip.xml)*

The reference to the transformation (XSL file) definition is present in line 3 of Figure 8.9. This is the most important part of the discussion for this section.

```
<?xml version="1.0" encoding="ISO-8859-1"?>

<xsl:stylesheet version="1.0"
xmlns:xsl="http://www.w3.org/1999/XSL/Transform">
<xsl:output method="html" encoding="utf-8" indent="yes"/>
<xsl:template match="/">

<h2>Match Results For
    <i><xsl:value-of select="trip/request/name"></xsl:value-of></i>
Route
    <xsl:value-of select="trip/request/from"></xsl:value-of> -
    <xsl:value-of select="trip/request/to"></xsl:value-of>
    (<xsl:value-of select="trip/request/when"></xsl:value-of>)
```

```
12.  </h2>
13.  <table border="solid">
14.      <tr>
15.        <th>Name</th>
16.        <th>When</th>
17.      </tr>
18.      <xsl:for-each select="trip/results/match">
19.      <tr>
20.        <td><xsl:value-of select="name"/></td>
21.        <td><xsl:value-of select="when"/></td>
22.      </tr>
23.      </xsl:for-each>
24.  </table>
25.
26.  </xsl:template>
27.
28.  </xsl:stylesheet>
```

Fig. 8.10 *XSLT/XPATH–Transformation definitions–trip.xsl*

The content of the document is a set of rules describing the transformation(s) to be performed. Each rule in the stylesheet contains an associated XPath pattern that matches the nodes in the source document to which that rule should apply. While XSTL defines the "how", XPath defines the "what" of a transformation (Figure 8.10).

The output method (line 4) immediately follows the XSL statement. The values for method typically are "text", "xml" or "html". The XPath statements define what elements are to be transformed (line 5 for example). The elements themselves are obtained by means of a filter defined by the "match" statement. The "/" in line 5 signifies the root element. It can also take complex matching patterns. The generic rule that can be summarized is that when a node in the source matches the pattern, the resulting sub-tree is considered for transformation in the template. This is the overall XSLT processing model. The template is shown in lines 5–25.

XSLT is quite powerful. The reader is encouraged to refer to the W3C at http://www.w3.org/TR/xslt for details.

Notice the XSD definition in line 2 in Figure 8.11. Though it is not relevant to our example, the Schema definition script has been included.

```
1.   <?xml version="1.0" encoding="utf-8"?>
2.   <xs:schema xmlns:xs="http://www.w3.org/2001/XMLSchema"
3.           xmlns:wmh="http://www.wmhelp.com/2003/eGenerator"
     elementFormDefault="qualified">
```

(*Continued*)

```
    <xs:element name=“trip”>
      <xs:complexType>
        <xs:sequence>
          <xs:element ref=“request”/>
          <xs:element ref=“results” minOccurs=“0”/>
        </xs:sequence>
      </xs:complexType>
    </xs:element>
    <xs:element name=“request”>
      <xs:complexType>
        <xs:sequence>
          <xs:element ref=“name”/>
          <xs:element ref=“from”/>
          <xs:element ref=“to”/>
          <xs:element ref=“when”/>
        </xs:sequence>
      </xs:complexType>
    </xs:element>
    <xs:element name=“name” type=“xs:string”/>
    <xs:element name=“from” type=“xs:string”/>
    <xs:element name=“to” type=“xs:string”/>
    <xs:element name=“when” type=“xs:string”/>
    <xs:element name=“results”>
      <xs:complexType>
        <xs:sequence>
          <xs:element ref=“match” maxOccurs=“unbounded”/>
        </xs:sequence>
      </xs:complexType>
    </xs:element>
    <xs:element name=“match”>
      <xs:complexType>
        <xs:sequence>
          <xs:element ref=“name”/>
          <xs:element ref=“when”/>
        </xs:sequence>
      </xs:complexType>
    </xs:element>
  </xs:schema>
```

Fig. 8.11 *Schema definition trip.xsd*

The output in Netscape is shown in Figure 8.12 for the input XML shown in Figure 8.3.

Match Results For *Ram@88990* Route BLR - PTP (01JAN2012 13:00)

Name	When
Shyam@99000	01JAN2012 13:30
Mike@79200	01JAN2012 15:30

Fig. 8.12 *XML transformation output*

8.9 XML PARSING

Parsing is one of the aspects of handling XML, as indicated in Figure 8.4. An XML document contains pieces of data. To make it available in a way that an application can consume (use) it, requires extraction of the same from the document. This is called parsing. It is used in a program through parsers. Two of the standard parsers are the SAX Parser and the DOM Parser.

XML is independent of the technology which is used as well as the vendor which implements. Support is provided by Microsoft as well as in Java environments or any other web development environment like Rails. The Java environment provides a high level API for processing XML within programs through JAXP (Java API for XML). It provides support for both SAX as well as DOM parsing.

8.9.1 SAX

SAX (Simple API for XML) parser enables an XML document to be processed using an event-driven model. This is implemented by callbacks methods. Events are fired during parsing in response to the flow of callback method invocations. Memory usage is significantly lower for large XML documents (as compared to DOM method), but the programming complexity could be high.

The SAX API defines several interfaces:

- org.xml.sax.XMLReader interface for SAX parsers. It allows to register a document event handler, the error handler, a DTD handler & an entity resolver
- org.xml.sax.ContentHandler is the main interface that is implemented to receive document events, notification of the following
    - The start or end of a document
    - The start or end of an element
    - Ignorable whitespace in element content
    - A processing instruction
- org.xml.sax.ErrorHandler interface to receive SAX error events, notification of errors (or warnings)
- org.xml.sax.DTDHandler interface to receive notification of basic DTD-related events
- org.xml.sax.EntityResolver interface for resolving external entity references

An application must provide at least a Content handler in order to catch relevant events and process them.

8.9.2 DOM

As per DOM (Document object model) model of parsing, it reads the XML and converts into a tree structure, which is essentially a set of nodes. This tree structure is then used for processing (manipulating). This is the same reference to DOM as mentioned in the client side part of this book.

The DOM API for XML defines interfaces as follows:

1. org.w3c.dom.Document interface representing the entire XML document
2. org.w3c.dom.Node and NodeList interfaces, representing a node (or a set of them) in the document tree. This defines methods to manipulate the Node.
3. org.w3c.dom.Element interface for representing an (XML) element
4. org.w3c.dom.Text interface representing the text of an Element

Whatever be the parser model used—SAX or DOM, Java does not have them in-built. The parsers are available as third party plug-ins, although they are made available in Java.

8.9.3 Choosing between DOM and SAX

Table 8.1 some guidelines on when to choose DOM over SAX or vice versa.

Table 8.1

Nature of Operation	DOM	SAX
Type of access	Suitable for random access	If it is required to traverse frequently over new nodes, SAX will score less over DOM approach
Memory usage	High, since the whole tree is brought into memory. Larger documents take significantly more time to process	Lower memory footprint since it is event driven—only the node(s) that are relevant, are loaded into memory. For smaller documents, it does not really matter if SAX or DOM is used (as far as performance is concerned).
Transformation intensive	DOM will be better since the entire tree is in-memory. However, if presentation is the only purpose of the transformation, use XSLT instead of parsing.	SAX will be less preferred
Data streaming	DOM will not be preferred since it has to rebuild the entire tree each time there is a change.	SAX will be better suited
Ease of use	Easier to use	Medium
Modification of XML	DOM is well suited	Not suited to modify XML documents

Overall, where performance is critical, use of SAX is recommended, otherwise, for smaller documents, DOM is preferred.

8.9.4 Java Support for Parsing XML

Java 5.0 and above has powerful and interoperable parsers as part of its package. The following are some of them:

- Org.xml.sax: Defines the SAX parser
- Org.w3c.dom: Defines the DOM parser
- Javax.xml.transform: Defines the XSL transformation functions, used along with XPATH.
- Javax.xml.xpath
- Javax.xml.validation

8.10 JSON

JavaScript Object Notation (JSON) is a format that has gained a good amount of traction as a replacement to XML, especially as a light-weight alternative.

Aside note

> Although JSON is a subset of JavaScript, it is completely independent of any programming language. Effectively it is a combination of two things—name–value pairs [hash table] and array-like [sequential] structures. Refer JSON Specifications at http://www.json.org/.

The basic principle used in JSON data structure is that data is considered to be occurring in name–value pairs. In many programming languages, this data structure manifests itself in several forms and names as a Class object (in Object oriented programming), a HashMap (in Java), Hash (in Ruby) etc. A JSON object begins with a opening brace, “{”, and ends with a closing brace , “}”. Within the braces are name–value pairs separated by commas. The name–value pair itself appears with a colon separator. An example is as follows:

```
{'locationcode' : {'type':'Text', 'alias':'Location', 'dispOpt':'Show'}}
```

The *locationcode* is the name of a name–value pair whose value is a set of name–value pairs. Take care to exclude cyclical definitions.

Individual members in the data structure could be retrieved using the dot notation (object notation) combined with subscripts if required (for array like structures).

Since JSON is a natural part of JavaScript, it is easier to manipulate data using JavaScript. For instance, in JavaScript, a text variable (like the one shown above) can be treated like a JSON object by the eval operator. An alternative which is more secure and robust is by using a JSON Parser.

There are JSON tools available to be used in Java as well (Figure 8.13).

```
package testj;

import org.json.JSONArray;
```

(Continued)

```
import org.json.JSONObject;
import org.w3c.dom.Element;
import org.w3c.dom.Node;
import org.w3c.dom.NodeList;
import rdr.JRdr;
import rdr.XRdr;

/*
* Demonstrate reading & parsing JSON file and also an XML file.
*/
public class JsonXmlDemo {
    public static void main(String[] args) {
            String entity = args[0];

            JRdr jr = new JRdr();

            JSONArray entities = jr.fetchDetails(entity);
            if ((entities == null) || (entities.length() <= 0)) {
                System.out.append(entity + ": No such entity (JSON)");
            } else {
                for (int i=0; i<entities.length(); i++) {
                    JSONObject fld = (JSONObject) entities.get(i);
                    System.out.println(fld.toString());
                }
            }
            //Now read the XML content
            XRdr xr = new XRdr();

            NodeList NList = xr.fetchDetails(entity);
            if ((NList == null) || (NList.getLength() <= 0)) {
                System.out.append(entity + ": No such entity (XML)");
            } else {
                for (int i=0; i<NList.getLength(); i++) {
                  Node node = NList.item(i);
                  System.out.println("==================================");
                  System.out.println(node.getNodeName() + ":" + node.
getTextContent());
                }
            }
    }
}
```

Fig. 8.13 *JsonXmlDemo.java*

The JSON reader is implemented in JRdr.java class as shown in Figure 8.14. Refer the JSON file as shown in Figure 8.15.

```
package rdr;

import org.json.JSONArray;
import java.io.BufferedReader;
import java.io.InputStreamReader;
import java.net.URL;
import java.util.ArrayList;
import java.util.Iterator;
import org.json.JSONObject;

public class JRdr {
    public JRdr() {

    }
    /*
     * Data is arranged such that each entity contains the fields, each of which contains a set of attributes
       * defining the field. Since the order is important, they are arranged in an array.The attributes themselves
      * are another JSON COnstruct. This method reads the JSON file and retrieves the field attributes.
      */
    public JSONArray fetchDetails (String ent) {
        BufferedReader reader;
        ArrayList a = new ArrayList();
        JSONObject defs = new JSONObject();

        String filename;
        JSONArray ja=null;
        filename = "entities";
        URL url = JRdr.class.getResource("/data/" + filename + ".json");
        try {

              reader = new BufferedReader(new InputStreamReader(url.openStream()));
```

(*Continued*)

```
            StringBuilder jsonData = new StringBuilder();
            String data = "";
            while( (data = reader.readLine()) != null ) {
                jsonData.append(data);
            }
            reader.close();

            defs = new JSONObject(jsonData.toString());
            ja = (JSONArray) defs.get(ent);
        } catch (Exception e) {
            return (null);
        }
        return (ja);
    }
    /*
     * Demonstrate getting value from the JSON object, given key
    */
    public Object getJO(JSONObject jo, String key) {
        Object myent=null;
        Iterator itr = jo.keys();

        while (itr.hasNext()) {
                String thiskey = (String) itr.next();
                if (thiskey.equalsIgnoreCase(key)) {
                    myent = jo.getString(thiskey);
                    break;
                }
        }
        return myent;
    }
}
```

Fig. 8.14 *JSONReader*

Here is the JSON formatted file (Figure 8.15). The data represents a list of entities—two in number—employee and department. Each of them has a set of fields defined with attributes represented in another JSON format. The fields are arranged in an array to preserve the order of fields. It is to be noted that it is important to understand the structure of a format in order to be able to parse it—this holds good for JSON as well as for XML.

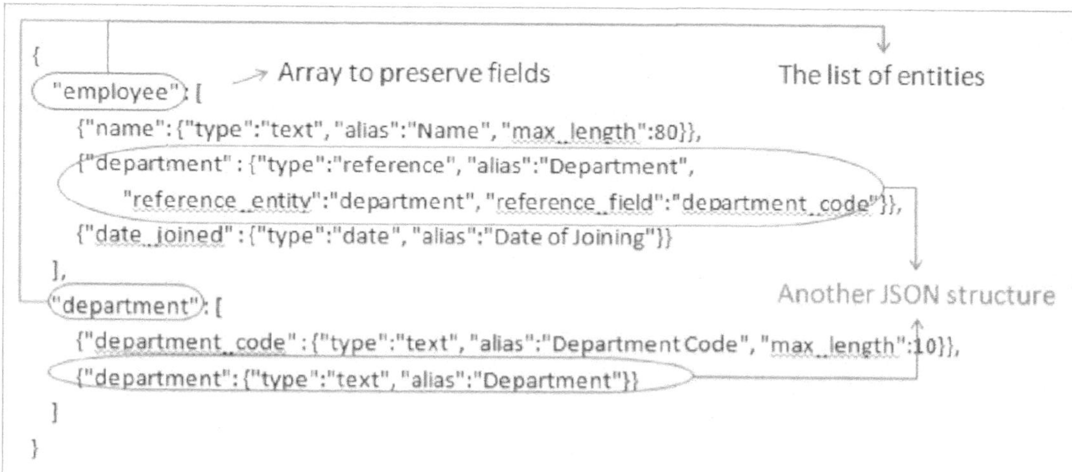

Fig. 8.15 *JSON file*

After demonstrating JSON, the same definition is created in an XML file. The following is the structure. XML reading and parsing is shown in the code listing in Figure 8.16.

```
package rdr;

import java.io.BufferedReader;
import java.io.InputStream;
import java.io.InputStreamReader;
import java.net.URL;
import java.util.ArrayList;
import javax.xml.parsers.DocumentBuilder;
import javax.xml.parsers.DocumentBuilderFactory;
import org.w3c.dom.Document;
import org.w3c.dom.NodeList;

public class XRdr {
    public NodeList fetchDetails (String ent) {
            BufferedReader reader;
            ArrayList a = new ArrayList();

            NodeList node;
            String filename;
```

(Continued)

```

            filename = "entities";
              URL url = JRdr.class.getResource("/data/" + filename + ".xml");
            InputStream is = JRdr.class.getResourceAsStream("/data/" + filename + ".xml");
            try {
                reader = new BufferedReader(new InputStreamReader(url.openStream()));
                StringBuilder jsonData = new StringBuilder();
                String data = "";
                while( (data = reader.readLine()) != null ) {
                    jsonData.append(data);
                }
                reader.close();

                  DocumentBuilderFactory dbf = DocumentBuilderFactory.newInstance();
                DocumentBuilder bld = dbf.newDocumentBuilder();
                Document doc = bld.parse(is);

                node = doc.getElementsByTagName(ent);


            } catch (Exception e) {
                return (null);
            }
            return (node);
        }
}
```

Fig. 8.16 *XML reader–class XRdr.java*

The XML reference is shown in Figure 8.17.

```
<?xml version="1.0" encoding="UTF-8"?>
<root>
  <employee>
          <name>
```

```
            <type>text</type>
            <alias>Name</alias>
            <max_length>80</max_length>
    </name>
    <department>
            <type>text</type>
            <alias>Name</alias>
            <reference_entity>department</reference_entity>
            <reference_field>department_code</reference_field>
    </department>
    </date_joined>
            <type>date</type>
            <alias>Date of joining</alias>
    </date_joined>
   </employee>
   <department>
            <department_code>
     <type>text</type>
     <alias>Department Code</alias>
     <max_length>10</max_length>
    </department_code>
    <department>
            <type>text</type>
            <alias>Department</alias>
    </department>
   </department>
 </root>
```

Fig. 8.17 *XML file*

An indicative output of the JsonXMLDemo (Figure 8.13) is shown below. Note that the output is in two parts—the top part shows JSON as-is (as per the toString() in line 26, Figure 8.13) and the bottom part shows the output of XML (as per the XML parsing code in Figure 8.13). Both modes, JSON as well as XML, permits parsing at lowest granular levels, however, the output shown is at different granularity.

```
{"name":{"max_length":80,"alias":"Name","type":"text"}}
{"department":{"alias":"Department","reference_field":
"department_code","type":"reference","reference_entity":"department"}}
{"date_joined":{"alias":"Date of Joining","type":"date"}}
================================
employee:

    Text
    Name
    80
    Reference
```

(Continued)

```
Department
department
department_code

Date
Date of Joining
```

8.11 SUMMARY

This chapter brought out the importance of an acceptable data format that can be used for any type of data, communicated over the web. Various means of XML manipulation were discussed—creation of data, parsing, manipulation and transformation. The last section of this chapter highlighted the importance of JSON which is fast replacing XML.

EXERCISES

Q1. Why is XML considered important?

Q2. In your view, why is XSD considered better than DTD?

Q3. What is an XML namespace?

Q4. Make a study of the parsers available in open source that can be plugged into Java.

Q5. Provide examples for the following XML document

a. Well-formed XML document, but not valid
b. Valid XML document

Q6. JAXP provides support for XSLT operations as part of its XML implementation. Refer Fig.8.9 and accordingly come up with a transformation mechanism using JAXP.

Q7. Create an XML document using Java.

Q8. Bring out the role of XML in Ajax.

Q9. RSS is a means to implement pull type data requests from a user. Research into the mechanism of RSS. List the format of an RSS XML document and bring out the concept of RSS Feeds and RSS Aggregators.

Project Activities

Q10. Study the schema of any specific XML implementation like MathML. Come up with a report.

Q11. Make a presentation on WSDL from an XML perspective.

Q12. Discuss the advantages of JSON data format as compared to XML.

Q13. A direct application of XML can be seen in Microsoft's middleware application called BizTalk, which enables systems to communicate with each other in XML. It implements EAI (Enterprise Application Integration) by using XML transformation techniques, and implementing business work flows. Come up with a report on the working of BizTalk. Refer to www.biztalk.org for details.

Q14. Compared to BizTalk, what are the other alternate equivalent technologies available?

Caselet Activity

Q15. Come up with a XML or JSON format for accepting data to add or update the list of product that are sold online.

9

WEB SERVICES

> ***Chapter Objectives:***
>
> - ***Understand the evolution of web services***
> - ***Discuss a few scenarios where web services can be useful***
> - ***Work out on the broad programming models available today—SOAP and REST***

"The web can grow significantly in power and scope if it is extended to support communication between applications, from one program to another."

—The W3C XML Protocol working group charter

The W3C defines a web service as "a software application identified by a URI, whose interfaces and bindings are capable of being defined, described and discovered by XML artefacts and supports direct interactions with other software applications using XML based messages via Internet-based protocols".

A web service is a facility that makes an application (or parts of the application) accessible to other applications. In this sense it is said to be "consumed" by other applications. Viewed conversely, the "consuming" application also needs to access the exposed web service in a certain fashion. Both these methods and processes come under the purview of web services.

9.1 TRACING THE PATH OF A REQUEST—A DIFFERENT VIEW

Recall the diagram explained in the first section on Web Essentials, where a typical HTTP request is traced out. Imagine the same scenario, but with a different conceptual view where it is split into two areas—the client which acts as a requestor and the service which acts as the resource. This way, the resource can cater to any number of such requests as long as they all follow a certain set of conventions and standardized interface while communicating between server and the client.

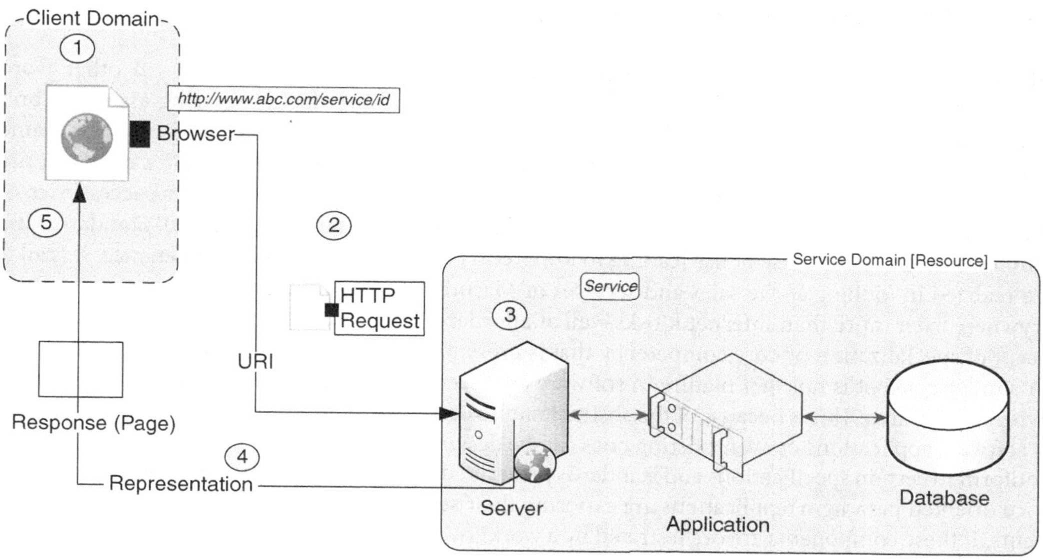

Fig. 9.1 *Web communication scenario–a different view*

The path that is traced is shown in the Figure 9.1. Removing the shaded blocks, it is actually the same figure appearing in the section on Web Essentials (Figure 2.8). Conceptually imagine that the two shaded portions are developed independent of the other. In other words, the requestor of a service can exist independent of the provider of service. This is the concept of services; since it is done over the web, it can be termed Web Services. They are also generically referred to as a Resource, since they perform some function, as shown in the figure.

In this context, just to give an idea of web services (resource), consider a few examples:

- credit card validation service, which could accept a credit card number then run the validation logic and then send out the result.
- temperature reporting service, where it could accept the name of a city (or such location indicator) and send the temperature.
- tracking of courier status, exposed as a service
- currency conversion service, server date/time service, etc
- and many more possibilities exist . . .

The architecture discussed above, supporting the concept of separation of a service and a client, throws open numerous and interesting possibilities. The service can be used by more than one client. A client can also use more than one service to achieve its purpose. This brings out a corollary (or rather a closed loop) that the service is designed in such a way to cater to multiple clients, being both flexible as well as hosting multiple tenants.

The patterns should be clear—any function that possibly is generic and reusable could be candidates for web services. Applications need not necessarily be in the public domain but can also be available in a private domain within the enterprise. Another pattern could be to use a web service (or a set of web services) to form an application, within a larger context.

9.2 EVOLUTION OF THE CONCEPT

In the manufacturing world, relatively many of the components are standardized—in other words, the interfaces are standardized. Cars, for example, have standard interfaces—steering assembly, brake system, accelerator, clutch, etc. Similarly, there exist standard processes and tools for its regular maintenance (servicing). Its components are also made of standard parts, as far as possible, for example, tires, steering assembly, brake linings, clutch parts, etc (what differentiates is its engine and accessories—in fact the engine is also made of standardized components for piston, crank shafts, etc). Standardization promotes reusability, and ease of use leading to lower costs of development and maintenance. It is all the more realized in looking at the sales and services of Maruti-800 cars in India—they are present almost everywhere even more than internet kiosks—all at affordable costs! At a deeper level, it aligns with the concept of specialization or core competency that is present in each of us and our companies.

A similar concept is not that mature in software engineering, though there is a continuous stream of activities in this area. This is because of the abstract nature of software and the flexibility it offers. However, new software applications or even existing ones can be designed (or redesigned for existing applications), to conform to certain specifications and standards prescribed by web services. Increasingly, more so in the service oriented paradigm, applications are exposing their services over the web, made available as components. If these components are orchestrated by a workflow, they could be used to implement a business process. Refer the diagram on the genesis of these concepts and how they evolved over time.

So far, in this book, the server side concentrated on building applications which are a mini world by themselves. Each method of a class was invoked and executed by classes within the same application, but what about using methods from a different application? It is to be recalled that the power of the web is in connecting various applications. In fact, the progress since Web 2.0 has brought forward the task of connecting people rather than just applications. So how do we build applications that connect together in the first place? The answer lies in Web Services, leveraging on XML's foundation on a similar philosophy.

Web Services is a concept that was not brought out overnight. The history of how it has evolved is rather interesting (see Figure 9.2).

In the beginning, the way applications talked to each other was by obviating the need for it—by building monolithic applications. Here, the idea was to build self-containing colonies of applications (modules) together. Needless to say, though it was effective, people realized that a significant disadvantage lay in the fact that it was both proprietary and prohibitively expensive to buy or maintain. It was probably cost effective only for large corporations or consortiums like airline companies, brokerage houses, railways, etc.

Client Server systems were less expensive but then not too effective when it comes to communicating across other applications. Moreover it was also proprietary so companies were locking themselves with a specific vendor, making the system inflexible. RPC paved the way for communications to be standardized, but each vendor (be it Microsoft or IBM) came with its own standard. CORBA and DCOM made it standardized but required both the client and server to have the appropriate CORBA/DCOM libraries installed. Moreover, many firewalls blocked these messages which were in binary format and coming in different ports (other than 80 which is an open port for firewalls). Then, with the growth in web-based standards including HTPP and XML, web services began to evolve. It enabled standardized, heterogeneous communication between applications in a distributed environment, over the web and across firewalls. This offers a platform for reusable components, orchestrating together, implementing a business process, achieved by BPEL (Business Process Execution Language). Software-oriented

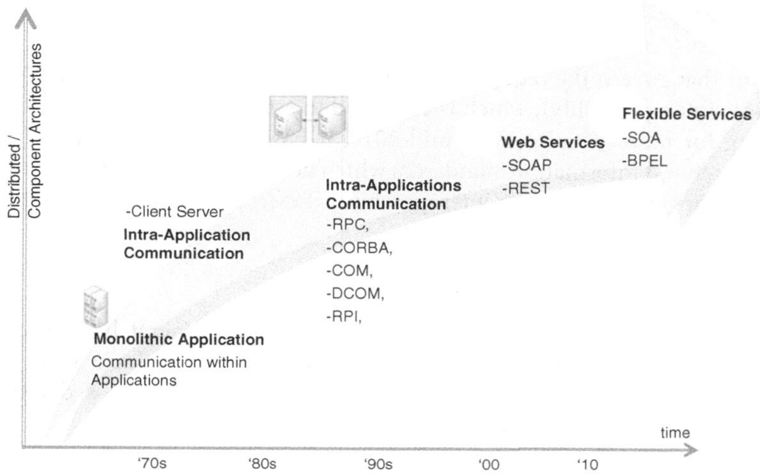

Fig. 9.2 *Tracing the evolution of the concept of web services*

connections between applications will automatically pave the way for business operations, previously requiring manual interventions. For example, if there was a way to connect an air travel reservation system with a hotel reservation system, any change in travel plans can be made to automatically cascade changes to hotel, and so on. Similarly, in a purchase-to-pay cycle in an organization, web services could play a part in streamlining procurement processes by connecting the process of accounts as well as goods receiving and inspection, even though these processes could belong to disparate systems. Done in a certain fashion, this could be the basis for service oriented architecture (SOA), which not only defines the processes but also service levels over a purely distributed environment, indirectly enabling outsourcing of functions.

The focus of this section is web services, which rightly balances out basic integration architecture with how business components can interact with each other, thus laying a good foundation for a strong web oriented architecture.

9.3 PURPOSE

The concepts mentioned above can be summed up into two main criteria for applications—being open and being interoperable. Being open does not necessarily mean open source, but here they refer to open standards (hence the two terms are being mentioned) which are a result of collective, transparent and industry-blessed processes or practices that are documented and widely followed. Interoperability is one of the main concerns of web service to be truly effective because clients can interoperate even if the services are written in different programming platforms. Much of the popular platforms like Java, Microsoft.NET, Ruby, Perl, etc. offer libraries for web services development that is interoperable. In fact, the generations prior to web services are differentiated predominantly by only the degree of interoperability, the core enabler being the ability to operate across firewalls.

The purpose of web services is thus to provide an interoperable, open framework for applications to communicate over the web, enabling application integration and component reusability.

9.4 STANDARDS

There are standards that govern the requirements of interoperability, earlier (since 2002) pioneered by WS-I (Web Services Interoperability), which is chartered to establish best practices for interoperability. Refer www.ws-i.org for more details. As of mid-2010, it has merged with OASIS (Organization for Advancement of Structured Information Standards) which develops and maintains many widely adopted open standards including those related to interoperability. Refer www.oasis-open.org for details.

9.5 USE CASES

Web services can be used not only while designing an application from scratch but also for legacy applications. When their services are cast through web services, they give a new lease of life to legacy applications. Whatever be the model, it defines how a piece of functionality can be exposed to the outside world. Some of the examples where it can be used are:

- Transactional environments
  - Means of communication with different modules
- EAI
  - Implemented on the intranet
  - As messaging
- Business web services
  - Trading partner communication
  - Multi channel integration

9.5.1 Sample Scenarios

For an e-commerce trading firm say in books on the web, customer support just to track order status is a vital function. The traditional way is for the customer to phone up (customer support) and ask for the status. Customer support in turn queries perhaps multiple databases and relays the status to the customer waiting on the phone. Instead, imagine if the process is made available on the web where using a web service could connect the application (on different databases) together and display the result. This will enable customer self-help, thus making the customer support leaner and also resulting in better customer satisfaction. A web service will fit in well, since it is not necessary to change the underlying applications or databases.

Another example scenario where web services could be leveraged is for a travel agent who wants to provide end-to-end services ranging from booking car, air travel, hotel, etc. for a tour. In the past a monolithic application would have been the approach (refer the diagram on evolution of web services) but with web services, information about the respective entities could flow in and aggregated to form a connected web of information. Furthermore, each individual piece of software (i.e. service) could have been or be built on different platforms and technologies. This, of course, brings in the additional responsibility of bringing in dynamism into the process should a particular entity change in its behavior.

It is thus realized that a proper orchestration of the events and entities are required, which leads to BPEL.

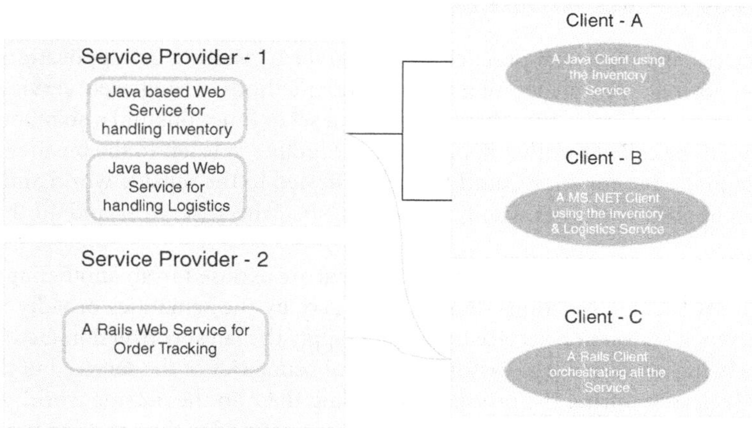

Fig. 9.3 *Web services scenarios*

In the Figure 9.3, there is a reference to multiple service providers and clients too using multiple service providers to satisfy the needs of their individual applications.

9.5.2 Roles

There are two significant roles in a web service architecture that is relevant—provider of the service, and a consumer of the service. This is also to be observed in the Figure 9.3. There is also a third role which is an intermediary—acts as the broker to connect the two together, as shown in Figure 9.4.

The service provider is responsible for creating the logic required for the function(s) and for running the service(s). In addition, the service provider is also responsible for defining the input and output specifications. In short, the service provider is responsible for creating (and maintaining) a self-contained system performing a specific set of computing functions.

The client uses the services provided by the service provider, in their own applications. Actually the relationship between the client and the service provider is a case of many-to-many. A service provider can cater to multiple clients. Likewise, a client can use multiple services, provided by multiple service providers, adhering to a distributed computing architecture.

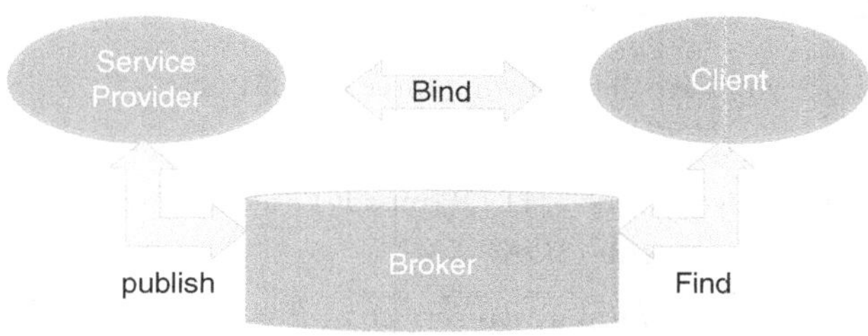

Fig. 9.4 *Web services roles*

9.6 PROGRAMMING MODELS

How do web services manifest? In practice, it is a style of writing an application. Most of it is programming the normal way of defining classes and methods. Using web services concepts, an application can be written in such a way that it performs a set of functions and also manifests or exposes itself, in some ways, to be called by other applications/programs. It is left to the business stakeholder or the designer to identify what functions need to be manifested to the outside world and how. There are instances where an application exists wholly to provide specialized services and all they do is expose their services.

An application can also be built using web services that are exposed from another application.

A service performs specific function—that is taken care by the semantics broadly by the business. For example, a currency conversion service is meant to apply the latest conversion factor and send back the result. What is being discussed here is not the logic or semantics of the service but the fundamental properties that are relevant during the process of exposing them to the outside world. Any service will involve passing messages as in the client to request the service and for the server to process it and send information in the form of a message back to the client. In doing so, a service can thus be standardized by these fundamental properties.

- The medium in which messages are sent
- The protocol by which they are sent
- The format by which they are sent

Broadly, a web service can be architected in two ways—SOAP based and REST based. SOAP was previously expanded as Simple Object Access Protocol. Earlier, most web services were SOAP based but the trend as observed in www.programmableweb.com is shifting more towards REST, because of its inherent simplicity. These approaches are discussed in detail in the subsequent sections.

Java environment provides support for SOAP and REST based web services through JAX-WS (Java API for XML based Web Services) and JAX-RS (Java API for RESTful Web Services) respectively.

Aside note

SOAP is governed by numerous standards. Refer SOAP specifications at **http://www.w3.org/TR/soap/**

9.7 SOAP BASED WEB SERVICES

A SOAP based (web) service will have the following three properties:

- The medium in which messages are sent—Web (Internet/Intranet/Extranet/LAN)
- The protocol by which they are sent—HTTP (mostly)
- The format by which they are sent—SOAP XML

The basic structural elements that form a web service in this model are XML (used by SOAP) and HTTP (as the mostly used protocol). Refer to the respective sections for more details about their individual capabilities. However, what is the significant is the combination of these two elements that make it powerful.

Platform elements used in a web service are SOAP, UDDI and WSDL. It is recalled that any service will involve passing messages between client and the server. These messages are called SOAP messages in this context. It, in fact, provides the envelope for sending messages.

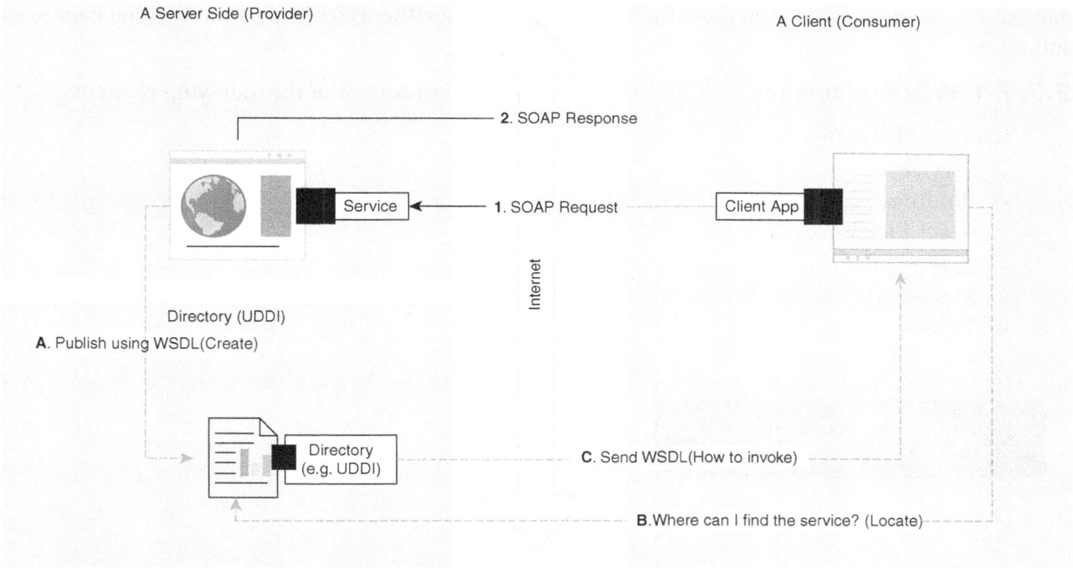

Fig. 9.5 *Steps involved in creating and using a SOAP based web service*

Figure 9.5 brings out the steps that are involved. Compared to Figure 9.3, this figure (Figure 9.5) represents a slightly lower level of detail, to enable a good understanding of what steps are required to create and use a web service. The diagram (Figure 9.5) shows a single instance of a pair of service provider and a client (consumer of a specific web service).

The steps with dashed lines of flow (represented alphanumerically as A, B and C, in that order) indicate those that need to be done as a preparatory set of activities before the calling SOAP service, the first time. The SOAP service calls, done by the client are abstracted as steps 1 and 2. It is to be noted that the activities associated with dashed-lines of flow need to be done only once, applicable during the following situations:

- On the Service Provider side, when the Service is created (or modified)
- On the Client side during discovery of the Service with the UDDI. During this time, the UDDI responds back with a WSDL.

Subsequently, the client is ready to use the WSDL to construct SOAP messages. Each time the service is invoked (this could typically be multiple times in the lifecycle of the client application), SOAP messages are constructed and sent to the service provider. These are indicated by solid lines of flow.

All messages that are transferred across systems follow SOAP. The directory serves as a means of discovering the service, using WSDL.

9.7.1 WSDL

The notion of a service that can be described in a technology-agnostic way is achieved by web services description language (WSDL). It is an XML document that facilitates dynamic discovery and invocation of the service.

As an XML file, WSDL is made of elements contained within the root (WSDL). This is shown schematically as in the diagram (Figure 9.6). It is used to describe the web service in a way that can even be automated.

9.7.1.1 *WSDL elements* A WSDL can be considered to consist of the following elements.

- Concrete Elements
  - Service
  - Binding
- Abstract Elements
  - Port Types
  - Messages
  - Types

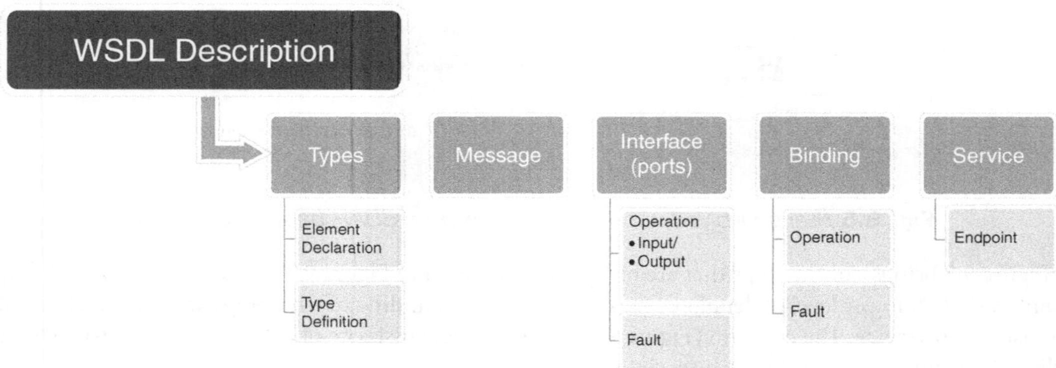

Fig. 9.6 *WSDL structure*

The representation shown in Figure 9.6 is actually in reverse order of the WSDL file and is done so to aid easier understanding of the concepts behind the file (see Figure 9.7).

```
<?xml version="1.0" encoding="UTF-8"?>
<definitions name="QuoteService" targetNamespace="http://ws1/"
xmlns="http://schemas.xmlsoap.org/wsdl/"
xmlns:xsd="http://www.w3.org/2001/XMLSchema"
xmlns:tns="http://ws1/"
xmlns:soap="http://schemas.xmlsoap.org/wsdl/soap/"
```

```
xmlns:wsam="http://www.w3.org/2007/05/addressing/metadata"
xmlns:wsp1_2="http://schemas.xmlsoap.org/ws/2004/09/policy"
xmlns:wsp="http://www.w3.org/ns/ws-policy"
xmlns:wsu="http://docs.oasis-open.org/wss/2004/01/oasis-200401-wss-wssecurity-utility-1.0.xsd">
<types/>
<message name="getRandom">
      <part name="arg0" type="xsd:string"/>
</message>
<message name="getRandomResponse">
      <part name="return" type="xsd:string"/>
</message>
<portType name="QuoteIF">
  <operation name="getRandom">
    <input message="tns:getRandom" wsam:Action="http://ws1/QuoteIF/getRandomRequest"/>
    <output message="tns:getRandomResponse" wsam:Action="http://ws1/QuoteIF/getRandomResponse"/>
  </operation>
</portType>
<binding name="QuotePortBinding" type="tns:QuoteIF">
      <soap:binding style="rpc" transport="http://schemas.xmlsoap.org/soap/http"/>
      <operation name="getRandom">
      <soap:operation soapAction=""/>
      <input>
      <soap:body namespace="http://ws1/" use="literal"/>
      </input>
      <output>
      <soap:body namespace="http://ws1/" use="literal"/>
      </output>
      </operation>
</binding>
<service name="QuoteService">
<port name="QuotePort" binding="tns:QuotePortBinding">
```

(Continued)

```
<soap:address location="http://localhost:8080/wstest/QuoteService"/>
</port>
</service>
</definitions>
```

Fig. 9.7 *WSDL listing for the example*

The Concrete elements comprise service and binding elements. The service element describes the collection of ports (or endpoints). Each of these in turn describes a binding (Figures 9.8 and 9.9).

As per JAX-WS, the following are the basic requirements of an end-point, similar to that for a Java Bean.

- The class (implementation class) must be annotated with @WebService (Figure 9.12)
- The business methods that expose the service should be public and must be annotated with @ WebMethod
- The class must have a default constructor

The example shows a WSDL for a web service that implements a RandomNumber Service (Figure 9.10). The service consists of a method called randomInt which is supposed to return a random number from 0 to a specified limit. This limit is passed as a parameter which is described in one of the Abstract elements.

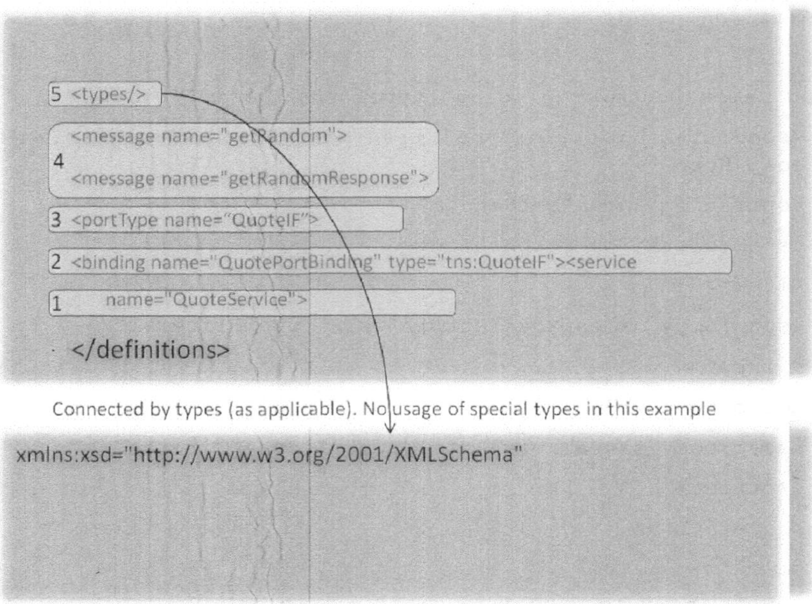

Fig. 9.8 *WSDL elements*

Fig. 9.9 *WSDL concrete elements–an example*

Fig. 9.10 *WSDL abstract elements–an example*

9.7.2 SOAP

SOAP defines a standard format of the messages used in web services. The message format is XML and communicates through HTTP. What this implies is that the communication mechanism and the protocol are independent of the underlying operating system and this is the secret of interoperability.

Aside note

SOAP with WSDL and XML Schema has become the standard for exchanging XML-based messages. SOAP was engineered to be extensible, consisting of a number of standards, often collectively referred to as WS-*, comprising of WS-Security, WS-Addressing, WS-Policy, WS-Federation, WS-ReliableMessaging, WS-Coordination, WS-AtomicTransaction, WS-Management, etc., concerning areas of Metadata, Security, Messaging, Privacy, Resource, etc. Hence the usage of SOAP seems very complex and indeed it is (unlike its earlier expansion). But, fortunately, one has to be concerned only about what is actually required for an application. Just like these standards have evolved over time, its implementation on a project can evolve too over time.

9.7.3 Structure of SOAP Messages

The Envelope contains the ROOT element, specifying the namespaces used in SOAP. It describes the message (and is frequently called by that name). It defines the scope of the message. The SOAP Header is optional. For simple web services, it may not be required. It is structured as a set of Blocks, each containing specific supplementary meta-data about the message. SOAP Body is best understood by referring to the flow of messages during a web service (Figure 9.11). The format is used both for request as well as the response. During Request, the Body contains the name of the method that is required to call, along with parameters, if any. During Response, the server sends back in the Body the return value(s), if any. If there is nothing to be returns it returns back empty.

The Envelope also houses a section called the SOAP Fault that is within the SOAP Body. The details of the error are housed in this part. This is also an optional part.

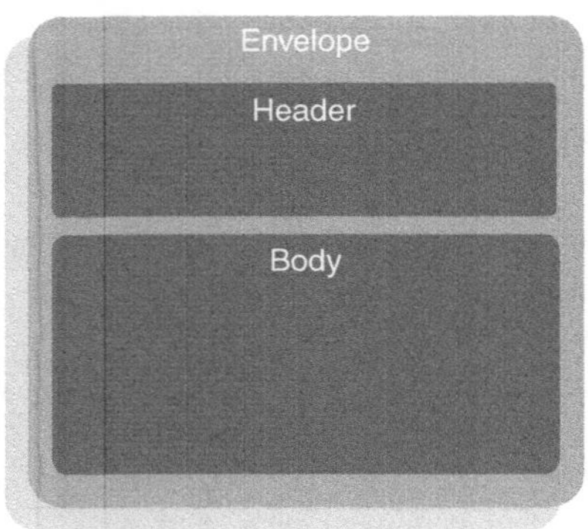

Fig. 9.11 *Essential elements of SOAP*

9.8 A BASIC EXAMPLE

Consider a simple example of fetching a random quote, used perhaps for flashing Thought-for-the-day kind of service. This could be used independently or as part of a web application, but in this example, it is simplified to be standalone. The service is implemented in a Java environment (service provider). Let us use the same WSDL as explained in the previous paragraphs.

For demonstrating interoperability, the example shows the client (service requestor) in a different environment, in this case Ruby on Rails, that is, the rails application calls the service that is running in a Java environment. It is equally easy to have the client in a different environment like Microsoft.NET or PHP or even in Java itself, in which the service provider is written. The service fetches the quote that is sent as a response from the service.

Java Service definition

```
package ws1;
import javax.jws.WebService;
import javax.jws.WebMethod;
import javax.jws.soap.SOAPBinding;
import javax.jws.soap.SOAPBinding.Style;

@WebService                              //Service Endpoint
                                         //Interface
@SOAPBinding(style = Style.RPC)          //WSDL & Service
Contract - basic data types

public interface QuoteIF {
    @WebMethod String getRandom(String category);
                                         //Service operation
}
```

Java Service Impl

```
/*
 * Implementation of the Quote Service. The service
   fetches a quote at random
 * from the list. Assume the list in memory and not from
   a database for simplicity
 * A simple parameter (category) is used to fetch from
   the appropriate category.
 */
package ws1;
import javax.jws.WebService;
import java.util.Random;
@WebService(endpointInterface = "ws1.QuoteIF")
public class Quote implements QuoteIF {
```

(Continued)

```
            //define a few categories of quotes
        String[] TFD_General = {
"An apple a day keeps the doctor away",
"Be good, see good, do good",
"Start early, finish the game",
"Love all Serve all"
};
        String[] TFD_Inspire = {
"Allow Your Inner Light to Guide You",
            "Be strong enough to at least try",
"Feel the calmness on a quiet sunny day",
            "Say hello to strangers and enjoy the people you know"
        };
        public String getRandom(String category) {
            String s;
            if (category.equals("General")) {
                int r = new Random().nextInt(TFD_General.length);
                s = TFD_General[r];
            } else {
                if (category.equalsIgnoreCase("Inspirational")) {
                    int r = new Random().nextInt(TFD_Inspire.length);
                    s = TFD_Inspire[r];
                } else {
                    s = "Ask for General or Inspirational";
                }
            }
            return (s);
        }
}
```

Web Service Client on Rails (Controller)

```
#Demo function to fetch a random quote from a Java Web Service
def myquote
#URI of the Service WSDL
qte_uri = 'http://localhost:8080/wstest/QuoteService?wsdl'
#
#get hold of the services object.
```

```
           7.  quot_svc = SOAP::WSDLDriverFactory.new(qte_uri).
               create_rpc_driver
           8.
           9.  #Invoke the method from service object and store in a
               local variable
          10.  @category = "Inspirational"
          11.  @quot = quot_svc.getRandom(@category)
          12.  #Ready to render the view for display
          13.  End
Rails View 1.  <!-- View the output from Java Web Service -->
           2.  <h1> <%=@category %> Quote of the Moment! </h1>
           3.  <h2>
           4.     <%=@quot%>
           5.  </h2>
```

Fig. 9.12 *Web service code sample–provider (in Java) and client (in Ruby-on-Rails)*

It does not matter if the reader is new to Ruby-on-Rails, however, with a little effort, the Ruby-on-Rails code shown in Figure 9.12, can be followed. Comments are shown after the hash (#) character. Variables with a prefix of "@" are available in the View part of the Rails' MVC. Actually Ruby-on-Rails aligns more closely with the MVC pattern and hence the three components (Model, View and Controller) are nicely kept separate in different parts of the code.

Running the Ruby-on-Rails client produces the output which prints a random quote. Notice that the Title is the H1 element in the Rails View (listing line 2) and the quote itself is written as H2 (line # 4). If the reader does not understand the syntax, just suffice to note that the variable (@quot —Figure 9.12. [Rails View] line 4) is coming from the Rails controller client (line 10), which comes from the Java-based web service, *getRandom*. Variable @category is set within the Rails Controller environment (line 9). The View is a combination of Ruby code and HTML.

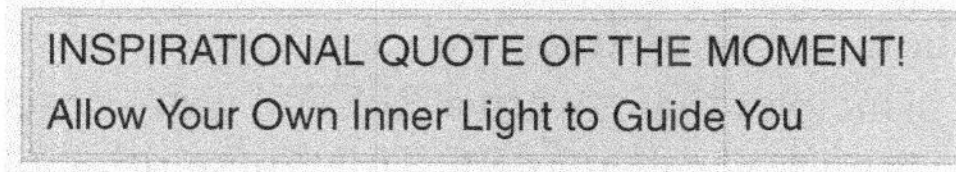

Fig. 9.13 *Output of the rails view*

An indicative output is shown in Figure 9.13. The idea is just to demonstrate how a simple web service is written in Java and how it is interoperable by calling the service from even a non-Java platform like RoR.

9.8.1 Generating a Web Service

There are a lot of tools available which have obviated the need to generate a web service manually. Using Annotations (in a Java environment) with good support from IDE has made the task very simple.

However, in the Java environment, for getting an insight into what goes behind the scenes, `wscompile`, as part of JWSDP, is used in a large part of the process. On the service provider side, it is used to generate the WSDL. On the client side, it uses WSDL to compile the java code referencing the service. It is evident from the example shown in Figure 9.12 that implementation of a web service is not very much different from implementing it otherwise.

9.9 REST BASED WEB SERVICES

It has been seen that SOAP is a protocol for exchanging information as part of Web Services. REST (short for Representational State Transfer) is another means for implementing Web Services, however it is not a protocol. It is an architectural style for distributed systems. Being an architectural style, it also implies that REST is not a specification, so it is not as concrete as SOAP. The key advantage of REST is that it leverages the already existing web infrastructure including HTTP. Not surprisingly, this has become the more popular way of connecting applications.

REST is a result of a doctoral thesis by Dr. Roy Fielding. According to him, REST is actually a reverse-engineer of the concept of web. In other words, the Web is something that uses the principles of REST or conforms to a RESTful architecture as it is commonly said.

Aside note

The web has seen increased usage of REST over the years, as a design style. Many of the major webservices on the web use REST as in Twitter, Yahoo web services, Flickr, del.icio.us, bloglines, technorati, etc. Salesforce.com, Amazon and eBay use both REST and SOAP. Those who are statistically inclined, may check in one of the blogs on **www.programmableweb.com**. There are other interesting information about the web in the site, that the reader may stumble upon

9.9.1 REST Principles

REST is a style that is oriented towards a concept called *Resources*, rather than oriented towards *messages*, as in SOAP. Strictly speaking, REST cannot be compared directly with SOAP, because they are two different things, though both can be used for Web Services.

There are certain guiding principles that govern a RESTful web service. Conversely, if an application conforms to these principles, it may be called as RESTful. These principles are in fact applicable to the general web as well. Here are the principles that govern each service in a RESTful application.

9.9.1.1 Resources A Resource is the most significant aspect in REST, just as an Object is in the world of OOP (Object Oriented Programming). Everything is a Resource in the context of the Web—pages, images, media, etc. A Resource is made accessible to a client where operations can be performed—it has to be addressable.

9.9.1.2 Addressability A Resource has to be addressable over the web, because otherwise, it cannot be reached or accessed. The Resource can be addressed by its URI. As far as REST is concerned, every Resource must have an URI. A Client can access multiple Resources just like a person surfing the web accesses multiple web pages in a web site, he/she has access to.

9.9.1.3 *Uniform means of communication* After addressing the "what" (which is URI), the "how" needs to be addressed! How a client communicates with the Resource is through standard means. In the context of the web, it is HTTP methods—Get and Post, for example. Having a uniform interface is the biggest differentiator of REST style. This dictates a uniform method, governed by HTTP specifications, on how components (clients and servers) communicate with each other. It is like the postal services offered, where if one knows the destination address along with zip (pin) code, any letter can be sent to anyone and the communication can be established. Fortunately, the infrastructure in the case of the web, is already available and hence made standard. For instance, no matter what URI it is or what resource type it is, GET can be used to retrieve the information.

9.9.1.4 *Stateless* True to the web, in its pure form there is no information pertaining to states of transactions in the server. Consequently no sessions or cookies are entertained. Each request from a client to a server is supposed to contain all the information required to perform a transaction. In practice some applications use Cookies for their otherwise RESTful application, but it cannot be termed as a pure RESTful, though it serves its purpose. Cookies bring in information that is global in nature as opposed to just being applicable for the transaction in question and this is the reason it is not purely object oriented. In other words, it does not follow pure inheritance.

9.9.2 Resource Orientation

The web is the best example of a truly distributed system, providing a framework for navigating across resources. The web intrinsically provides the infrastructure to navigate resources through links. A resource could be an URI, a Data file, an image, a media file, etc., represented by standard (mime) types. Retrieval of information of a resource can be thought of as a representation of the current state of the resource and hence the origination of the term REST.

In summary, in REST everything is a Resource, which can be accessed through an HTTP method.

Java supports REST through the JAX-RS (Java API for Restful Web Services). The specifications are defined in JSR 311. A popular reference implementation of JSR311 is code named *Jersey* and supports the annotations defined in the same (JSR 311). Conceptually, a Resource is mapped to a Class (POJO—Plain Old Java Objects). The HTTP Verbs (Get, Post, etc.) are mapped to methods within the Class.

Aside note

Just another school of thought...! REST uses standards already available, like XML, JSON, MIME, URL, HTTP, HTTPS, & SSL. Compare it with WS-* from SOAP.

9.10 REST BASED WEB SERVICES—AN EXAMPLE

The example being considered is about an example implementation of a Question Bank service. The QB is a single source of questions meant for exams. There is a facility to call the service for getting the questions. For the demo, it is also good to have a facility where only a part of the questions are to be delivered, and accordingly, the questions are organized based on chapters. For instance, if questions are required from Chapter 1, they can be sent across in a URL and the questions will be delivered accordingly.

To keep the demo implementation simple, let us have the questions hard-coded into memory rather than the ideal case of serving it from a database. There are two parts to the demo—one the service provider that delivers the requests and two, the client that needs the service.

First let's take a look at the main part of the Service provider code.

9.10.1 Service Provider Side

Create a web project in Netbeans and then create a new web service. Select RESTful web service from patterns, as a simple root resource (Figure 9.14).

```
Package qbsp;

import java.io.StringWriter;
import java.util.ArrayList;
import java.util.logging.Level;
import java.util.logging.Logger;
import javax.ws.rs.core.Context;
import javax.ws.rs.core.UriInfo;
import javax.ws.rs.PathParam;
import javax.ws.rs.Consumes;
import javax.ws.rs.PUT;
import javax.ws.rs.Path;
import javax.ws.rs.GET;
import javax.ws.rs.Produces;
import javax.xml.parsers.*;
import javax.xml.transform.OutputKeys;
import javax.xml.transform.Transformer;
import javax.xml.transform.TransformerFactory;
import javax.xml.transform.dom.DOMSource;
import javax.xml.transform.stream.StreamResult;
import org.w3c.dom.Document;
import org.w3c.dom.Element;
import org.w3c.dom.Text;

@Path("Quest")
public class Quest {
     //private HashMap QAList;
     StringWriter sw = new StringWriter();
     Document doc=null;
     /* This is the main data structure that forms the purpose of this demo
```

```
     * In reality this data shoould reside in a database. Lets simplify.
     * Data consists of Questions, Answers and Chapters - They are connected
     * by the array list sequence.
    */
    private class QAStruct {
        private ArrayList Questions;
        private ArrayList Answers;
        private ArrayList Chapters;
        public QAStruct() {
            this.Questions = new ArrayList();
            this.Questions.add(“Explain the difference between a Process and a Thread in Java”);
            this.Questions.add(“Explain different ways of creating a Thread in Java”);
            this.Questions.add(“What does EJB stand for?”);
            this.Questions.add(“Name the different types of EJB’s”);
            this.Questions.add(“Which is the EJB not used directly by a Client?”);
            this.Answers = new ArrayList();
            this.Answers.add(“A process is an execution of a program but a thread is a single execution sequence within the process”);
            this.Answers.add(“Extending Thread class and Implementing Runnable”);
            this.Answers.add(“Enterprise Java Beans”);
            this.Answers.add(“Entity Beans, Session beans and Message drive bean”);
            this.Answers.add(“Message driven bean”);
            this.Chapters = new ArrayList();
            this.Chapters.add(“Chapter1”);
            this.Chapters.add(“Chapter1”);
            this.Chapters.add(“Chapter2”);
            this.Chapters.add(“Chapter2”);
            this.Chapters.add(“Chapter2”);
                //This list could go on... Here is just a
                //sample.
 //It is important to be ordered by chapter (i.e.) not to mix
 //chapters
        }
    }
    private QAStruct QAList;
```

```
    @Context
    private UriInfo context;

    /** Creates a new instance of Quest */
    public Quest() {
        this.QAList = new QAStruct();
    }

    @GET
    @Produces("application/xml")
    public Document getQuestions() {

        try {
            DocumentBuilderFactory dbf = DocumentBuilderFactory.newInstance();
            DocumentBuilder db = dbf.newDocumentBuilder();
            //Create the document root qith node name "questions"
            doc = db.newDocument();
            Element myRoot = doc.createElement("questions");
            doc.appendChild(myRoot);

            createXML("ALL", myRoot);

            //Preparing to write it out
            TransformerFactory tf = TransformerFactory.newInstance();
            Transformer tr = tf.newTransformer();
            tr.setOutputProperty(OutputKeys.OMIT_XML_DECLARATION, "yes");
            tr.setOutputProperty(OutputKeys.INDENT, "yes");

            StreamResult res = new StreamResult(sw);
            DOMSource src = new DOMSource(doc);
            tr.transform(src, res);
            //XMLString = sw.toString();
        } catch (Exception ex) {
            Logger.getLogger(Quest.class.getName()).log(Level.SEVERE, null, ex);
        }
        return (doc);
    }

```

```
    @Path (“{chap}”)
    @GET
    @Produces(“application/xml”)
   public Document getChapterQuestions(@PathParam(“chap”) String chap) {

        try {
            DocumentBuilderFactory dbf = DocumentBuilderFactory.newInstance();
            DocumentBuilder db = dbf.newDocumentBuilder();
           //Create the document root qith node name “questions”
            doc = db.newDocument();
            Element myRoot = doc.createElement(“questions”);
            doc.appendChild(myRoot);

            createXML(chap, myRoot);

            //Preparing to write it out
                TransformerFactory tf = TransformerFactory.newInstance();
            Transformer tr = tf.newTransformer();
          tr.setOutputProperty(OutputKeys.OMIT_XML_DECLARATION, “yes”);
            tr.setOutputProperty(OutputKeys.INDENT, “yes”);

            StreamResult res = new StreamResult(sw);
            DOMSource src = new DOMSource(doc);
            tr.transform(src, res);
            //XMLString = sw.toString();
        } catch (Exception ex) {
             Logger.getLogger(Quest.class.getName()).log(Level.SEVERE, null, ex);
        }
        return(doc);
    }

    @PUT
    @Consumes(“application/xml”)
    public void putXml(String content) {
    }

```

(*Continued*)

```
137.        public void createXML (String chap,Element myRoot) {
138.
139.                String lastChapter = "";
140.                Element ChapterNode = null;
141.
142.              for (int idx=0; idx < QAList.Questions.size(); idx++) {
143.                    String q = (String) QAList.Questions.get(idx);
144.                    String a = (String) QAList.Answers.get(idx);
145.                    String c = (String) QAList.Chapters.get(idx);
146.
147.                    if (!lastChapter.equals(c)) {
148.                     if (!c.equals(chap) && (!chap.equals("ALL"))) {
149.                            continue;
150.                        }
151.                        ChapterNode = doc.createElement(c);
152.                        myRoot.appendChild(ChapterNode);
153.                        lastChapter = c;
154.                    }
155.                    //create the Question node belonging to the
                        //chapter node
156.                Element QuestionNode = doc.createElement("question");
157.                    Text txt = doc.createTextNode(q);
158.                    ChapterNode.appendChild(QuestionNode);
159.                    QuestionNode.appendChild(txt);
160.
161.                    //create the Answer node belonging to the same
                        //chapter node
162.                   Element AnswerNode = doc.createElement("answer");
163.                    Text anstxt = doc.createTextNode(a);
164.                    ChapterNode.appendChild(AnswerNode);
165.                    AnswerNode.appendChild(anstxt);
166.                }
167.        }
168.    }
```

Fig. 9.14 *Quest.java*

Refer the code listing on Figure 9.14. there are two methods that are relevant here since they are the ones that are exposed as RESTful Web Services. The methods are:

- public Document getQuestions() (line 73)

- public Document getChapterQuestions (chapter)

The first method (getQuestions) are available through a URL as http://127.0.0.1:8080/QBank/questRes/Quest where the last element (of the URI)—Quest—comes from the Annotation on line 25.

```
@Path("Quest")
```

Since it is declared global to the class (above the Quest class definition), all methods have this path, unless supplemented. Observe lines 101–104 (reproduced below).

```
    @Path ("{chap}")
    @GET
    @Produces("application/xml")
   public Document getChapterQuestions(@PathParam("chap") String chap) {
```

The path is supplemented as shown. It can be a hard-coded string which is easier to handle, or a variable (as given in the example, by name chap, signifying chapter name). So the relative path will become /Quest/{chap}.

The braces {} signify that a variable name. This is referenced in the method definition (getChapterQuestions). @PathParam is another Java annotation which signifies variable "chap" as a (String) parameter.

Both these methods imply getting data from the Service. Though the client need not be concerned about how data is being created into the QBank, it is a question that will arise if a systems viewpoint is taken. For this, there is another (web service) putXML method defined in line 134. However this is not used in this application (for a reason). If used, this signifies that HTTP method, PUT (as per the @PUT Annotation in line-132) is leveraged to get data into the QBank. The reason it is not used here is that it does not make sense in this context, when there is no data persistence, that is, when DB access is not being done for making it simplistic. Even if the data is used to post new Questions into the QBank, it will not be available for the user since each request is treated differently and they are stateless. In combination with EJBs this will be an effective means to add entries.

In summary, the following are the methods. Note that the URLs are intuitively easy to create and use.

Path (URL)	HTTP Method	CRUD	Description of the Service
/Quest	GET	R	Deliver all questions
/Quest/{chapter}	GET	R	Deliver all question for the chapter specified
/Quest	PUT	C	Inserting data into the Question Bank

Note the equivalent CRUD operations that are satisfied by each URL. Similar operations for Delete and Update can be introduced.

9.10.2 The XML Document from the Service

The output from the service cannot be run because it does not have a client component (Figure 9.15). However, the IDE offers a means to test the output, which is shown in Figure 9.16. The method createXML

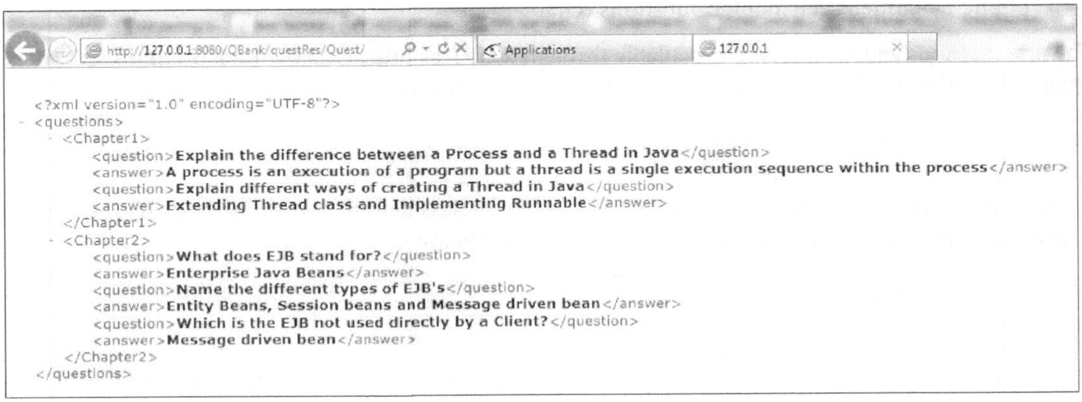


```
<?xml version="1.0" encoding="UTF-8"?>
- <questions>
  - <Chapter1>
      <question>Explain the difference between a Process and a Thread in Java</question>
      <answer>A process is an execution of a program but a thread is a single execution sequence within the process</answer>
      <question>Explain different ways of creating a Thread in Java</question>
      <answer>Extending Thread class and Implementing Runnable</answer>
    </Chapter1>
  - <Chapter2>
      <question>What does EJB stand for?</question>
      <answer>Enterprise Java Beans</answer>
      <question>Name the different types of EJB's</question>
      <answer>Entity Beans, Session beans and Message driven bean</answer>
      <question>Which is the EJB not used directly by a Client?</question>
      <answer>Message driven bean</answer>
    </Chapter2>
</questions>
```

Fig. 9.15 *REST service–the XML output*

is responsible for producing this output. Any client web service that is called by a REST client will get the XML similar to the listing shown. Notice the URL in the address box shown in the browser.

9.10.3 Client Side

The client is open to use Microsoft.Net, Java, rails or any such environments. However, for the purpose of this demo, a Java environment is taken.

Create a project as a Web application, and create a RESTful client.

```
<%@page import="java.util.ArrayList"%>
<%@page contentType="text/html" pageEncoding="UTF-8"%>

<!DOCTYPE html>
<html>
    <head>
        <meta http-equiv="Content-Type" content="text/html; charset=UTF-8">
        <link href="expCSS.css" rel="stylesheet" type="text/css" />
        <title>JSP Page</title>
    </head>
    <body>
        <h1>Question Bank Client</h1>
         <form action="mys">
            <p>
                Chapter: <input type="text" name="thisChapter" /> (blank for all)
```

```
            </p>
            <button type="submit">Get Questions</button>
        </form>
        <br />

        <%
            ArrayList quest = (ArrayList) session.getAttribute("questions");
            ArrayList answers = (ArrayList) session.getAttribute("answers");
            ArrayList chaps = (ArrayList) session.getAttribute("chapters");
            int sz = 0;
            if (quest != null) {
                sz = quest.size();
            }
        %>

        <% if (sz > 0) { %>
        <table class="gradient-style">
            <thead>
            <tr><td>Chapter</td><td>Question</td><td>Answer</td></tr>
            </thead>
            <% for (int i=0; i<sz; i++) { %>
            <tr>
                <td><%= (String) chaps.get(i) %></td>
                <td><%= (String) quest.get(i) %></td>
                <td><%= (String) answers.get(i) %></td>
            </tr>
            <% } %>
        </table>
        <% } %>
    </body>
</html>
```

Fig. 9.16 *RESTClient–index.jsp*

The home page (index.jsp) renders the Form which accepts the Chapter name, if supplied. On clicking the button (Get Questions), the servlet routine is invoked. The servlet code is given in the following code listing (Figure 9.17).

```
package su;

import java.io.IOException;
import java.util.ArrayList;
import javax.servlet.RequestDispatcher;
import javax.servlet.ServletException;
import javax.servlet.http.HttpServlet;
import javax.servlet.http.HttpServletRequest;
import javax.servlet.http.HttpServletResponse;
import javax.servlet.http.HttpSession;
import org.w3c.dom.*;

public class QuestServlet extends HttpServlet {

    @Override
    protected void doGet(HttpServletRequest request,
    HttpServletResponse response) throws ServletException,
IOException {
        doPost(request,response);
    }

    @Override
    protected void doPost(HttpServletRequest request,
    HttpServletResponse response) throws ServletException,
IOException {
         Document doc;
        //Get chapter from Form. Null implies all chapters
         String chap = request.getParameter("thisChapter");

         Quest quest;
        //Instantiate the client class for accessing the questions
        //from REST server
         quest = new Quest();

         HttpSession sess;
         sess = request.getSession();
        //Get all questions if chapter is not specified, else get
         //chapter specific questions
         if (chap == null) {
             doc = (Document) quest.getQuestions();
```

```
            } else {
                //demonstrates use of arguments passed to a web service
                  doc = (Document) quest.getChapterQs(chap);
            }

            /*Retreive the data from XML obtained thru REST web service
            This maps to the definition in the REST Service provider. However, this
                can map into a class or any other way of describing it
            */
            ArrayList Questions = new ArrayList();
            ArrayList Answers = new ArrayList();
            ArrayList Chapters = new ArrayList();

            if (doc != null) {
                ArrayList nodeNames = new ArrayList();

                //there is only node (root) called questions
              Node rootNode = doc.getElementsByTagName("questions").item(0);
                NodeList chapterNodes = rootNode.getChildNodes();
                //Get all chapter node names
              for (int idx=0; idx < chapterNodes.getLength(); idx++) {
                nodeNames.add(chapterNodes.item(idx).getNodeName());
                }

                for (int idx=0; idx < nodeNames.size(); idx++) {
                    String nodeName = (String) nodeNames.get(idx);
                //first element of the tag named by chapters is the
                //main chapter node
                 Node ChapNode = doc.getElementsByTagName(nodeName).
                 item(0);
                 //all child nodes under the chapter consists of q/a
                    NodeList QA = ChapNode.getChildNodes();
                    int nCh = QA.getLength();
                  //Loop for each Chapter Node. Take all child nodes
                  //- consists of Question, Answer
                    for (int qaidx=0; qaidx<nCh; qaidx++) {
                        Node n = QA.item(qaidx);
```

(Continued)

```
69.                     String typ = n.getNodeName();
70.
71.                     //Expect the node name (typ) to be answer or
                        //question
72.                     if (typ.equals("question")) {
73.                         Questions.add(n.getTextContent());
74.                         Chapters.add(nodeName);
75.                     }
76.                     if (typ.equals("answer")) {
77.                         Answers.add(n.getTextContent());
78.                     }
79.                 }
80.             }
81.         }
82.         sess.setAttribute("questions", Questions);
83.         sess.setAttribute("chapters", Chapters);
84.         sess.setAttribute("answers", Answers);
85.         //Transfer control from where it came!
86.       RequestDispatcher rd = request.getRequestDispatcher("index.
    jsp");
87.         rd.forward(request, response);
88.     }
89.     @Override
90.     public String getServletInfo() {
91.         return "Short description";
92.     }// </editor-fold>
93. }
```

Fig. 9.17 *RESTClient–questservlet.java*

Lines 33–38 handle the task of calling the REST web service through the Quest object, the definition of which is given in Figure 9.18. Notice that the web service returns the document object (line 34 and line 37), which is the XML document (from org.w3c.dom.Document) that is returned by it. Lines 49–80 deal with (DOM) parsing the XML and pushing them into the Questions, Answers and Chapters ArrayList. This is much the same way it was stored in the server provider (QBank) program, though it is not necessary to mimic the same structure.

```
package su;

import com.sun.jersey.api.client.Client;
```

```
import com.sun.jersey.api.client.UniformInterfaceException;
import com.sun.jersey.api.client.WebResource;
import org.w3c.dom.Document;
public class Quest {
    private WebResource webResource;
    private Client client;
    private static final String BASE_URI = "http://127.0.0.1:8080/
    QBank/questRes";
public Quest() {
    com.sun.jersey.api.client.conFigure ClientConfig config = new
    com.sun.jersey.api.client.conFigure DefaultClientConfig();
    client = Client.create(config);
     webResource = client.resource(BASE_URI).path("Quest");
}
  public Document getQuestions() throws UniformInterfaceException
{
        WebResource resource = webResource;
        Document x;
     x = resource.accept(javax.ws.rs.core.MediaType.APPLICATION_
XML).get(Document.class);
        return (x);
    }
    public void putXml(Object requestEntity) throws
UniformInterfaceException {
       webResource.type(javax.ws.rs.core.MediaType.APPLICATION_
XML).put(requestEntity);
    }
    public Document getChapterQs(String chap) throws
UniformInterfaceException {
        Document x;
        WebResource res = webResource;
          x = res.path(chap).accept(javax.ws.rs.core.MediaType.
APPLICATION_XML).get(Document.class);
        return (x);
    }
```

(Continued)

```
35.
36.        public void close() {
37.            client.destroy();
38.        }
39.
40.    }
```

Fig. 9.18 *REST client–quest.java*

Notice the client class method names. The names need not match with the names on the Service Provider. For instance, the method, getChapterQs, does not match with any method on the Service provider. What is significant is in fact the URL.

Notice Line 11, which defines the base URL. Since the path is supplemented with the Chapter name for getChapterQuestions service, the same is passed as an argument to the getChapterQs method defined in the client. Also notice the corresponding HTTP method—GET, PUT, etc.

The output is rendered back to index.jsp, which uses the ArrayList to construct the table showing the questions and answers, arranged by chapter.

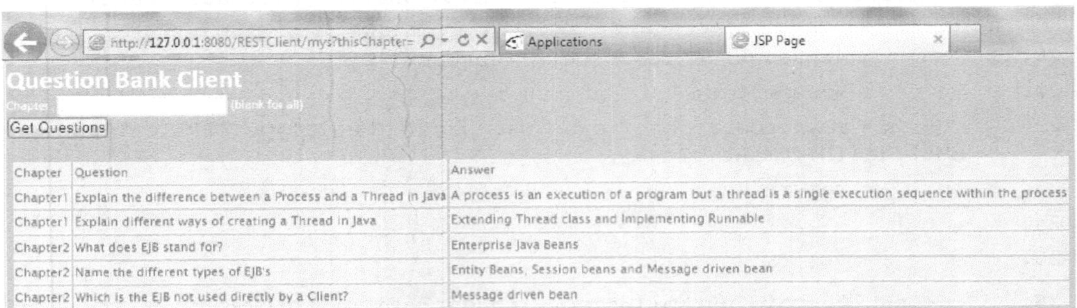

Fig. 9.19 *REST service–the output*

The output is rendered in HTML (Figure 9.19). This demonstrates the ability of rendering a service, converting output data into XML, and then invoking through a different client, rendering back into HTML.

9.11 SOAP VS. REST

Both SOAP and REST are relevant technologies that are being used and will continue to be used. How do we make a decision whether it is SOAP or REST (or both!) that will be well suited to an application? It all depends on what really is required, from a business and an architectural point of view. The following table summarizes the categories that are applicable to both the schools of thought.

Category	SOAP	REST
Classification	Middleware interoperability standards	Architectural style for web services
Comprehensiveness	Generic (more comprehensive)	Specialized (less comprehensive)
Integration styles	RPC and Messaging—Heterogeneous	RPC—Heterogeneous
Contractual obligations	Contractual since it includes WS-Reliability, WS-Transactions, rigid type checks, etc.	Not Contractual
Transport Protocols supported	Many (includes HTTP, TCP, SMTP, JMS, etc)	Predominantly HTTP
Mode of messages (payload)	XML	XML, JSON, YAML, MIME
Security	WS-Security, HTTPS	HTTPS
Overheads	Heavy	Light weight

This can be applied to the specific web initiative (an application or product) depending on what categories can be considered important. Overall, REST is simpler to develop because it leverages the web, which is already in place and the degree of freedom is limited (less choices to make, so simpler). SOAP offers a number of alternatives and is also slightly more difficult to develop, but offers more alternatives and areas to work.

9.12 CASE STUDY OF AN ONLINE STORE

This section is meant to impart the distinction of how web services can enable do business better and more efficient.

9.12.1 Online Store Front

Imagine an online storefront consisting a seller of sports goods—badminton rackets, tennis equipments, etc. There is a catalog of items that are available to be displayed along with images, prices, data sheets and all the information necessary to make a purchase. The Storefront is mainly a distributor and in that sense it is agnostic about the manufacturers of these products. There are multiple sources of supply—either from manufacturers themselves or from suppliers or from storefront's own distribution centers. Whatever be the case there is a notional local inventory that is available during the customer's online buying process.

Lets us analyze two broad scenarios lying on two different sides of the spectrum—one without web services and the other using web services.

When none of the applications (or modules) is developed without any web service, the store front can service customers as long as local inventory is well maintained. If an item runs out of stock, it has no automatic visibility into any of the other sources and hence has no other option but to deny the service to the customer. It can be argued that the sources of supply can be made to publish their inventory each day as a matter of routine, but then it may not be cost-effective. Practically, the sources of supply (represented by manufacturer/suppliers/distributors) do business with multiple such store fronts, just like this particular store front does business with multiple sources. Hence updating inventory turns out to be a complex problem. Furthermore, the store front has to account for new sources of supply on a continual basis. It is manifested by either tightly coupled systems or fractured business processes, made up by manual interventions like phone or fax. Thus business performance gets affected (Figure 9.20).

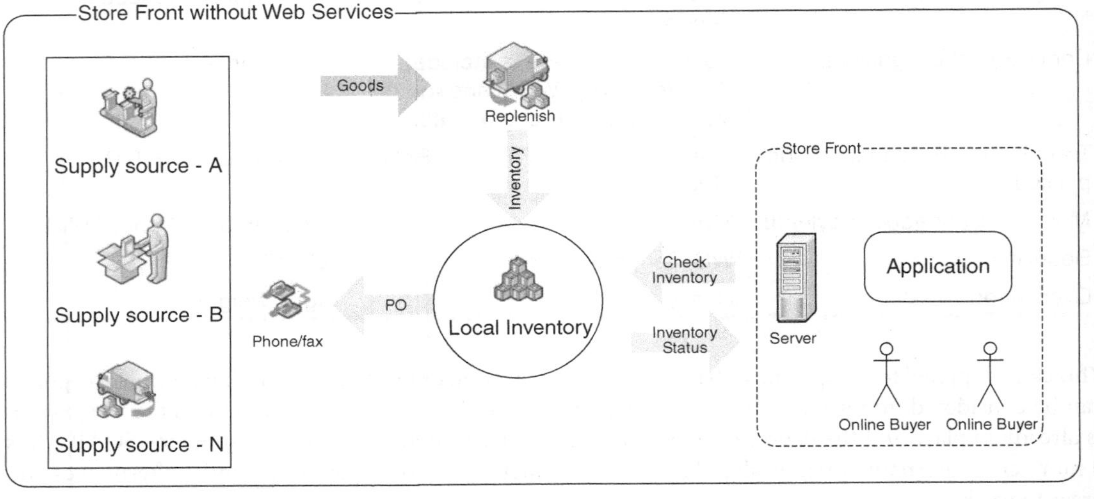

Fig. 9.20 *Store front without web services*

Web services promote standardized channels for communicating between the applications. When there is a standard means, a process can be established easily. For instance, a purchase order can be

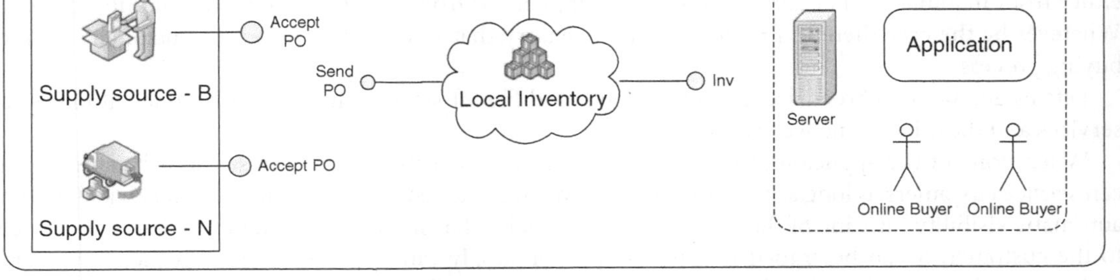

Fig. 9.21 *Store front with web services*

automatically created when inventory levels reach a certain stage. This can free purchasing organizations from the mundane tasks of creating POs and the effort saved can be spent on defining purchasing contracts so as to get the best bargains possible from the suppliers. So this can throw open numerous possibilities. Again, for example, automatic price comparisons can be shown to the customers, thereby increasing customer satisfaction. Also, stock out situations can be minimized by tapping into other inventory sources and by raising purchasing orders at the right times. There are obviously many ways of doing this with various degrees of web services implementation. One of such scenarios is represented in Figure 9.21.

Any new source of supply can join using the same WSDL for the PO web service. From a business perspective, it means that the system is automatically ready to accept any supplier (as long as they conform to the WSDL), without the need for massive integration efforts or changes to the system. The process for handling new suppliers can align with business processes as required by the system, thus enabling a future-proof automated procurement system.

9.13 WEB SERVICES ENDNOTE

It took nearly 100 years for the telecom industry to establish a standardized, interoperable network. It generally takes an enormous amount of time for a technology (or a set of technologies) to converge to any standards. Given the ubiquitous nature of the web, it is expected to take a long time for standardization to occur and conform to standards. However, in this context of standards, and interoperability, there are two levels which can be talked about—one is within the web community itself and the other level is across business.

Web services pave the way to standardize within the web community. This in turn can be leveraged by business to converge on business standards.

9.14 SUMMARY

Web services is one of the most important technologies that enable reaching out to other applications. It has a rich history of technological developments that led to the state of web services we have today—in SOAP and REST. It is thus supporting one of the strong philosophies of the web by promoting interoperability. We have also seen how the Java environment provides full stack support for web services. It was also observed that it was interoperable by having a Rails client call a Java based web service.

EXERCISES

Q1. An airline or rail reservation system operates on the basis of city codes rather than by city names. Write a SOAP Web Service to access city codes, given a city name. First create a simplistic service where it is assumed that the city name is perfectly given (i.e. city name without spelling mistake). A slightly complex scenario is one in which city names are approximately given (i.e. expect city name with spelling mistake). A more complex scenario would be to output multiple city codes for a given city name which is not correctly typed.

Q2. Implement a basic client mechanism for the above mentioned SOAP service.

Q3. List out the Annotations available in Java, with respect to SOAP web services.

Q4. Examine the XML Schema (XSD) in the light of a WSDL file.

Q5. In the example of the REST demo, enhance the web application to access a database. Also enhance it by adding a service to create new questions.

Q6. How does the philosophy of the web services align with that of the web?

Q7. Make a list of scenarios that you can think of using the concept of web services. Research the web to find out. The stronger the scenario, the better it is.

Q8. Make a list of Annotations that Java offers for REST based web services.

Q9. Study the example of the REST demo again. (Figure 9.14–9.18) Examine the features that are normally required to make it production-class. By this, it is meant as to what additional functionality is required to make it robust, and reliable—in short usable. Some of the essential functionalities are mentioned below:

a. Login functionality and user registration (for both service provider and the client)
b. Database persistence
c. Ability to add, modify or delete questions
d. Ability to add attachments (for a question and its answer)
e. Ability to view the attachments

Try to implement the above functionality as an exercise. Use as much of client and server technologies that can be used. Be as much creative as possible.

Project Activities

Q10. A Mashup is an application that uses different web services available in the web (or otherwise) to create new possibilities. For example you can create an application that could accept an area code (say PIN/ZIP code) for a location, get a map from Google Maps, read weather information from Yahoo weather and present to the user. This process involves registering with Yahoo and getting an ID for using its services. Demonstrate an example which does the above.

Q11. Create a (collocated or distributed) team of at least three people. Implement the case study involving the Store Front. Refer Figure 9.21 for a high level architecture of the system.

Caselet Activity

Q12. In continuation with the Caselet activities, in the previous chapters, enhance the web application to expose some of the services. Some examples are given below:

a. Fetch product details given item code
b. Fetch multiple product details given a family of products

APPENDIX

A.1 JAVA REFRESHER

According to current trends, Java is the most widely used language, supporting a variety of environments—standalone applications, web applications, mobile environments, etc. This section is meant as a refresher or act as a basic introduction guide to running Java. It is not meant to be an elaborate course on Java lest the book get diluted from its main focus. For a detailed overview on the language, the reader is advised to consult various tutorials available on the web.

Java was promoted by Sun Microsystems (now a part of Oracle) during the 1990s, first targeted towards embedded systems like VCRs and PDAs. Since the market did not evolve as expected, the focus got shifted to the web since the core principles of platform-independence was required in both environments.

Java promotes the philosophy of "Write once Run anywhere". This is a simple statement but having a profound impact in reality. Though this philosophy is yet to be achieved 100%, the degree of compliance to this is much better than before and is among the best in class of computer languages. The single most important factor that enables towards achieving this goal is the JVM or the Java Virtual Machine.

A.1.1 JVM

The Java Virtual Machine is the bridge between the underlying hardware and a Java application. It is an interpreter program that emulates the underlying processor executing byte code instructions. The reason it runs on any hardware is that JVMs are available on many platforms. These platforms include not only operating systems like Linux and Windows but also on devices like mobiles, set-top boxes and many hand-helds.

Oracle (Sun) provides JVM implementations for its own operating systems, other Linux systems and also for Microsoft Windows platforms. There are other vendors like Apple providing JVM for their platforms.

As a web programmer, it is interesting to note the best thing about JVM is that there are other modern and innovative languages that could run on it, besides of course Java. These languages include Groovy, JRuby and Scala that can run in the JVM, with Groovy being the most promising and popular among these. Groovy itself brings out the best of Java, Ruby and Smalltalk and can be used in the course of web development.

A.1.2 Getting Started

The major editions of Java available are the following:

- Java SE (Standard Edition)—this is by default commonly referred to as Java. Works on desktop applications, applets, etc. It is also used as the base to build web applications.
- Java EE (Enterprise Edition)—this was originally termed J2EE. This is build and deployed (run) in application servers that are commonly accessed. Various components include Servlets, JSP, JSF (Java Server Faces), etc. A lot of frameworks like Spring and Hibernate are have also been a part of this edition.
- Java ME (Micro Edition)—this refers to Java that is used in small devices like mobiles, hand-held's, etc. It enables convergence of such devices into the larger enterprise types of applications and thus is one of the most promising areas of web development today. Some of the popular examples include Android, Kindle, etc.

The following are the minimum pre-requisites:

- Java SDK or J2SE which contains the essentials components to run a Java program. The components include the Java Complier (javac), interpreter (java), applet viewer (appletviewer) and Class libraries. The SDK is freely down-loadable from the internet.
- Documentation to refer API's for use in programs.

The JRE or Java RunTime Environment is needed for running java programs. The JRE is an implementation of the Java Virtual Machine which actually executes Java programs.

The JDK is the Java Development Kit for Java application developers. The JDK is a bundle of software which contains one (or more) JREs along with the various development tools like the Java source compilers, bundling and deployment tools, debuggers, development libraries, etc.

A.1.2.1 Environment variables It is important to set the right operating environment. The following are especially of interest in a Java environment:

- PATH: The PATH variable should include the path for the Java executables, pointing to the bin directory of Java compiler.
- JAVA_HOME: This variable is used by application servers like Tomcat, JBOSS, etc. Set this variable to point to the JDK directory. It may be recalled that JDK is JRE plus tools for Development. True to its expansion (Java Runtime Engine), JRE is just required for running java programs. For development, the Java Development Kit (JDK) is required.
- CLASSPATH: This is a set of directories that Java uses to use JAR files required for the application. This is an optional parameter, but useful for including a large set of libraries.

The process of setting these environment variables is simple, but depends on the operating system which is being used.

A.1.2.2 Running a Java program Consider a sample program like the one shown in Figure A.1.

```
public class myArgs {

```

```
    public static void main(String[] args) {
        String[]  order  =  {"First","Second","Third","Fourth","Fifth",
        "Sixth"};
        if (args.length > order.length) {
        System.out.println("Do not know more than" + order.length);
        return;
        }
        for(int i=0;i<args.length;i++){
        String s = order[i] + "argument is" + args[i];
        System.out.println(s);
    }
  }
}
```

Fig. A.1 *myArgs.java–display variable number of arguments*

The program is compiled using the Java Compiler. There are certain naming conventions that need to be followed. The name of the file should be the same as the class name with extension, java. The package name (which is not shown in the sample code) should be the same as the directory name. The usual convention in package names is to have it with the reversed domain name. In that case, each of the sub domains will form a directory. The compilation of the java code is done as follows:

```
javac myArgs.java
```

The output is a class file by name myArgs.class. This class file is executed through the following command line:

```
java myArgs arg1 arg2 arg3
```

The program accepts a variable number of arguments, accordingly arg1, agr2 and arg3 are shown as arguments in the example. In general, there are two ways of launching a Java program.

- Java classFile
- Java –jar jarFile

A.1.3 Java Data types

Primitives are the basic types in any language. Java supports the basic types as listed in Figures A.2.

Type	Values Range
boolean	true or false
Char	Unicode character
Byte	Signed integer
Short	Signed integer

(Continued)

(Continued)

Type	Values Range
Int	Signed integer
Long	Signed integer
Float	IEEE 754 floating point
Double	IEEE 754 floating point

Excepting Boolean, Java allows conversion of values from one primitive to another.

A.1.4 Classes in Java

It is assumed that the reader is familiar with basics of Java types—primitives, literals, operators and statements. However, the fundamentals of Java's object orientation in the form of Classes are discussed in this section.

Classes form the fundamental part of the Java language. A class is a module of Java code that defines its (class') data structure (a set of properties) and a set of methods that operate on its data. They are the most fundamental structure that forms a Java program.

Any Java program relies on a set of predefined classes. These classes comprise the Java platform and are organized into related groups known as packages. These packages are organized by functionality such as IO (Input/Output), graphics, user-interface creation, security, and much more.

Classes could also be defined by the developer. For example a Shape class can be defined below:

```
Public Class Sphere {
    public static final double PI = 3.14;     //Class property - a
                                               //Constant
    public static String sphereCh { // Class Method - Sphere charecteristics
                                    // Return("spherical facts…");
    }
    Public Sphere() {};             //empty constructor
    public Double r;                //instance property
    public Double volume() {        //instance method
    Return ((4/3) * PI * r**3);     //can also use this.r to be explicit
    }
    ...                             //other methods
}
```

The property/method attributes (modifiers) for each property/method can assume public, private or protected. They control the access of the fields within the class, thus achieving encapsulation.

Static methods can be invoked on the class rather than an instance of the class, which means that the JVM allows it (static method), to be accessed even without instatiation of the class.

An object is an instance of a class. A class is like a template and an object is an occurrence using the template. There are multiple ways of creating an object in Java. Here are some of the ways which it can be done:

- Using keyword "new": This by far is the most common way to create an object.
  - Sphere mySphere = new Sphere();
- Using Reflection API— Class.forName(): An example of this can be seen while initializing the Driver class for connection to a database. It is a part of the Java Reflection API which enables instantiation of classes at runtime. For example, if the name of the class is determined at

runtime (in a String), this method can construct the class and invoke the constructor (through the newInstance() method) to get the object (instance).

- Using clone(): As the name suggests, it is used to create a copy of the object (that already exists).

There are other ways of creating an object like deserialization which results in a new object, but the primary goal relates to serialization/deserialization aspects rather than creating a brand new object.

A.1.4.1 Extending a class In Java, inheritance is achieved through the Extends keyword. For example, if there is a Mammal class, a class called Dog can extend Mammal which implies that a Dog is inherited from the Mammal class.

```
Public class Dog extends Mammal {
      <properties and methods for Dog>
}
```

Here, Mammal is considered the "Super" class. In plain words, "a Dog is a Mammal", so it (inheritance or *extends*) is sometimes expressed as IS-A relationship. Similarly, if the relationship (between two classes) is based on usage then they are related by a "HAS-A" relationship. For example if the Dog has a reference to a property (like PlaceOfResidence, for instance), which is another class then the two classes (Dog class and Place_Of_Residence class) are related by a HAS-A relationship.

In fact, all objects (except one) have a super class. If no class is specified as the super class, that is, no "Extends" keyword, then it is considered to be extended from the Object (java.lang.Object) class. The object class is the only exception since it is the root of the hierarchy.

If a class were declared with the "final" keyword, it implies that no class can inherit from it. For example, primitive-wrapper classes are declared final so it cannot be extended.

A.1.4.2 Abstract class Imagine a class, SolidShape, which could potentially act as a super class to the Sphere class that was declared earlier in this section. The definition of such a class is indicated below:

```
public abstract class SolidShape {
      public abstract double volume(); //Abstract method
}
```

Note that the method, volume, is defined as an abstract method because the body of this function is empty. It is, in fact, waiting to be overridden by the inherited method's class definition.

A.1.4.3 Wrapper classes A wrapper in the general context of programming (languages and API) is meant to encapsulate or wrap the functionality of an object. Since primitives types in Java are not classes by themselves, the language offers a set of wrapper classes on these primitives. Each primitive type in Java has a corresponding wrapper class so that the developer can treat them as classes, in pure object oriented style. Wrapper classes are declared Final. The following table is a summary of the wrapper types.

Primitive	Wrapper	Allowed Arguments
Boolean	java.lang.Boolean	string/boolean
Byte	java.lang.Byte	string/byte
Char	java.lang.Character	char

(Continued)

Continued

Primitive	Wrapper	Allowed Arguments
Double	java.lang.Double	string/short
Float	java.lang.Float	string/double/float
Int	java.lang.Integer	string/int
Long	java.lang.Long	string/long
Short	java.lang.Short	string/short
Void	java.lang.Void	

The main advantage is ease of use. While primitives are passed by value across functions, wrappers are passed by reference. A few type-conversions are also made available by the wrappers. For example, consider the following ways to initialize a wrapper class and the relevant conversion functions.

```
Integer myInt = Integer.valueOf("12AB", 16);
    //Wrapping a primitive using the wrapper's static (class) method.
    //myInt assumes a value of 4799 which is 12AB to the base 16.
Short convMyInt = myInt.shortValue();
    //Convert into a short. Observe the Integer's instance method,
    //shortValue()
Boolean myBool = new Boolean("true");
    //another method to initialize a wrapper class by using the new
    //operator
Int myPrimitiveInt = Integer.parseInt("123");
    //Using the Integer class method to quickly convert a string to
    //integer.
```

Note that a wrapper can be defined through two methods as shown in the example. Observe the conversion methods of the Integer. The shortValue() (instance) method of the Integer class is one of the many conversion methods to convert an object back to a primitive. Integer.parseInt(s) is a conversion method (available as a class method on Integer), to convert a string to a primitive integer. Likewise there are other functions available to convert into other types.

The process of wrapping a primitive into a (wrapper) class is also refered to as *Boxing*. The reverse is called *unboxing*. Since this process (of boxing and unboxing) is done quite frequently, there is a facility available to automatically do this. The process is called auto-boxing and has been introduced since JEE 5. For the recent entrants, it will appear that wrappers are treated like primitives, but that is not so, since the process of conversion is done automatically, in the background. Auto-boxing works with their corresponding types only, for example from Integer to int (and vice versa), Float to float (and vice versa), and so on. Auto-conversion from other types (as in short to Integer, etc.) is not being discussed here.

A.1.4.4 Enumerated types Enumerated (enum) types were first introduced from EE5. It is used when a variable needs to hold only a specified set of values. It can be thought of as a special type of class.

```
enum mobileBrands {INDICOM,SAMSUNG,MOTOROLA,NOKIA};
mobileBrands nm = mobileBrands.NOKIA;
```

The enum cannot be declared within a method.

A.1.4.5 Interfaces An interface is a class template that contains declarations. As for methods, it provides only declarations, not their implementation. But that is not sufficient to understand the concept of an Interface. Visualize the car manufacturing industry where an engine needs to be fitted into a particular (brand of) car. The Engine is manufactured by a different unit and all they need to expose to the car unit is simplified to just about the following—fixtures that are required to hold the engine, the inputs to the engine and the output shaft for consuming the engine power. The car unit need not be concerned about how the engine is built or structured. For the sake of simplicity, let us assume the basics and cut out all complexity of the manufacturing required for the engine. Essentially, it is required to treat this interface as an engineering contract between the engine unit and the car unit. The concept of an engine in a car also signifies that this is used during the manufacture of the car but not to be used by the end user (unlike a tyre for instance).

In a similar way, an Interface in Java is a contract between two parties—the provider of the interface and a consumer of the interface.

The implementation is defined on the class that inherits the interface.

```
interface stimuli {
     Boolean sensitive = true;     //this is considered constant (final)
     string[] touch ();            //returns combination of
                                   //[comfort,pain,hot,cold,none,...]
     string taste();               //returns sweet/sour/pungent..
     ...
}
class Dog extends Mammal implements stimuli {
     ...
     public string touch () {
     //implementation of touch
         int nSensorPoints;
         string ret = "none";
         ...
         return (ret);
     }
     public string taste (f) {
         //implementation of touch
         int pH;
         string ret = "acidic";
         ...
         return (ret);
     }
}
```

Interfaces form a contract between the class and the outside world, because they interact with the outside through the defined methods only. This contract is enforced at build time by the compiler, that is, all methods defined by the interface must appear in its source code.

Note that an interface can extend another interface but cannot implement it. A class can implement more than one interface, so this is considered as another way to multiple inheritance (through interfaces only). However, the concept of multiple inheritances is actually not necessary to model real life instances for all scenarios. Rightly so, it has been discontinued after C++ as it makes the language unnecessarily complicated.

Some of the most popular implementations of Java interfaces include Iterator, Serializable, Cloneable, Runnable,

A.1.5 Handling Application Exceptions

There are three ways to deal with application runtime failures or exceptions. They are exception handling, assertions and logging.

Java offers a comprehensive mechanism to deal with exceptions. An *exception* is said to be "thrown" when an error occurs at runtime. It is "thrown" probably because it changes the normal flow of execution. Internally, *exceptions* manifest as a set of classes, which are incidentally arranged as a hierarchical set of classes. The root class of such a set is the class called throwable. This class has two subclasses—error and exception. Errors represented by the error class refer to runtime errors and occur in the JVM (not the application). Application errors are trapped by the exception class.

There are some important keywords that are used as part of exception handling—try, catch, throw, and finally. A catch block, with an exception identifier, is a piece of code in the program that is executed (rather transferred to) only if it catches the corresponding exception. If no catch is found (for the exception) then the program stops at the point where the fault was found.

Here are some examples of exceptions that can be trapped.

- NullPointerException
- IllegalStateException occurs when the method is invoked at an inappropriate time
- StackOverflowError
- NoClassDefFoundError occurs when attempting to load a non-existing class
- ArrayIndexOutOfBoundsException occurs due to negative index on an array (or an index which is greater than the size of the array)
- AssertionError ensures to check that certain conditions are true when the program executes

Exception handling is an important part of programming web based application development. However much precautions are taken to handle conditions, exceptions will happen because the program has no control over the external data that is encountered. Checked exceptions are the ones to take care of by including them in the code.

A.1.6 Java File I/O

Java has the standard package, java.io, to handle file operations. It has the File class to enable working with the local file system. Since the path is absolutely OS specific, internally Java translates the path into its own format by using the concept of abstract path names. For example, Unix/Linux based systems use forward slash (/) whereas Windows based systems use the backward slash (\) for specifying the path.

A File object can be created by specifying the path of the file. This instance can then be used to interact with the file system of the OS. The following are the operations that can be handled by the File object.

In a generic way, I/O is handled as if there is a source of data and there is a target (destination) for the data. Data flows from the source to the destination by means of a stream (of data). So the high level steps to read data from a file is to open the stream, keep reading from source, keep writing to destination (if necessary) and then close the stream.

File Method	Return Type	Description
f.canRead()	boolean	Indicates if the file can be read or not
f.canWrite()	boolean	Indicates if the file can be written or not
f.createNewFIle()	boolean	Creates a new file, if it does not exist
f.exists()	boolean	True if file exists
f.getCanonicalPath()	String	Path that is in conformance with the underlying OS
f.getName()	String	Retruns the name of the file
f.isDirectory()	String	Returns true if it is a directory
f.mkDir()	Boolean	Creates a directory

At a high level there are low level Streams and high level Streams, where raw data is read or written as bytes. The IO package includes the class FileInputStream for this purpose, whose signature is shown below.

```
Public FileInputStream(file) throws FileNotFoundException
```

In the statement above, file could be either a file descriptor or a File object or a filename (with path). Similar signature exists for the FileOutputStream. The important methods for both classes are summarized in the following paragraph.

Stream Method	Return Type	Description
inf.read()	Int	Returns the file's next byte of data. Returns -1 if EOF
inf.read(bytes[] b)	Int	Reads the file's next set of bytes in b (governed by b.length); returns number of bytes read or -1 if EOF
Inf.read(bytes[] b, int offset, int size)	Int	Reads the file's next set of bytes in b (governed by size) from offset; returns number of bytes read or -1 if EOF
Inf.close()	Void	Closes the stream and releases buffer
Outf.write(int b)	Void	Writes b bytes into the out stream
Outf.close()	Void	Closes the out stream

While low level streams are useful for handling raw data like images and other binary forms of data, high level streams are useful for handling data types like integer, float, etc. Java offers DataInputStream and DataOutputStream for such high level I/O. However, internally they go through the process of low level handling of raw data so these classes are logically viewed as a wrapper on the low level streams.

```
public DataInputStream(InputStream inf)
```

There are methods for reading each primitive data type, for example dif.readInt(), dif.readChar(), dif.readByte(), dif.readFloat(), and so on. On similar lines, this can be extrapolated for DataOutputStream. To simplify the understanding of the maze of various types of I/O possible in Java, a snapshot is shown in Figure A.2.

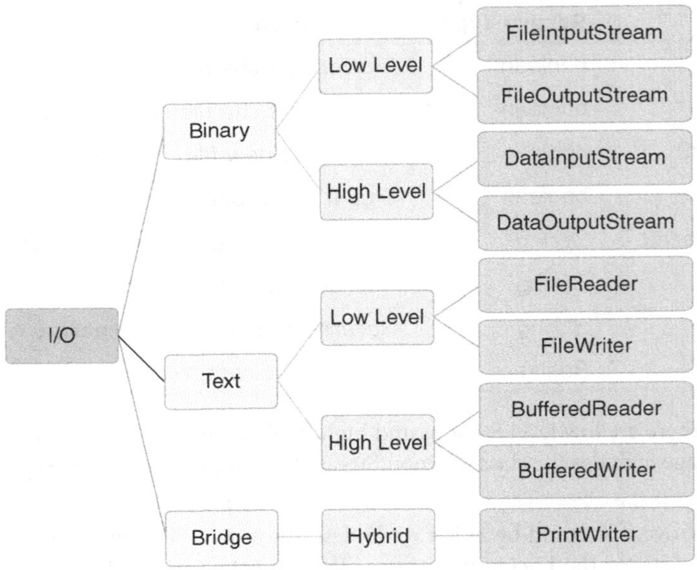

Fig. A.2 *Java I/O*

Complicated as it appears, fortunately, the methods have a very good naming convention. It follows that the programmer can extrapolate the method names as long as the class names are known.

A.1.6.1 PrintWriter PW is a subclass of the Writer and deserves a special mention. It tries to bridge the two broad means of accessing data—binary and text. Print and Println, the most common methods encountered during development of a java program, are methods belonging to PrintWriter class.

A.1.6.2 Serialization So far we have seen reading/writing of bytes, and primitive types. In an object-oriented language, we deal with objects. So, how do we write objects into some persistent storage? The process of writing an object to storage is called object serialization. The inverse of this operation is called deserialization.

A.1.7 Collections in Java

We have touched upon the different nature of data that need to be processed to get going, as part of a process, symbolized within a Java program. We have also seen the granularity of data—ranging from primitives to objects. Often we need to deal with multiple types of data related to each other in some fashion. Java offers a facility to deal with such groups of data, by having them together in a single object. This is referred to as Collections in Java.

The Collections framework in Java provides a convenient set of APIs aligned with the abstract data types from computer science data structures—maps, sets, lists, trees, arrays, and hashtables. The Java classes in the Collections Framework encapsulate the data structures and the algorithms associated with these abstractions, in true object oriented style. The following list mentions the type of collections that are available in Java.

Collection Type	Description	Usage Scenario
List	List is like a variable sized array; order is preserved; Duplicates OK	Array of objects; Iteration possible; Duplication possible
Set	Similar to the concept of Sets. Order of items may not be preserved; Needs to be unique.	Inclusion / exclusion of items in a set are of importance rather than sequence. Uniqueness is important.
Map	Implementation of Key-Value pairs. Equivalent terminology in other languages are Hash (Rails), JSON (JavaScript), etc.	Scenarios where it is required to retreive a Value for a specified Key.
Queue	Similar to List.	If Order is significant, as in FIFO, use Queues.

Under each of the types, there are a lot of structures available. There are so many options that are possible, but how does one choose which type(s) of Collection is/are to be used. Let's try to demystify the process of choosing the right type of Collection.

The dimensions to consider the choice of the Collection usually are ease of search, storage considerations, uniqueness of items, sensitivity to speed of access, speed of indexing, need for synchronization (multi threading), and sequence preservation. The first decision to make is to identify the most relevant high level Collection Type—among List, Set, Map and Queue. Hash based storage improves search but indexing might be slow. LinkedList structures are slow in searching but relatively fast for addition of new items.

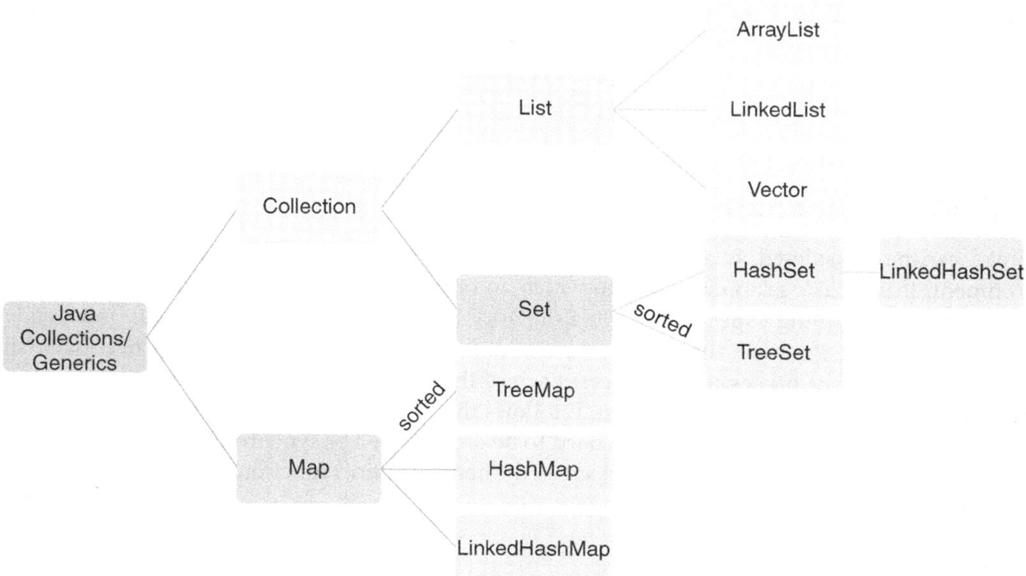

Fig. A.3 *Java collections*

The structure of Java Collections is summarized in Figure A.3. Here "Collections" refer to class but "Collection" (singular) refers to interface.

An example of ArrayList is shown below:

```
//An ArrayList to store Books
ArrayList<myBook> myBookCollection = new ArrayList<myBook>();
//Initialize some book objects
myBook book1 = new myBook("Web Technologies");
myBook book2 = new myBook("Software Engineering");
//other books...
//Now add them to the collection
myBookCollection.add(book1);
myBookCollection.add(book2);
```

The collection is a list of books. Each book follows a structure, defined in a Class, myBook (which is not shown). Instead of the structure, *myBook*, the ArrayList could also be a collection of String, Integer or any of the standard class items.

The above example also introduces the concept of Generics in Java.

The basic operations that can be done on a Collection include the following:

- Add objects to the collection
- Remove objects from the collection
- Find out if an object (or group of objects) is in the collection
- Retrieve an object from the collection (without removing it)
- Iterate through the collection, examining each element (object) one after another

When handling a Collection, Iteration is one of the most common operations performed. The Collection class extends an iterator class called *Iterable*. The iterator lets us use the following methods:

- hasNext
- next
- remove

A.1.8 Multithreading

A thread can be considered as a light-weight form of a process, operating within a main process environment. It is a basic processing unit to which an operating system allocates a certain amount of processor time, performing a specific task (or a subtask). It is efficient to perform several (independent) tasks concurrently, at the same time taking care of not spawning more threads than necessary, since a thread itself consumes processing resources. Each of these tasks is performed by means of a thread. Several threads can be created by a program. It follows that if they are to be tuned towards performing something useful and coherent, the threads need to be orchestrated or synchronized together.

Each Java program has at least one thread, created when the main() function is invoked. A Thread can be invoked in Java in two ways as under:

- By extending the Thread class
- By implementing the Runnable interface

A.1.8.1 Extends thread The class that wants to use threading, can extend Java's *Thread* class. The *run* method of the class should be overridden as in the following snippet.

```
class myThread extends Thread {
public void run() {
   //override the method...
}
}
public class threadExtend {
public static void main(String[] args) {
   myThread thread = new MyThread();
   thread.start();
   }
}
```

The *myThread* class should implement the *run* method, which is invoked as soon as the *start()* method is called on the thread.

However, using this method of creating a thread is not always practical as Java does not allow for multiple inheritance. When a class has to be subclassed, and at the same time needs to use multi-threading, it is not straight forward using the "Extends Thread" method. In these cases providing a *Runnable* object can be used.

A.1.8.2 Implements runnable The Runnable interface is another way to create a thread. This interface also has a run() method that needs to be implemented (same as in the earlier method). Refer to an example in Figure A.4.

```
/*
 * Initialize 2 threads and start them sequentially. Notice the result
   would contain
 * inter-twining tasks.
 */
public class threadTest {
 public static void main(String[] args) {
     t1 test1 = new t1();
     Thread test1Thread = new Thread(test1);
     t2 test2 = new t2();
     Thread test2Thread = new Thread(test2);

     System.out.println("Thread1 Thread2");
     System.out.println("------- -------");
     //Start Thread1 and then Thread2
     tes1Thread.start();
     tes2Thread.start();
 }
```

(Continued)

```
18.   }
19.   //use the Runnable
20.   class t1 implements Runnable {
21.    public void run() {
22.        for (int i = 1; i <= 10; i++) {
23.        System.out.println("  " + i);
24.
25.        try {
26.        Thread.sleep(1000);
27.        } catch (InterruptedException e) {
28.        }
29.        }
30.        }
31.   }
32.   //Thread2 definition
33.   class t2 implements Runnable {
34.    public void run() {
35.        for (int i = 1; i <= 10; i++) {
36.        System.out.println("  " + i);
37.
38.        try {
39.        Thread.sleep(800);
40.        } catch (InterruptedException e) {
41.        }
42.        }
43.        }
44    }
```

Fig. A.4 *threadTest.java-thread example*

Both classes t1 (line 20) and t2 (line 33) implement the Runnable interface. The run() method is defined which displays a counter from 1 to 10. The thread sleeps for a definite amount of time such that t1 sleeps for more time than t2. The output is displayed arranged in a columnar like fashion (lines 23 and 36).

Notice that sleep method stops the thread for a definite amount of milliseconds as given in its argument. Each thread goes through a lifecycle, comprising a set of states. At any point of time, a thread is in one of the definite states. It can be read from a method called getState() on the thread.

The following are the states of a thread:

- NEW
- RUNNABLE
- BLOCKED

- WAITING
- TIMED_WAIT
- TERMINATED

A State diagram is represented in FigureA.5. It starts with the state New, where things are being set ready to start. JVM schedules a runnable thread to run at the earliest opportunity. From this state of Runnable, a thread can go to any of the states—Blocked, Waiting or Timed Wait, if not terminated. A thread can wait on sleep() or join(). After the thread has completed its execution of the task, it goes into the TERMINATED state.

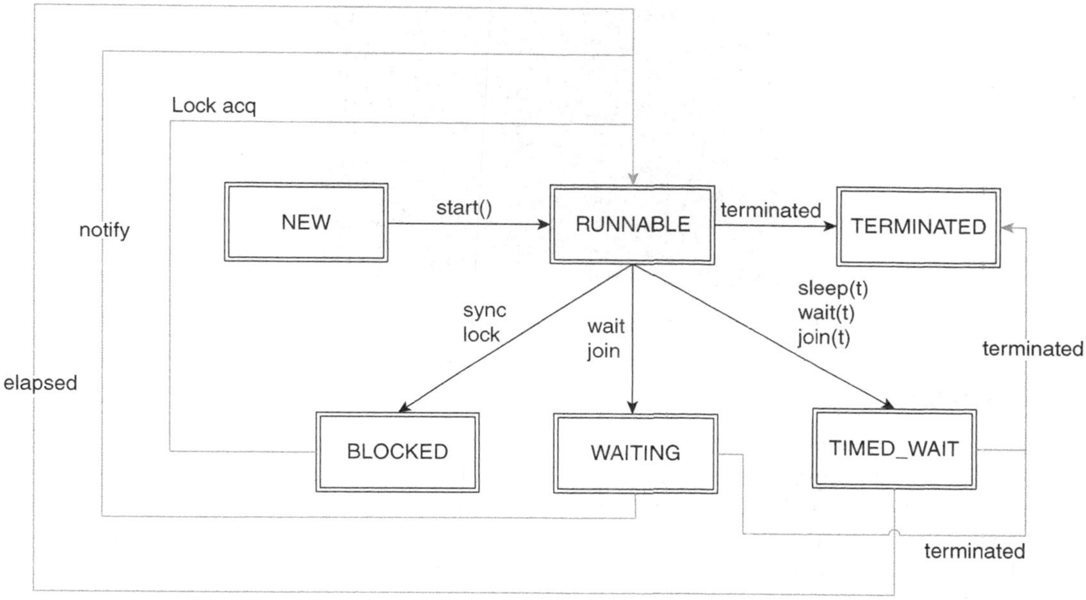

Fig. A.5 *Thread states*

The output of the testThread.java is shown in the Figure A.6.

It is to be observed that the threads execute simultaneously, manifested in the staggered output as shown in the figure. During the time first thread sleeps (line 26 in code in Figure A.4), it executes the second thread and vice versa. The first thread sleeps for more time; hence it takes a longer time to finish (though it starts off first) as compared to the second. The reader is encouraged to play around with different values for sleep() and arrive at a better understanding.

A.1.8.3 Synchronization Threads run independent of one another, but then sometimes there will be situations where exactly one thread needs to be working on a specific resource. For instance, in a highway, imagine if there is one toll booth servicing multiple lanes (threads). Then, at any one point of time, only one vehicle can be serviced by the toll collection agent. Similarly, certain methods need to be guaranteed access to only one thread at a time. This is achieved using the synchronized modifier on the method. On similar lines, a block of code can also be synchronized, which is used to enable atomic transactions.

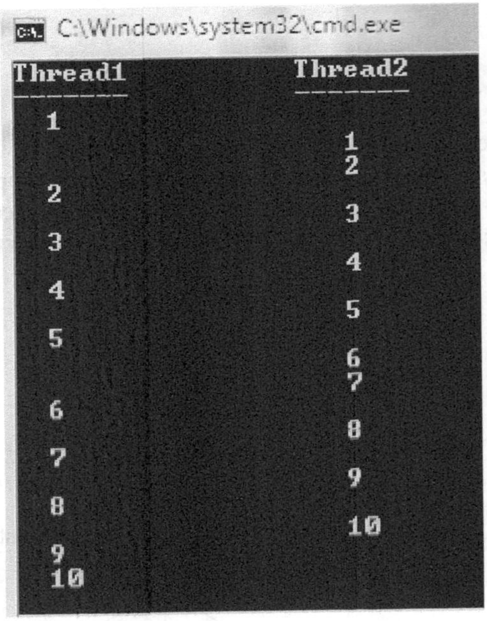

Fig. A.6 *testThread.java–an indicative output*

A.1.9 JNDI

The JEE platform has evolved over the years, supported, directed and sponsored by the industry. It offers a development model comprising a collection of APIs, providing standardized and Open set of enterprise solutions. Besides Servlets and JSP, the important APIs include JDBC, JTA, RMI/IIOP, JNDI and EJB.

JNDI is an important JEE API that provides naming and directory services. To understand the role of JNDI in web development, it is important to get an overview of a naming & directory service.

A.1.9.1 Naming and directory systems—a background There are various contexts in which a Naming and Directory service is involved. A Directory service goes along with the Naming service, in fact it can be considered as an extension of a naming service. For example, the Directory service enables association of attributes (like contact number as an attribute for an employee name).

The most common application is Active Directory (from Microsoft), based on a generic protocol called LDAP (Lightweight Directory Access Protocol), which is supported by JNDI. AD is used to store and retrieve a set of users (employees, & their hierarchy) and resources (like laptops, printers, etc). In a different context, CORBA Naming Service (COS) enables clients to access CORBA server objects based on names. A DNS (Domain Name Service) enables getting IP address, given names. RMI (Remote Machine Interface) Registry is another example of a naming service.

In some sense, even a Windows (or Unix) file system is a naming service—given the complete file path, it gives you a handle to the file. In other words, given a name, an object is retrieved. Thus a naming system is a means to handle the following:

- A provision to associate an object with a name (technically called Binding)
- A means to retrieve the object, given the name (resolution)
- A scope which comprises a set of bindings, following the same naming convention (context)

A.1.9.2 JNDI architecture The reason JNDI is brought out here is that the backbone of a naming and directory service in an application server is JNDI itself. A lot of these APIs are used in Java programming as part of the web, though, a majority of them are handled by easy to use Annotations, helped by the IDE.

JNDI is seen to be generic enough to handle a wide range of naming services like LDAP, DNS, RMI and CORBA. It also provides a significant role in distributed environments like EJB. JNDI is designed to be independent of any specific naming and directory service by providing a common API. It is layered into three different areas as shown in Figure A.7.

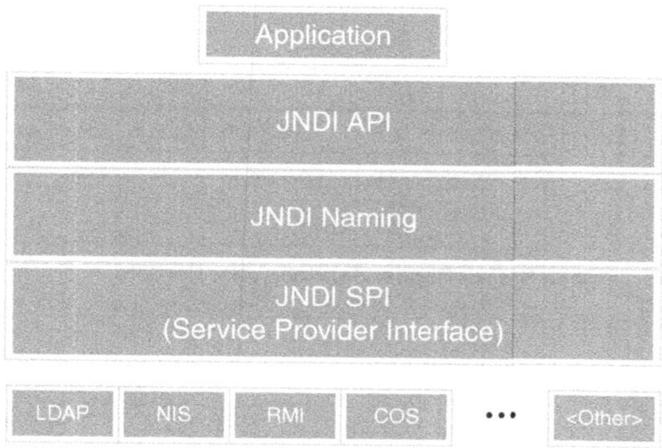

Fig. A.7 *JNDI layers*

The layers are manifested as Java packages, as described below:

- package javax.naming is the basic API. It is normally used to look up names such as from a registry.
- package javax.naming.directory API used for filtered searching and modifying of hierarchical values in directory and naming services such as LDAP
- package javax.naming.spi is more basic level, used by service providers. The package provides a number of interfaces. Most enterprise developers will not need to use this API, because it is used for mapping JNDI calls to a specific service provider.

Typically, the higher-level calls in the javax.naming and javax.naming.directory packages are used by application developers. Here is a summary of JNDI within JEE development.

- Application servers have a JNDI implementation to maintain the resources
- JNDI can be used to look up Beans to get reference to the Bean.
- It can connect to common resource like JDBC DataSource or Java Message Service (JMS) drivers. Using DataSource to connect (instead of Driver Manager offers better portability because only the configuration file needs to be changed, rather than code.
- Connecting to the Java Transaction API's (JTA) for transaction management

A.1.10 The Big Picture

It can be seen that Java is more of a platform, rather than just a language. The big picture is shown in Figure A.8.

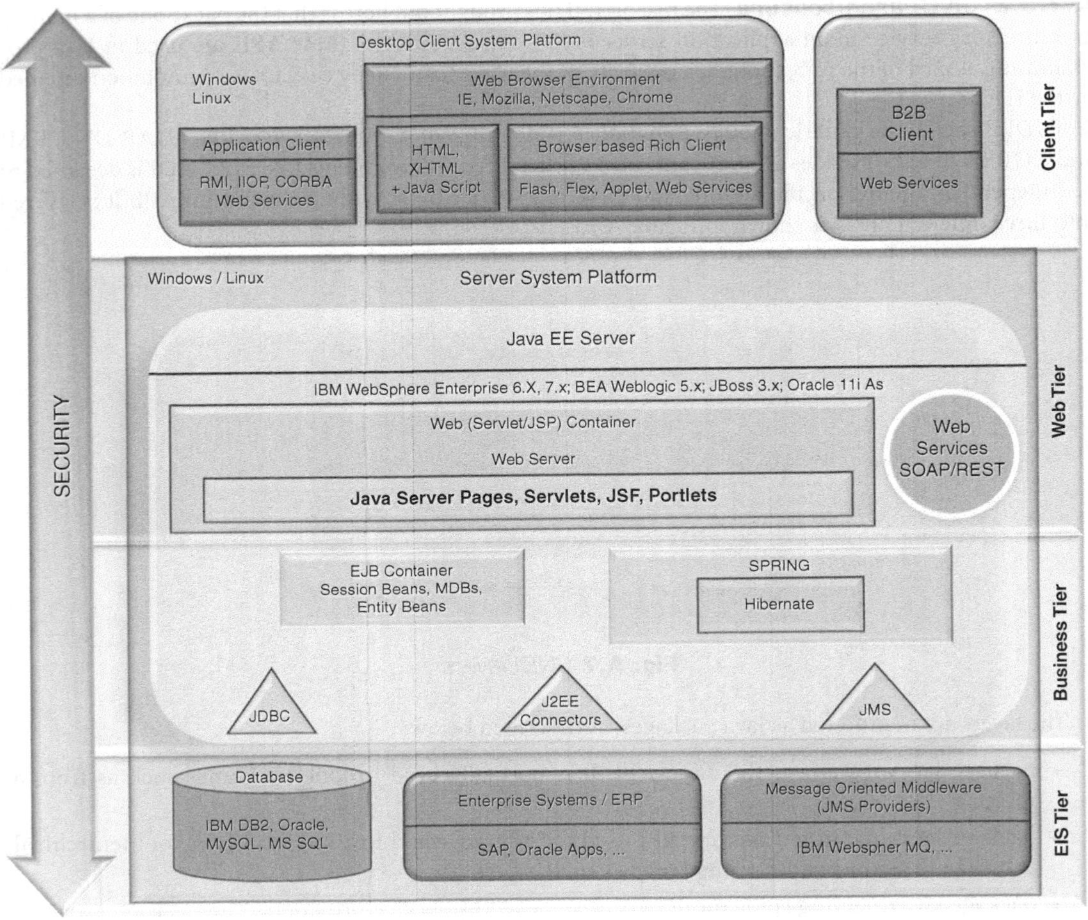

Fig. A.8 *Java EE–the big picture*

A.2 JAVA VS. JAVASCRIPT

JavaScript is quite different from Java, though they share a similar name. Both are powerful languages in their own areas, being descendants of C/C++, but have progressed in different directions. Nevertheless, a comparison table is included below:

Area	Java	JavaScript
Model	Object Oriented	Server-side JavaScript is Object Oriented.
Positioning in the MVC Stack	Client side and Server side	Client-side JavaScript operates on the View part of MVC, though Server-side JavaScript can be used on Server side

Runtime dependencies	Considered Standalone, though running on a JVM	Client side as part of HTML, through a browser. Could face browser incompatabilities.
Mode of running	Complied code	Scripting
Libraries	-NA-	JavaScript based libraries are available which also takes care of browser related inconsistencies.
Design influence	Promotes MVC	Promotes Unobtrusiveness
Type style	Strongly typed	Loosely typed

A.3 ARCHITECTURAL STYLES

It is a common practice to logically present architecture into layers of distinct functions. It is a logical model, implying physically that they can be different but that does not matter. The logical layering is required to architect the system that is easily manageable and maintainable. After all, one of the goals of an application architecture is to build systems that are flexible to change rather than building to last.

The early generation of software was procedural. All layers of code—presentation (with the console), business logic and data storage were all in the form of procedures in blocks. This was enough at that time since major emphasis was in implementing business logic, interacting with a database. With user interfaces getting richer and clients getting diverse (ranging from a plain browser to a mobile phone interface), the need for core sets of skills arose. Furthermore, it needs to be better maintainable, hence the need for separation or layering.

Logical layering also aligns with people's core competency in these layers, so that a team is made of a User Experience specialist, a Database architect and a Domain expert for instance. The logical separation of layers brings out the application architecture as belonging to various tiers. The client–server model paved the way for this kind of separation.

A.3.1 Client–Server

The client–server model brought about advantages of separation of concerns into two broad parts—the server side and the client side. Business logic was bundled with the client (as in a thick client with thin server) or with the server (thin client, thick server). But a third layer was added, in the 1990s, as the foundation for a n-tier architecture. The 3-tier model comprises three layers—the Presentation tier, Business Logic tier and the Data tier.

A.3.2 3-Tier

The Presentation layer is responsible for rendering information or views to users, but does not take part in processing the information. In fact, it does not care about how it gets the data and from where. In the context of the web a view is mostly done through HTML rendered by browsers. It does not actually matter whether it is HTML or any other—it could even be a mobile device interface.

The middle tier is responsible for processing. It takes care of implementing the application's business logic, handling a workflow, aggregating data, etc. It abstracts the aspects of the domain into the application. This layer does not in any way take part in how the information is displayed (or exchanged) on (with) the client.

3-Tier

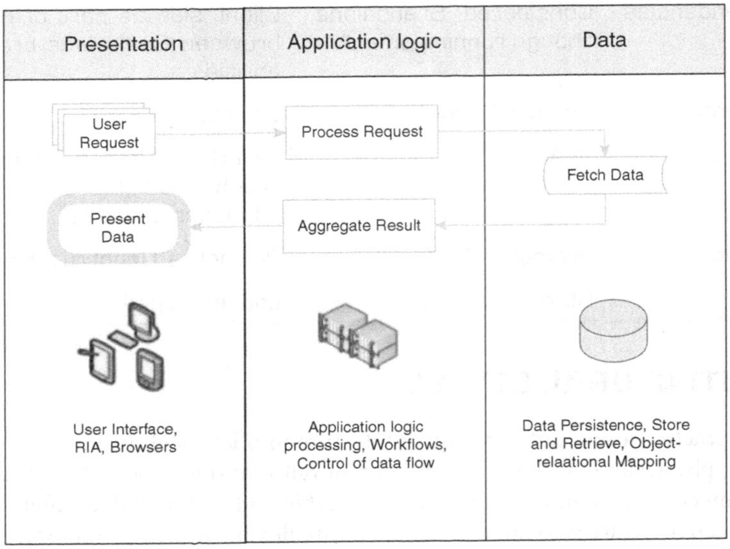

Fig. A.9 *Three-tier architecture representation*

The Data tier is responsible for data persistence and retrieval. It takes care of translating object models into relational database models, what is called as ORM.

A.3.3 n-Tier

In the 3-tier architectural style, a few of the tiers can be further split into more layers, depending on the size, necessity and complexity of the application. For example, the Application logic tier can be split into a Workflow tier and Business logic tier if it is a workflow-intensive application. This means that the architecture can be represented as a 4-tier structure consisting of Presentation, Business Logic, Workflow and Data layers. The point is that the architecture can be split into layers that as per the applications' focus areas to form a n-tier style. The value of n is normally 4 or 5.

The idea behind splitting into multiple units is summarized into a combination of the following factors:

- Reduce complexity
- Promote core competencies and separation of skills
- Increase scalability by having multiple servers. This may or may not translate into additional hardware. For example an organization might split its order processing into two parts—an Order entry and Order tracking systems since it intends to expose its Order tracking to its users. The organization could then selectively scale-up its Order tracking servers to meet the anticipated increase in usage.
- Leverage existing framework(s) or products. For example, a workflow intensive application may include a 3rd party workflow product to be integrated into the application, which could be leveraged to reduce development time.

Imagine a scenario about an online order processing system for books from a publisher. The architecture is required to cater to a growing need for a system which tracks orders that have been processed. It is required to facilitate self-help where a user tracks for shipment(s) that have been ordered by him/her. It is anticipated that the tracking transactions could be voluminous and also facilitate third party logistics interfaces. A sample 4 tier style is presented in Figure A.10.

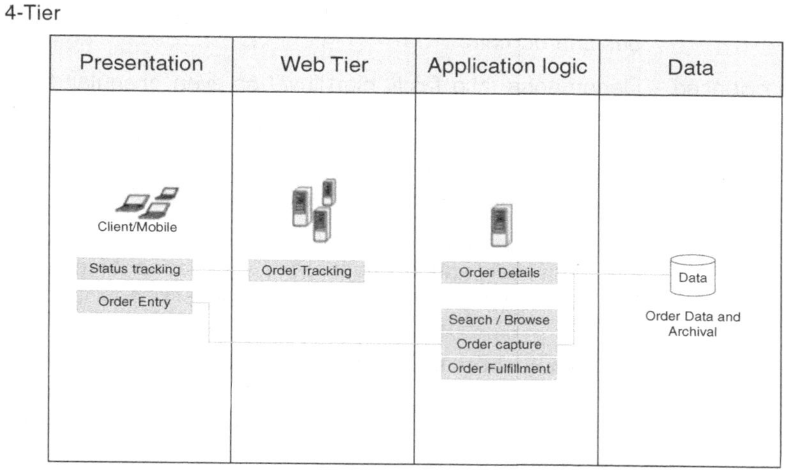

Fig. A.10 *Four-tier architecture representation of an online order process*

A.3.4 Summary of Architectural Styles

It is important to conceptualize on paper the architecture of systems that are being designed. An understanding of the architectural style will lead into several benefits. First and foremost, it is independent of any technology—meaning it can be used in any technology, commonly referred to as technology-agnostic. They can also identify their key focus areas. For example, an initiative where integration to outside systems is extremely important will take care to include an integration layer (tier) as part of the architecture. An application that emphasizes on communication (through business process orchestration and workflow), for instance, will be oriented towards SOA (Service Oriented Architecture). There are numerous examples of styles that can be followed. Some of the common styles are summarized in this section. It also includes those that are discussed in previous sections.

Style	**Remarks**
Client/Server	Client is separate from a server. Client renders the screen—could be thick or thin. Server holds all the processing logic including application logic and database handling
3-Tier	Generic separation of concerns in the form of Presentation tier, Application or Business logic tier and Data tier.

(Continued)

(Continued)

Style	Remarks
n-Tier (4 or 5 tier)	Separation of concerns is more granular as compared to a 3-tier. More examples of cases where additional tiers are necessary include Integration tier, Workflow tier, Object relational mapping, Business Intelligence tier, Web Services, etc. They also could be specific as per the domain.
Web Service oriented	Decompose into fairly high level or even granular functionality that expose services which can be consumed by multiple applications or components. It promotes object oriented benefits like reuse, encapsulation and being self also contained. Can use (or facilitate to be used) frameworks that are available.
SOA	When there are a number of (granular) services or components that act together and orchestrated by means of messages and contracts, they can be structured as a Service Oriented Architecture.

Many factors will influence the choice of an architecture style and most of these factors will be towards business or domain, as opposed to technology. Quite frequently, many of these styles can even be used in combination either as a whole or in parts. For example each component could conform to parts of MVC and be integrated over SOA approach.

A.3.5 Relationship with MVC

MVC stands for Model-View-Controller. It is a pattern that is commonly used. Whatever be the style of architecture, the MVC as a pattern can be conformed to. This is important for a web based application and signifies that the three aspects be separated in logical terms. M stands for Model, used to denote the data model or data aspects of an application. C stands for Controller which signifies the flow of control, that is, the process part of the application. V stands for View which signifies the presentation aspects of an application.

A.4 COMMON E-BUSINESS APPLICATIONS

The concept of e-Business (electronic) denotes enterprise applications that are transacted over the web. Needless to say, more and more applications automatically fall into this category. This is also manifested in a variety of tools that are made available by the open source community and also by corporate. A number of components are also available, some of which fall under broad categories like content management systems, e-commerce systems, etc. It is very difficult to name each vendor and the product that fall in these categories as their number will easily span multiple sections. However, there are websites which make available this information. One such example is as follows.

A.4.1 e-Commerce

e-Commerce is a set of transactions that enable online shopping. Though the shopping experience varies depending on the products that are sold (online), the transaction of buying is similar. For example, the shopping experience of buying a piece of jewellery is different from buying a book online. This is also different from the view of the seller, so it follows that the concept of selling jewellery is different from the concept of selling books.

The major similarity in the above transactions is that they are B2C. Transaction on a B2B environment comes with a host of pre and post-processing from a business point of view—things like Negotiation, Contracts Management, Preferred Supplier, Alternate items, etc. will be required to support the purchasing process. These modules generally come in the purview of an ERP or a Supply chain system like Oracle Apps, SAP, JDA(i2), Ariba or also specific purchasing engines that need to be incorporated as part of a bigger package, though they are still form part of e-Commerce systems. This section, however, is focused on the B2C eCommerce engines.

Popular eCommerce engines that are available include Microsoft eCommerce Server 2009, IBM WebSphere eCommerce, which has a fair degree of sophistication built in. Open Source also offers a variety of such systems, Notable ones include Open Commerce.

A.4.2 Portals and Web Content Management

Dynamic websites need automated systems in place to manage content. Organizations have exhibited growth organically (growth in sales) as well as inorganically (through mergers and acquisitions). Unless there is a robust content management system, websites will be difficult to manage. A centralized mode of delivery of web site information, coupled with decentralized operational content mechanism has been known to be a good design from a business standpoint.

A website can double up not only as a means for information dissemination, but also act as a portal for vendors and partners for doing business. Consequently, a lot of intranet portals have become popular, resulting in website design work leading to a lot of System Integration work as well.

As such, a typical set of workstreams that can be expected in such an initiative are as follows:

- Websites by Goegraphy (Internet)
- Department sites (Intranet)
- Partner/Vendor login (Internet)
- System Integration (Web Services, SOA, etc.)

The following table summarizes the kind of approach towards these initiatives.

Initiative	What It Constitutes?	Typical Technologies
Web Sites by Geo	Web Page design, Navigation, i18N,	Internet based design, HTML, CSS, JavaScript, jQuery, Web Content Management systems
Department Sites	Departmental Web pages, Navigation, Localization	
Partner/Vendor login		

A.5 INSTALLING NETBEANS

An IDE is very much essential for web development, because there are many different components and libraries to be linked, placed in a definite directory structure. Some of the popular IDEs that are available to be used under Open Source are Eclispe and Netbeans. The reader is free to choose any IDE for trying out the exercises. However, this book follows Netbeans to a large extent. It is recommended to use Netbeans 7.01 along with Java 6 or 7.

URL of the IDE: `www.netbeans.org`. This was first launched by Sun Microsystems (now Oracle) in 2000 when it took over Netbeans Ceska, a Czech firm.

The IDE is available for Windows as well as most favors of Linux. Netbeans itself is written in Java, so it requires the Java environment to be available during installation.

A typical web application development environment will involve multiple developers working on various parts of code. It is recommended to use a version control mechanism along with the IDE to ensure that development is streamlined. Various version control software include Visual Source Safe (licensed from Microsoft), Git (Open Source), SVN (Open Source), etc.

A.6 INSTALLING RUBY ON RAILS

Ruby-on-Rails is one of the most modern frameworks available on the web. It is based on a pure object-oriented model, aligned with the principles of MVC and offers remarkable simplicity to developing web applications. Moreover, it is a complete stack solution—from Client side to Server side; from Development environment to Production environment. This way it is a uniquely positioned web development and deployment environment. RoR is available as Open source at http://rubyonrails.org/. Netbeans IDE for Java can double up as the preferred IDE for Rails as well, through a plug-in.

In this book, there is only a small reference to Ruby-on-Rails as part of web services. But that should not deter the reader from missing out the goodies that the framework offers.

A.7 INSTALLING MYSQL

A database is very much a part of any Enterprise application. It is a separate topic by itself, vast and offers plenty of variety. For examples used in this book, mySQL is the preferred choice of database. The reason that this it is chosen is not only because it is available as part of open source, but also because this is powerful enough to be used in a production scenario. MySQL Clustering offers a good level of performance, though it is not required for the samples that are available in this book.

The reader is expected to be familiar with basic database concepts. mySQL can be downloaded from the internet at `http://dev.mysql.com/`. Any version above 5.0 is recommended.

Index

A

abstract class, 345
actions, 249
active, 56
Ajax. *See* Asynchronous JavaScript and XML (Ajax)
anchor tag, 33
anonymous functions, 91–92
AOP. *See* Aspect Oriented Programming (AOP)
application server, 18
architectural styles, 359–362
  client–server, 359
  n-tier, 360–361
  3-tier, 359–360
  arrays, 73, 86–89
  implementation aspects, 86–87
  string operations and, 87–89
Aspect Oriented Programming (AOP), 273
Asynchronous JavaScript and XML (Ajax), 137–141
  code, 139–141
  example of, 138
  steps involved in, 139
  technology components required for, 138
  XMLHttpRequest object, 138–139

B

basic string operations, 80–84
block elements. *See* block tags
block tags, 45
Boolean, 75
Box Model, 57–58
  concept of, 57–58
  padding, 58
browser, 16–17
browser caches, 17

C

Cascading Style Sheets (CSS), 48–64
  benefits of, 64
  declarations, 48–49
  sample file, 51–52
  selectors, 52–57
  use of, 49–51
class selector, 52–53
classes, 27, 101–112
  creating objects, 101–102
  in Java, 344–348
  inheritance, 104–112
  objects through function constructors, 102–103
  prototype, 103–104
clear, 60–61
client–server, 359
client-side cookies, 99–100
closures, 92–97
configuration file, 159–162
constants, 75
conversions, 78–80
cookies, 99–100, 195–207
CSS. *See* Cascading Style Sheets (CSS)

D

date object, 84–86
data types, 73–78
  primitive, 73
  reference/composite, 73
  trivial, 73
declarations, 239, 245
default event listener, 123–126
Denial of Service (DOS) attacks, 15
descendant selector, 53–54
DHTML, 151
directives, 239, 245–246

Document Object Model (DOM), 112–119, 296
- accessing nodes directly, 117
- comparison with SAX, 296–297
- manipulation, 117–119
- representation of, 113–114
- traversal, 114–116

Document Type Definition (DTD), 28, 287–289
DOM manipulation, 117–119
DOM traversal, 114–116
DOM. *See* Document Object Model (DOM)
DTD. *See* Document Type Definition
Dynamic HTML. *See* DNTML

E

e-commerce, 362–363
EDI. *See* Electronic Data Interchange (EDI)
EJB. *See* Enterprise JavaBeans (EJB)
EL. *See* Expression Language (EL)
Electronic Data Interchange (EDI), 290
e-mail related protocols, 8–9
end tag, 31
Enterprise Java Beans (EJB), 266–280
- components of, 269–271
- life cycle of, 271–273
- with servlets, 268–269
- usage, 269
- versions, 269–271

entity beans, 270–271
enumerated class, 346
environment parameters, 165–171
event driven tracking, 207–233
event handling, 119–130
Event Onload, 122
event propagation, 127–129
Expression Language (EL), 249
expressions, 240, 248
Extensible Markup Language (XML), 282–304
- building blocks, 284–285
- characteristics of, 286
- operational mode of, 285–286
- parsing, 295
- scenario for handling, 286–287
- validity of, 287–290
- XML Schema Definition (XSD), 289–290
- XML Stylesheet Language (XSL), 290–295

F

FavConnect, 210–232
- attribute scope for, 232–233
- data model used, 232
- database access, 215
- database connection manager, 229–231
- login servlet, 212–214
- login.JSP, 210–211
- organization and modules, 210
- user information, 215–229

Federal Networking Council (FNC), 2
firewalls, 15
- importance of, 15

first-child, 54–56
float, 58–61
FNC. *See* Federal Networking Council (FNC)
focus, 56
frames, 40
FTP, 7–8
function, 73
- ways to use, 98–100

function arguments, 90–91
function literals, 89–90

G

GET method, 12
GlassFish, 18

H

Hadoop algorithms, 17
higher level protocols, 7–14
- e-mail related protocols, 8–9
- FTP, 7–8
- Hyper Text Transfer Protocol (HTTP), 10–14
- Telnet, 8

hover, 56
HTML5, 45
HTML validator, 44
HTTP. *See* Hyper Text Transfer Protocol (HTTP)
Hyper Text Markup Language (HTML), 25–45
- common tags, 30–40
- embedded server-side scripts in, 153–155
- file structure, 28–30

forms, 40–42
HTML5, 45
tags used in, 26–28
XHTML, 40, 43–44
Hyper Text Transfer Protocol (HTTP), 10–14
response, 14
architectures of, 10–11
use of, 11–12

I

IAB. *See* Internet Architecture Board (IAB)
IANA. *See* Internet Assigned Numbers Authority (IANA)
ID selector, 53
id, 27
IESG. *See* Internet Engineering Steering Group (IESG)
IETF. *See* Internet Engineering Task Force (IETF)
IMAP, 9
inheritance, 104–112
inline elements, 45
inner functions, 92
Inner HTML, 136
interfaces, 347
Internet
applications of, 3
Internet Architecture Board (IAB), 21
Internet Assigned Numbers Authority (IANA), 20–21
Internet Engineering Steering Group (IESG), 19, 20
Internet Engineering Task Force (IETF), 19–20
Internet Research Task Force (IRTF), 21
IPv6, 6–7
IRTF. *See* Internet Research Task Force (IRTF)

J

Java
collections in, 350–352
data types, 343–344
file operations in, 348–350
handling application exceptions, 348
vs. JavaScript, 358–359
Java EE 5, 266
Java Server Pages (JSP), 236–264
elements in, 239–240
equivalent technologies and, 262–264
example of, 251–258
exceptions, 246–249
Expression Language (EL), 249
FavConnect example modified, 241–244
history and background of, 237
implicit objects, 240
lifecycle of, 238–239
object scope, 240–241
overview of, 237–238
reasons for use, 237
standard tag library, 250–251, 259–262
tags, 244–246
Java servlets, 155–165
example of, 158–159
an intermediate web application architecture, 159–165
life cycle of, 157–158
server creation and life cycle, 156–157
Java Virtual Machine (JVM), 341
JavaScript, 67–145
Ajax with, 137–141
closure scenarios, 98
concept of classes, 101–112
in context of execution, 112
example of, 68
history of, 66
organization of language, 68–69
security, 141–142
variables and functions, 89–97
vs. Java
JavaScript Object Notation (JSON), 297–304
JBoss, 18
JNDI, 356–357
architecture of, 357
background of, 356
JSON. *See* JavaScript Object Notation (JSON)
JSP. *See* Java Server Pages (JSP)
JVM. *See* Java Virtual Machine (JVM)

L

last-child, 56
layering, 266–268
link, 56
listeners, 208–210
steps involved in, 210

M

MDS. *See* Message Driven Beams (MDS)
Message Driven Beams (MDS)
meta, 31
MIME, 9
Model-View-Controller (MVC), 362
mouse events, 122–123
multithreading, 352–355
MVC. *See* Model-View-Controller (MVC)
MYSQL, 364

N

netbeans, 364
networks, 4–7
n-tier, 360–361
NULL, 73

O

OASIS. *See* Organization for Advancement of Structured Information Standards (OASIS)
object relational mapping (ORM), 270
object, 73
Onchange event, 121–122
Onclick event, 121
Organization for Advancement of Structured Information Standards (OASIS), 310
ORM. *See* object relational mapping (ORM)

P

padding, 58
parameter data, 171–183
  access of, 171–183
portals, 363
POST method, 12–13
primitive data types, 73
  Boolean, 75
  special numbers, 74
  strings, 73
PrintWriter, 350
prototype, 103–104
pseudo selector, 54–57

R

RAI. *See* Rich Internet/Interactive Applications (RIA)
reference, 83–84
regular expression, 84
Resources, 322
REST, 312
  principles of, 322
Rich Internet/Interactive Applications (RIA), 137
routers, 15–16
Ruby-on-Rails, 364

S

SAX parsers, 295
scriptlets, 240, 249
selectors, 52–57
  class selector, 52–53
  descendant selector, 53–54
  ID selector, 53
  pseudo selector, 54–57
serialization, 350
service oriented architecture (SOA), 309
servlet code, 162–165
session attributes, 233
session beans, 270
SGML. *See* Standard Generalized Markup Language (SGML)
SMTP, 8–9
SOA. *See* service oriented architecture (SOA)
SOAP, 312, 318
  structure of messages, 318
  vs REST, 336–337
  with WSDL and XML schema, 318
special numbers, 74
Standard Generalized Markup Language (SGML), 24–25
  framework of, 24–25
start tag, 31
state management, 183–207
string encoding, 82–83
strings, 73

T

TCP/IP, 4
  Internet address structure, 5–6

Telnet, 8
thread safety, 182–183
3-tier, 359–360
TLDs. *See* top level domains (TLDs)
top level domains (TLDs)
transfer control, 240
Typeof, 76–78

U

unboxing, 346
undefined data types, 73
unordered collection, 73

V

variables, 89–92
  functions and, 89–92
VB program, 207
visited, 56

W

W3C. *See* World Wide Web Consortium (W3C)
web
  components of, 15–17
  evolution of, 1–2
  history of, 2–3
web content management, 363
web layering, 266
web search engines, 17
web server vendors, 154
web servers, 17–18
web services description language (WSDL), 314–317
web services, 306–339
  evolution of concept, 308–309
  generation of, 322
  programming models, 312
  purpose of, 309
  REST based, 322
  SOAP based, 312, 318
  soap based, 312–318
  standards, 310
  use cases, 310–311
WebLogic, 18
WebMail, 9
website, 63
WebSphere, 18
World Wide Web, 17
World Wide Web Consortium (W3C), 21
wrapper class, 345–346
WSDL. *See* web services description language (WSDL)

X

XHTML, 40, 43–44
  HTML validator, 44
XML Schema Definition (XSD), 289–290
  advantages of, 290
XML Stylesheet Language (XSL), 290–295
XML. *See* Extensible Markup Language (XML)
XMLHttpRequest object, 138–139
XSD. *See* XML Schema Definition (XSD)
XSL Formatting Objects (XSLFO), 290
XSL Transformation, 290–295
XSL. *See* XML Stylesheet Language (XSL)
XSLFO. *See* XSL Formatting Objects
XSLT. *See* XSL Transformation

Z

Z-index, 61–64